Foreign Trends in American Gardens

Foreign Trends in American Gardens

A HISTORY OF EXCHANGE, ADAPTATION, AND RECEPTION

Edited by
RAFFAELLA FABIANI GIANNETTO

University of Virginia Press
CHARLOTTESVILLE AND LONDON

University of Virginia Press
© 2016 by the Rector and Visitors of the University of Virginia
All rights reserved
Printed in the United States of America on acid-free paper
First published 2016

1 3 5 7 9 8 6 4 2

Library of Congress Cataloging-in-Publication Data
Names: Fabiani Giannetto, Raffaella, editor.
Title: Foreign trends in American gardens : a history of exchange, adaptation, and reception / edited by Raffaella Fabiani Giannetto.
Description: Charlottesville : University of Virginia Press, 2016. | Includes bibliographical references and index.
Identifiers: LCCN 2016015326 | ISBN 9780813939131 (cloth : alk. paper) | ISBN 9780813939292 (pbk. : alk. paper) | ISBN 9780813939148 (ebook)
Subjects: LCSH: Gardens—United States—Foreign influences—History.
Classification: LCC SB451.3 .F67 2016 | DDC 635.0973—dc23
LC record available at https://lccn.loc.gov/2016015326

Cover art: Garden project by Wilson Eyre for the University of Pennsylvania Museum. (Wilson Eyre Collection, Architectural Archives, University of Pennsylvania)

Contents

Preface

The essays collected in this book address various aspects and consequences of the translation, imitation, adaptation, and naturalization of distant trends onto the American territory. The focus in all of the contributions is on the role of the foreign in shaping American gardens, the perception and use of foreign plants, and Americans' ability to read their own natural landscape. The essays are organized around major geographical areas of influence (France, England, Italy, and the East) with the exception of part 4, which addresses three topics: the reaction to anything foreign in an effort to find a true American identity rooted in the nation's soil; the attempt to conceptualize a regional horticultural character in the American South; and, finally, the distinctiveness of modern American landscape architecture, curiously defined by the work of a foreign immigrant, as perceived and construed beyond the United States.

This book does not claim to offer an exhaustive overview of the foreign trends that influenced American gardens, and more research is indeed needed that addresses, for example, the role of Dutch, German, Spanish, Portuguese, and Chinese garden traditions in shaping American landscape architecture. In addition, by purposefully leaving out any aspect of the history of landscape architecture that is solely American, this book hopes to inspire further research on the subject as a full comprehensive history of place-making in the United States remains to be written.

The study of foreign influences vis-à-vis the American landscape architectural tradition is not a new undertaking, and this work builds on the research of garden and landscape historians who have preceded us, especially Robin Karson's *Influences on American Garden Design: 1895 to 1940*, a publication that resulted from the Garden Conservancy symposium of 1994 in New York. The essays collected here expand the scope of Karson's book both temporally, by including the eighteenth century and colonial America, and topically, by considering the reception and value not only of landscape styles, but also of foreign plants and the cultural, social, and economic aspects that explain their exchange, propagation, and shifting significance.

Questions about indistinct national identities, the unique horticultural and topographical qualities of certain regions, and the legacy and value of past artistic traditions that were asked by the protagonists of American landscape history are very much relevant today. Landscape architects work in an increasingly global world, in which boundaries are blurred and cultural differences softened. The challenge is therefore to create a sense of place in any new project by addressing not only the ecological demands and environmental constraints of a site, which may or may not be immediately perceptible to the uninitiated eye, but also its history, which resonates differently according to the cultural background of the designer. This may choose to confront the cultural past, or palimpsest, of a given site by pondering how it may be interpreted creatively in order to enrich the experience of the beholder.

Most essays contained in this book, here in expanded and edited form, were presented at the Foreign Trends on American Soil symposium that took place at the University of Pennsylvania School of Design in March 2011. The volume editor wishes to thank James Corner, former chair of the Department of Landscape Architecture and Regional Planning, and former dean Marilyn J. Taylor for their generous support; David Leatherbarrow and Aaron Wunsch for offering critical advice at various stages of the editing process. Thanks are also due to the symposium's moderators and audience, who all contributed to a successful forum, and to the speakers for their work and for the most useful and enriching conversations that ensued afterward. Last and not least, this editor should like to acknowledge those who, in an effort to be helpful, are willing to look farther and beyond everyday bureaucratic hurdles and in so doing show a most uplifting aspect of humanity: Elizabeth Beck and Constance Mood of the Fine Arts Library Image Collection at Penn have been exemplary in this regard.

Raffaella Fabiani Giannetto

Introduction

In the discourse of landscape architecture, the American garden has often been a source of confusion, due to its multiple meanings and often ambivalent definitions that defy the order of a distinct type. Indeed, the idea of the American garden has meant different things to people living either centuries apart or, notably, at the exact same time. The history of garden design and landscape architecture in the United States is a history of adaptation, transformation, and invention, which have been made possible—as the essays in this book show—by a critical consideration of the foreign. In particular, the use of foreign styles and exotic plants on American soil has been seen either as a means to strengthen a timid local artistic identity or, alternatively, as an unwise practice that would weaken and hamper the development of a national design idiom.

But plants and gardens of other countries have also attracted the interest of Americans independently of their impact on local practices and forms. In such cases the foreign has been seen as a symbol of otherness that could be conquered (mastered), transformed, and displayed as an interesting exotic specimen standing out amid native flora. Debates about the merits of the foreign versus the native softened whenever critics and designers shifted their attention toward more abstract questions, such as the essence of and quest for the beautiful or the autonomy of the creative act that preoccupied many modernist designers.

Postmodern critiques stimulated an increased interest toward local, vernacular traditions but also prompted a realization that the *genius loci* in this country is often far from being solely American and in many cases owes much of its own character to something brought in from elsewhere. Thus, the foreign has again been acknowledged, but without dogmatism, and if on one hand the last quarter of the twentieth century has authorized eclecticism and historicism, on the other it has championed the need for stewardship and encouraged the rewriting of history from a cultural rather than a purely formalistic lens, as shown in the pages that follow.

The search for a truly American style was particularly earnest at the turn of the twentieth century. "Except for the Pueblos and the cliff-dwellers," wrote architect Louis Boynton in an issue of *House and Garden*, "the only 'indigenous style' [in America] is the wigwam."[1] But the wigwam was obviously not enough; therefore, the application of foreign, but flexible modes of design seemed to be the logical next step for a nation that lacked a clear stylistic identity. The same view was shared by architectural critic Herbert Croly, who argued that "the old world may or may not need a new art, which violently breaks away from established forms, but the new world certainly needs in the beginning an old art, in which those forms are not only preserved, but cherished. For in this country all art, however old in its origin, is in a very real sense new."[2]

The need for a stylistic identity informed specifically the discourse on gardens, which were considered "an expression of the genius of the republic." And by the last quarter of the nineteenth century the republic had already produced great examples of landscape architecture, such as Central Park, the Boston Metropolitan Park system, and the Columbian Exposition.[3] These examples included different approaches to design that had been born across the ocean from the old continent. But deciding what imported mode of garden design, or which "old art," would be most appropriate for the new country was cause for controversy, as there was lack of consensus on the essence of the foreign styles adopted. Louis Boynton went to great lengths to prove the flexibility of the Italian mode of design by insisting on its lack of absolute symmetry and obvious balance, which "accounts in some measure for the strange compelling charm of the style,"[4] and arguably made it more adaptable to a different soil than the native. On the contrary, for Harvard professor and chair James Sturgis Pray, "The shape of the Italian garden seems to have been usually rectangular . . . [its] different architectural and horticultural features" "grouped symmetrically" about the main axis.[5] Landscape designer Beatrix Farrand insisted on the predominance of contrasts of light and shade in the gardens of Italy, and her colleague Charles Platt added to it the importance of colorful flowers, while others, like the author and art critic Edith Wharton, ignored the flowers altogether. Lastly, in his lecture on Italian gardens at the 1905 meeting of the American Society of Landscape Architects, member Ferruccio Vitale claimed that "if I should be asked what an Italian garden is, it would be difficult to reply. It would be much easier to say what it is not. It is not such a concentration of stone or marble benches, wells, statues, and pergolas, in a small, geometrically shaped and generally flat piece of ground, as I have mostly seen called by the name."[6]

Notwithstanding the different definitions of the Italian or the formal garden,[7] as John Charles Olmsted preferred to call it, there were many who thought it the most appropriate form of garden design for the United States. For art critic Charles Caffin it ought to be so because "nature abhors straight lines," and the most important sign of civilization is precisely man's detachment from it.[8] But for others, the geometric or Italian type was never going to be as restful and calming "as the Arsenal garden in Tokyo, and even a Fern-crowned rock by a mossy streamlet," and while they conceded that it may "excite admiration," they thought that it could not "stir the profoundest feelings of the soul," as the naturalistic garden could do, whether adopted from China, Japan, or England.[9] Criticism of the more general category of the formal garden was equally harsh. Seen as a matter solely of form and color, its beauty was regarded as a quality that may "give the keenest pleasure," but its lack of "inner meaning" was just as disappointing as that of its Italian subtype, and in any case neither could compete, the critics argued, against "the natural landscape or a genuine work of landscape-art" that could "move the feelings and touch the heart."[10]

The essence of the landscape garden was less the subject of debate in that, according to American garden critics, it had been theorized and naturalized by earlier generations and for a longer time. The process of naturalization had been favored by the fact that the style, which had its roots in the late-eighteenth-century British phenomenon of picturesque travel, was actually applicable to American landscape features. "Since the 1820s, tourism, painting, and literature had converged in the United States in a common fascination for the description and celebration of [native] landscape scenes, from the Hudson River eventually to the Far West." Through the identification of the republic with its unique landscape scenery, Americans could also shore up "an insecure sense of national accomplishment."[11] In addition, Andrew Jackson Downing and Frederick Law Olmsted imbued the picturesque with a moral message, the betterment of society and in particular the improvement of the lower classes that had no access to public grounds. Against the lofty scope of the landscape garden, Italian gardening was sometimes referred to as "extreme cultivated barbarism."[12]

For some critics, neither garden styles could truly represent the spirit of the nation, which they saw best expressed in the native woodland, marsh, and copse. For the horticulturalist Horace McFarland, writing in 1899, it was only natural that his forefathers "looked for models to their old homes across the Atlantic. In England and on the Continent the adornment of private and public grounds . . . [was] the growth of centuries of living beyond the struggle for mere existence." On the contrary, on the American soil "[seventeenth-century] pioneers saw little beauty in the wild tangle of the woodlands they had to cut off for home sites [because] the rich flora of the meadows and marshes [needed to] be subdued to make pastures."[13] For McFarland, when the Europeans showed an appreciation for American plants such as the laurel and the rhododendron, "the ubiquitous American tourist learn[ed] with astonishment that the common bushes and weeds of his generous home land [were] esteemed as rarely beautiful abroad."[14]

In fact, a widespread American appreciation for the beauty of the native flora began to manifest itself only in the first half of the nineteenth century, thanks, ironically, to the work of two foreigners, André Parmentier, a Belgian native who established himself in Brooklyn, and Thomas Affleck, who, as James Schissel explains in this book, moved to the United States from Scotland and finally settled in Washington, Mississippi.[15] Both men advocated the use of native plants, in addition to foreign ones proven hardy, through their writings and horticultural activities.[16] Later in the century, scientific farmer turned landscape gardener Horace W. S. Cleveland showed Americans the beauty of the midwestern native landscape and the importance of preserving its flora. Cleveland's ideas were expounded and put into practice by the next generation of landscape visionaries, including Ossian Cole Simonds, Jens Jensen, and Wilhelm Miller, author of the 1915 manifesto *The Prairie Spirit in Landscape Architecture*.[17]

McFarland championed Jensen's contemporary, Warren Manning, as the best interpreter of the American native landscape. Describing Dolobran, a garden Manning designed near Philadelphia, he exclaimed, "Here is no tailor-made lawn! No geranium-beds or coleus borders of monotonously continuous coloring meet the eye; no 'carpet gardening' of mosaic plants offends the taste. Just the natural beauty of American plants, located cunningly where they like to grow, unrestrained, untrimmed. True, the plants are cared for—fed, if need be, watered on occasion—but no attempt is made to guide them into preconceived forms."[18] The use of native materials in their natural conditions—the study of which will be named plant ecology in the years to follow[19]—was a pragmatic solution suitable to the American situation, where many of the plants familiar to European designers were not found or, if imported, were difficult to acclimate, and where large-scale earth moving and plantings were too costly. McFarland's criticism may have also been prompted by the vogue for exotic plants in many so-called gardenesque designs.

Among the participants in the debate about the merits of different styles, or different plants, some maintained a more moderate stance. Landscape architect Charles Eliot, for example, wrote in *Garden and Forest* that the quarrelling about styles was a useless or at best puerile pastime: "Is beauty . . . won by following shifting fads or fashions, by heaping up decorations, by gathering architectural or botanical specimens, however remarkable or even lovely? [. . .] The right planning or the arrangement of lands for private country-seats or suburban houses, for public squares, playgrounds or parks, for villages or for cities, is not a question of 'the gardenesque' or 'the picturesque,' 'the artificial' or 'the natural,' 'the symmetrical' or 'the unsymmetrical.' Whoever, regardless of circumstances, insists in any particular style or mode of arranging land and its accompanying landscape . . . has overlooked the important basal fact that, although beauty does not consist in fitness, nevertheless all that would be fair must first be fit," meaning that good design should be driven solely by "usefulness and adaptation to purpose."[20] Thus, for Eliot, beauty, intended as a consequence of fitness, released American landscape architecture from the tight boundaries of foreign styles, a merit that was attributed to the concept of space-composition in the years to follow. Like Eliot, others considered beauty to be above the styles. It was beauty that apparently made Frank Lloyd Wright say of Charles Platt that he "was a very dangerous man—he did the wrong thing so well."[21]

If some raised themselves above the quarrel about the styles, others avoided the issue of a national stylistic identity altogether. Beatrix Farrand wrote sarcastically, yet perceptively, that "the art of gardening at its best is as strongly national as that of painting or sculpture; in the England of old days gardens which were honestly supposed to be Italian were in reality British, just as the so-called 'English gardens' of the eighteenth century were either French or Italian when they were made in one or the other country."[22] And Platt himself, who was acclaimed as the most faithful interpreter of the Italian garden, and who also admitted to be guided mainly by principles of design derived from the Italian examples, argued, "I should not call [any one of my gardens] an 'Italian' garden any more than I should call any one of my houses an Italian house."[23]

But the adoption of foreign modes of design was not exclusively linked to the search for national identity. At the beginning of the twentieth century a taste for foreign traditions developed that was distinctively motivated by the appeal of the exotic. For example, Japanese-style gardens were created, sometimes as stand-alone symbols of otherness, sometimes as part of an eclectic ensemble that included both Western and Eastern garden traditions. In addition to being a dominant feature of the Arts and Crafts aesthetic, eclecticism was sanctioned at the thirty-fourth annual meeting of the American Institute of Architects.[24] The papers on Italian, French, English, and Japanese gardens read at the meeting were published in a 1902 volume entitled *European and Japanese Gardens.* The latter were particularly popular in the regions of California and the Pacific Northwest, whose topography, vegetation, and dramatic landscape views resembled those of Japan. In addition, the popularity of the Japanese garden was augmented by the presence of a large number of Japanese immigrants and Japanese Americans who facilitated the country's exposure to Japanese culture, with its appealing gardening traditions and fine arts, which were first re-presented in Philadelphia on occasion of the Centennial International Exposition of 1876. The great variety of Japanese gardens constructed on American soil, however, differed significantly from the original Japanese models in that they were often conceived as Japanese-inspired outdoor rooms "adapted for modern American living patterns, which valued nature as a visual amenity and backdrop, rather than as a conceptual and philosophical abstraction central to life."[25] An interesting example is the Kubota garden created by Fujitaro Kubota in Seattle, Washington, in which the visual diversity and the variety of flora were not only meant to be experienced at close range and on foot, as in a typical Japanese stroll garden, but also appreciated during a drive-through along a gracefully curving road.

In some cases, the exotic garden blended with more autochthonous forms and native plants in an attempt to define a regional identity very much influenced by Hispanic cultures. For example, several California gardens displayed native flora, characterized by brightly colored plants adjacent to more monochromatic and largely flowerless compositions. Less literal and obvious Japanese influences were also present in the works of mid-twentieth-century modernist designers who made use, in their gardens as well as in their architecture, not so much of Japanese forms as of Japanese principles of design, such as irregular pathways, unsymmetrical balance (often defined as "hidden" or "occult"), the composition of pictorial views gradually revealed along a path, *shakkei* or borrowed scenery, principles of miniaturization, and the employment of local materials.[26]

The emphasis on principles, rather than on explicit forms, was a characteristic of modernism, whose apostles' focus on space composition freed the American garden discourse from the rhetoric of historical styles. But modernist landscape architecture in the United States was itself indebted to the work of overseas designers and theorists. Unlike European modernism, however, which rejected references to the past and any overt meaning, modernism in American landscape architecture was inclusive and diverse, as the works and writings of Fletcher Steele and Christopher Tunnard indicate. In a 1937 essay for the catalog *Contemporary Landscape Architecture and Its Sources,* Steele called the classical tradition and the landscape garden of English origins "mere surface decoration," but he also argued that space composition "in landscape design may be achieved by either method or by combination of both."[27] In his most famous work, the Blue Steps at Naumkeag, in western Massachusetts, Steele created a highly original and modern interpretation of a garden feature that dates to the Italian Renaissance, rendered with concrete and tubular steel and accented by color contrasts between the mineral and vegetal elements.

Like Steele, Tunnard recognized the importance of new scientific advancements as he wrote in 1938 in his most influential work, *Gardens in the Modern Landscape:* the garden of the future "must necessarily be influenced by new materials and their methods of application—for example, by plant importation and hybridization, and the amelioration of soil and weather conditions."[28] Although Tunnard admired Eastern garden traditions, in particular the Japanese way of reaching "the beautiful by means of the necessary,"[29] he also abhorred the direct borrowing of forms, or styles, as he implied in the manifesto that he and Belgian landscape architect Jean Canneel-Claes wrote for the Association Internationale des Architectes Jardinistes Modernistes in 1938. That document, Tunnard later recalled, "stressed the probity of the creative act" and the need for the designer to rely "on his own knowledge and experience and not on the academic symbolism of the styles or outworn systems of aesthetics to create by experiment and invention new forms which are significant of the age from which they spring."[30] Yet, many of Tunnard's own landscape designs failed to produce new forms, presenting instead "the same awkward blending of traditional formal elements and biomorphic forms that he criticized as inappropriate to a twentieth-century design canon that sought to be genuinely responsive to the new realities of modern life."[31] A more concentrated effort at responding to the necessities and ideals of Americans living in the twentieth century occurred at a regional scale. Thomas Church, Garrett Eckbo, and later Lawrence Halprin produced designs that incorporated the very essence of California's *genius loci* and that responded to the lifestyle of its residents. Their work has been said to belong to a "loosely defined California School of Modernists," whose common characteristic is a sensitive response to the particularities of place and climate.[32]

With the critique of mainstream modernism that developed in the United States during the last quarter of the twentieth century, the distinctive qualities (cultural, ecological, and environmental) of many more American regions and places became object of interest, while critics and designers shifted their attention toward the significance of the vernacular.[33] This new tendency was influenced, in part, by a postmodern sensibility that affected such disciplines as cultural geography and cultural studies. Critical developments in such related fields of study have sparked the interest of landscape architects and critics in multiculturalism and polyvocality, which doubtless have contributed to the writing of more nuanced histories of landscape architecture and more site-sensitive projects.

But have these latest developments made obsolete the question of the meaning and essence of the American garden in its relationship to the foreign? Certainly not. What has emerged, instead, is an acceptance of diversity as a form of identity in and of itself that is no longer perceived as threatening but that may be embraced and productively celebrated. This ultimately explains why the importance of the foreign trends imported, translated, and adapted to the American territory has not been forgotten and comes to life both in contemporary design practice and, as Herbert Croly predicted, through preservation efforts that value the incomparable mosaic that forms the very essence of American landscape architecture.

Notes

I would like to thank Thaïsa Way and Eric MacDonald for their thoughtful remarks on an early draft of this introduction.

1. Louis Boynton, "Italian Adaptations for American Homes," *House and Garden* 17, no. 5 (May 1910): 172.

2. Herbert Croly, "The New World and the New Art," *Architectural Record* 12 (June 1902): 149.

3. Mary Caroline Robbins, citing these three Olmsted designs in "Imagination in Gardening," *Garden and Forest* 7 (December 12, 1894): 493.

4. Boynton, "Italian Adaptations for American Homes," 171.

5. James Sturgis Pray, "The Italian Garden—II," *American Architect and Building News (1876–1908)* 67 (February 17, 1900): 51.

6. Ferruccio Vitale, "Italian Gardens," in *Transactions of the American Society of Landscape Architects from Its Inception in 1899 to the End of 1908,* ed. Harold Caparn, James S. Pray, and Dawning Vaux (Harrisburg, PA: J. H. McFarland, Mt. Pleasant Press, 1912), 37.

7. Also the essence of the generic "formal garden" was subject to debate as the following excerpt shows: "The first essential of a formal garden is, of course, its formality, or perhaps we should say its mathematical symmetry both in surface and outline. In connection with this we are accustomed to see conspicuous brightness of color, but the very best examples of formal garden art may exist without brilliant colors, and, indeed, formal flower-beds where carpet patterns are reproduced in emphatic colors are often used in places where rigidity of outline and vividness of color are conspicuously out

of place that they have done very much to prejudice persons against the very name of formal gardening." This excerpt is from the editorial titled "Formal Gardening" that appeared in *Garden and Forest* 5, no. 219 (May 4, 1892): 205.

8. Charles H. Caffin, "Formal Gardens and a New England Example," *Harper's New Monthly Magazine* 99, no. 592 (September 1899): 558.

9. Charles Eliot (attributed), *Garden and Forest* 6, no. 284 (August 1893): 322.

10. "Formal Gardening," *Garden and Forest* 5, no. 219 (May 4, 1892): 205.

11. Ethan Carr, *Wilderness by Design: Landscape Architecture and the National Park Service* (Lincoln: University of Nebraska Press, 1999), 11.

12. Horace McFarland, "An American Garden," *Outlook* 63, no. 6 (October 7, 1899): 327.

13. Ibid.

14. Ibid.

15. A century earlier, John Bartram, a Quaker farmer from Philadelphia, had contributed to popularize the taste for American plants across the ocean thanks to his shipments of native seeds, cuttings, and bulbs from his nursery along the banks of the Schuylkill River to collectors in Europe.

16. According to Andrew Jackson Downing, Parmentier developed a periodical catalog where "he arranged the hardy trees and shrubs that flourish in this latitude in classes, according to their heights, etc." See Downing, *A Treatise on the Theory and Practice of Landscape Gardening Adapted to North America,* with an introduction by Therese O'Malley (Washington DC: Dumbarton Oaks Research Library and Collection, 1991), 41.

17. About the development of landscape architecture in the Midwest and the promotion of regional identity, see William H. Tishler, ed., *Midwestern Landscape Architecture* (Urbana: University of Illinois Press, 2000). On Cleveland and on Simonds and Jensen, see Lance M. Neckar, "Fast-Tracking Culture and Landscape: Horace William Shaler Cleveland and the Garden in the Midwest," and Robert E. Grese, "The Prairie Gardens of O. C. Simonds and Jens Jensen," both in *Regional Garden Design in the United States,* ed. Therese O'Malley and Marc Treib (Washington DC: Dumbarton Oaks Research Library and Collection, 1995), 69–123.

18. McFarland, "An American Garden," 328. On Manning see Lance Neckar, "Developing Landscape Architecture for the Twentieth Century: The Career of Warren H. Manning," *Landscape Journal* 8 (Fall 1989): 78–91, and more recently Robin Karson, "Warren H. Manning, 1860–1938," in *A Genius for Place: American Landscapes of the Country Place Era* (Amherst: University of Massachusetts Press, 2007), 25–45.

19. Edith Roberts and Elsa Rehmann, eds., *American Plants for American Gardens: Plant Ecology—The Study of Plants in Relation to Their Environment* (New York: Macmillan, 1929). I thank Thaïsa Way for this reference.

20. Charles Eliot, "What Would Be Fair Must First Be Fit," *Garden and Forest* 9, no. 423 (April 1896): 133.

21. Wright is quoted by Keith N. Morgan, *Charles A. Platt: The Artist as Architect* (New York: Architectural History Foundation; Cambridge, MA: MIT Press, 1985), 69.

22. Beatrix Farrand, "The Garden as a Picture," *Scribner's Magazine* 42, no. 1 (July 1907): 4.

23. Charles Platt's quote is in Wilhelm Miller, "An 'Italian Garden' That Is Full of Flowers," *Country Life in America* 7, no. 5 (March 1905): 492.

24. David Streatfield, "The Influence of Japan upon Gardens in California and the Pacific Northwest," in *Influences on American Garden Design: 1895 to 1940*, ed. Robin Karson (Cold Spring, NY: Garden Conservancy, 1995), 39.

25. Ibid., 47.

26. Ibid.

27. Fletcher Steele, "Modern Landscape Architecture," in *Contemporary Landscape Architecture and Its Sources* (San Francisco: San Francisco Museum of Art, 1937), 25.

28. Christopher Tunnard, *Gardens in the Modern Landscape* (London: Architectural Press; New York: Charles Scribner's Sons, 1948), 62–63.

29. Ibid., 87. Tunnard borrowed this sentence from Raymond McGrath's *Twentieth-Century Houses* (1934). See David Jacques and Jan Woudstra, eds., *Landscape Modernism Renounced: The Career of Christopher Tunnard (1910–1979)* (London: Routledge, 2009), 97.

30. Cited by Dorothée Imbert, "The AIAJM: A Manifesto for Landscape Modernity," *Landscape Journal* 26, no. 2 (2007): 233n11.

31. Catherine Howett, "Modernism and American Landscape Architecture," in *Modern Landscape Architecture: A Critical Review*, ed. Marc Treib (Cambridge, MA: MIT Press, 1993), 32.

32. Ibid., 33.

33. On this topic see O'Malley and Treib, *Regional Garden Design in the United States.*

PART 1

British Influences

The American Translation of the Picturesque

EMILY T. COOPERMAN AND
JOHN DIXON HUNT

The arrival of the picturesque in North America in the late eighteenth and early nineteenth centuries depended in large part upon the ideas for its practice and theory developed in Europe, especially England, where the picturesque had enjoyed a considerable exposure. Its translation into North America, rather than losing usefulness and point, saw the vocabulary of the picturesque and its application to a newfound land acquire both a renewed vitality and, more importantly, a new sense of its relevance. Yet by the end of the twentieth century, the picturesque developed a rather negative reputation, with landscape architects in particular lamenting its bland, unstrenuous usage and its supposed dependence upon a merely "pictorial" model. These diminished expectations belie what was originally central to the picturesque, so it is worth revisiting, very briefly, some of the elements that sustained the picturesque in England, most of which are ignored in modern discussions of the picturesque.[1] Six in particular are crucial.

1. The word first entered the English language in 1685 when William Aglionby's *Painting Illustrated* noted that some north Italian artists were "working à la *pittoresk,* that is to say boldly."[2] The reference was primarily to the medium of representation, techniques for rendering subject matter, and implied little if any specific reference to landscape. A modern equivalent might be the paintings of Jackson Pollock. The application of paint on a canvas, bold and vigorous manipulation of brushwork, or the detailed work of the engraver's burin on the engraved plate, produced work that provided, as the later painter Thomas Gainsborough explained, "business for the eye," by which he meant busy work on the surface of the representation. That both Gainsborough himself and other engravers saw the technique as especially useful in depicting landscapes became of greater importance by the end of the eighteenth century.

2. In discussing paintings by the end of the seventeenth century, it was always assumed that paintings represented human nature and that "Nature imitated," the usual phrase for describing the work of a painting, meant that *human* nature was imitated; thus the Italian critic Giovan Pietro Bellori stated in his *Vite de' pittori . . . moderni* (1672) that the essence of painting consists in imitating human action. Hence the central role of humans in paintings by Poussin, Claude, or Salvator Rosa, all of which had a huge impact on the picturesque, either through direct viewing of their canvases or in engravings of their work that enjoyed a wide circulation. Even when landscape became a more prominent genre (as opposed to historical paintings), it still addressed or implied similar concerns for finding in it some human element: it was not visual or pictorial for its own sake. This aspect was largely lost sight of by the end of the eighteenth century in England but had a powerful role to play in America.

3. It followed that places, or scenery, were representations of how and why *people* belonged in a particular place. Rubens's painting of his own property, *Het Steen* (London, National Gallery), was (if you like) its "portrait," even if the owner was not personally figured there. It showed people at work in the fields, a considerable repertoire of human activity. This is exactly what Joseph Addison has argued in *The Spectator* (no. 414, 1712), when he called for a landscape design that represented those who owned it and for which he used the Dutch term *landskip* (i.e., how a painter would represent a view, prospect, or "opening of a country"): "Fields of corn make a pleasant Prospect, and if the Walks were a little taken care of that lie between them, if the natural Embroidery of the Meadows were helpt and improved by some Additions of Art, and the several Rows of Hedges set off by Trees and Flowers . . . *A Man might make a pretty Landskip of his own possessions*" (emphasis added). Similarly, William Kent's well-known drawing of Alexander Pope in his garden at Twickenham was "picturesque," not because of the garden forms and layout (though the Shell Temple could be seen as being a picturesque item), but because it showed the poet in his proper habitat and surrounded by an appropriate, personal, and iconographical landscape.

4. The picturesque was not static—whether seen through the windows of a moving stage coach or by the pedestrian movement of visitors through a site and by the movement of their eyes as they scanned what they saw; the picturesque was always mobile, and we make a big mistake if we think simply of camera viewfinders and static sketches, which are anyhow rarely able to capture lateral views of territory around the visitor. That the Claude glass was much invoked by English artists (though never by Claude himself) was a tool for apprehending and understanding something of a landscape,

but not a means of capturing a literal representation.[3] We needed the arrival of the video camera to appreciate the importance of movement. But even a careful scrutiny of many "static" images from the eighteenth century shows artists particularly alert to the suggestion or implication of persons moving through the scenery: Kent's image of Pope's garden seems like a "freezing" of the poet's walk in his grounds. Some paintings even declare—against the grain of the image itself—how people moved through gardens: in the painting by Pieter Andreas Rysbrack of the *Orange Tree Garden at Chiswick* in the late 1720s (Trustees of the Chatsworth Collection), you see two groups actually emerging through the outer hedges of the enclosure, one of them gesturing to what the group will see once they emerge into the garden space.[4]

5. Physical and visual movement promoted a movement of the mind, the imagination, and the memory, without which an experience would be empty; this put a central emphasis upon associationism, that fundamental aspect of seventeenth- and eighteenth-century psychology whereby the mind stored ideas and memories that could be triggered by encounters with different sceneries and events. Movement of the mind cannot be illustrated visually, but a look at Gilpin's *A Dialogue on the Gardens of Stowe* (1748), the earliest publication of one who would become famous for descriptions of journeys throughout England, Wales, and Scotland, narrates how its two characters discuss and debate what they see as they move through the gardens.

6. In its earliest days the picturesque sprang from the same empirical understanding that gave birth to the Royal Society in England, founded in 1662 and dedicated to a whole range of European empirical enquiry.[5] (So it is perhaps no accident that the introduction of the term *pittoresk* occurred shortly after the empirical enquiries into English landscape.) The Royal Society promoted an interest in local history, recovering the meaning and association of places, mapping their terrain, listing and identifying monuments, ruins, and other archaeological remains and records of antiquity; one of its members, Henry Oldenburg, drew up a document on which to base "inquiries for all Counties" in England—asking about such items as "air, water, earth, plants, animals, minerals, and famous inhabitants of particular locales."[6] These habits of enquiry and recording were much needed and well used in North America when immigrants confronted a strange and unknown land. And though it has been largely ignored, the new scientificism associated with the Royal Society contributed markedly to what came to be termed the picturesque, which provided a means of viewing and assessing landscapes, offering a complex language and syntax for looking, drawing, and writing

about the surrounding landscapes. We have forgotten that the picturesque was a means of understanding how the land looked, but was not a model for creating a landscape. It was essentially a tool for comprehension, for learning how to look, how to seize the substance of a place, to parse what you saw, and learn about its components. For that skill, one could certainly learn from looking at carefully composed landscape paintings, and that scrutiny (that "tutorial") sharpened the mind in its other inquiries beyond paintings. Obviously some people did this well, others more clumsily or superficially.

These English developments were well attested and published in England. One of its later exponents was the enamel painter and engraver William Birch, who emigrated to Philadelphia in 1794. He had explored Great Britain in his volume of 1791 that combined text and descriptions of aspects of the whole nation, *Les Délices de la Grande Bretagne;* once he arrived in the United States, he began to explore that country too, utilizing all of the picturesque elements from his British experience in his views of Philadelphia (since the urban picturesque was vital in America) and of the nation's new country seats.[7]

By the end of the eighteenth century in Britain the picturesque was defined as an aesthetic category: an unsorted middle term between the beautiful—in landscape terms what was small, well formed, and smooth—and the sublime—what was vast and in some way awesome, that is, inspiring awe. Related to this aesthetic category, by the 1790s, the picturesque was also coupled with an appreciation of wilder, less refined nature, both in landscape understanding and in landscape garden design. However, during the time when the American colonies were becoming the American nation, the picturesque was not understood merely as an aesthetic category for landscape intervention; the notion of what we would now call a picturesque landscape park (the best known examples are arguably Central and Prospect Parks by Olmsted and Vaux in New York City), or a national park created on picturesque principles (such as Yellowstone and Yosemite) was, of course, in the future. But earlier, the picturesque had developed (as it had been in England) as a cluster of intellectual strategies: ways of comprehending landscape, experiencing it, and, of course, using and shaping it, concurrent with others that related directly to the understanding of the New World landscape.

Chief among these, and going back to empirical endeavors, are land survey and map making. As Martin Brückner details in *The Geographic Revolution in Early America,* geodesy, or "the art of land surveying or the measurement of land" "became both a trope and a narrative structure."[8] Today, geodesy is conventionally conceived of as primarily visual, that is, manifest in maps themselves; but Brückner rightly charts the course of a surveying verbal language and its important role in establishing American identity.

A familiar passage gives us an example of the relationship between geodesy and the picturesque. Thomas Jefferson's description of the Natural Bridge (fig. 1) in his *Notes on the State of Virginia* is primarily told in geodetic tropes (or to use Robert Clark's apt and somewhat more elegant characterization, "the language of utility").[9] In describing the Natural Bridge, Jefferson uses language that is empirical, noting the specific "admeasurements" of the opening under the arch: "The fissure, just at the bridge, is by some admeasurements, 270 feet deep, by others only 205. It is about 45 feet wide at the bottom, and 90 feet at the top."[10] Its quasi-manmade qualities, as well as the industrial capacity ("sufficient in the driest seasons to turn a grist-mill") of the "stream passing under" the arch, are contrasted with the dramatic physical effect the site has on Jefferson, causing him to literally fall to his knees: "you involuntarily fall on your hands and feet, creep to the parapet and peep over it. Looking down from this height about a minute, gave me a violent headache."[11] After this rapturous (if brief) characterization, Jefferson seems to pause. It is as if he manages to look up from his prone position on the upper side of the bridge to which he has been thrown by the enormity of the sublime experience. He looks up and notices what is beyond it, but his comment is terse. The landscape view is only "short" and "pleasing": "a short but very pleasing view of the North mountain on one side, and Blue ridge on the other, at the distance each of them of about five miles."[12] Neither geodesy nor the terms of the sublime are sufficient for a parallel analysis of the larger American landscape beyond the arch.

The shortcomings of geodetic description with respect to achieving a full understanding of the American landscape were clear to Jefferson's contemporaries. Most eloquent on the subject was America's first novelist, Charles Brockden Brown. In 1806–7, as the founding editor of the *Literary Magazine and American Register,* Brown reprinted portions of William Gilpin's *Three Essays: On Picturesque Beauty, on Picturesque Travel, and on Sketching,* which provided detailed, almost cookbook-like instructions for his subjects. Although Gilpin's volume was available in this country shortly after its publication in 1792 in such places as the Library Company of Philadelphia, it was given significantly greater distribution by Brown through this means. As editor also, from 1799, of the *Monthly Magazine, and American Review,* Brown published several articles on the picturesque and its relationship to American landscape.

Fig. 1. Isaac Weld, *View of the Rock Bridge,* from *Travels through the States of North America,* engraving, 1800.

In an 1800 article titled "On a Taste for the Picturesque" he presents a dialogue on the subject, writing under the pseudonym "Looker-On."[13] In this, Brown observes the tendency of "cultivated" Americans, when they "gaze upon a rural landscape," to experience "a pleasure higher than most of those that may be called sensual," even with "a delight bordering upon rapture." Despite this enthusiasm, Brown notes that his fellow citizens respond in ways that are "strangely meager, jejune, and vague" with only a few "trite and insignificant phrases to denote all the variety of kinds of scenery, and the degrees of pleasure the scenery produces."

In a clearly satirical voice, Brown itemizes the terms most often used. First he takes on *fine* with reference to the visual experience of sites near New York City, including the Hudson River Highlands and the Passaic River ("*'tis very fine indeed!*"; emphasis in the original). Both of these areas had been noted for their beauty for some time and were among the subjects of early engraved views of American landscape, including a view of the falls of the Passaic River at Paterson, New Jersey, published in London in 1761 (fig 2).

The inadequacy of the terms Brown singles out becomes clearer as he itemizes them. After addressing *fine,* he moves on to *sweet,* discussing a conversation between two women who take an evening excursion to a summerhouse over a waterfall. "Lady Clara" characterizes virtually every landscape item they encounter with this term, culminating in Clara's exclamation to her companion that "never, Maria, never saw you so *sweet* a rock," thus making Brown's attitude clear.

Pretty is skewered in the same vein. Brown notes that "sometimes the admiring gazer sees nothing in the wide extent of nature but what is *pretty.*" The ineptitude if not bathos of the application of this adjective to the American landscape is evinced by Brown noting that he had encountered someone

Fig. 2. Paul Sandby, after Thomas Pownall, *A View of the Falls on the Passaick . . . ,* engraving, published 1761.

who "once confirmed a description of the wonders of Niagara [Falls], by an assenting nod, and a—'Very pretty, indeed. The very prettiest cataract I ever saw in all my travels.'"

Brown's discussion of *handsome,* however, begins to move toward the relationship between human action (in the "human imitators" of Nature), drama, and landscape experience. Within a single paragraph, Brown notes the application of the term to *Othello* ("a very *handsome* composition"), to Cicero's defense of Quintus Ligarius ("a very handsome piece of eloquence"), to a neighborly act of charity ("a very *handsome* action"), and to the "grandeurs of the Blue-ridge, and the solemn beauties of the Leheigh [River—*sic*]."

Brown's satirical critique of the terms misused in their application to an understanding of the American landscape concludes by noting that some observers compound the crime by simply piling them into one account of a place: "'Tis very seldom that we meet with one who occasionally diversifies his praise with all these [linguistic] flowers, and who distributes, with due judgment, his *handsome* skies, his *sweet* rocks, his *pretty* water-falls, and his *fine* lakes."

Brown ascribes this "poverty and indistinctness of expression . . . not [to] sluggish feelings, but [to a] want of accurate conceptions" and the failure to differentiate "the peculiar character of different scenes." Equally important (and key to solving the shortcomings of Jefferson's geodetic approach to American landscape) is Brown's attention to his countrymen's propensity to "distinguish not between the different emotions which scenes of different kinds produce," resulting in the confusion of "the gentlest impulses of pleasure . . . with the most impetuous" and therefore in the absurd usage of terms he has been inventorying to this point in the article. Brown thus sees this problem as a failure of the scientific classification of emotional experience of landscape rather than of its intrinsic physiographic attributes.

It will not surprise those who attended to the early manifestation of the picturesque in England that Brown offers the picturesque as an antidote to the problem. In fact, he equates the "study of landscape" with "*picturesque beauty*" and assures his readers that this study "not only furnishes distinctness, and thus multiplies and renders accurate our language, but also serves, at the same time, a much more useful purpose."[14] Specifically, Brown asserts that his suggested study will "unspeakably augment and extend our pleasures" and "invigorate, diversify, and prolong a gratification the nearest a kin [*sic*] and most friendly to the ennobling and domestic virtues, of any that the sense possess." He goes on to itemize its health benefits "by strengthening the inducements to wholesome exercise," and its accompanying sensual stimulation ("physical delight in inhaling a pure breeze"; "the music of the groves," which he compares favorably to "senseless squeakings of the pipe"; and "the sense of smelling . . . no less gratified by the aromatic exhalations of which the vegetable tribes are so liberal"). Thus, Brown suggests, the picturesque will enrich not only the intellectual but also the moral and physical experience of the American landscape through sensual, physical endeavors.

In response to a query in the dialogue from one of the protagonists—"'How is landscape to be studied?'"—Brown urges the examination of "the works of this kind of celebrated painters" but acknowledges that "this is an advantage scarcely to be hoped for by us who stay on this side of the ocean." Given this American lack, he urges his readers to seek literary sources for the "principles of landscape," recommending the travel writing and romances of Ann Radcliffe and particularly those of Gilpin, "whose works ought to be perfectly familiar to every mind endowed with virtuous propensities and true tastes." The article concludes with the statement that "to examine with a picturesque-discerning and a cause-inquiring eye every scene that really occurs"—thus combining both picturesque and geodetic registers—"to ponder in like manner on the landscapes of painters and picturesque travellers, many of whom delineate and describe at the same time, seems to be the best mode of opening, in your breast, this source of high and beneficial pleasure."[15]

We want to make two more points about Brown because, despite this article, he does not simply look slavishly to Gilpin's publications and travel literature and to the study of paintings to understand the American landscape. And this, of course, is where the translation of the picturesque begins to become clear.

The first point comes out of his novels, in particular *Edgar Huntly,* first published in 1799. In this, the protagonist is represented as a kind of picturesque traveler, much along the lines of the activities for which Gilpin provides such clear formulas. Traveling in Connecticut, Huntly encounters multiple dangers of the American wilderness—storms, caves, mountain lions, and Indians. Brown's novel is a cautionary tale about the limits of picturesque study of the American landscape he lauds in the shorter article.[16] The author thus recognizes the shortcomings of the picturesque, in its specific focus, in a vein similar to that of Thomas Rowlandson's satirical sketches of Gilpin's single-minded pursuit of the picturesque in the British landscape of the following decade (fig. 3).

Fig. 3. Thomas Rowlandson, *Dr. Syntax Falling into the Water,* hand-tinted etching, 1809.

The second point about Brown's writing arises out of another article. In 1805, he published a short piece called "American Prospects" in his *Literary Magazine.* In this brief essay, he touches on several crucial points.[17] The first is the refutation of the common idea in the period that the American landscape was not picturesque in character: "I have often heard it observed by travelers, that America contained nothing of the picturesque."[18] Brown notes that this is primarily attributed to the lack of evidence of human intervention and activity, as it would be seen in Europe. In the United States, travelers find "no crumbling walls scattered over our vallies; no ivy-clad tower repos[ing] on the brow of our hills," which trigger the imagination "by these memorials of former generations."[19] Brown acknowledges that "those who are accustomed to see nature constantly accompanied by ancient turrets or modern obelisks, by palaces and spires, by artificial lakes and water-falls, grow fastidious." He further reports that the critics from whom he has heard find no evidence for this activity in "uncultivated nature, which contains no vestige of other times, nothing to hint of battles, sieges, or murder."

As a rejoinder to this perceived lack, Brown offers the activity of European settlement ("those districts, which have been settled eighty or a hundred years") within the wild American landscape as "abound[ing] with all those ingredients of the picturesque" and "worthy of the Claudes and Poussins of the age." As an example, he provides a description by the explorer

Alexander Mackenzie of an expedition into what is now northwest Canada. In this, Mackenzie's sees his "people" from an "elevated situation," working at communal activities of "pitching their tents in a charming meadow" and repairing their canoes in a river valley that broadens into a vista that displays "the most delightful intermixture of wood and lawn."[20] Mckenzie's expedition appears "diminished," like the figures in a Claude painting, from the vantage point from which he views them. Buffalo and elk "pasture" on the "lawn" rather than cattle in the Claudian Roman countryside. This is a remarkable vision in which European settlers live productively as communities in the benign bounty of American "uncultivated nature," in Mackenzie's terms "completing the picture." Group activity, then, provides a better strategy for the experience and understanding of the American landscape than the fate of the solitary picturesque traveler like Edgar Huntly.

It is this clear connection between human action and the understanding of and intervention in the American landscape that brings us back to William Birch.[21] Birch also allows us to make the connection between picturesque landscape understanding, landscape representation, and landscape intervention in the form of garden making. Birch spent his early career in London, where, in 1791, he issued his first book-length publication, *Les Délices de la Grande Bretagne.* The *Délices* registers the popular state of the British picturesque at the end of the eighteenth century but also prefigures the content of his work in the United States, which included the first two sets of picturesque views to be published in this country, accounts of picturesque travel on the East Coast, and designs for landscape gardens.

Salient among the aspects of the *Délices* are, first, the tone of the volume, as it is announced in his introduction, which is assertively nationalistic, even boosterish. He claims that British landscape "comprehends whatever is beautiful in nature" and the "singular excellence of Britain for picture scenes."[22] Second is the associationist operation of the picturesque already noted. This hinges on the inextricable relationship between words and images in the picturesque. For example, the role in the narrative of British history played by Roslin Castle might be guessed at by this image in which the castle is seen, in the manner perhaps of antiquarian research along the lines of the Royal Society[23] (fig. 4). But one would not guess by simply looking at this image of Saltram that the narrative associated with it concerns a royal visit to the site, because this visit is not visible in the image but noted in his text: "Their Majesties made this ['the seat of the Right Honorable Lord Borington'] their residence for a fortnight, in the course of their late tour"[24] (fig. 5).

Words play a complementary and vital role in understanding not just the meaning of images of places, but the meaning of places themselves, and Birch was not the first or only person to bring this maneuver to the shaping and understanding of American place. Just as picturesque views (and sites) came to be associated with nationalistic narratives and values in England, this British procedure was adapted in the United States to the purpose of developing American identity.

This dual operation can be seen in the association of what is now a familiar narrative with the Pennsylvania State House, better known today as Independence Hall. This image, engraved after the background of a portrait by Charles Willson Peale, originally appeared in the *Columbian Magazine*, at the moment of the Constitutional Convention in 1787[25] (fig. 6). Yet the image shows no hint of what was going on inside. It is only in the text for which the image is simply the accompanying illustration that we learn of the relative significance of the events taking place in the building on the stage of world history. The titular subject of the article is characterized as "a building which will, perhaps, become more interesting the history of the world, than any of the celebrated fabrics of Greece or Rome."[26] It is important to

Fig. 4. William Russell Birch, *Roslin Castle*, etching, from *Les Délices de la Grande Bretagne*, 1791.

Fig. 5. William Russell Birch, *Saltram, Devonshire,* etching, from *Les Délices de la Grande Bretagne,* 1791.

note that this narrative, one that we take for granted today, was constructed through picturesque operation as part of the larger enterprise of American nation-building. When Birch came to represent the State House in the *City of Philadelphia in 1800,* his second book and the first set of picturesque views successfully to be published in the United States, the site was already understood to have a multilayered narrative associated with it. One more crucial point needs to be made about the *Délices* to bring us finally to aesthetics and landscape making as well as its understanding for the United States. Among the picturesque equipment Birch brought with him when he arrived in Philadelphia in 1794 was both the appreciation of the wild landscape and the importance of its role in garden making (in the vein of Richard Payne Knight and Uvedale Price).[27] This is very clearly articulated in a long poem Birch wrote about the creation of his own garden at Springland,[28] his property at the mouth of the Neshaminy Creek at the Delaware River north of Philadelphia, and is seen in the images he created of it. Birch engraved this watercolor (fig. 7) for his third and final set of engravings, *The Country Seats of the United States,* which he published from Springland in 1808. In the introduction to this volume, he positions his subject as the confluence

Fig. 6. Charles Willson Peale, *A N.W. View of the State House in Philadelphia taken 1778*, engraving, illustration to "Account of the State-House of Pennsylvania," *Columbian Magazine*, July 1787.

Fig. 7. William Russell Birch, *View from the Elysian Bower, Springland, Pennsylvania, the Residence of Mr. W. Birch*, hand-colored engraving, 1808, from *The Country Seats of the United States of North America.*

Fig. 8. William Russell Birch, *The Sun Reflecting on Dew, a Garden Scene. Echo, Pennsylvania, a Place Belonging to Mr. D. Bavarage [Beveridge],* hand-colored engraving, 1808, from *The Country Seats of the United States of North America.*

of the picturesque understanding and appreciation of what he calls the "variegated" "face" of American nature, the creation of estates, and the advancement of the emerging American culture (fig. 8). This aspect is shown most vividly in one particular image for the text of which Birch not only extols the virtue of that nature but also associates the site with a nationalistic American narrative of the Revolution. Shared landscapes in the form of the elite villa districts along the Schuylkill River in Philadelphia and in Upper Manhattan in New York are also featured in the *Country Seats* (fig. 9). In these, gardens merge into a larger landscape if not into the American whole.

The succeeding generations after Jefferson, Brown, Birch, and their contemporaries continued the process of translating the British picturesque for American purposes. The threads of landscape description and understanding, design, and representation found together in Birch's work show up in a variety of ways. Without picturesque understanding of place, and the values associated through it, we would not have preserved Independence Hall, nor created Yosemite Park, nor appreciated American landscape sufficiently to see it depicted in park designs like the Ravine in Prospect Park. The pic-

Fig. 9. William Russell Birch, *York-Island, with a View of the Seats of Mr. A. Gracie, Mr. Church & c.*, hand-colored engraving, 1808, from *The Country Seats of the United States of North America.*

turesque narrative of collective settlement in the bounties of the American landscape that Brown records leads, on the one hand, to the doctrine of Manifest Destiny, just as, coupled with Birch's perception of the suburbs as the picturesque middle term between wilderness and city, we come to A. J. Downing's "smiling lawns and tasteful cottages."[29]

Notes

1. The topic of the picturesque has generally been well treated. See, in particular, Christopher Hussey, *The Picturesque; Studies in a Point of View* (London: Putnam, 1927, with reprints); Sidney K. Robinson, *Inquiry into the Picturesque* (Chicago: University of Chicago Press, 1991); John Dixon Hunt, *Gardens and the Picturesque: Studies in the History of Landscape Architecture* (Cambridge, MA: MIT Press, 1992); Kim Ian Michasiw, "Nine Revisionist Theses on the Picturesque," *Representations* 38 (1992): 76–100; Stephen Copley and Peter Garside, eds., *The Politics of the Picturesque: Literature, Landscape and Aesthetics since 1770* (Cambridge: Cambridge University Press, 1994); John Dixon Hunt, *The Picturesque Garden in Europe* (London: Thames and Hudson, 2002). An essay on the modernity of the picturesque by Hunt was published as "John Ruskin, Claude Lorrain, Robert Smithson, Christopher Tunnard, Nikolaus Pevsner, and Yve-Alain Bois Walked into a Bar . . . ," *Hopkins Review* 5, no. 1 (Winter 2012): 81–94.

2. William Aglionby, *Painting Illustrated in Three Dialogues* (London, 1685), 24.

3. On the Claude glass, see Arnaud Maillet, *The Claude Glass: Use and Meaning of the Black Mirror in Western Art,* trans. Jeff Fort (Cambridge, MA: MIT Press, 2004). That these glasses were still sold as late as the end of the nineteenth century in Philadelphia suggests as much the need for amateur artists to assemble suitable scenery to depict; see Deborah Jean Warner, "The Landscape Mirror and Glass," *Antiques,* 105, no. 1 (1974), 158–59.

4. The painting and a detail of the walkers are illustrated in John Dixon Hunt, *A World of Gardens* (London: Reaktion Books, 2012), 345–46.

5. This is a topic not explored, as far as we know, in any discussion of the picturesque. For the Royal Society, see Charles Webster, *The Great Instauration: Science, Medicine and Reform, 1626–1660* (London: Duckworth, 1975); Michael Hunter, *Science and Society in Restoration England* (Cambridge: Cambridge University Press, 1981), and his essay "John Evelyn in the 1650s," in *John Evelyn's "Elysium Britannicum" and European Gardening,* ed. Therese O'Malley and Joachim Wolschke-Bulmahn (Washington, DC: Dumbarton Oaks Research Library and Collection, 1998), 79–106. For work on two precursors of the Royal Society and their work in landscape, see Michael Leslie and Timothy Raylor, eds., *Culture and Cultivation in Early Modern England: Writing and the Land* (Leicester: Leicester University Press, l992), and Mark Greengrass, Michael Leslie, and Timothy Raylor, eds., *Samuel Hartlib and Universal Reformation: Studies in Intellectual Communication* (Cambridge: Cambridge University Press, 1994). See also the CD-ROM edition of *The Hartlib Papers: A Complete Text and Image Database* (Ann Arbor: UMI, 1995).

6. Royal Society "Classified Papers," 19, no. 43. Also published in Robert Boyle, *General Heads for the Natural History of a Country, Great or Small; Drawn out for the use of Travellers and Navigators* (London, 1692).

7. For Birch, see William Russell Birch, *The Country Seats of the United States,* ed. Emily T. Cooperman (Philadelphia: University of Pennsylvania Press, 2009), and the study of his work, including discussions of the *Délices,* in Emily T. Cooperman and Lea Carson Sherk, *William Birch: Picturing the American Scene* (Philadelphia: University of Pennsylvania Press, 2010).

8. Martin Brückner, *The Geographic Revolution in Early America* (Chapel Hill: University of North Carolina Press, 2006), 17.

9. Robert Clark, "The Absent landscape of America's Eighteenth Century," in *Views of American Landscapes,* ed. Mick Gidley and Robert Lawson-Peebles (Cambridge: Cambridge University Press, 1989), 81–98.

10. Thomas Jefferson, *Notes on the State of Virginia* (London, 1787), 35.

11. Ibid.

12. Ibid., 36.

13. [Charles Brockden Brown], "On a Taste for the Picturesque," *Monthly Magazine, and American Review* 3, no. 1 (July 1800): 11–13. (Brown later reprinted the same piece in the *Literary Magazine and American Register* 2, no. 9 [June 1804]: 163–65).

14. Ibid.

15. Ibid.

16. See Beth L. Lueck, *American Writers and the Picturesque Tour: The Search for National Identity, 1790–1860* (New York: Garland, 1997), 31–48.

17. Anonymous, "American Prospects," *Literary Magazine, and American Register* 3, no. 17 (February 1805): 97.

18. Ibid.

19. Ibid.

20. Ibid.

21. For Birch, see note 7 above.

22. William Russell Birch, *Délices de la Grande Bretagne* (London, 1791), i.

23. The English material is engagingly set out in the catalog of the exhibition on the British Society of Antiquaries: *Making History: Antiquaries in Britain, 1707–2007* (London: Royal Academy Books, 2007).

24. Birch, *Délices,* n.p. (text for plate *Saltram, Devonshire).*

25. "Account of the State-House of Pennsylvania," *Columbian Magazine* 1, no. 11 (July 1787): 513.

26. Ibid.

27. Richard Payne Knight, *The Landscape: A Didactic Poem* (London, 1794), with his later *An Analytical Inquiry into the Principles of Taste* (London, 1805); Uvedale Price, *Essay on the Picturesque as Compared with the Sublime and the Beautiful,* 2 vols. (London, 1784–98), with a third edition in three volumes, 1805.

28. See Cooperman and Sherk, *William Birch,* 205–15.

29. A. J. Downing, *The Architecture of Country Houses* (New York: D. Appleton, 1851), v.

Studying Peculiarities

Andrew Jackson Downing's Multifaceted Adaptation of British Principles to American Practices and Ways of Life

CAREN YGLESIAS

Almost as a farewell caution, a month before Andrew Jackson Downing (1815–1852) died, he wrote an editorial essay for his popular monthly journal the *Horticulturist.*[1] In it, Downing decried the inability of immigrant British gardeners to adapt their horticultural skills to American climate, topography, and soil. Downing's first two books—a well-received treatise on landscape gardening (1841) and another on rural domestic architecture (1842)—included the words "Adapted to North America" in their titles. Specifically, Downing adapted British principles of fitness (form appropriate to use), expression of purpose, and expression of style primarily known to him from the writings of John Claudius Loudon (1782–1843) and other British authors.[2]

Loudon, a botanist, landscape gardener, and prolific writer working first in Edinburgh and then England, formulated the principle of the Recognition of Art as a design approach that informed his gardenesque style. Principles of garden design had been debated throughout England long before Loudon, however, in response, for example, to the work of such landscape designers as Lancelot "Capability" Brown (1716–1783) and Humphry Repton (1752–1818) and later as a consequence of the new aesthetic theories of the beautiful and the sublime, with which Downing was familiar.

Downing, however, did not simply offer an original synthesis of British debates on landscape design. Along with his goal of adapting British principles and techniques to the needs and hopes of the American middle classes, one of his significant achievements was paving the way for the advancement of the practice of landscape gardening to professional status, albeit with the same aspirations of gentility earlier associated with the noble pursuits of the privileged.[3] Thus, while Loudon "had few illusions that the wealthy would voluntarily fulfill their obligation to encourage the taste and elevate the standing of the lower classes,"[4] Downing optimistically believed that they could do precisely so, even though he never explicitly acknowledged their existence. Despite his assertions, Downing's remarks and artistic advice were primarily directed to the upper class—as Dell Upton has shown—whose cultivated taste he distinguished from the mass taste of the working class, including farmers, who, in Downing's opinion, needed guidance if they wanted to express anything more than their own simplicity. The wealthy, on the contrary, grasped the principle of individuality of expression, which entitled them to make use of historical styles to give shape to their own character. This, as a quality inseparable from moral traits, traditionally linked to the land, was reflected in the proprietor's improvements to all domestic buildings including rural cottages, farmhouses, and villas.

The English press published books in the early nineteenth century by architects working in various styles, but what made them different from earlier publications and surely inspiring for Downing was that they illustrated a shift in thinking about designing smaller houses that were no longer the gate lodges, vicarages, and accessory structures of manor houses, but were worker housing. Downing believed—albeit unrealistically for those times—that any American worker could own a comfortable cottage on land with vegetable gardens and flower beds located between dense cities and the retreating wilderness and could participate in social systems that were decidedly middle class. Downing took this emerging interest in what had previously been considered an unsuitable subject for design and addressed the ideal suburban village as free of class distinctions. He adapted Loudon's principles, with some notable exceptions, for American practices based on the ability of design to link *peculiarities* of people, place, and artifice. In doing so Downing anticipated expectations for domestic design and suburban land planning still evident today. In addition, by observing practices and skills mastered by British designers, Downing promoted the scientific advancement of the discipline.[5]

Downing's writings directed the attention of Americans toward domestic accomplishment, arguing against the imitation of European fashions without considering a direct link between the particular proprietor and his land. In so doing, as Therese O'Malley has argued, "Downing and colleagues presented landscape gardening as a patriotic pursuit, using bold rhetoric to obscure their wholehearted imitation of European models and the contradiction this wrought in their republican world."[6] But not only the adaptation of European models to the New World would have been contradictory; also, the attempt to confine Americans of various social strata within the limits and boundaries of their own class—as is evident from Downing's explanation of the social basis of taste—was more conservative than liberal or democratic. By failing to acknowledge the presence of a class-based society, Downing in effect came closer to the adaptation of the trappings of Old World social privileges than he ever allowed in his writings. But he did so with a precise purpose: the necessity to invest the person of means with the role once performed by the patron, while promoting the architect and landscape designer from the position of expert technician to that of a learned professional, who shared with his clients a cultivated, if not innate, good taste.[7]

Thus, Downing made clear that determining what was appropriate required the guidance of an expert professional, knowledgeable in the science of his own discipline, because previous experience would not necessarily be useful to those building in locations with unfamiliar conditions. Professional design assistance, by contrast, provided information about consistent architectural style elements and the latest technical devices for homes, and about climate and soil preparation for planting, which could mean the difference between successful and failed crops. Also critical to consider were the reasons that spurred immigration in the first place: political and religious freedom and economic opportunity. Among Downing's stated objectives was to encourage settlement and cultivation, to elevate refinement and taste, and to support ethical and social ideals through design, and in order to accomplish this goal propriety was to be the guide.[8] These values and their expression in built form became the foundation for designs Downing thought were distinctly American.

Importing Plants and Developing Horticultural Skills

In his 1852 editorial comparing American and British horticultural practices, Downing explained the need for British gardeners to know the American climate and flora: "The ugly words of English gardening, are *damp, wet, want of sunshine, canker.* Our bugbears are *drought, hot sunshine, great stimulus to growth, and blights and diseases resulting from sudden checks.*"[9] Although Downing expressed his disappointment at British gardeners' inability to adapt their knowledge to the American landscape (about which he proclaimed himself to be, for reasons of self-promotion, very knowledgeable),

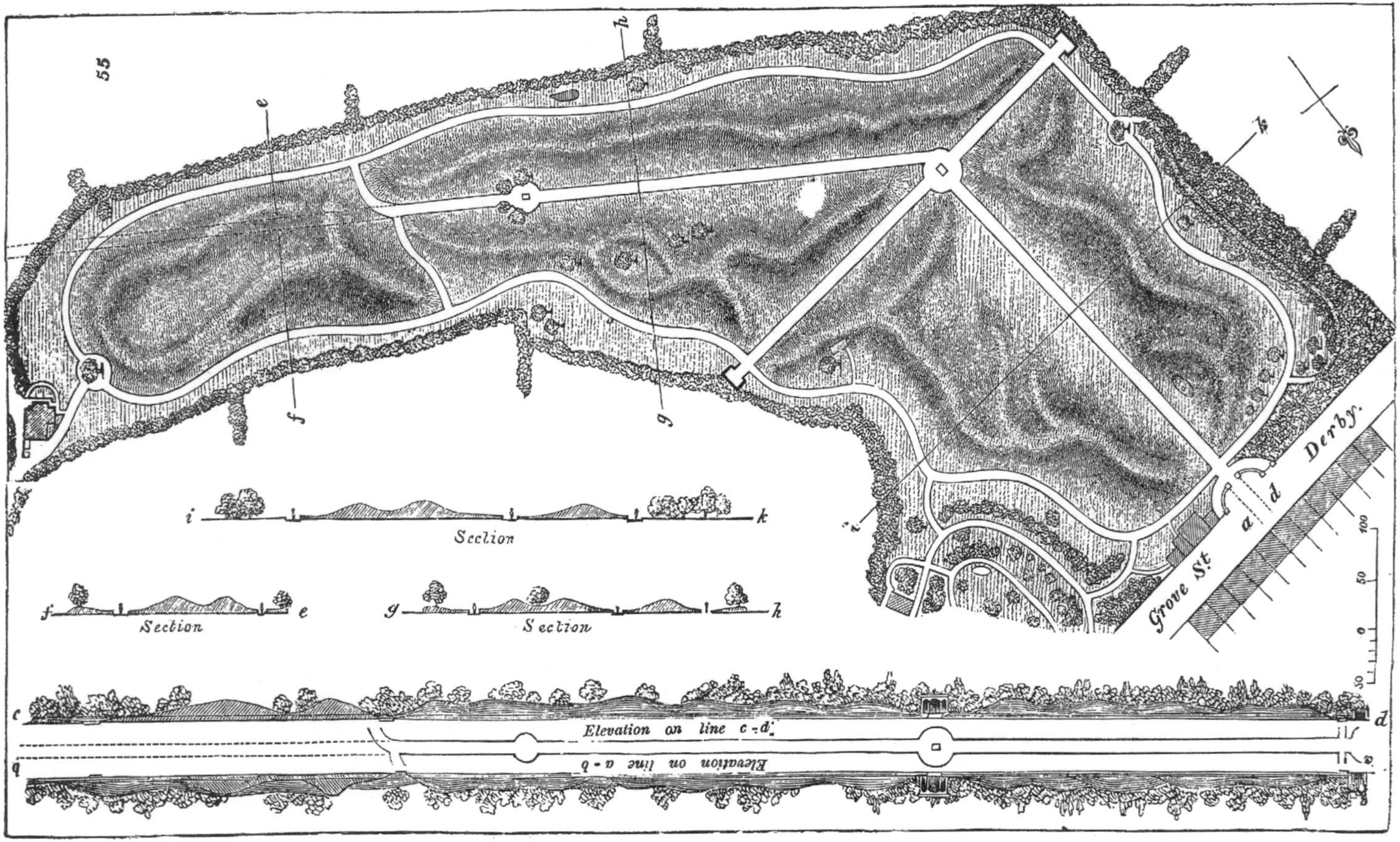
55
Derby.
Grove St.
a
d
100
50
0
50
Section
Section
Section
i
k
f
e
g
h
Elevation on line c - d.
Elevation on line a - b
c
d
b
a

he had, earlier in his life, admired the horticultural prowess of the British, particularly their skills in acclimatizing foreign plants, including American ones.

Loudon had argued for the correct and singular placement of specimen trees, native and foreign, so as to allow ideal form growth. In addition, he maintained that "the true modern gardener must introduce 'other species of trees,' for if he did not, 'however beautiful the scene copied, the beauty produced would be merely that of repetition.' "[10] These ideas informed Loudon's principle of the Recognition of Art, which, according to Downing, was the "first principle in Landscape Gardening."[11] Loudon's principle had three requirements. First, garden designs were not to imitate nature or be mistaken for a work of nature. Rather, the use of foreign plants or exotics would aptly reveal the artificial nature of the design. Single specimen trees were thought to have great presence if they were allowed to grow into full form; shrubs were to be planted sparingly along water edges, replacing indigenous species; and turf expanses were to be visually distinguishable from adjoining fields of crops.

Second, design compositions were to have geometric forms, of which the circular flowerbed with a single species was preferred. Simple regular shapes were thought to be the great evidence of design because they are seldom found in nature. Such botanical displays satisfied those who obliged landscape designs to stir the senses *and* the mind. Finally, gardens were to be kept in the highest possible order displaying a high degree of care and never be allowed to appear unkempt.

All of Loudon's requirements were in place at Derby Arboretum, his most important commission and the first English park designed to be public that was open to all social classes[12] (fig. 1). The park included over eight hundred native and nonnative trees and shrubs suited to the climate, each described on brick tallies noting their common and botanical names, native country, year of introduction to England, and potential height. Trees were placed to show their full natural shape and habit of growth. Loudon prepared detailed maintenance instructions recommending that encroaching trees be removed and replaced when the growth interfered with an adjacent form. Even if Loudon's maintenance recommendations, in the end, were not carried out,[13] his design strategy must have been equally appreciable to an expert eye, as Downing's observations show. When he visited the park

Fig. 1, opposite. J. C. Loudon, *Derby Arboretum,* engraving, published in *Gardener's Magazine* 16 (1840): 536.

ten years after it opened, he remarked that if the "ridges had been cleverly planted with groups and masses of trees and shrubs, the effect would have been very good; but dotted as they are with *scattered* single trees and shrubs, the result is a little harsh, with neither the ease of nature nor the symmetry of art."[14] Notwithstanding what he thought were design flaws, Downing still admired the fact that British gardeners had horticultural skills beyond the traditional practices of local farmers.

Adapting a foreign plant to a new habitat required the expertise to select a site with favorable aspects in terms of light and shade, to amend the soil by adding peat, sand, or humus, and to make elevated beds for better drainage given the rainy English weather. Further, successful plant cultivation from seed and propagation from cuttings called for specialized skills requiring those who worked the land to become more versatile gardeners. In his 1849 book, *A Treatise on the Theory and Practice of Landscape Gardening,* under the last section called "Embellishments," which included quotes from Loudon's *Encyclopaedia of Gardening* (1822), Downing described several methods the English used to acclimatize exotic plants including relying on pots kept under glass or with removable nightly protection; building a glass frame, hothouse, greenhouse, or conservatory; or keeping spare plants in a reserve garden and rotating them to the beds as blooms fade[15] (fig. 2).

When Downing had the opportunity to admire firsthand the horticultural skills of British gardeners during his trip abroad in 1850, he visited, in addition to Derby Arboretum, several English estates about which he wrote in the *Horticulturist.*[16] Two estates in particular were mentioned for their exotics. While Downing did not particularly like Dropmore, the seat of Lady Grenville near Windsor, he did appreciate its scientific collection of rare evergreen trees collected in a pinetum with every species of the pine tribe that could grow in England.[17] Downing noted that the collection also had trees from Chile, California, India, and Japan. Downing also saw Woburn Abbey and praised the advancement and maturity of its landscape due to the estate remaining in the same family for three centuries. Contrasting it to Chatsworth and its continental influences, Downing thought the landscape of Woburn Abbey's thirty thousand acres was thoroughly English, possessing, in his words, "grandeur of extent and substantial completeness, united with the most systematic and thorough administration of the whole."[18] Within the pleasure grounds, Downing described the American Garden as having "several acres of sloping velvety turf, thickly dotted with groups of rhododendrons, azaleas, &c., forming the richest masses of dark green foliage that it is possible to conceive." "The soil for them had all been formed

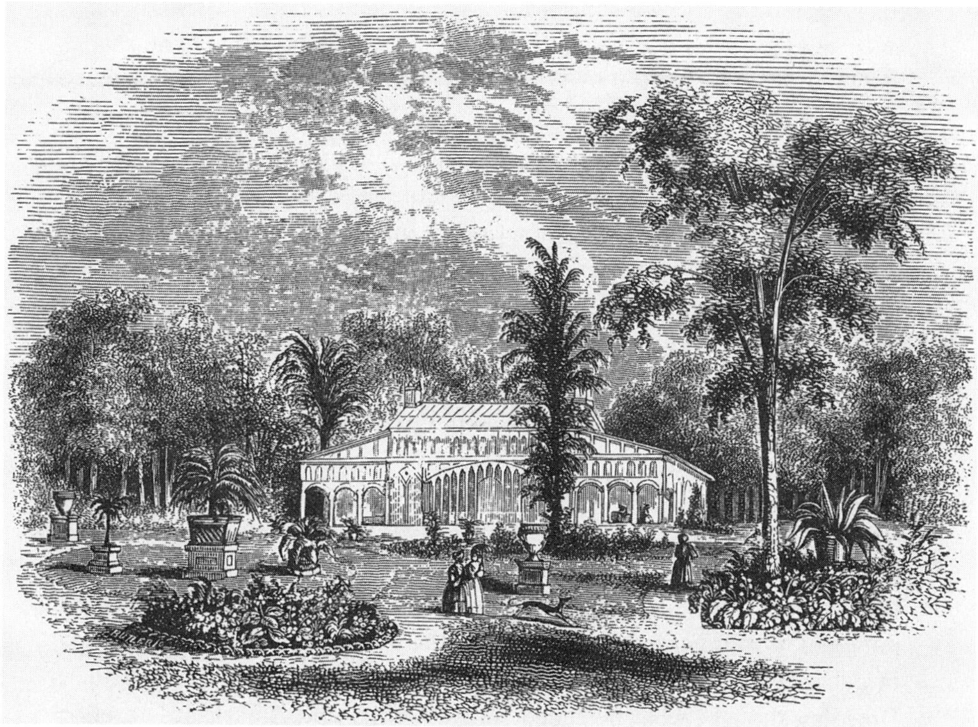

Fig. 2. A. J. Downing, *The Conservatory and Flower Garden at Montgomery Place,* 1839, engraving from *A Treatise on the Theory and Practice of Landscape Gardening,* 6th ed., 1859, Figure 73.

artificially, and consisted of a mixture of peat and white sand, in which the rhododendrons and kalmias seemed to thrive admirably."[19] Similarly praiseworthy were Loudon's words, written more than twenty years earlier: "The collection of heaths, hardy and exotic, is the most complete in the world, and not less so the collection of willows."[20]

Inspired by British gardeners' efforts, Downing championed the horticultural knowledge of the professional designer and initially espoused the use of exotics in American gardens while later—as Judith Major has shown—he prioritized the cultivation of American plants that were highly prized in Europe for their exotic character and paradoxically underutilized in their homeland.[21]

Even before his trip to England in 1850, Downing recommended techniques for adapting foreign fruit trees for American orchards in his *The Fruits and Fruit Trees of America.* Priorities began with the earth. Soil exhausted by long cultivation needed the addition of inorganic food supplying lime, potash, and phosphates found in wood ash, bone dust, and blacksmith cinders. After that, suitable climate and its conditions of light, shade, and humidity were critical to consider. The cultivation of fruit trees, in particular, was important because newly introduced foreign varieties might be weak due to poor grafting choices and techniques that enfeebled stock through successive generations. In this book, Downing first identified the source country with each fruit description and then suggested soil amendments to support new varieties, admitting that, "In this country, we have soil varying from the poorest sand to the richest alluvial, climate varying from frigid to almost torrid—a range wide enough to include all fruit trees between the apple and the orange."[22]

Wealthy Americans were interested in foreign plants for their estates for similar reasons as the British aristocracy to the point that Downing noted the irony of neglecting native American plants seen as worthy of export to the finest English gardens but not appreciated at home. Downing lamented: "azaleas, kalmias, rhododendrons, cypripediums, magnolias and nysas—the loveliest flowers, shrubs, and trees of temperate climates—you never put them in your gardens, but send over the water every year for thousands of dollars worth of English larches and Dutch hyacinths."[23] In particular, Downing thought what he called Native Hollies and American Laurel or Kalmia as being unreasonably underappreciated. Contrary to his earlier recommendations, Downing eventually prioritized the use of native plants in an effort to give shape and celebrate American identity.

Adapting British Principles to American Practices

Downing's work, built and published, adapted selectively Loudon's design principles—in particular his focus on botanical correctness—along with British landscape theory on the beautiful and picturesque, clarifying these principles for American practices.

Downing lived in Newburgh, a thriving town halfway between New York City and Albany along the Hudson River. There his family nursery supplied plants, and later he supplied landscape designs for estates along the Hudson River, now made more accessible from New York City with quicker and more reliable rail and steamboat service. Downing's direct involvement with the nursery ended in 1847 due to financial difficulties, at which time he devoted himself to his writing and professional practice.[24] In order to enhance the latter, however, Downing expounded, in his writings, on the benefits of availing oneself of the services of a professional designer. But who were his clients? "In Downing's universe, all men lived in the beautiful countryside, each satisfied with his villa or cottage, envy and pretension buried forever. Downing wished not every man a democrat, but every democrat an aristocrat—so far as was possible."[25] The new landowner, born into the world with or without any hereditary advantage, needed guidelines on what to build in a country still in the process of defining itself. Downing observed: "Foreign architects are finding their way to this country very plentifully. Some among them who follow rules and not principles, do us great harm by building expensive and unmeaning copies of foreign houses. Others do us service, by studying the peculiarities of climate and mode of life, and adapting their designs to meet the peculiarities."[26] And foreign principles did need adaptation.

For architecture, Downing specifically criticized copying styles that held no meaning to Americans, such as the Persian and Chinese styles, and even the English, whose interiors are characterized by "narrow passages, disconnected rooms, and no verandas for the warm climate of the middle States."[27] For gardens and landscapes, the principles defined in Loudon's theory of Recognition of Art became less important than the expression of individual choice that displayed a close correspondence between the land and what was built. Downing scholar George Tatum considers that "Downing's greatest achievement may have been his ability to turn the abstruse aesthetic theory developed in England during the eighteenth century into a system that middle-class Americans could comprehend and utilize in designing their own houses and gardens in the nineteenth century."[28]

Working with advances in image printing allowed a new type of book—which has been called a style book—that was directed primarily to the prospective client and not to the builder hoping to elevate what he could offer.[29] Before Calvert Vaux, Downing teamed with architect Alexander Jackson Davis, who self-published a book of his designs entitled *Rural Residences* in 1837. It was a financial disaster for Davis and did not reach the American middle classes as intended because of its high cost.[30] Downing's books on horticulture and architecture also spoke to the prospective client but were far more successful.[31] His books began with chapters on taste and design principles based on social ideals rather than formulas for copying architectural styles. Downing's cottages (requiring fewer than three servants) and villas (requiring more) were different not only in size. Cottages were to take their ornament from nature. For instance, climbing vines indicated intimacy and expressed a general domesticity. Villas were to include libraries showing intellectuality, art to display a love of the beautiful, and pleasure grounds suggesting an air of hospitality.[32] Downing recognized his audience had to set aside their many cultural traditions if they were to adapt to their new country. After all, unlike the lower classes in highly stratified European societies, many Americans bought land and built their own homes and farms, sometimes taking advantage of rising land values and repeating the process by moving farther west every few years.[33] Downing observed homesteaders had what he called a Great Spirit of Unrest and needed to settle in one place. Settlement would then lead to the cultivation of the land and the people, and eventually to developing a national identity of cultural, educational, and social institutions. England offered the inspiration, if not the model, for Downing's social vision in that he realized that, "in the best English tradition, prosperous landed interests would counteract the 'disposition to change which is characteristic of our people,' and place society on steadier supports."[34]

For the settler, Downing provided guidelines for design, not by offering model houses and landscape designs to imitate, but rather with a request for self-reflection. In so doing Downing averted the main criticism that eventually tarnished Loudon's encyclopedic production. In fact, Downing's mentor was criticized for introducing too many foreign architectural styles unsuited to the English situation and for not providing sufficient guidance directing tasteful and consistent selection of unusual ornament. For instance, Loudon published interchangeable "jackets of style" that could be draped over basic building forms for varying effect. Readers were left to wonder about how to make design decisions satisfying their desire to build nostalgic recollections of their foreign travels and what the chosen style might say about their character (fig. 3).

Displaying character through architectural and landscape forms was a way to express morals, and "moral character"—as Karen Halttunen has shown—"was closely linked to social position."[35] Aware of this, Downing forcefully raised the social responsibility, and therefore indispensability, of the professional designer. As a consequence of linking together aesthetic and moral judgment, Downing, adapting the principles of Scottish "Common Sense" philosophy already espoused by Loudon, held the view that moral claims could be made on the grounds of appearances, and that "directly perceivable moral and psychological truths were available to anyone with well-developed sensory skills," particularly the visual.[36]

Thus, Downing's procedure began precisely with the proprietor, who recognized his character as one of three possible types: that of sentiment and feeling, of imagination, or of common sense.[37] This would correspondingly

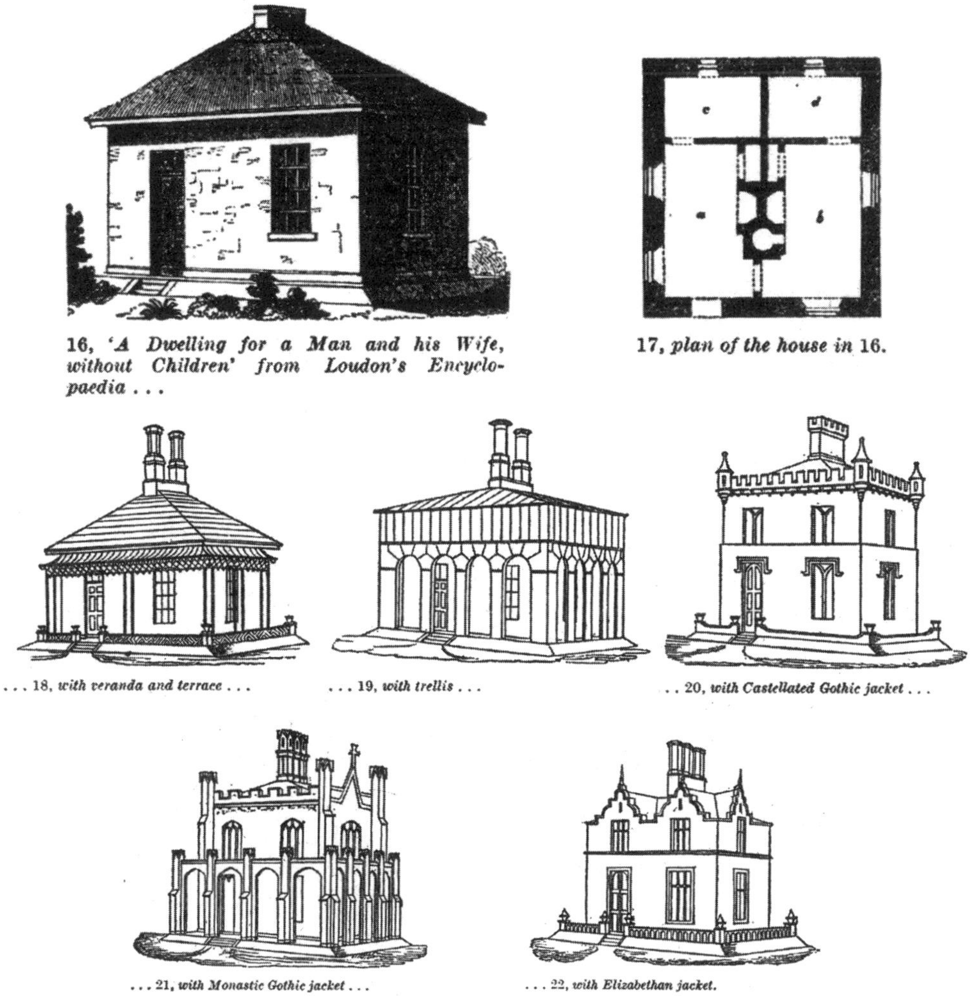

Fig. 3. J. C. Loudon, *Jackets of Style,* drawings from Loudon, *An Encyclopaedia of Cottage, Farm, and Villa Architecture and Furniture,* 3rd ed., 1835, Figures 16–22.

lead to preferring land with primarily either beautiful or picturesque qualities and to preferring architectural styles that complemented the nearby landscape or contrasted to the distant background.

In his *Cottage Residences,* Downing compiled ten designs for houses, each with a layout of their grounds. Design descriptions ended with long lists of the finest foreign and native plants available in America at that time. If a reader compiled the lists, the book identified the hardy varieties of flowers and shrubs that would thrive in temperate climates as well as trees that would produce fresh fruit ten months of the year. The first design was the smallest cottage in no identified style and was meant for a suburban location. Another design was a farmhouse he also felt needed no pretension of style. The other designs had titles that identified a distinct architectural style. Of these, Downing offered three for the man of sentiment and feeling, four for the man of imagination, and one for the man of common sense in what he hoped would become the American style.

Downing thought the man of sentiment and feeling would tend to prefer the vertical, more poetic, and aspiring lines of the Italian or Tuscan house styles, set, in his words, on a "smiling" plain or meadow diversified by hill and dale and sprinkled with groups or masses of deciduous trees avoiding straight lines. This landscape Downing called "graceful"[38] (fig. 4). In this design, the curved drive (*b*) approached on the diagonal allowed the view of the house to show its full form (fig. 5). The areas with the best soils were set aside for the kitchen garden (*f*) and orchard (*e*), separated by the stable (*d*) and laundry yard (*n*), all well concealed from the house and pleasure grounds. The meandering walks were to take advantage of distant prospects and river views. A hill and broad open glades of turf were to be "kept constantly mown, and in the highest order, so as to heighten, and render more forcible by contrast, the wilder and more picturesque beauty of the sylvan walks"(*i*). An oval lawn and ornamental beds (*m* and *l*) of "handsome flowering plants" were kept close to the house. Downing considered these grounds, with gradual topographic variation and improved with intimate nooks and shady vales, to exemplify the beautiful.[39] He summarized, "Landscape gardening, as an art, does not consist, as many seem to suppose, in producing a counterfeit of nature, but in *idealizing* natural beauty in a lawn, park, or garden."[40] This was a principle that had been mastered by Lancelot "Capability" Brown in England. Brown did not "simply [let] country estates become natural, but [represented] in its most perfect forms a nature that was British, and to do so he invoked the general, abstract forms of his materials—trees, woods, waters, hills."[41] But where Brown used solely the materials of nature to create the artifice, Downing added those of man to call attention to the illusion.

Downing defined the man of imagination as one who would appreciate boldness and originality and favor in architecture the asymmetrical and capricious forms of the English or Rural Gothic, Old English, Pointed, or Tudor styles (fig. 6). The ideal site would be near rugged mountains or in a sequestered valley full of dense evergreen forests (fig. 7). In this design, the house location and thick shrubbery (*f*) divides the front pleasure grounds

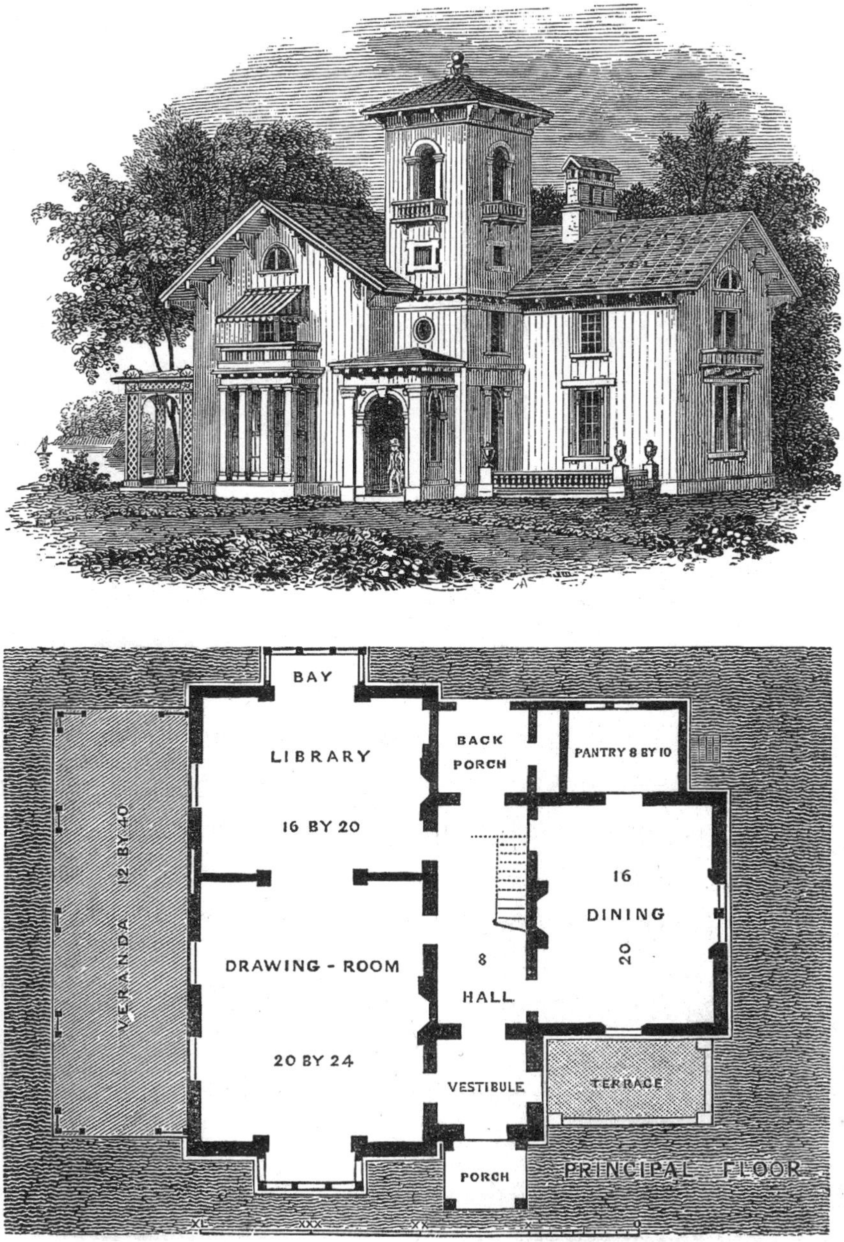

Fig. 4. A. J. Downing, Design VI, *A Villa in the Italian Style, Bracketed,* engraving, Exterior elevation/Principal floor plan from *Cottage Residences,* 4th ed., 1852.

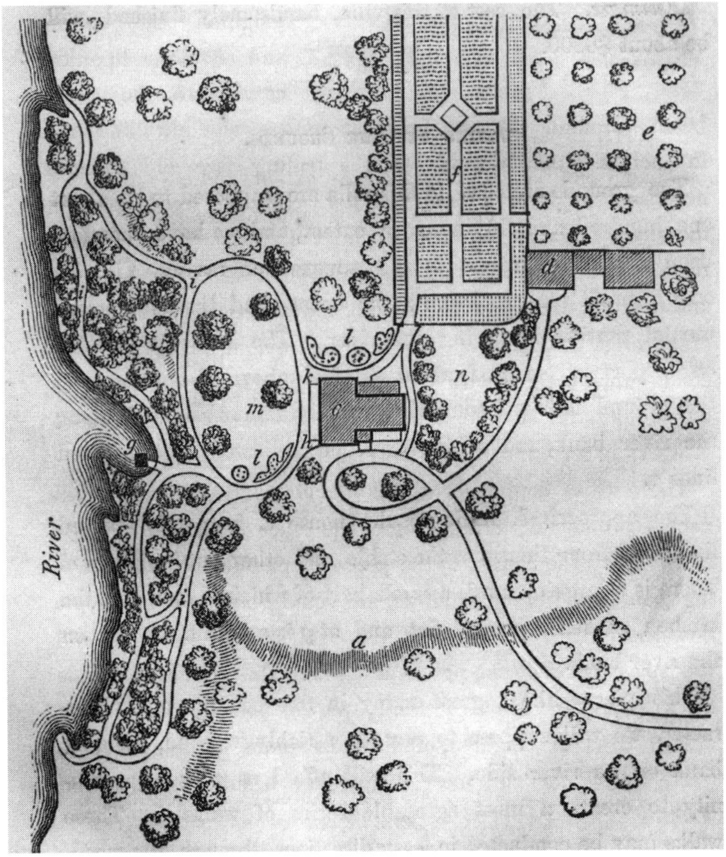

Fig. 5. A. J. Downing, Design VI, *A Villa in the Italian Style, Bracketed,* engraving, Site Plan from *Cottage Residences,* 4th ed., 1852.

from the rear productive fields. Flower beds (*e*) were kept to the perimeter with the central space reserved for turf and trees with bold and spiry-topped shapes that would harmonize with the architecture. Downing considered this a picturesque landscape.[42]

Downing's man of common sense would prefer a house in the American Bracketed style with regularity and symmetry that was built on level land with neat productive gardens and fields and with irregular pleasure grounds offering beautiful *and* picturesque characteristics. Downing's recommendations for the man of common sense are not dissimilar from those of Humphry Repton, who challenged Capability Brown's design approach as impractical for estate operations.[43] Repton thought a house should not rest "in a sea of lawn," but that it needed a balustrade terrace as an architectural

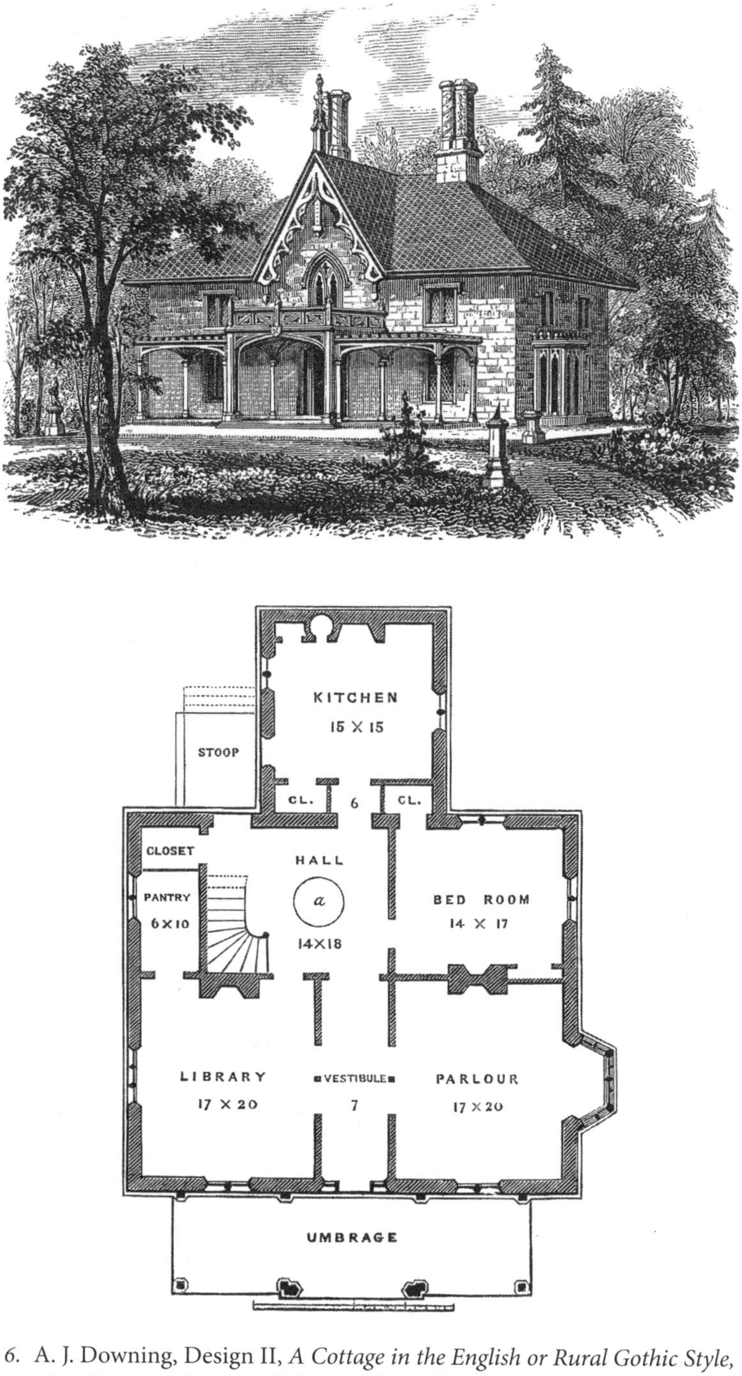

Fig. 6. A. J. Downing, Design II, *A Cottage in the English or Rural Gothic Style*, engraving, Exterior elevation/Principal floor plan from *Cottage Residences*, 4th ed., 1852.

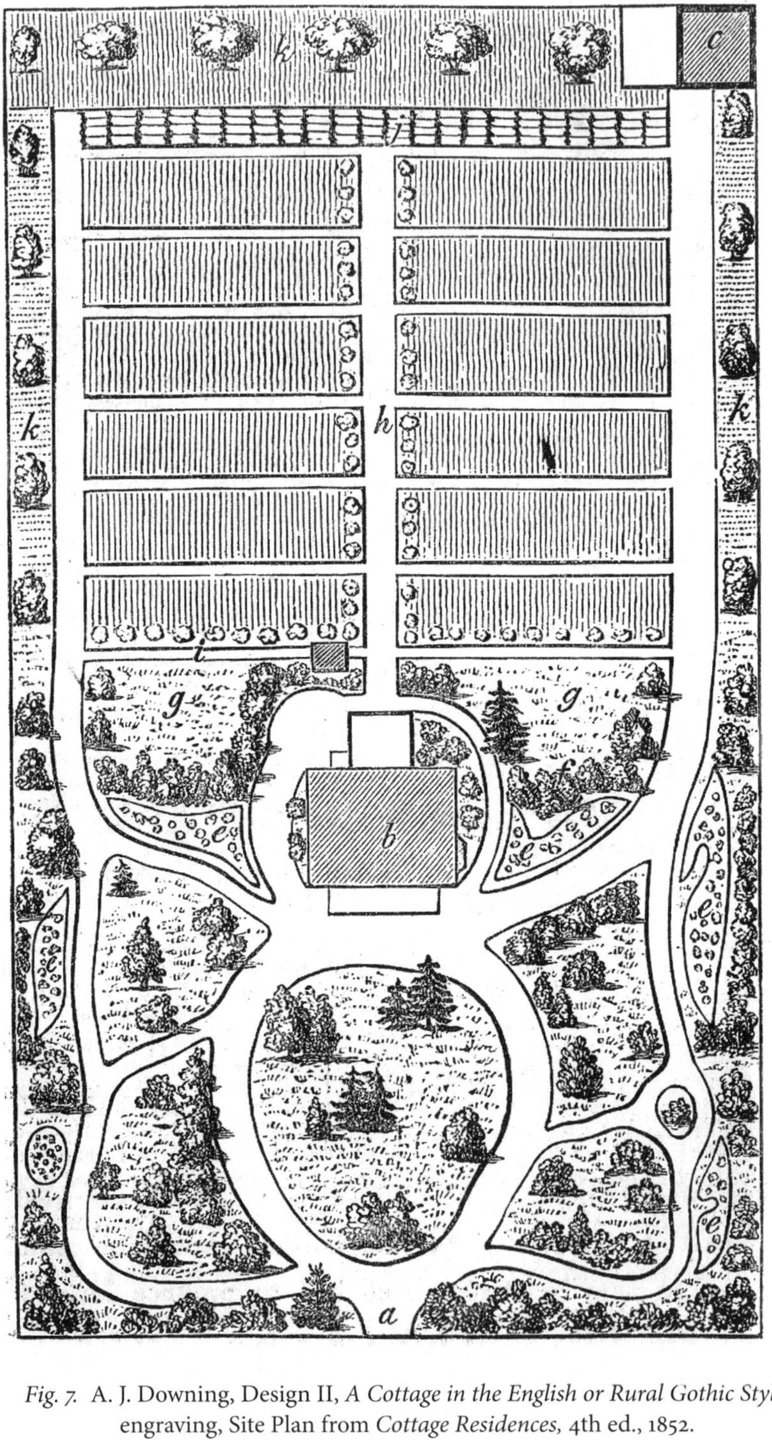

Fig. 7. A. J. Downing, Design II, *A Cottage in the English or Rural Gothic Style,* engraving, Site Plan from *Cottage Residences,* 4th ed., 1852.

base. Further, the approach need not wind endlessly before arriving at its destination. Short or long, a carriage drive could take advantage of pleasing displays in sequential presentation.[44] Downing's "A Cottage Villa in the Bracketed Mode" included everything he thought desirable, where "its domestic, comfortable air" in an "elegant expression" would be "highly suitable to North America"[45] (fig. 8). The generous roof overhangs, ornamental chimney tops, and articulated window and door hoods and sills indicated the domestic character of the building, which exemplified Downing's principle of the Expression of Purpose. The wraparound veranda, entry porch, and second-floor balconies offered places for leisure activities located between house and grounds. The interior was outfitted with the latest technical devices for comfort and convenience including a built-in window seat (*a*), water closet off the back hall (*b*), a casement window door (*c*), and closets as storage rooms. The two-acre site had gardens with flower borders and cut beds in the beautiful style around the house "to create an airy, cheerful aspect" (fig. 9). The oval lawns had ornamental trees and shrubs planted, as Loudon preferred, with "some being allowed to grow alone and assume all their beauty of development, and others planted in groups, or thickets, for effect or shelter," as Repton advised. The picturesque landscape had a meandering path through a thickly planted hill to a rustic summerhouse (*c*), about which Downing said, "from whence a prospect of the surrounding country is obtained."[46] Kitchen gardens and the orchard were concealed from the pleasure grounds with a privet or hedge, which, according to Downing, "will scarcely appear barriers."[47] Loudon's gardenesque style is found in the round flower beds (*j*) "filled with choice double dahlias" in geometrically shaped botanical displays. The detached greenhouse (*r*) is located on the diagonal to the house in order to be less visible from interior view.[48]

In sum, Downing's hypothetical design proposals enabled his audience to imagine a relationship between land and building qualities and to expect this harmony to reflect the proprietor's character and morality. Variety was achieved in the regular arrangement of various species. Unity was achieved when beds or belts of similar plants were massed in an irregular composition. Downing's approach made sense for Americans interested in building their country. For Downing, "A home revealed the character of the man who built it; the perceptive observer easily detected expressions of pride or egotism. Domestic architecture reached perfection only when it expressed the beauty and truth of the builder's life."[49]

The best example of Downing's ideas applied to practice is Springside, his most complete built project[50] (fig. 10). The forty-four-acre estate belonged to

Fig. 36.

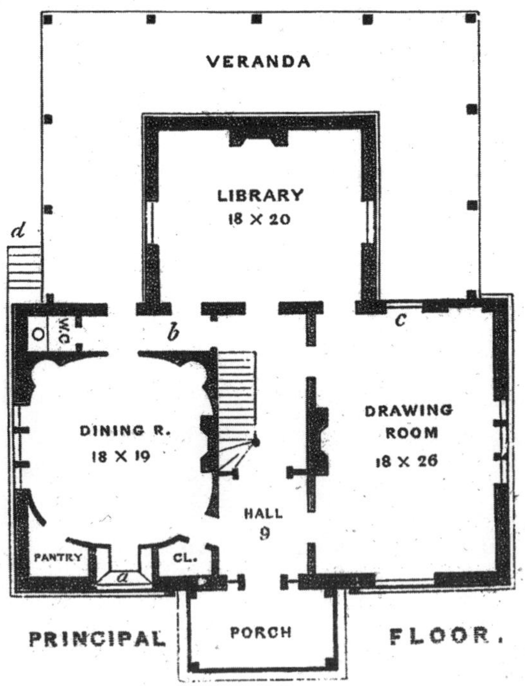

Fig. 8. A. J. Downing, Design V, *A Cottage Villa, in the Bracketed Mode,* engraving, Exterior elevation/Principal floor plan from *Cottage Residences,* 4th ed., 1852.

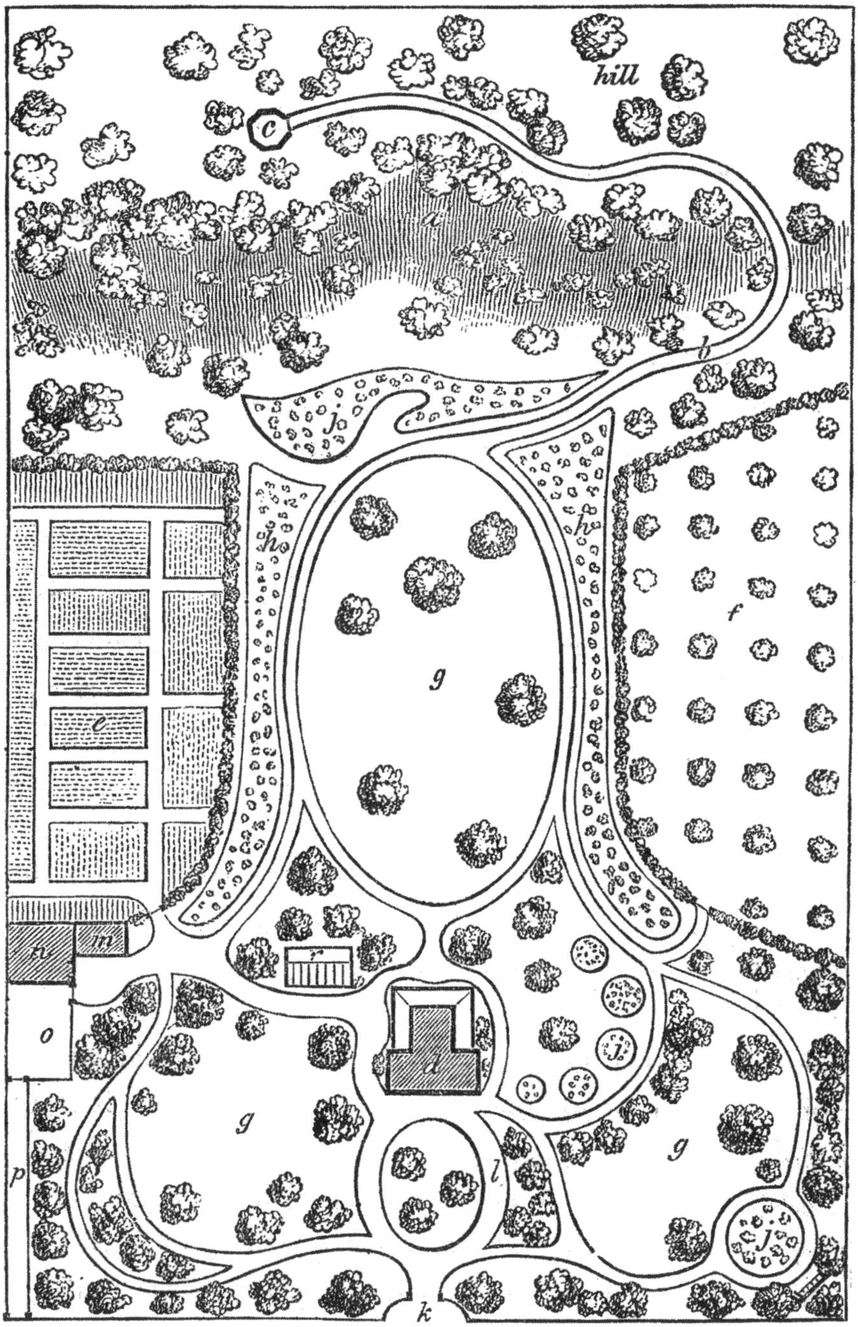

Fig. 9. A. J. Downing, Design V, *A Cottage Villa, in the Bracketed Mode,* engraving, Site Plan from *Cottage Residences,* 4th ed., 1852.

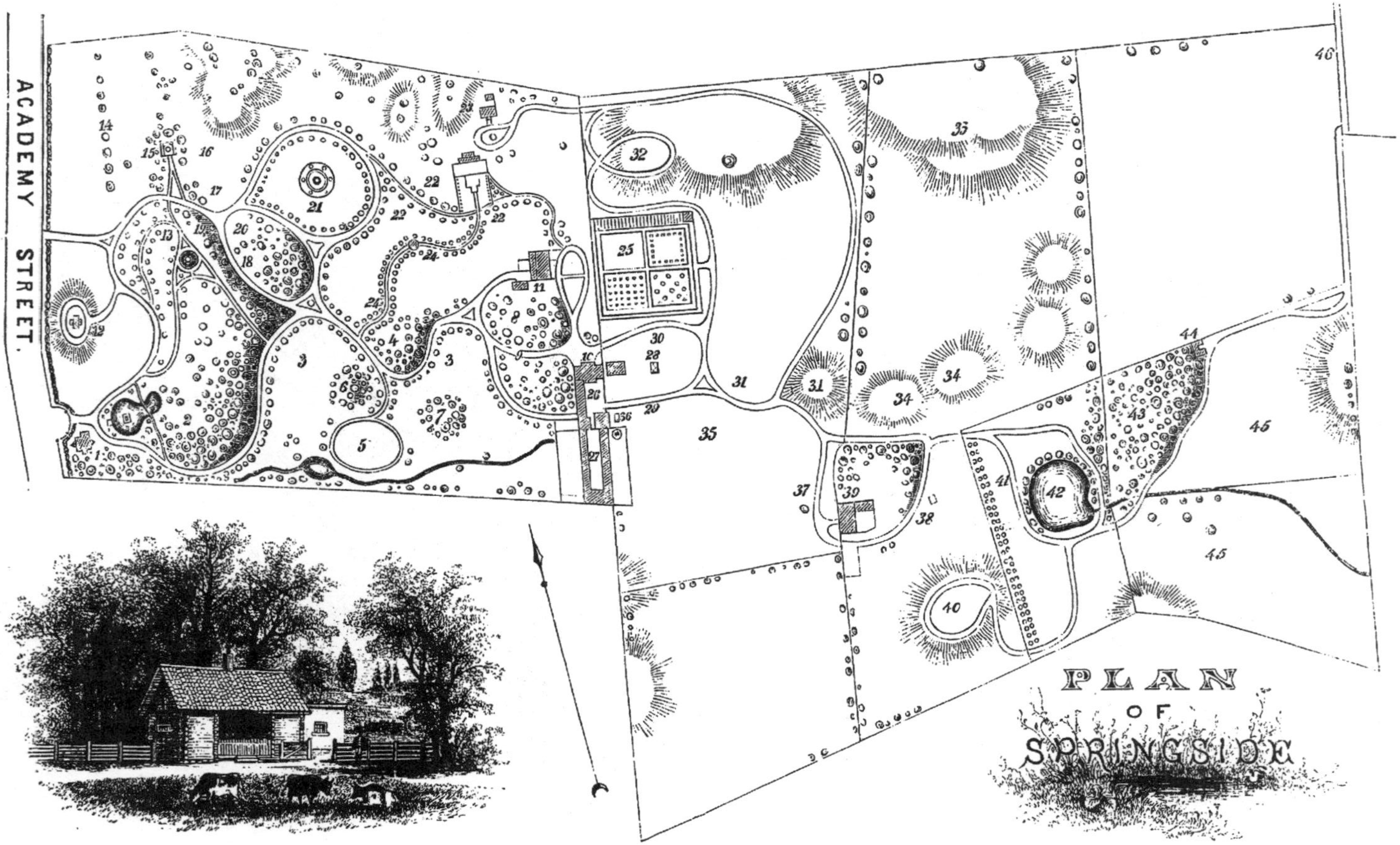
ACADEMY STREET.
PLAN
OF
SPRINGSIDE

the industrialist and philanthropist Matthew Vassar of Poughkeepsie, New York, and founder of Vassar College for Women. Vassar originally acquired the land for a public rural cemetery, but when the town chose another site, he developed the property for his own use. Beginning in the autumn of 1850, Downing designed eight buildings and laid out the grounds with seventeen gardens and landscapes, some designed as beautiful, others as picturesque. The wooden buildings were covered with vertical board-and-batten siding and had deep roof overhangs with carved verge boards and ornamental window hoods in what Downing called the Rustic Pointed style.

In Downing's landscape design, the beautiful is found in the curved gravel drives and paths, rambles, meandering streams with ponds, springs, and fountains in places called Jet Vale (13), Willow Spring (17), and Center Circle (21). The smoothed park-like lawns with specimen trees and shrubs were for herd grazing in places such as Deer Park (3) and Little Belt (7). The picturesque is found in the rocky knolls and outcroppings of Stonehenge (4), Group Gap (5), Rock Roost (6), and Evergreen Parks (19 and 20). Rustic seats were located to enjoy distant prospects of the Hudson River.

While Downing may have learned his discipline from British landscape theory and practice, it was his adaptation of its principles to his understanding of the American mode of life, in addition to his self-promotion as a talented designer, that made his work so popular and influential both at home and abroad. But in addition to adapting design principles to the peculiarities of American soil, Downing was instrumental in articulating the identity and purpose of the professional landscape designer, for whom he carved a specific place in the American social structure. Relying on the strength of his scientific knowledge and ability to judge taste and propriety, the designer entered social circles from which his earlier role of laborer or gardener would have excluded him. In spite of his assertion about the democratic nature of American society, Downing's private commissions were for the upper class, the only one that could support his profession.[51] In order to promote the latter Downing aimed to counter the "great spirit of unrest" that characterized American people, and he preached instead the importance of growing roots, shaping and cultivating the land for many generations, and in so doing giving shape to individual character while also contributing to the development of a national identity. Perhaps this was Downing's most subtle adaptation of a long-lasting, but soon waning, British tradition. As

Fig. 10, opposite. A. J. Downing, *Springside,* 1850, drawing from Benson J. Lossing, *Vassar College and Its Founder* (New York: C. A. Alvord, Printer, 1867).

Neil Harris states, "Downing's most enduring legacy was his identification of aesthetic reform with a set of ethical and social ideals, his rural commonwealth of men of honor whose rationality was strengthened by the natural beauty which [the professional] architect and gardener had assembled."[52] The design of the American landscape, then, was to be less about building copies of fashionable foreign styles in architecture and the landscape and more about the potential harmony among peculiarities of people, their land, and what they built, united in an ability to define their interests. Downing's understanding of this circumstance as integral to a prosperous and free society—admittedly dependent on individual land ownership and eventually the automobile—is a premise and a problem that remains true today.

Notes

The author thanks Raffaella Fabiani Giannetto and Aaron Wunsch for their thoughtful guidance during the development of this essay, and Magenta Livengood for her careful reading and helpful suggestions as well as her well-crafted work on the images.

1. Andrew Jackson Downing, "American vs. British Horticulture," June 1852, in *Rural Essays*, ed. George W. Curtis (1853; rpt., New York: Da Capo Press, 1974), 83–87. Downing was the editor of the *Horticulturist* from its inception in July 1846 until his death in July 1852. Publisher Luther Tucker claimed that it was the most widely read text in America after the Bible.

2. Downing corresponded with and contributed to Loudon's *Gardener's Magazine* (1826–44) and admired Loudon's *Arboretum et Fruticetum Britannicum* (1838). See Melanie Simo, *Loudon and the Landscape: From Country Seat to Metropolis, 1783–1843* (New Haven: Yale University Press, 1988), 10, 142, 203. Numerous lengthy quotations from J. C. Loudon, *Encyclopaedia of Gardening* (1822) appear in Downing's *A Treatise on the Theory and Practice of Landscape Gardening.* Downing included designs similar to those found in Loudon's *The Suburban Gardener and Villa Companion* (1836–38). See David Schuyler, *Apostle of Taste: Andrew Jackson Downing, 1815–1852* (Baltimore: Johns Hopkins University Press, 1996), 40. Downing recommended Loudon's *An Encyclopedia of Cottage, Farm, and Villa Architecture and Furniture* (London: Longman, 1832–33) to his readers in his *A Treatise on the Theory and Practice of Landscape Gardening, Adapted to North America*, 4th ed. (1850; rpt., Washington, DC: Dumbarton Oaks Research Library and Collection, 1991), 417.

3. Therese O'Malley, "From Practice to Theory: The Emerging Profession of Landscape Gardening in Early Nineteenth-Century America," in *Botanical Progress, Horticultural Innovations and Cultural Changes*, ed. Michel Conan and W. John Kress (Washington, DC: Dumbarton Oaks Research Library and Collection, 2007), 223–37.

4. Dell Upton, "Pattern Books and Professionalism: Aspects of the Transformation of Domestic Architecture in America, 1800–1860," *Winterthur Portfolio* 19, no. 2–3 (Autumn 1984): 126.

5. Loudon introduced the term *landscape architecture* to describe the work of Humphry Repton, who called himself a landscape gardener in that his art combined the "powers of the *landscape painter* with those of the *practical gardener.*" Humphry Repton, *Sketches and Hints on Landscape Gardening* (London, 1794), introduction, xiii. For Loudon, landscape architecture expanded the expertise of the landscape gardener by including the skills of grading and redirecting waterways.

6. O'Malley, "From Practice to Theory," 234.

7. Upton, "Pattern Books and Professionalism," 128.

8. See Neil Harris, *The Artist in American Society: The Formative Years, 1790–1860* (New York: George Braziller, 1966) for a review of the social and intellectual climate for American artists during the first third of the nineteenth century. For Downing's contribution, see 208–16.

9. Downing, "American vs. British Horticulture," 84, emphasis in the original.

10. Alan A. Tait, "Loudon and the Return to Formality," in *John Claudius Loudon and the Early Nineteenth Century in Great Britain,* ed. Elisabeth B. MacDougall (Washington, DC: Dumbarton Oaks Research Library and Collection, 1980), 72, quoting Loudon, *Gardener's Magazine* 8 (1832): 701.

11. Downing, *A Treatise on the Theory and Practice,* 75.

12. "Admission was open to subscribers who paid an annual fee," and a small entrance fee was charged five days a week to fund operations and maintenance; it was free on Sunday afternoons and on Wednesdays. Simo, *Loudon and the Landscape,* 199.

13. Ibid., chapter 11 for a full account.

14. Downing, *Rural Essays,* 516, 517, emphasis in the original.

15. Downing, *A Treatise on the Theory and Practice,* 433–35.

16. Downing, *Rural Essays,* July, August, and September 1850, 475–557.

17. Ibid., 538–40, emphasis in the original.

18. Ibid., 532.

19. Ibid., 535.

20. John Claudius Loudon, *In Search of English Gardens: The Travels of John Claudius Loudon and His Wife Jane,* ed. Priscilla Boniface (Herts: Lennard, 1987), 22. Repton prepared a Red Book in 1805 for changes to Woburn Abbey including opening views that Loudon noticed during his visit in the summer of 1829.

21. For the evolution of Downing's thinking on exotics versus natives through the multiple revisions of *A Treatise on the Theory and Practice of Landscape Gardening,* 1841, 1844, and 1849 editions, as well as in the *Horticulturist,* see Judith K. Major, *To Live in the New World: A. J. Downing and American Landscape Gardening* (Cambridge, MA: MIT Press, 1997).

22. Andrew Jackson Downing, *The Fruits and Fruit Trees of America,* 14th ed. (New York: Wiley & Halsted, 1856), 555.

23. Downing, *Rural Essays,* 340, quoting "an enthusiastic collector in Belgium" and correspondent.

24. See Caren Yglesias, *The Complete House and Grounds: Learning from Andrew Jackson Downing's Domestic Architecture* (Chicago: Center for American Places at Columbia College Chicago, 2011).

25. Harris, *The Artist in American Society,* 213.

26. Andrew Jackson Downing, *The Architecture of Country Houses* (1850; rpt., New York: Da Capo Press, 1968), 265n.

27. Ibid.

28. George B. Tatum, "The Emergence of an American School of Landscape Design," *Historic Preservation* (April/June, 1973): 34.

29. Upton, "Pattern Books and Professionalism," 122–24.

30. Unfortunately its appearance coincided with the Financial Panic of 1837. The hand-colored portfolio included designs for a cottage, gatehouse and farmhouse, three villas, and a village church and schoolhouse. Its title page states its purpose: "with a view to the improvement of American country architecture." Alexander Jackson Davis, *Rural Residences: Consisting of Designs, Original and Selected, for Cottages, Farm-Houses, Villas, and Village Churches* (New York: Da Capo Press, 1980). Davis never published the remaining sections of the intended six-part series.

31. Andrew Jackson Downing, *Cottage Residences; or, A Series of Designs for Rural Cottages and Cottage-Villas, and Their Gardens and Grounds, Adapted to North America* (1842) was reissued in 1844 and 1847 and expanded in 1852. The *Architecture of Country Houses* was first published in 1850 and was reissued before Downing died in 1852. Both books went through numerous subsequent reissues.

32. Harris, *The Artist in American Society,* 212.

33. Immigrants without money worked on transportation projects, in mills, or in factories or provided domestic service.

34. Harris, *The Artist in American Society,* 214.

35. Karen Halttunen, "From Parlor to Living Room: Domestic Space and the Culture of Personality," in *Consuming Visions: Accumulation and Display of Goods in America, 1880–1920,* ed. Simon J. Bronner (New York: Norton, 1989), 159.

36. Adam W. Sweeting, *Reading Houses and Building Books: Andrew Jackson Downing and the Architecture of Popular Antebellum Literature, 1835–1855* (Hanover, NH: University Press of New England, 1996), 94, 95.

37. Downing, *The Architecture of Country Houses,* 262–63, and *A Treatise on the Theory and Practice,* 66, 73–79.

38. Downing's term *graceful* corresponds to Edmund Burke's *beautiful* as discussed in his *Philosophical Inquiry into the Origin of our Ideas of the Sublime and Beautiful* (1756). Burke's *beautiful* exemplifies what is small and smooth, with shapes of gradual and non-angular variation, delicate frame, and with colors clear and bright that are not very strong or glaring (Part 3, §XIII–XVIII). By contrast, the sublime has qualities of irregularity, roughness, and boldness with dim light and dark colors (Part 2, §I–XVIII). The latter qualities were eventually attributed to a buildable version of the sublime termed the picturesque.

39. Andrew Jackson Downing, *Cottage Residences* (1852; rpt., New York: Dover, 1981), 114–27.

40. Ibid., 68.

41. John Dixon Hunt, "The Garden as Cultural Object," in *Denatured Visions: Landscape and Culture in the Twentieth Century,* ed. S. Wrede and W. H. Adams (New York: Muscum of Modern Art, 1991), 27.

42. Downing, *Cottage Residences,* 40–49.

43. Downing owned a copy of Loudon's *The Landscape Gardening and Landscape Architecture of the Late Humphrey Repton,* which Loudon published three years before he died in 1840. Downing referred to Repton's four books on landscape design theory (1795, 1803, 1806, and 1816) mostly in his *A Treatise on the Theory and Practice of Landscape Gardening* (1841), although Repton's influence is also apparent in the numerous quotations included by the other authors Downing recommended, such as Peter Robinson, Robert Lugar, Francis Goodwin, Thomas Hunt, and Augustus Pugin.

44. Edward Hyams, *Capability Brown & Humphry Repton* (New York: Scribner's, 1971), 132, 133, 140.

45. Downing, *Cottage Residences,* 89.

46. Ibid., 98.

47. Ibid., 99.

48. Ibid., 89–113.

49. Harris, *The Artist in American Society,* 212.

50. See Harvey K. Flad for a complete account, "Matthew Vassar's Springside: '. . . the hand of Art, when guided by Taste,'" in *Prophet with Honor: The Career of Andrew Jackson Downing, 1815–1852,* ed. George B. Tatum and Elisabeth B. MacDougall (Washington, DC: Dumbarton Oaks Research Library and Collection, 1989).

51. Downing's public commissions, however, such as the Public Grounds at Washington (now known as the Washington Mall) were meant to encourage the cultivation of all people.

52. Harris, *The Artist in American Society,* 215.

PART 2

French Exchanges

"These Beautiful Pleasure-Grounds of Death"

Nineteenth-Century America's Adaptation of the Parisian Rural Cemetery

JILL SINCLAIR

The American landscape tradition was deeply affected by the adaptation of the innovative rural cemetery model from its origins in early-nineteenth-century Paris to a new situation at Mount Auburn in eastern Massachusetts. The analysis of inceptive responses to both cemeteries demonstrates how design trends and commemorative practices borrowed from Europe became transformed into an intensely American tradition of naturalistic pleasure grounds, with Mount Auburn as the progenitor of the rural cemetery movement in the United States and a model for later nineteenth-century public parks throughout the country.

Père Lachaise was the first metropolitan rural cemetery, laid out on fifty-five acres beyond the Paris city walls in 1804. It was a replacement for squalid, overflowing urban churchyards, where graves were unmarked and transient, and planting of any sort was discouraged by the Church. Visiting such sites to grieve for lost loved ones was unimaginable, and concerns had grown about dangers to health from the mass of rotting corpses left half-buried in communal trenches. Created as part of the social reforms that followed the French Revolution, Père Lachaise was a radically new style of designed landscape for mourning, using picturesque elements from fashionable English landscapes. It allowed a secularized form of burial that celebrated the importance of the family over the old order of Catholicism and veneration of the monarchy, and provided the first example of picturesque individual and family burial plots that could be purchased in perpetuity. Originally an Edenic, idealized landscape, with curving pathways designed for sweetly melancholic promenades, its popularity meant that it soon became crowded with commemorative monuments and family mausoleums.

Created in response to social, medical, and political changes similar to those that produced its French predecessor, Mount Auburn cemetery was laid out in 1831 on the outskirts of Boston and was explicitly inspired by Père Lachaise.[1] Located on a seventy-two-acre site of wooded hills and streams, it provided the setting for nondenominational, permanent burial in family lots in a picturesque, horticulturally rich landscape. Romantic, accessible, and imbued with a new sense of calm and hope about the afterlife, Mount Auburn quickly became Boston's chief tourist attraction, popular for Sunday outings and social picnics.

Imported ideas and funerary practices from France thus directly influenced the emerging landscape tradition of the new Republic, but European designs were not simply replicated once they crossed the Atlantic: they were shaped and molded into distinctive new forms by American values, practices, attitudes, beliefs, and perceptions.

Character of Site

The cemetery at Père Lachaise was intended as a radical shift from past practice, a new style of burial ground on a new site. Mount Auburn's founders followed the same model, choosing a seemingly pristine location for their pioneering institution. As William W. Stowe has shown, the character and qualities of Mount Auburn then evolved, in part through the language used to describe the place in the early years after it was founded.[2] But in truth each site had a long history before it was chosen for its respective cemetery, and we can trace, through the continued use of old names and telling of old stories, how the past seeped through into the perceptions and attitudes of the present and created disparate associations and values for these two seemingly similar and radically new cemeteries.

When Napoleon Bonaparte seized on the long-debated idea of a rural burial ground for Paris and ordered the creation of three cemeteries just outside the city, the first property acquired was on high ground to the east, offering fine views over Paris. The chosen site had already played a lengthy and significant role in the history of the capital. Once medieval grazing lands owned by the diocese of Paris and appropriately known as Champ l'Evêque (the Bishop's Field), the site had been turned into a country seat by rich spice merchant Regnault de Wandonne in the late fourteenth century and for many years was called La Folie-Regnault. Despite some interpretations to the contrary, the name probably meant simply the country house or leafy retreat of Regnault, with none of the sense of extravagance or fool-

Fig. 1. "Vue de la Maison du Père Delachaise au XVIème Siècle," from Messieurs Roger, père et fils, *Le Champ du Repos, ou le Cimetière Mont Louis, dit Du Père Delachaise,* published Paris, 1816.

ishness associated with the later use of the word *folly* in English.[3] Following Regnault's death, the property was acquired by the powerful congregation of the Jesuits and, at their request, was subsequently renamed Mont-Louis after an incident in 1652 in which the boy-king Louis XIV had observed a crucial battle during the Fronde (French civil war) from the site. Later that century the king greatly expanded and enhanced the estate to turn it into a suitable retreat for his Jesuit confessor, Père (Father) François d'Aix de la Chaise (fig. 1). When the once-feared Jesuits became the object of hostility and suppression in the religious and political turmoil of pre-revolutionary France during the 1760s, the property passed through various hands and was almost a ruin by the time it was acquired for the new burial ground.[4]

The site was then officially renamed le Cimetière de l'Est (the eastern cemetery), in keeping with the revolutionary desire to use classical, geographical names rather than those rhetorically associated with the old order.[5] Parisians, however, quickly began calling it le Cimetière du Père Lachaise, after the king's confessor, whose once-revered name by the time of the Revolution had been reduced to little more than a curse.[6] Many felt it was only right after the French Revolution that such a magnificent place, a symbol of pride and elitism, should now become a cemetery.[7] Through its various titles, the site was thus acknowledged as a place linked to the monarchy and to the political and religious in-fighting of the *ancien régime.* Guidebooks to the new cemetery discussed at length the role of the Jesuits and of Père Lachaise himself in French history.[8] More than one contemporary writer saw it as a place with a moral message: the monarchy challenged, Jesuits exterminated, and philosophy vindicated through the Revolution.[9]

In Massachusetts, the site chosen for its cemetery was wooded land, four miles outside Boston, once a colonial farm established by the Stone family, early settlers of Watertown, but now deserted and overgrown (fig. 2). Harvard students affectionately called the site Sweet Auburn after the village in Oliver Goldsmith's sentimental English poem left gradually to decay until "Desolation saddens all thy green," and the author walks alone "Amidst thy tangling walks and ruin'd grounds."[10] It had a melancholic, romantic feel that caught the spirit of the age, a sense of the real America as expressed through its threatened, picturesque landscapes. One poet wrote of Sweet Auburn's "untrained loveliness," remembering it as "a sweet, lovely spot, a fairy place / Of gentle beauty, and of quiet grace."[11] The new cemetery was

Fig. 2. Deacon Simon Stone farmhouse on the Charles River, before the founding of Mount Auburn, painting by Josephine M. Stone, c. 1830. (Courtesy of the Watertown Free Public Library)

named Mount Auburn after the highest point in the grounds, a title carefully chosen by its founders to suggest a godly place of rural simplicity, while preserving something of the students' fond epithet.[12]

The site continued to hold romantic associations for those who had known the plot as Sweet Auburn: visitors still linked it "with the recollections of boyhood" while one looked again "upon our gorgeous woods and heard the song of the wind in the pine groves. I should like to sleep there, with that beautiful soul sighing my requiem."[13] Some resented the arrival of the masses in what had once felt a private place: "Probably few persons, of contemplative minds, now visit this sacred spot without feeling that there is too much *life,* too much of the world collected there."[14]

The differing histories, titles, and associations of the chosen sites are a key factor in explaining how the American adaptation of the rural cemetery came to differ from the original French model. On its creation, Père Lachaise was already a bittersweet reminder of the monarchy and the Jesuit history of turmoil and hatred, of public events, prominent people, and conflicting loyalties; it was clearly what we today would call a cultural site. The plot chosen for its American interpretation was, by contrast, perceived as romantic and natural, private and intimate, provoking feelings of nostalgia and warm affection.

Role of the State

French philosopher Alexis de Tocqueville famously stated in 1840 that Americans "are forever forming associations. . . . In every case, at the head of any new undertaking, where in France you would find the government . . . in the United States you are sure to find an association."[15] Much is made in contemporary analysis of this contrast between the static, centralized administration of Catholic France and the self-organizing Protestant communities of the young America.[16] Applying the distinction to the rural cemetery movement, James Ackerman is one of several scholars who has argued that Père Lachaise was "fundamentally different in conception" from Mount Auburn principally because it was generated by the government.[17] In fact, Napoleon and his *préfecture* (regional government) created Père Lachaise, while attempts in the 1820s by the mayor of Boston to establish a similar cemetery for his city failed, and Mount Auburn was subsequently founded by a voluntary association formed by men of influence and industry to promote the common good. Some of the challenges of working in an elective

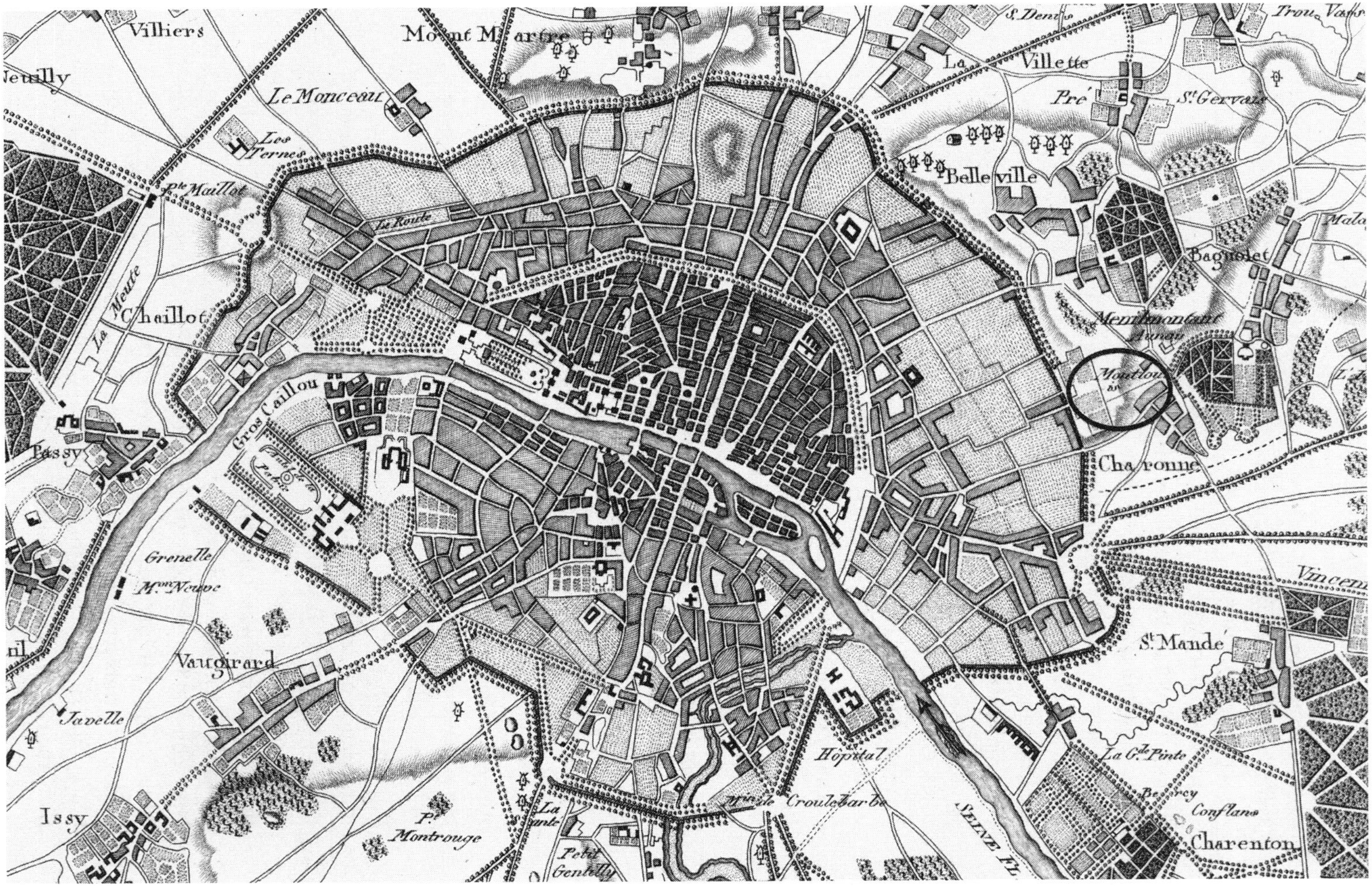
Villiers
Mont Martre
Le Monceau
Les Ternes
La Villette
Pré St. Gervais
Belleville
Baguolet
Chaillot
La Meute
Passy
Gros Caillou
Grenelle
Vaugirard
Javelle
Issy
Montrouge
Petit Gentilly
Croulebarbe
Hôpital
Charonne
St. Mandé
Vincennes
La Gde. Pinte
Conflans
Charenton
Seine Fl.

alliance are apparent in the early history of Mount Auburn, most notably when an original wish to construct both an experimental garden and a rural cemetery on the site—to meet the needs of the various parties involved in the association—foundered on the inability of the individuals concerned to work together successfully. Yet confrontations and unexpected events also buffeted the early years of Père Lachaise, from the strong personalities jostling for initial control of the project to the lack of funds as a result of the cost of the Napoleonic Wars in the first decade of the nineteenth century and the sudden deaths in 1813 of both cemetery designer Alexandre-Théodore Brongniart and the *préfet* (state representative) Nicolas Frochot.[18]

Thus perhaps the most obvious distinction between the government-ordered French cemetery and its self-organizing American adaptation is, in reality, difficult to detect on the ground. Certainly, there is surprisingly little evidence of the difference in inceptive responses to the two cemeteries: occasionally we can just glimpse American satisfaction that their rural cemeteries were created by "noble spirits" with philanthropic motives; or, conversely, concern that such an approach could lead to pride and ostentation.[19]

Location of Site

More important in creating the character of the two cemeteries was their relative proximity to the cities they served. Designed to replace congested urban burial grounds, Mount Auburn followed the Parisian model in being deliberately placed outside the city, allowing individual graves to be arranged within a spacious designed landscape. Père Lachaise had been located just beyond the tollgates of the unpopular Farmers' General wall, which had been built around the city in the 1780s as a means of collecting custom duties on goods being brought into Paris.[20] Nestled so close to the city (fig. 3), it offered a striking contrast between the dead and the still living, the rural landscape and the city fabric, the past and the present. One visitor in 1826 described how from a seat in the cemetery he saw the city as an anthill, full of people oblivious to how soon their lives would end; the proximity of Paris was a reminder of the meaninglessness of the city bustle.[21] Similarly in 1835, the president of Amherst College, who knew Mount Auburn, visited

Fig. 3, opposite. Detail of Plan der Stadt Paris mit ihren umliegenden Gegenden / Plan de la Ville de Paris et ses Environs (detail), drawn by Jos[eph] Lantz, engraving by Joh[ann] Spiegl, published Vienna, 1805. Circle added showing the location chosen for the new Paris cemetery. (Library of Congress, Geography and Map Division)

BOSTON HARBOUR
SUFFOLK
CHELSEA
Noddles Island
Bell Isle
Pulling
Governors I.
Fort Warren
Fort Independence
SOUTH BOSTON
BOSTON
Receiving Bason
Common
PORT
CAMBRIDGE
Harvard University
Botanical Garden
Fresh Pond
Fresh Pond Hotel
Little Pond
WATERTOWN
U.S. Arsenal
Contemplated
BRIGHTON
BROOKLINE
Charles River
Malden River
Winter Hill
Newbury port Turnpike
Leehmore Point
Beaver Brook
N. Amory
Dr. Aspinwall
Dr. Spooner
T.H. Perkins
Punch Bowl
Tide Mills
A. Davis
T. Williams
Five Corners
Corner
Road

Père Lachaise and commented: "What sudden and admonitory transitions! Now you are in the heart of Paris, walking in the gardens of the Tuileries, or sauntering along the Boulevards, where all is health, and bustle, and pleasure; and in half an hour you are lost in the dark cypress labyrinths of Père la Chaise, where, under a few shovelfulls of earth, all distinctions find one common level, and where uncounted multitudes are silently gathering together, to await the last summons."[22]

Mount Auburn, in comparison, was located farther from Boston (fig. 4) and seen as quite separate from the city. Although no nineteenth-century images survive that capture the distant views of Boston, there were many descriptions of the fine prospect available from the cemetery's summit and the relationship between the new cemetery and the city it served. For one Mount Auburn visitor in the 1830s, "Boston may be seen enveloped, as it were, in a dark fog. Neither bustle nor noise is perceptible. Here stands man alone in the presence of his Creator and his conscience. . . . His breast, hitherto filled with worldly passions, now heaves with sublime and holy feelings."[23] Rather than gloomy thoughts about the pointlessness of city life, Mount Auburn's more distant location allowed visitors to contemplate the necessary balance between the natural and the urban world, and to "ponder on those themes which are neglected by the multitude, during the hurry of business or in the idle whirl of pleasure."[24]

And so a landscape form that in Paris was perceived as almost part of the city, a place for mournful reflection on human frailty, became transformed through its more remote location in Massachusetts into a rural sanctuary, separate from the urban noise and providing opportunities for uplifting contemplation. Arguably the respective choice of locations may have been a reflection of a wider cultural divergence between the two countries: Andrew Jackson Downing, later musing on the emerging American character, discussed the nature of various European personalities, including the Frenchman: "He eats, talks, lives in public. He is only happy when he has spectators. In town, on the boulevards, in the café, at places of public amusement, he is all enjoyment. But in the country—ah, there he never goes willingly . . . it is plain, from our love of the country, that we are not French at heart."[25]

Fig. 4, opposite. Detail of Map of Boston and its vicinity from actual survey, drawn and copublished by John G. Hales, engraving by Edwin Gillingham, published Boston and Philadelphia, 1819. Circle added showing the location subsequently chosen for the new Boston cemetery.

Purpose of Commemoration

By the end of the eighteenth century, Parisian cemeteries had become little more than communal pits for the disposal of human remains, and a grim reminder that, in death, all are equal. Replacing these urban burial grounds, Père Lachaise was instead a place fundamentally about remembrance, designed with curving pathways and carriage roads wending past carefully designed monuments in a picturesque landscape as a way of creating accessible, permanent memorials. Americans duly followed this model, creating at Mount Auburn a landscape of commemoration that replaced the Puritan notion of burial grounds as places of horror, where barely concealed corpses signified the pointlessness of earthly success or material worth. Yet, despite these similarities, we can trace a shift in what was being venerated at—and through—each site. By the time Père Lachaise was created, the French were little interested in celebrating national heroes. Recent history was painful and complex, and it was no longer easy to feel pride in the country's past. Many felt numbed by the horrors of the Revolution; those who emerged triumphant did not wish the vanquished remembered, while the ravages of the Terror robbed people of their respect for the masses of the dead.[26] Instead people turned to a comforting view of the new cemetery as a place to express familial affection, where they could for the first time erect permanent memorials and mourn lost relatives. In those monuments they were able to invest associations and emotions and, through regular visits to the cemetery, to proclaim their grief.[27]

Many initially felt uncomfortable that, with the old hierarchical orders gone, Père Lachaise became a place "where all Paris repose, the rich and the poor, the mean and the mighty"[28] and that the graves were arranged without obvious social or economic distinctions. So it became fashionable for families to perpetuate their standing and express the worth of their ancestors through the splendor of their tombs (fig. 5). Jacob Bigelow, one of Mount Auburn's founders, visited Père Lachaise in 1833 and wrote home in admiration of the many "magnificent monuments."[29] But the practice was condemned by some French writers who saw the tombs reflecting vanity more than sadness; while one English visitor disapprovingly described how "wealth, rank, and pride heap decorations over the worthless clay, striving vainly to conceal its nothingness."[30]

In contrast, after their Revolution, Americans were seeking to create a distinct civilization and commemorative culture for the new country. The Puritans had established no monuments, rejecting such ostentation and

Fig. 5. Père La Chaise: Monument de la Famille Bouchée, drawn by J. Nash, engraving by W. Faithorn, from *Paris and Its Environs, Displayed in a Series of Picturesque Views,* The drawings were made under the direction of Mr. Pugin and engraved under the superintendence of Mr. C. Heath, published London, 1831.

the postmortem creation of heroes. But now the new Republic wanted to encourage patriotism, a national culture distinct from Europe, and a "usable past," creating a common purpose, shared values, and social stability through the celebration of war heroes and commemoration of recent events.[31] It was this very different attitude to recent history and future development that infused the creation of Mount Auburn.

As historian Gunther Barth has explained, natural scenery and indigenous plants played a significant role in creating this new American culture: the wild, primitive beauty of the East Coast's already disappearing primeval forests was clearly distinct from the long-cultivated, manicured landscapes of Europe and represented the potential and promise of the new Republic and its democratic ideals.[32] Barth quotes an 1853 visitor to Mount Auburn who declared, "Freedom rules the infinite spaces of the cosmos, freedom rules according to any American's precept, and therefore free nature shall be the heir and guardian of his dust."[33] Indeed, this belief in the distinctive quality of their surroundings led the founders frequently to argue that American nature was so perfectly provided and so bountiful that it had virtually created the ideal landscape for the cemetery, with little extra work necessary.[34]

Time and again, early-nineteenth-century Americans wrote of Mount Auburn as an outstanding example of American culture, created from distinctive American scenery, superior to any European model, and deserving replication throughout the Republic.[35] From the beginning, its founders declared that they were creating "a holy and pleasant resort for the living—the whole will present one of the most instructive, magnificent and pleasant promenades in our country . . . it will attract universal interest."[36] In an attempt to emphasize the triumphantly local character of the cemetery, poet Caroline Orne played down the role of European practices and attitudes in the creation of Mount Auburn and instead sought to establish its origins as the honoring of the dead in Native American antiquity: "Not in the Old World only may we view / This reverend care, but also in the New."[37] Similarly, Joseph Story, in his consecration address at Mount Auburn in 1831, was probably alluding to local Indian practices as part of the inspiration for the new cemetery when he urged Bostonians to follow the example of heathens who "strewed flowers, and garlands" at the burying spot of the their loved ones and allowed the "secret indulgence of sorrow."[38]

The short-lived experimental garden at the cemetery was designed to encourage Americans to turn against plants bought from foreign nurseries and the "anti-national prejudices" they embodied. Instead they would develop native plants and so "depend more upon our own resources."[39] In the same vein, Henry Dearborn, one of the cemetery's founders, argued that the time was right to "develope the vast vegetable resources of the Union . . . advance the prosperity, and improve the general aspect of the whole country."[40] He sought to increase people's pride in the new Republic in other ways as well, arguing, for instance, that Mount Auburn was immediately more popular than Père Lachaise had been, and that this was a sign of the strength and national character of America and its citizens' patriotism.[41] Even schoolchildren were given texts that praised Mount Auburn over its French predecessor: "The celebrated and far-famed Père La Chaise, in the vicinity of Paris, so far as nature is concerned, is as far inferior to it, as pigmy mountains to the towering Alps."[42]

So in these inceptive responses we can perceive how the purpose of commemoration shifted in the adaptation of the rural cemetery to America. Père Lachaise reflected the complex, weary views of Parisians, focusing on the veneration of their ancestors through the splendor of their tombs, rather than celebrating national history. At Mount Auburn, we see the unequivocal American desire to commemorate their new country and emerging culture, an almost desperate need to celebrate the Mount Auburn landscape as different from and superior to anything in the Old World, and a wish to encourage the replication of the new cemetery as something quintessentially American.[43]

God and Mortality

Père Lachaise marked a clear break with the old order of Catholic cemeteries, being a secular burial ground owned by the state rather than the Church and remaining as a whole unconsecrated ground. Mount Auburn was similarly a nondenominational cemetery, intended from the outset to serve the whole local community, its consecration address given in a civic ceremony by a respected lawyer. In practice, both places were infused with religious—largely Christian—associations, motifs, and attitudes toward death, some common to both cemeteries and others reflecting the very different religious histories and beliefs of the two countries.

While this essay is not the place to explore this subject in any depth, it is clear that in France, burial customs were defined by the Catholic Church's traditional views of the essentially sinful nature of man and the threat of eternal damnation, tempered by the long-held belief in the power of repentance: the chance to save one's soul, even on one's deathbed, through confession and receipt of the sacraments. A further tenet of Catholic belief is that of purgatory, seen as a place or condition of temporal punishment after death for those who have not fully repented their sins while on earth. Those in purgatory are in need of the consolation of the living through prayers and other offerings to God for the repose of their souls, particularly on funeral days and the anniversary of their death. Catholics argue that such a belief makes funerals more meaningful and continues the bond between the living and the dead, offering real comfort both to the departed and those left behind.[44] This tradition clearly played a part in the ceremonies and burial customs at Père Lachaise: one 1825 visitor described the cemetery on All Souls' Day, when "immense crowds perform a solemn pilgrimage to Mount Louis, bearing garlands and decorations of every description, to be strewed upon the graves of their departed relatives, recollections of whom are annually revived."[45]

A second set of beliefs is also apparent at Père Lachaise: eighteenth-century thinkers such as Voltaire and Jean-Jacques Rousseau had challenged the Catholic Church's traditional teaching on death and instead posited a celebration of virtuous lives as a way of offering moral instruction to the living.[46] Before and after the Revolution, many French writers were as a result proposing secular, rural cemeteries in wooded locations, typically with simple tombs celebrating deserving lives and a respect for ancestors, and melancholic views to encourage contemplation of the shortness of man's time on earth and the need for harmony and virtue.[47] Thus one early visitor to Père Lachaise saw the sepulchers as the finest moral instruction save for the Bible, while a guidebook in the 1820s describes how the cemetery soon became famous for its depiction of morality and the lessons it presented to the human heart.[48]

Puritan New Englanders had shared this dread of death and eternal damnation, with unmarked graves in overflowing burial grounds intended as a grim warning against earthly pride and the valuing of material wealth.[49] But as Tracy Fessenden has explained, Catholicism itself was viewed by early Americans as synonymous with popery, corruption, intolerance, and arrogance; it was seen as a religion based in ceremony and church, with much ostentation, cult, and drama. Protestantism was welcomed instead, as offering freedom, tolerance, and what one eighteenth-century preacher called "religious liberty." It was a faith founded in the everyday, with religion and civil life barely distinguishable, and heaven available to those who had lived a good life in preparation for death.[50] With the hope and optimism created by the founding of the new Republic and the influence of Romantic ideals appearing in literature and art, the old Puritan fear and foreboding was gradually replaced by a view of death as a welcome release from worldly toil, with those who had lived Christian lives confident of immediate entry into heaven and the possession of eternal life.

Mount Auburn reflects these changing views. One of its founders described the afterlife as a return to the Garden of Eden, with monuments "amidst the quiet verdure of the field, under the broad and cheerful light of heaven, where the harmonious and ever changing face of nature reminds us, by its resuscitating influences, that to die is but to live again."[51]

Indeed, early responses to Mount Auburn show a striking sense of hopefulness about the afterlife and calmness in the face of death: one visitor described its "cheerful glades" and believed that "the consecration of this place to hope and triumph would make it too sad for the hesitating and hopeless; and that such probably turn away from the spot where all is too bright and lovely for the desolate of heart."[52]

Similarly, an English visitor described Mount Auburn's pastoral scenery as an "Eden for the dead" and wrote that, in contrast to her homeland, "death does not seem a thing to be dreaded or deplored in America, as with us."[53] Visiting Mount Auburn, one French writer noted with surprise and admiration how young couples did not fear death and were calm and serene about choosing where in the cemetery they would one day lie.[54] While much of the cheerful atmosphere came from the naturalistic scenery, the monuments themselves were frequently made from marble, for its optimistic bright coloring and suggestion of purity and hope for the afterlife, in comparison with the Puritans' dour, grey slate.[55] Even the birdsong was found to be cheerful.[56]

Emerging Transcendentalist views on religion, spirituality, and the regenerative role of nature are also apparent in early perceptions of Mount Auburn.[57] Emerson found there a particular communion with nature "from the vault to the moss and lichen on which I lay," while a protégé of his experienced the cemetery as a new Eden where "Each sense forever found a new delight, / Such as the spirit's vision only knows."[58] For Margaret Fuller the cemetery provided a fitting place to find hope and solace before her departure for a new life in New York, as she spent an afternoon walking "gently among the graves."[59]

From these early responses, we can see how Protestant attitudes toward religion and mortality affected the use and associations of the American version of the rural cemetery. A French funerary tradition, which combined Catholic belief in the postmortem power of prayer and ceremony with a celebration of the individual lives of the dead as moral examples to the living, was transformed by American beliefs and values into a new certainty and hope for the future and a consoling belief in the regenerative power of nature.

Interpretation of the Picturesque

Both France and the United States had seized on the modern English fashion for rugged, naturalistic landscapes—all "mould'ring hues and mosses"[60]—embellished with artfully placed classical ornaments, as a sign of their rejection of previous traditions and values. In France, influential writers argued against the static, aristocratic style of geometric gardens and in favor of this new naturalistic, more seemingly egalitarian approach.[61] An early example of a picturesque landscape appeared at Ermenonville, north of Paris, where the Marquis de Girardin famously laid the body of Rousseau on an island under trees in 1778.[62] He described himself as inspired by the classical approach to burial, which celebrated "great men in some picturesque situation" rather than dumping their bodies in abhorrent urban burial grounds.[63] Other fanciful examples followed, full of fabricated neoclassical

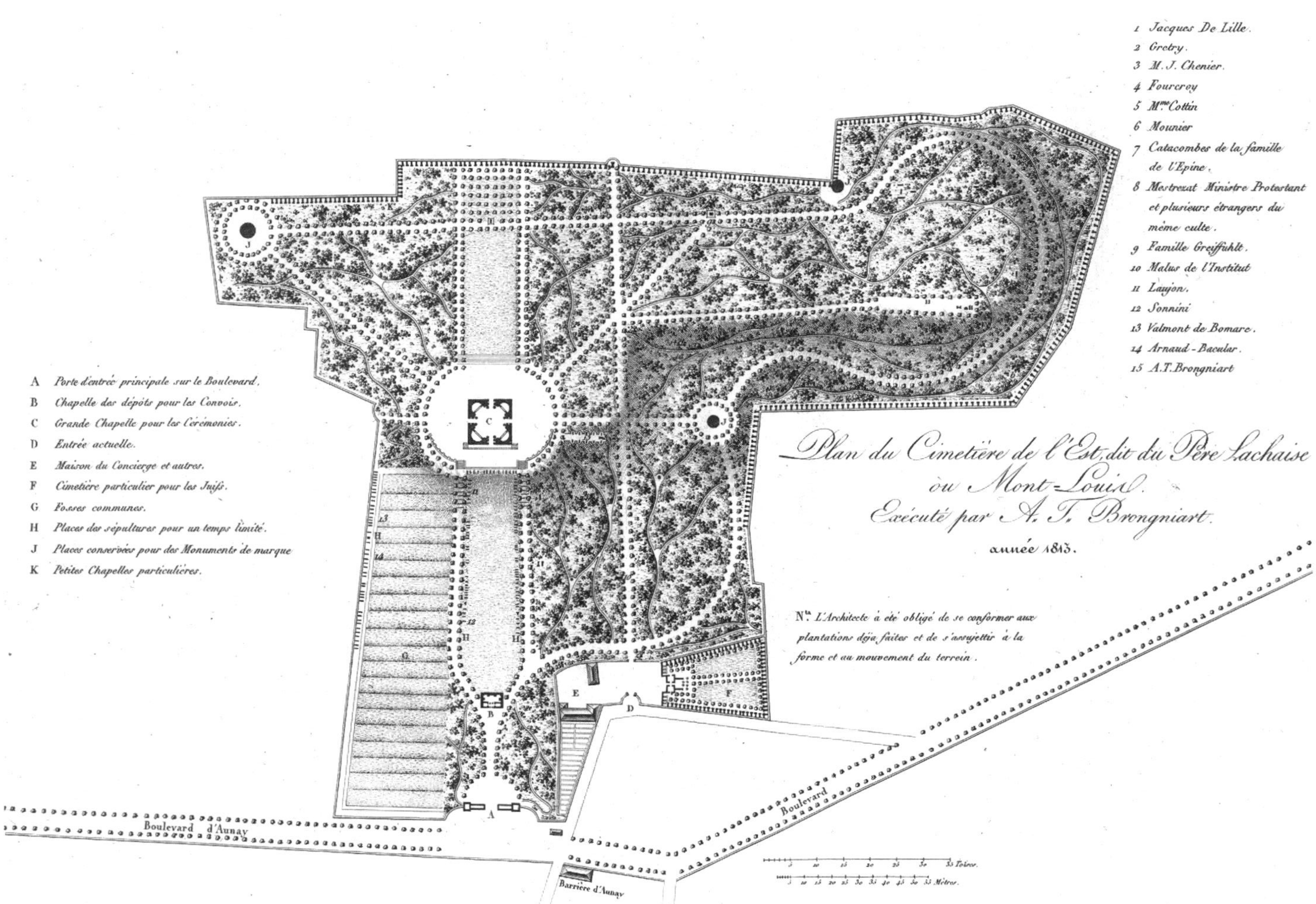
Plan du Cimetière de l'Est, dit du Père Lachaise ou Mont-Louis.
Exécuté par A. T. Brongniart.
année 1813.
A Porte d'entrée principale sur le Boulevard.
B Chapelle des dépôts pour les Convois.
C Grande Chapelle pour les Cérémonies.
D Entrée actuelle.
E Maison du Concierge et autres.
F Cimetière particulier pour les Juifs.
G Fosses communes.
H Places des sépultures pour un temps limité.
J Places conservées pour des Monuments de marque
K Petites Chapelles particulières.
1 Jacques De Lille.
2 Gretry.
3 M. J. Chenier.
4 Fourcroy
5 Mme Cottin
6 Mounier
7 Catacombes de la famille de l'Epine.
8 Mestrezat Ministre Protestant et plusieurs étrangers du même culte.
9 Famille Greiffuhlt.
10 Malus de l'Institut
11 Laujon.
12 Sonnini
13 Valmont de Bomare.
14 Arnaud-Bacular.
15 A.T. Brongniart
Nta. L'Architecte a été obligé de se conformer aux plantations déja faites et de s'assujettir à la forme et au mouvement du terrein.
Boulevard d'Aunay
Boulevard
Barrière d'Aunay
Toises.
Mètres.

ruins and tombs, from the Désert de Retz to Parc Monceau. It was this emblematic version of the picturesque that inspired the architect Brongniart in his designs for Père Lachaise, as he replaced geometry with "the beauty of nature" and sought to create "a character of sadness without terror, and of religious melancholy."[64] Thus, although he retained elements of the old Jesuit country house garden with its axes, straight lines, and allées of horse chestnut trees, Brongniart added sinuous paths, carriage roads, and plantings of trees including cypresses, poplars, and weeping willows[65] (fig. 6). As an architect, he focused on structures and monuments to create much of the character of the place, and soon the cemetery was celebrated as the most picturesque and varied site anywhere near Paris, heralded by visitors for its "great number of beautiful monuments" and the names inscribed upon them.[66]

In the United States, the picturesque was also welcomed as a sign of rebellion against Tory values and power. Thomas Jefferson was one of the early proponents of the style at Monticello, deciding to "improve [the grounds] in the style of the English gardens" with lofty trees, thickets of shrubs, and vistas revealing rivers, cultivated grounds, and villages.[67] The adoption of an English-style landscape was seen as the logical choice for Mount Auburn, marking a break with Puritan traditions and allowing a return to the burial styles used for ancient heroes such as Simon Peter, Aristides, and Homer, who were laid to rest not in tombs but simply in the earth; the approach reflected the ideals of the new country, "where all are equal" in life as well as death.[68] From the outset, early proponents of Mount Auburn pictured a cemetery, both derived from English models and "similar in its design to that of Père Lachaise," with rural embellishments such as weeping willows, cypress, and native laurels, and flowers with their "budding and bloom and decay."[69] The classical structures and tombs were generally simpler in style than their French counterparts, and Americans largely resisted the European enthusiasm for fabricated ruins, given common fears about the young Republic crumbling.[70]

As well as references to Greek and Roman antiquity, both cemeteries looked to ancient Egypt for inspiration. Obelisks and pyramids had become such common design motifs in Europe after the Renaissance, widely appearing in eighteenth-century English gardens, for instance, that their explicit history as part of the Egyptian tradition was frequently overlooked.[71]

Fig. 6, opposite. "Plan du Cimetière de l'Est dit du Père Lachaise ou Mont Louis," in Alexandre-Théodore Brongniart, *Plans du Palais de la Bourse de Paris et du cimetière Mont-Louis en six planches,* published Paris, 1814.

Interest in the original Egyptian sources was reawakened by the scholarly research and publications like *Description de l'Égypte* ordered by Napoleon as part of his Egyptian campaign of 1798–1801 and appearing in print from 1809. Egypt was particularly valued by the founders of both rural cemeteries because it was perceived as the cradle of civilization, while, as Richard Etlin has argued, the majestic pyramid was seen as able to withstand the ravages of existence and so bestow on the new burial grounds an appropriate sense of enduring timelessness.[72]

Thus, around 1810, Brongniart proposed a two-hundred-foot-high chapel in the shape of a pyramid at the center of Père Lachaise. Although this was never realized, the tombs of many individuals who had been involved in Napoleon's campaigns in Egypt were clearly Egyptian in style. Similarly, at Mount Auburn, Jacob Bigelow designed monumental entrance gates explicitly in imitation of those at Thebes and elsewhere, which were installed in timber in 1831 and reconstructed in granite in 1842. Other Egyptian-inspired funerary designs followed, most notably a vast sphinx in memory of the Union casualties of the Civil War. While the use of Egyptian motifs was controversial and sometimes attacked as inappropriate for a largely Christian burial site, the defenders of the Egyptian Revival style argued that ancient Egyptian culture was not pagan but somehow pre-Christian, providing the source of much contemporary divine imagery and that, like nineteenth-century Christians, ancient Egyptians buried their dead and believed in divine protection and human resurrection.[73]

Despite the design of both cemeteries thus being inspired by the English picturesque and its incorporation of architectural references to antiquity, a comparison between early guidebooks and memoirs for the two sites reveals striking differences in the perceptions of the landscapes. For Père Lachaise, descriptions focus in detail on individual graves and the history of the person buried there, with moral and philosophical meanings derived from the carefully transcribed epitaphs. Images are almost invariably detailed renditions of single monuments or small groups.[74] The elaborate and plentiful monuments impressed an American visitor: "It is already so thickly set with marble, that there is hardly room for any more, and it would be difficult to find two monuments alike, among all the thousands that arrest your attention."[75] Père Lachaise thus exhibited what Thomas Whately had characterized as an "emblematical" version of the picturesque, with statues and inscriptions requiring examination and explanation to be appreciated.[76] In contrast, guides to Mount Auburn summon up Whately's "expressive" picturesque style, describing and illustrating the naturalistic scenery, and the feelings it generated, with only occasional references to the monuments. A typical visitor describes in detail the terrain "beautifully undulating in its surface, containing a number of bold eminences, steep acclivities, and deep shadowy valleys," before briefly mentioning the tombs, which from the main carriageway are seen "starting up from the surrounding verdure, like bright remembrances from the heart of earth."[77] Popular engravings of Mount Auburn created an image of rural scenes, meadows, forests, views, tree-lined paths, solitary mourners, and lofty graves, with visitors in pensive reflection, their hearts calmed by the pure sentiments engendered by the scenery[78] (fig. 7).

Those who knew both burial grounds drew sharp distinctions between them: one American writer described with affection how a cemetery like Mount Auburn was created simply "from nature, and the love of it" while criticizing Père Lachaise for teeming with names, monuments, and "historical and classical accumulations," and, as he saw it, striving to provoke "sensations . . . [of] mere excitement."[79] Another compared the "picturesqueness" of Mount Auburn with Père Lachaise and its "morbid sentimentality,

Fig. 7. Forest Pond, Mount Auburn Cemetery, engraving by James Smillie, 1847. (Courtesy Mount Auburn Cemetery Historical Collections, Cambridge and Watertown, Mass.)

done up in bronze, and marble, and silver-gilt . . . a splendid illustration of the French passion for effect."[80] Many compared the style of monuments at the two cemeteries: a French visitor to Mount Auburn noted how much simpler were its graves than those at Père Lachaise; he felt that vanity and glory played no part in their design, and that the simplicity of style present throughout the Massachusetts cemetery acknowledged that death was the great leveler.[81] Others judged that the elaborate tombs at Père Lachaise were "jewels of great intrinsic value, with cameos of rare workmanship."[82] Overall, any attempt at drawing parallels was as absurd as trying "to compare St. Peter's church at Rome with the Falls of Niagara," so different were their respective attitudes to art and nature.[83]

In France, the fashion for the picturesque passed as, by the end of the nineteenth century, people were coming again to a patriotic appreciation of the merits of classically geometric gardens and their reflection of the national character.[84] In any event, as John Claudius Loudon disparagingly argued, the fad for English-style landscapes in France had in reality often produced little more than "crooked walks" and much fanciful ornamentation.[85] But, as we can see in responses to Mount Auburn, the picturesque landscape style resonated deeply with Americans as a reflection of the new Republic and its uplifting natural scenery; it came for many to symbolize the real America.

Evolution in Context

Père Lachaise was vastly influential as the model for a new kind of cemetery, which spread throughout Europe and North America. Its particular interpretation at Mount Auburn led to the establishment of a new type of American landscape, with Downing describing how, "[n]o sooner was attention generally roused to the charms of this first American cemetery, than the idea took the public mind by storm."[86] The rural cemetery movement spread rapidly across the new Republic, from Philadelphia's Laurel Hill Cemetery and Green Mount in Baltimore to Brooklyn's Green-Wood Cemetery, Cincinnati's Spring Grove, and Graceland in Chicago. By 1880, the influential Irish garden writer William Robinson was describing the rural cemeteries inspired by Mount Auburn as if they were an American institution.[87]

In contrast with Père Lachaise, Mount Auburn was also to play a significant part in shaping the subsequent development of public parks. The French cemetery's lack of influence on park design was to some extent because it remained principally a place for public sorrow, for people to visit and mourn their lost loved ones, with many groups performing public lamentations.[88] An Englishwoman who knew both cemeteries commented on the forlorn visitors at Père Lachaise, where "every expression of mourning is to be found; few or none of hope. . . . In Mount Auburn, on the contrary, there is nothing else."[89] The French cemetery also remained linked closely in people's minds with the realities of death and the new distaste for its decaying, polluting, revolting nature.[90] There were continuing fears about the dangers to public health from rotting corpses, which had been one of the factors behind the original decision to replace city graveyards with a rural cemetery.[91] As a result, during the modernization of Paris in the 1860s, Père Lachaise was perceived as a problem: the cemetery was too close to the city, too small, and a potential risk to urban water supplies. It was even proposed (unsuccessfully) that it should be closed down and a new cemetery built away from Paris.[92]

In addition, the long-standing French love of strolling in public, with all its attendant "spectacle and social rivalry," meant that there were already many places of popular resort in the city available for promenades, from the Tuileries and the Champs Elysées to the Palais-Royal, Luxembourg gardens, and Jardin des Plantes.[93] There was no need for Parisians to appropriate their new cemeteries for such a purpose. Subsequently, when Napoleon III and Georges-Eugène Haussmann were planning new public parks for working people, they turned for inspiration to a model from abroad, in the London parks and squares familiar to the emperor from his time in exile.[94]

In contrast, Mount Auburn was intended from the outset as a place of "general resort."[95] Even so, the founders were soon reporting that "visitors were numerous beyond all expectation"; the grounds were closed at night, entry was restricted, and various activities involving loud noise and refreshments were banned.[96] Guidebooks proliferated, and soon articles were being written not just about the recreational pleasures of Mount Auburn, but also about its surprising lure for all of society, from the working classes gathering there on Sundays to fashionable groups deciding on a whim to take their carriages "and away they dash, full of life, and health, and beauty, to visit the mansions of Death."[97] One French visitor to Mount Auburn was greatly surprised by how much more spacious than Père Lachaise the cemetery was, and how like a park; he noted that indeed it was used for family walks, like the Bois de Boulogne in Paris, but with a rather more melancholic feel.[98]

In this way, the popularity of Mount Auburn as a pleasure ground directly led to both Downing and Frederick Law Olmsted identifying the need for American public parks.[99] Downing argued that the appeal of Mount Auburn, and the other cemeteries it inspired, was not as burial ground, or place for melancholy reflection, or home of funerary art, but "in the natural beauty of the sites, and in the tasteful and harmonious embellishments of these sites by art." Public parks or gardens would, he argued, be visited by even more than the "thousands and tens of thousands" of Bostonians who visited Mount Auburn in a season, and would fulfill the American "passion for rural pleasures."[100]

Olmsted was less comfortable than Downing with the popular use of rural cemeteries, arguing that they should be "a place of rest, silence, seclusion, and peace," rather than "a constant resort of mere pleasure seekers, travelers, promenaders, and loungers." It was this inappropriate use that for him indicated "as much as anything else, the need that exists in every town and village for a proper pleasure ground."[101] Similarly, visitors to Mount Auburn, faced with the increasing number of prominent memorials and tombs, began to wonder "whether it might not be better to have it all without the graves," and so "fashion and pleasure looked about for a garden where death was not so frequent a visitor."[102] From the middle of the nineteenth century, Downing and Olmsted's dreams of public parks became a reality, directly modeled on the success and style of America's rural cemeteries, and so the "rage" for Mount Auburn as a tourist attraction in its own right gradually fell away, thus bringing to a close this first, extraordinary stage in its history.[103]

Conclusion

This essay has explored the adaptation of the rural cemetery model from its origins in Paris to a new situation in eastern Massachusetts and has attempted to demonstrate how key foreign funerary and design trends were directly borrowed from Europe, including the adoption of a radically new and more secular approach to burials, the choice of spacious rural locations for cemeteries, creation of densely planted landscapes in the fashionable picturesque style, a widespread use of architectural references to Greco-Roman and Egyptian antiquity, and the construction of pathways and carriage roads among monuments to form accessible commemorative landscapes. Yet these foreign trends were not simply replicated in the new Republic, but were intentionally and unintentionally fashioned to become part of a distinctive new landscape tradition. A wide range of factors influenced the adaptation of the rural cemetery to Massachusetts, from the vigor, optimism, and essential newness of the Republic, and its wish for cultural enrichment, to the country's more primitive, wild scenery, and its citizens' attitudes to freedom, nature, and death, born of the country's particular religious and political history. It was thus that, from its French origins as a bittersweet source of philosophical and moral reflection, an expression of familial grief and ancestral pride, and an essentially urban display of man's artistic mastery, the rural cemetery became at Mount Auburn a nostalgic representation of the East Coast's disappearing natural scenery, an example of distinctive new culture, and ultimately an expression of the hopes and ideals of the new American Republic.

Notes

The author would like to thank the following people for help in the production of this essay: Blanche Linden, whose seminal work *Silent City on a Hill* is the starting point for any scholar of Mount Auburn; Meg L. Winslow, curator of historical collections, and Brian A. Sullivan, former archivist, both at Mount Auburn Cemetery; Maureen Horn, librarian at the Massachusetts Horticultural Society; the research staff at the British Library, the Bibliothèque Nationale de France, and the Centre des Archives de Paris; the Friends of Père Lachaise (l'Association des Amis et Passionnés du Père-Lachaise); and the chair and participants at the University of Pennsylvania Foreign Trends on American Soil symposium where an earlier version of this paper was presented.

1. There is some scholarly debate on how far Mount Auburn was based on the model of Père Lachaise, but research suggests the influence is undeniable. Abel Bowen, "Burial in Cities," *Boston News-letter and City Record*, March 4, 1826, 126–29; Blanche M. G. Linden, *Silent City on a Hill: Picturesque Landscapes of Memory and Boston's Mount Auburn Cemetery* (Amherst: University of Massachusetts Press, 2007), 147; Carl David Arfwedson, *The United States and Canada, in 1832, 1833, and 1834* (London: Richard Bentley, 1834), 1:210.

2. William W. Stowe, "Writing Mount Auburn: Language, Landscape, and Place," *Proceedings of the American Philosophical Society* 150, no. 2 (June 2006): 296–317.

3. Ernest Weekley, "Folly," in *An Etymological Dictionary of Modern English* (New York: Courier Dover, 1967), 586.

4. François Gabriel Théodore Busset de Jolimont, *Les mausolées français* (Paris: Firmin Didot, 1821), 16.

5. Lynn Avery Hunt, *Politics, Culture, and Class in the French Revolution*, 20th anniversary ed. (Berkeley: University of California Press, 2004), 19–51.

6. Pierre François Pietresson de Saint-Aubin, *Promenade aux cimetières de Paris, aux sépultures royales de Saint-Denis et aux catacombes* (Paris, c.1817), 33–34.

7. François Marie Marchant de Beaumont, *Manuel et Itinéraire du Curieux dans le Cimetière du Père La Chaise*, 3rd ed. (Paris: Emler Frères, 1828), 22.

8. See, for example, Messieurs Roger, père et fils, *Le Champ du Repos, ou le Cimetière Mont Louis, dit Du Père Delachaise* (Paris: Lebègue, 1816), vii–xiv.

9. Antoine Caillot, *Voyage religieux et sentimental aux quatre cimetières de Paris* (Paris: L. Haussmann, 1809), 145–54.

10. Oliver Goldsmith, *The Deserted Village* (1770; rpt. Chicago: Fountain Press, 1965).

11. Caroline Frances Orne, *Sweet Auburn and Mount Auburn with Other Poems* (Cambridge: John Owen, 1844), 14.

12. Robert Manning, ed., *History of the Massachusetts Horticultural Society, 1829–1878* (Boston: Massachusetts Horticultural Society, 1880), 85.

13. William A. Brewer, "Mount Auburn," in *Recreations of a Merchant; or, The Christian Sketch-book* (Boston: Crocker & Brewster, 1836), 165–71; Mary Tyler Peabody, letters, 1835, quoted in Linden, *Silent City on a Hill*, 165.

14. Caroline Howard Gilman, *The Poetry of Travelling in the United States* (New York: S. Colman, 1838), 163–64, emphasis in the original.

15. Alexis de Tocqueville, *Democracy in America*, vol. 2, 1840, qtd. in Amy A. Kass, *The Perfect Gift: The Philanthropic Imagination in Poetry and Prose* (Bloomington: Indiana University Press, 2002), 22–27.

16. See, for instance, Helmut K. Anheier, *Nonprofit Organizations: Theory, Management, Policy* (New York: Routledge, 2005), 25–27.

17. James S. Ackerman, "On Public Landscape Design before the Civil War, 1830–1860," in *Regional Garden Design in the United States*, ed. Therese O'Malley and Marc Treib (Washington, DC: Dumbarton Oaks Research Library and Collection, 1995), 191–208.

18. Richard A. Etlin, *Symbolic Space: French Enlightenment Architecture and Its Legacy* (Chicago: University of Chicago Press, 1995), 169–71; Linden, *Silent City on a Hill*, 76–77.

19. Stephen Duncan Walker, *Rural Cemetery and Public Walk* (Baltimore: Sands & Neilson, 1835), iv; Mary Abbott, "The Family Circle: Our Birth Place," *Valley Farmer* 6, no. 12 (December 1854): 473–75, and "Ornamental Cemeteries," *Yale Literary Magazine* 11, no. 2 (November 1855): 45–49.

20. The cemetery was enclosed within the fortifications of Paris in the 1840s and became part of the city's new twentieth arrondissement in 1860 when Napoleon III annexed the capital's suburban communes.

21. Jean-Pons-Guillaume Viennet, *Promenade philosophique au cimetière du Père Lachaise*, vol. 2 of *Oeuvres Diverses* (Brussels: Hayez, 1826), 294.

22. Heman Humphrey, *Great Britain, France and Belgium: A Short Tour in 1835* (New York: Harper & Brothers, 1838), 2:325.

23. Arfwedson, *United States and Canada*, 1:210–13.

24. Judge Story's 1831 address on the consecration of Mount Auburn, as discussed in Thomas Bender, "The 'Rural' Cemetery Movement: Urban Travail and the Appeal of Nature," *New England Quarterly* 47, no. 2 (June 1974): 196–211; Wilson Flagg, *Mount Auburn: Its Scenes, Its Beauties, and Its Lessons* (Boston: James Monroe, 1861), 35–36.

25. Andrew Jackson Downing, "On Feminine Taste in Rural Affairs," *Horticulturalist and Journal of Rural Art and Rural Taste* 3, no. 10 (April 1849): 449–50.

26. Richard [Jean-Marie-Vincent Audin], *Le Véritable Conducteur aux cimetières du Père Lachaise, Montmartre, Montparnasse et Vaugirard* (1830; 4th ed., Paris: Baudouin, 1836), 55–56.

27. Marchant de Beaumont, *Manuel et Itinéraire,* i–x. See also Philippe Ariès, *Western Attitudes toward Death: From the Middle Ages to the Present,* trans. Patricia Ranum (Baltimore: Johns Hopkins University Press, 1975), 55–84, and Ariès, *The Hour of Our Death,* trans. Helen Weaver (New York: Alfred A. Kopf, 1981), 529–34.

28. Augustus Pugin and Charles Heath, *Paris and Its Environs: Displayed in a Series of Two Hundred Picturesque Views* (London: Jennings and Chaplin, 1831), 129. See also James Smillie and Cornelia W. Walter, *Mount Auburn Illustrated: In Highly Finished Line Engraving, from Drawings Taken on the Spot* (New York: R. Martin, 1847), 118–19.

29. Jacob Bigelow, letter to his family, May 2–4, 1833, qtd. in Linden, *Silent City on a Hill,* 159.

30. Pietresson de Saint-Aubin, *Promenade aux cimetières,* 37; Frances (Fanny) Milton Trollope, "Letter 22: Père Lachaise," in *Paris and the Parisians in 1835,* 2nd ed. (London: Richard Bentley, 1836), 1:190.

31. Linden, *Silent City on a Hill,* 95–116.

32. Gunther Paul Barth, "The Park Cemetery: Its Westward Migration," in *American Public Architecture: European Roots and Native Expressions,* ed. Craig Robert Zabel and Susan Scott Munshower (University Park: Pennsylvania State University Press, 1989), 61; Philip Pregill and Nancy Volkman, *Landscapes in History: Design and Planning in the Eastern and Western Traditions* (New York: John Wiley, 1999), 454–55.

33. "Report on Mount Auburn Cemetery," *Meyer's Universum,* 1853, qtd. in Gunther Paul Barth, *Fleeting Moments: Nature and Culture in American History* (New York: Oxford University Press, 1990), 133.

34. See Edward Everett, "The Proposed Rural Cemetery," qtd. in Linden, *Silent City on a Hill,* 155.

35. For instance, "History of Mount Auburn," in *The Picturesque Pocket Companion, and Visitor's Guide, through Mount Auburn* (Boston: Otis, Broaders, 1839), 3–4.

36. Henry A. S. Dearborn, "General Dearborn's Report," in *Picturesque Pocket Companion,* 48.

37. Orne, *Sweet Auburn and Mount Auburn,* 34–35.

38. Aaron Sachs, "American Arcadia: Mount Auburn Cemetery and the Nineteenth-Century Landscape Tradition," *Environmental History* 15, no. 2 (2010): 206–35.

39. Zebedee Cook Jr., *An Address Pronounced before the Massachusetts Historical Society in Commemoration of Its Second Annual Festival, the 10th of Sept. 1830* (Boston: Isaac R. Baits, 1830), qtd. in Linden, *Silent City on a Hill,* 160.

40. Dearborn, "General Dearborn's Report," in *Picturesque Pocket Companion,* 42.

41. Manning, *History of the Massachusetts Horticultural Society,* 95–96; Linden, *Silent City on a Hill,* 162.

42. John Lauris Blake, *The Young Orator: Consisting of Prose, Poetry, and Dialogues for Declamation in Schools* (Boston: Lilly, Wait, Colman and Holden, 1833), 12–13.

43. Americans smarted at any hint that the new Republic was culturally impoverished, the most famous European taunt on this score being the dismissive line "Who reads an American book?" from Sydney Smith, Review of "Adam Seybert, Statistical Annals of the United States of America," *Edinburgh Review* 33 (January 1820): 69–80.

44. See, for instance, the Catholic text *A Dialogue on Purgatory; or, The Existence of a Middle State of Suffering after Death, and the Propriety of Praying for the Dead: Con-*

taining a Comparative View of the Catholic and Protestant Burial Services (Manchester: Ambrose Clarke Robinson, 1831).

45. Nathaniel Carter, qtd. in Richard A. Etlin, *The Architecture of Death: The Transformation of the Cemetery in Eighteenth-Century Paris* (Cambridge, MA: MIT Press, 1984), 367.

46. Linden, *Silent City on a Hill,* 20, 64–65.

47. Exponents included Jacques-Henri Bernardin de Saint-Pierre, Christian Cajus Lorenz Hirschfeld, Jean Lecointe, Alexandre Lenoir, Joseph Fouché, Amaury Duval, Abbé Mulot, and others, as discussed in ibid., 65–72.

48. Caillot, *Voyage religieux et sentimental,* 160; Marchant de Beaumont, *Manuel et Itinéraire,* 47.

49. Linden, *Silent City on a Hill,* 16–17, 25–28, 120.

50. Tracy Fessenden, *Culture and Redemption: Religion, the Secular, and American Literature* (Princeton, NJ: Princeton University Press, 2007).

51. Jacob Bigelow, "On the Burial of the Dead," in *Nature in Disease, Illustrated in Various Discourses and Essays* (Boston: Ticknor and Fields, 1854), 194.

52. Harriet Martineau, *Retrospect of Western Travel* (London: Saunders & Otley, 1838), 2:278.

53. Lady Emmeline Stuart-Wortley, *Travels in the United States, etc., during 1849 and 1850* (New York: Harper & Brothers, 1851), 65–66. See also Arfwedson, *United States and Canada,* 210–13.

54. Jean-Henri Grandpierre, *Quelques mois de séjour aux États-Unis d'Amérique* (Paris: Grassart, 1854), 107.

55. Linden, *Silent City on a Hill,* 180. Many of the monuments were modeled on those at Père Lachaise, using designs copied and imported by Massachusetts Horticultural Society president Henry Dearborn.

56. Wortley, *Travels in the United States,* 47–48, and Enoch Cobb Wines, "Letter VII: Mount Auburn Cemetery, July 26, 1838," *A Trip To Boston: In a Series of Letters to the Editor of the United States Gazette* (Boston: Charles C. Little and James Brown, 1838), 42–53.

57. Sterling F. Delano, *The Harbinger and New England Transcendentalism: A Portrait of Associationism in America* (Rutherford, NJ: Fairleigh Dickinson University Press, 1983), 111–24.

58. Ralph Waldo Emerson, *The Journals and Miscellaneous Notebooks of Ralph Waldo Emerson,* vol. 4, 1832–1834, ed. Alfred R. Ferguson (Cambridge, MA: Belknap Press, 1964), 272–75; Jones Very, "The Garden," in *Essays and Poems* (Boston: Charles C. Little and James Brown, 1839), 132.

59. Margaret Fuller, journal entry, qtd. in Jeffrey Steele, *Transfiguring America: Myth, Ideology, and Mourning in Margaret Fuller's Writing* (Columbia: University of Missouri Press, 2001), 177. For another Transcendentalist response, see James Russell Lowell, "To a Voice Heard in Mount Auburn, July, 1839," *Dial,* January 1841, 366.

60. Richard Payne Knight, *The Landscape: A Didactic Poem,* 1794, in *The Genius of the Place,* ed. John Dixon Hunt and Peter Willis (Cambridge, MA: MIT Press, 1988), 342–48.

61. See, for example, Claude-Henri Watelet, *Essay on Gardens: A Chapter in the French Picturesque,* 1774, trans. Samuel Danon (Philadelphia: University of Pennsylvania Press,

2003), and Christian Cajus Lorenz Hirschfeld, *Theory of Garden Art,* 1779–1785, trans. Linda B. Parshall (Philadelphia: University of Pennsylvania Press, 2001).

62. Michel Baridon, "Cross-Channel Exchanges and the Rise of the Landscape Garden," in *"Better in France?" The Circulation of Ideas across the Channel in the Eighteenth Century,* ed. Frédéric Ogée (Lewisburg, PA: Bucknell University Press, 2005), 51.

63. Réné-Louis Girardin, *An Essay on Landscape,* 1777, trans. author (London: Dodsley, 1793), 121–22, qtd. in Linden, *Silent City on a Hill,* 65.

64. "Brongniart, Alexandre-Théodore," entry in Louis Gabriel Michaud, *Biographie universelle, ancienne et moderne, ouvrage rédigé par une société de gens de lettres* (Paris: Desplaces, 1854), 5: 605–6.

65. Marchant de Beaumont, *Manuel et Itinéraire,* 35–46; Linden, *Silent City on a Hill,* 72–75, 79.

66. Girault de Saint-Fargeau, *Guide pittoresque du voyageur en France* (Paris: Didot, 1838), 6:143.

67. Thomas Jefferson, letter to William Hamilton, July 1806, qtd. in Frederick Doveton Nichols and Ralph E. Griswold, *Thomas Jefferson, Landscape Architect* (Charlottesville: University Press of Virginia, 1993), 87–89.

68. Fellow of the Massachusetts Medical Society, *Remarks on the Dangers and Duties of Sepulture; or, Security for the Living, with Respect and Repose for the Dead* (Boston: Phelps & Farnham, 1823), 67. Similar views were expressed by Boston mayor Josiah Quincy. See Linden, *Silent City on a Hill,* 129.

69. Zebedee Cook Jr., *An Address Pronounced before the Massachusetts Historical Society,* qtd. in Walker, *Rural Cemetery and Public Walk,* iii–iv.

70. Linden, *Silent City on a Hill,* 102. See also "Mount Auburn," *New England Magazine* 1 (September 1831): 237–39, as qtd. in Stowe, "Writing Mount Auburn," *American Philosophical Society,* 296–317, a nightmarish vision of the future city laying ruined as part of the universal cycle of creation and destruction and remembered only in the graves of Mount Auburn.

71. Richard G. Carrott, *The Egyptian Revival: Its Sources, Monuments, and Meaning, 1808–1858* (Berkeley: University of California Press, 1978), 82.

72. Etlin, *The Architecture of Death,* 109.

73. Scott Trafton, *Egypt Land: Race and Nineteenth-Century American Egyptomania* (Durham, NC: Duke University Press, 2004), 158–61. In a further attempt to counter their pagan associations, Egyptian-style monuments also featured biblical inscriptions.

74. See, among many examples, Roger, *Le Champ du Repos,* and Jolimont, *Les mausolées français.*

75. Humphrey, *Great Britain, France and Belgium,* 234–35. See also Trollope, *Paris and the Parisians,* 193.

76. Thomas Whately, *Observations on Modern Gardening,* 1770, qtd. in Hunt, *The Genius of the Place,* 37–38.

77. Isaac Smith Homans, *Sketches of Boston, Past and Present: And of Some Few Places in Its Vicinity* (Boston: Phillips, Sampson, 1851), 103–9. Many other early visitors used similar language to describe Mount Auburn; see, for instance, [Fanny Kemble,] *Journal by Frances Anne Butler* (Philadelphia: Carey, Lea and Blanchard, 1835) 2:131; and Arfwedson, *United States and Canada,* 210–13.

78. Barth, *Fleeting Monuments,* 133; David Schuyler, *The New Urban Landscape: The Redefinition of City Form in Nineteenth-Century America* (Baltimore: Johns Hopkins University Press, 1986), 52.

79. "Church-yard Sketches," in *Picturesque Pocket Companion,* 193–209.

80. "Visit to the Père Lachaise at Paris," in *The Christian Parlor Book* (New York: George Pratt, 1850), 6:346–49. See also Charles Sumner, qtd. in Barth, "The Park Cemetery," 61.

81. Grandpierre, *Quelques mois,* 107.

82. Augustus Kinsley Gardner, *Old Wine in New Bottles; or, Spare Hours of a Student in Paris* (Dublin: James M'Glashan, 1849), 242–43.

83. Ibid. See similar views in John Ross Dix, "A Visit to Mount Auburn," *Local Loiterings and Visits in the Vicinity of Boston* (Boston: Redding & Co, 1845), 17–43, and Blake, *The Young Orator,* 12–13.

84. Lucien Corpechot, *Jardins de l'intelligence* (Paris: Emile-Paul, 1912), qtd. in Monique Mosser, "Henri and Achille Duchêne and the Reinvention of Le Nôtre," trans. Barbara Mellor, in *The Architecture of Western Gardens: A Design History from the Renaissance to the Present Day,* ed. Monique Mosser and Georges Teyssot (Cambridge, MA: MIT Press, 1991), 446–50.

85. John Claudius Loudon, *An Encyclopaedia of Gardening* (London: A&R Spottiswoode, 1824), 33–43.

86. Andrew Jackson Downing, *Horticulturist,* July 1849, qtd. in Janet L. Heywood, "Mount Auburn Cemetery: National Historic Landmark Nomination," March 2001, U.S. Department of the Interior, National Park Service.

87. Noël Dorsey Vernon, "Adolph Strauch: Cincinnati and the Legacy of Spring Grove Cemetery," in *Midwestern Landscape Architecture,* ed. William H. Tishler (Urbana: University of Illinois Press, 2000), 18.

88. Jolimont, *Les mausolées français,* 12–13; Trollope, *Paris and the Parisians,* 190–91. See a similar view in Humphrey, *Great Britain, France and Belgium,* 234–35.

89. Martineau, *Retrospect of Western Travel,* 276–77.

90. Thomas W. Laqueur, "The Places of the Dead in Modernity," in *The Age of Cultural Revolutions: Britain and France, 1750–1820,* ed. Colin Jones and Dror Wahrman (Berkeley: University of California, 2002), 19.

91. Félix Vicq d'Azyr, *Essai sur les Lieux et les Dangers des Sépultures* (Paris, 1778), qtd. in Laqueur, "The Places of the Dead in Modernity," 27.

92. Georges-Eugène Haussmann, *Mémoires Du Baron Haussmann* (Paris: Victor-Harvard, 1893), 3:404–34.

93. Daniel Rabreau, "Urban Walks in France in the Seventeenth and Eighteenth Centuries," trans. Barbara Mellor, in Mosser and Teyssot, *Architecture of Western Gardens,* 314; Haussmann, *Mémoires,* 172–73. See also Thomas Von Joest, "Haussmann's Paris: A Green Metropolis?," trans. Barbara Mellor, in Mosser and Teyssot, *Architecture of Western Gardens,* 387–98.

94. Haussmann, *Mémoires,* 183, 239–40.

95. Joseph Buckingham, "Cemetery at Mount Auburn," *Boston Courier,* 1831, rpt. in Massachusetts Horticultural Society, *Constitution and By-laws of the Massachusetts Horticultural Society* (Boston: Tuttle, Weeks and Dennett, 1836), 27–29.

96. Massachusetts Horticultural Society Records, 1832, qtd. in Shary Page Berg, *Historic Landscape Report,* vol. 2 of *Mount Auburn Cemetery Master Plan* (1993), 13.

97. George Ticknor Curtis, "Mount Auburn," *New-England Magazine* 7 (1834): 316. The article, which praises Mount Auburn for its ability to bring calm and contemplation equally to the mourner and the casual visitor, provided the title for this essay ("these beautiful pleasure-grounds of Death").

98. Grandpierre, *Quelques mois,* 105–7.

99. Etlin, *Symbolic Space,* 149–50.

100. Andrew Jackson Downing, "Public Cemeteries and Public Gardens," *Horticulturalist* 4, no. 1 (July 1849): 9–12.

101. Frederick Law Olmsted, "Parks at Home and Abroad," in *The Papers of Frederick Law Olmsted,* ed. Charles E. Beveridge and David Schuyler (Baltimore: Johns Hopkins University Press, 1983), 3:356–57.

102. Clarence Cook, *A Description of the New York Central Park* (New York: F. J. Huntingdon, 1869), 14–15.

103. Linden, *Silent City on a Hill,* 237–58.

Of Monarchical Climates and Republican Soil

French Plants and American Gardens in the Revolutionary Era

ELIZABETH HYDE

In 1787, the Reverend Manasseh Cutler traveled from Massachusetts to New York and Philadelphia as part of a mission to present to Congress plans for the settlement of the western frontier. Cutler was a Yale graduate, had studied medicine in addition to religion, and had practiced both in the American Revolution. He was also a botanically curious man—he traveled with equipment he needed to gather plant specimens. And on his journey he consulted libraries and scientific collections at universities, including Yale, Columbia, and Princeton, and organizations such as the American Philosophical Society, along the way. He was delighted to find certain botanical texts he did not own in some collections and disappointed that British soldiers had "carried off" other volumes (at Columbia, volumes belonging to Dr. Hill's *Natural History*, a thirty-volume folio text, only one copy of which existed in America).[1] He also carried with him letters of introduction to dignitaries he planned to encounter along the way. Upon reaching New York City, he cataloged his impressive stack of letters intended for Benjamin Franklin, Benjamin Rush, Reverend Witherspoon (president of Princeton), William Livingston, and members of Congress. Among the letters was one intended for Mons. "Le Mechard," "Superintendent [of the] French King's Botanical Garden" in New Jersey.[2] What did Cutler expect to learn from "Le Mechard" (André Michaux) and his garden? And what might those expectations reveal about French influences on American soil? Cutler's expectations—and, as will be seen, subsequent disappointments—reveal an American association of French gardens with taste and botanical sophistication.

Cutler traveled at a crucial moment in the botanical history of the young United States: while private collections such as William Hamilton's in Philadelphia, and the uniquely private, commercial, *and* scientific example of

Bartram's garden also in Philadelphia, were flourishing, the idea of the botanical garden as public or educational institution was, spurred in part by the French, just entering public discussion in America, hence Cutler's interest in the French example.[3] Cutler's detailed diary of his journey described a lively and lengthy audience with Benjamin Franklin. He described his trip to John Bartram's garden that was the hub of botanical networks in North America. And back in New York, he recorded his impressions of "Congress Chamber," on the second floor of City Hall, where the United States Congress convened. In addition to a full-length portrait of George Washington, the chamber included "the portraits of the King and Queen of France, as large as life. They were drawn by the King's own portrait painter," he continued, "and [were] presented by his Majesty to Congress. The drapery infinitely exceeds any thing of the kind I ever saw before. They are dressed in their robes, and life and animation is imitated to perfection. When the damask curtains, which covered them, were drawn, their eyes were fixed upon us with a vivacity that bespoke life itself, and their majestic countenances seemed to chastise our insolence in approaching them with so little reverence."[4]

Cutler's remarks, while acknowledging the republican impudence of the Americans, betray a fascination with, if not outright approval of, the French style and sophistication on display in the portraits.[5] So Cutler's disappointment must have been all the more keenly felt when he passed through Bergentown where he "was determined to make Mons. Mechard a visit, to whom I had letters. He is the French botanist sent to America for the purpose of establishing a botanical garden, where he collects American trees and plants of every species, and gives in exchange foreign trees and plants, which are sent to him from France at the expense of the King." When Cutler finally reached the garden, he found no one to whom to present his letter and nothing to satiate his curiosity. He wrote:

> Unfortunately he [Michaux] was gone to the Carolinas. There were several gardeners, but they appeared to understand little of Botany. They, however, showed me the Gardens, and were very complaisant. There were a considerable collection of exotic shrubs and plants, set in a kind of beds for transplanting. The American plants they had received were mostly sent to France. There was no order nor beauty in the gardens, the soil remarkably sandy and poor, the situation wretched, and the way to it as bad as can well be conceived. Of all the places in America, this would have been the very last I should have thought of for such a purpose. What could induce Mechard to fix down in the awful, gloomy, lonely, miserable spot, is

> beyond my power to conceive. I was never more disappointed, and regretted the pains I had taken to see the ill taste and judgment of this Botanical Frenchman.[6]

The garden Cutler had gone to see was the garden constructed near Hoboken, New Jersey, by André Michaux on behalf of the French king. Its purpose was exactly what Cutler described: to serve as a nursery for trees and other plants gathered by the botanist Michaux as he traveled around the mid-Atlantic of North America. He had been charged by the king of France and Charles-Claude Flahaut de la Billarderie, Comte d'Angiviller, the head of the king's botanical gardens in France, with locating specimens that might be acclimatized in France to aid both in the reforestation of France and in the furnishing of timber for the construction of a French navy capable of competing with the British.

Michaux's garden was, in fact, the culmination of escalating French attempts to gather North American specimens. Until Michaux's arrival, French diplomats were directed to collect and purchase plants and seeds from landed Americans and seedsmen.[7] Michaux, however, wanted a nursery garden in which to gather and propagate North American plants for study and to optimize chances of successful shipment to France.[8] He therefore decided to purchase land in New Jersey for such a purpose. New Jersey laws prohibited the purchase of land by noncitizens, so Michaux appealed to William Livingston, governor of New Jersey, for help. Livingston was inclined to be sympathetic. A member of the Hudson River Valley of New York Livingston family political dynasty, Livingston studied at Yale and built his professional reputation practicing law in New York City. As a young man, however, he wrote and published *Philosophic Solitude, or the Choice of a Rural Life,* a poem praising the virtues of rural living.[9] In the 1760s, Livingston made plans to retire from his law practice and retreat to an estate he had purchased in Elizabeth, New Jersey. On the estate he built a home, now called Liberty Hall, and gardens that he furnished with native and imported ornamental and fruit trees.[10] In New Jersey, Livingston was drawn into American Revolutionary military and political affairs and was elected governor of the state in 1777, serving until his death in 1790. He found little of the solitude he celebrated in his poem, but he had become the quintessential American version of the gentleman farmer: intellectually and culturally sophisticated, politically engaged, and curious about agriculture and botany.

Michaux's appeal was not Livingston's first contact with the French. As governor, Livingston had been given a questionnaire by François, Marquis de Barbé-Marbois, secretary to the French consul general Anne-César, Chevalier de la Luzerne in Philadelphia, regarding the population, economy, and natural history of each of the thirteen states. Livingston answered the questionnaire, and in thanks Marbois sent him a packet of seeds to be shared between himself and his cousin Robert R. Livingston. Livingston thanked Marbois for the seeds, writing, "Thanks to heaven that the times [the American Revolution having ended] again permit me to pursue my favourite amusement of raising vegetables which with the additional pleasure resulting from my Library I really prefer to all the bustle and splendour of the world."[11] And he expressed hope that "our republican soil" would not harm "the products of a monarchical climate."[12]

So when contacted by Michaux in 1786, Livingston urged the New Jersey State Assembly to grant Michaux permission to purchase the land. The assembly complied with passage of a special act, and Michaux made the purchase, began construction of the garden and a house, and proceeded with his primary mission: the gathering and study of North American specimens. He would travel widely around the mid-Atlantic region and establish a similar garden in Charleston, South Carolina.

Meanwhile, word of the garden began to spread. Manasseh Cutler clearly had prior knowledge of it, for he carried with him his letter of introduction to Michaux. Its creation had been publically reported in New Jersey: news of Michaux's appeal to the New Jersey State Assembly circulated in New Jersey newspapers, the *New Jersey Gazette* reporting on April 3, 1786, that the House met and "The bill, intitled, 'an act to enable Andrè [*sic*] Michaux to purchase a certain tract of land,' was read a second time, and the title amended to read as follows: 'an act to enable Andrè [*sic*] to purchase lands in the state of New-Jersey, under certain restrictions.' The bill was also further amended in the house, and ordered to be engrossed."[13] The news was also reported in the *Political Intelligencer and New-Jersey Advertiser* published in Elizabeth Town.[14] Subsequent accounts of the garden could have heightened expectations. The *Political Intelligencer and New-Jersey Advertiser* reported from Elizabeth Town, New Jersey, on April 19 that "Mr. Michaux, Botanist to His Most Christian Majesty, having purchased a lot of ground at Wehocken, near the Three Pigeons, is erecting a garden there, which, for magnificence, & c. will far surpass any thing of the kind in America—in it is introduced many exotic and domestic Botanical curiosities."[15]

In just over a year, not only had the garden begun to grow, but, warranted or not, so had its reputation. On June 27, 1787, the *New-Jersey Journal, and Political Intelligencer* recorded passage of the act to create a "garden and a fruitery," but further reported, "Part of this space is at present inclosing with a stone wall, and a universal collection of exotic, as well as domestic plants, trees and flowers, are already begun to be introduced to this elegant spot, which in time will rival if not exceed the most celebrated gardens of Europe. The situation is naturally wild and romantic between two considerable rivers, in view of the main ocean, the city of New York, the heights of Staten-Island, and a vast extent of distant mechanisms on the western side of the landscape."[16] The exaggerated account is revealing. First, the garden had grown in reputation to rival not only any garden in America but also "the most celebrated in Europe." Second, and more interestingly, the (anonymous) author of the passage, seemingly untroubled by the presence of neither "order nor beauty" that had bothered Cutler, described the situation as "naturally wild and romantic."[17]

The contrasting descriptions of Michaux's garden are rooted in competing aesthetics of eighteenth-century garden and landscape design. While Cutler's desire for "order" might reflect the hope that Michaux's garden was organized according to botanical principles, that he linked it to "beauty" suggests Cutler expected a garden laid out in a formal geometric garden style perfected in continental European gardens in the sixteenth and seventeenth centuries in which order, expressed through geometry, axiality, and symmetry, contributed much to the perception of the garden's beauty.[18] Indeed, Cutler critiqued Michaux for failing to exhibit "taste" in his garden. By contrast, the newspaper account, citing the wild and romantic setting of the garden, uses language of the picturesque, the aesthetic that had emerged triumphant over the course of the eighteenth century in England. The eighteenth-century picturesque landscape garden strived for the appearance of "natural" (the "art" of improvement having been applied with a seemingly easy hand) through asymmetry, with visual interest supplied through the texture and colors of plants—especially the new textures and colors supplied by the newly tapped botanical riches of the North American colonies.

The contrasting judgments of Michaux's garden demonstrate that Americans were aware of a range of garden aesthetics. While garden historians have asserted that a geometric style of gardening was predominant in eighteenth-century American gardens, some historians have found piecemeal elements of the picturesque in the eighteenth-century American garden: the ha-ha could be found in Virginia gardens by 1740, while mid-eighteenth-century descriptions of Middle Place in Virginia, at Van Cortland Manor in New York, and at Morven, in Princeton, New Jersey, suggest that if, bit by bit, picturesque elements were invading the gardens, more importantly, observers were identifying them, or at least using the vocabulary of the picturesque to describe what they saw.[19]

Eighteenth-century Americans were reading books on agriculture, botany, and gardening from both England and France that represented different garden tastes and traditions. Livingston assembled a library with English and Continental works, including John Evelyn's *Sylva,* Philip Miller's *Gardener's Dictionary,* and Batty Langley's *Principles of Gardening,* as well as volumes by John Ray, Joseph Pitton de Tournefort, and Marcello Malpighi.[20] His cousin Robert R. Livingston built a greenhouse and extensive garden on Clermont, his Hudson River estate, as well as a library, the contents of which he published in 1800. It included a variety of English and French works, listing Young "on agriculture," Bradley's *Improvements on Gardening,* and Mawe's *Gardiner's Calendar,* as well as Duhamel's *Practical Treatise of Husbandry, L'Ecole de Jardin Fruitier,* and a translation of the *Dictionnaire jardiniers et supplement.*[21] Thomas Jefferson's (more extensive) library held a broad range of books on botany (including Dioscorides and Theophrastus, Parkinson, Boerhaave, Tournefort, Linnaeus, Rousseau, and Bradley, as well as volumes specifically on North America).[22] He owned English, Italian, and French works on agriculture, including the *Maison Rustique,* Olivier de Serres, Duhamel, Fabbroni, Bradley, and Maupin. Among books on gardening, he owned English works including Evelyn's *Sylva,* Miller's *Gardener's Dictionary* (in English and in French), Heely's *Letters on the Beauties of Hagley,* Bradley's *General Treatise of Husbandry & Gardening,* Mawe's *Every Man His Own Gardener,* and Whately's *Observations on Modern Gardening,* that Jefferson used as critical guidebook on his tour of English gardens with John Adams.[23] He owned French volumes including Duhamel du Monceau, Liger's *Jardinier solitaire,* Mallet's *Le Parfait jardinier,* Maupin's *L'Art de la vigne,* and de la Brosse "de la culture du Figuier."

The libraries of the incomparably well-read and well-traveled Jefferson—and the much smaller ones of the still erudite Livingstons—are hardly typical of what most eighteenth-century Americans could have accessed. But they demonstrate that Americans could draw from a range of gardening traditions. William Livingston's example is instructive: in his 1747 *Philosophic Solitude,* he described the setting for his ideal rural home:

> Full in the center of some shady grove,
> By nature formed for solitude and love;
> On banks array'd with ever-blooming flow'rs,
> Near beauteous landskips, or by roseate bow'rs;
> My neat, but simple mansion I would raise, . . .[24]

The house itself, set near the "beauteous landskips," would be entwined in grape vines while

> Along my mansion, spiry firrs should grow,
> And gloomy yews extend the shady row;
> The cedars flourish, and the poplars rise
> Sublimely tall and shoot into the skies.[25]

From this setting, "varied prospects glad the wandring eyes":

> Where meadows flourish and fields look gay;
> From bliss to bliss with endless pleasure rove,
> Seek crystal streams, or haunt the vernal grove,
> Woods, fountains, lakes, the fertile fields or shades,
> Aërial mountains, or subjacent glades.[26]

Livingston's verse is ripe with the sensual pleasures of nature and anticipates the romantic or sublime. And yet there is no evidence that he employed the picturesque in his gardens at Liberty Hall. Together, however, these references demonstrate an awareness of both English and continental geometric garden aesthetics so that an eighteenth-century American like Cutler could assume that a "Frenchman's garden" would combine "beauty" and "order" in displaying taste, while another, perhaps aware of more recent fashion for the picturesque, could appreciate the wild beauty of the garden's setting.

Surviving plans for Michaux's garden confirm Cutler's observation that the garden was organized purely around its utilitarian goals, rather than sophisticated formal French garden aesthetics (fig. 1). Indeed, for Michaux, the genius of the place lay in its proximity both to "grands bois pour aller recueiller des semences et arracher des jeunes arbres," and to "New York et de la riviere pour communiquer avec les Paquebots": he could easily transport the carefully packed crates of seeds and plants to ships in the New York harbor that would carry them to France.[27] The garden, then, was planned and organized around its very utilitarian mission.

As we have seen, Cutler assumed that because Michaux's garden was French, it would be sophisticated in layout *and* botanical content. The bo-

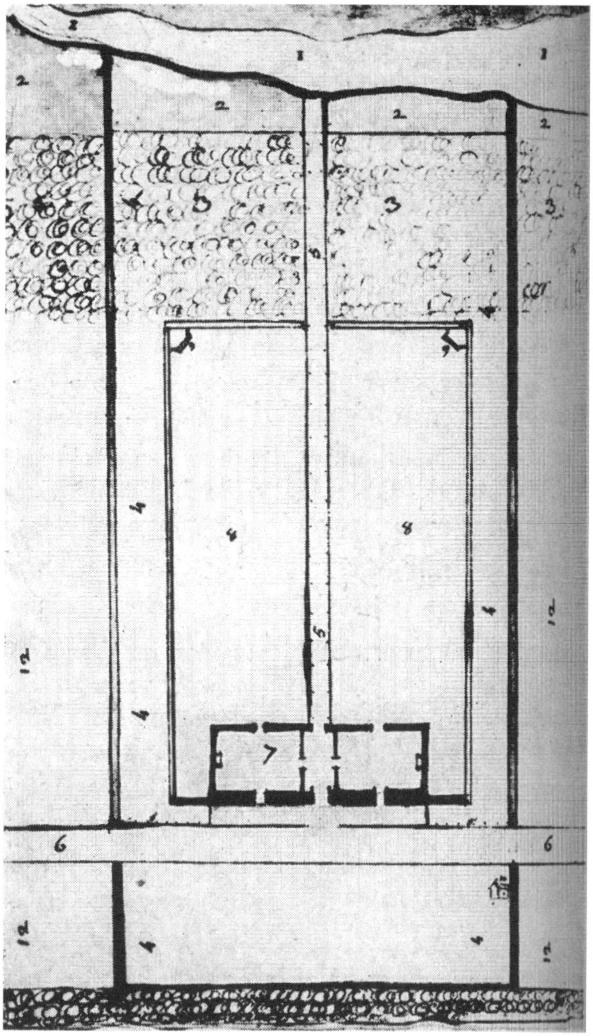

Fig. 1. André Michaux's garden plan reproduced in William J. Robbins and Mary Christine Howson, "André Michaux's New Jersey Garden and Pierre Paul Saunier, Journeyman Gardener," *Proceedings of the American Philosophical Society* 102, no. 4 (August 1958): 356.

tanical reputation of the French had preceded Michaux. Indeed, the French had touted their botanical superiority in appealing to the Americans for access to their collections. In 1779, Conrad Gérard, French envoy to the Continental Congress, contacted Philadelphia physician Thomas Bond in hopes of acquiring American plants. In exchange for American plants, he promised French specimens. Bond, writing to nurseryman Humphry Marshall from whom he would acquire the desired plants, explained: "It is in his power—it is his wish, to improve the useful productions of this new world. He wants our curiosities and novelties: we want his valuable collections from all other parts of the world."[28] Bond requested that Marshall fill the order, and when the promised French plants were delivered, he wrote "the collection, though small, is valuable and curious. I wish to keep up a correspondency in Europe, on a small scale, and solely with a view of furnishing each country, reciprocally, with such things as may be useful."[29] In 1783, Hector St. John de Crevecoeur, serving as French consul to the states of New York, New Jersey, and Connecticut, extended a formal proposal that should the states establish a botanical garden, the French would share specimens from their collections in exchange for American plants. William Livingston responded by submitting the French proposal to the State Assembly and reported to Crevecoeur that the Assembly expressed thanks and "to assure him that whenever this state hath formed an Establishment of a Botanical Garden, His Most Christian Majesty's offer will be gratefully accepted."[30] When Michaux appealed to the New Jersey Assembly in 1786, he promised the Assembly that he had "full powers to draw from France at the King's expence any Tree, Plant and Vegetable that might be wanting in this Country" in the form of a "depository not only of French and American plants, But of all other productions of the World, which might be drawn from the King's Garden at Paris."[31] Such French promises served to whet the appetites of Americans who were curious about botany.

For however much ambivalence eighteenth-century Americans may have had about geometrically laid-out gardens as opposed to picturesque parks, Americans were aware of the superiority—and desirability—of French plants and French collections of plants. Indeed, surviving epistolary and commercial evidence reveals Americans valued French specimens and French knowledge. While the French and American exchange was not as vigorous as the better-documented trade in plants between the British and the Americans, it nonetheless existed—and contributed to planting a public-minded spirit of botanical exchange on American soil.

As the botanical diplomacy carried out by the French in advance of Michaux's mission suggests, the French had a strong desire for American plants that was fueled by concern for French geopolitical power. The French believed that their acquisition of botanical specimens and creation of botanical knowledge was indicative of their power. Louis Guillaume Otto, French chargé d'affaires in New York from 1785 until 1791, had been charged by the Comte d'Angiviller, the director of the Bâtiments du Roi, with gathering

North American plants. But Otto urged the Comte d'Angiviller to instead send a French botanist to do the job: "The Emperor is already ahead of us in this measure, for around two years ago, he sent to America a botanist charged with gathering all the specimens cultivated in the United States and sending to his court the seeds and plants of different trees that they found there."[32] To Otto, the botanical mission of Joseph II, Holy Roman Emperor, represented a challenge to French botanical supremacy to which the French must respond.

But it was not only the French government that sought North American plants. Humphry Marshall, Philadelphia seedsman and cousin to John Bartram catered to an international clientele that included French men and women. In 1785, Marshall published his *Arbustrum Americanum: The American Grove, or, An Alphabetical Catalogue of Forest Trees and Shrubs, Natives of the American United States,* one of the first books published on American plants by an American. Marshall directly addressed a global audience: "The *foreigner,* curious in American collections, will be hereby better enabled to make a selection suitable to his own particular fancy. If he wishes to cultivate timber for oeconomical purposes, he is here informed of our valuable Forest Trees: if for adorning his plantation or garden of our different ornamental flower shrubs."[33] The work circulated in England and was translated into French in 1788 by M. Lézermes, assistant director at the Pépinières du Roi in Paris. He dedicated the volume to d'Angiviller, writing, "It is due to your care that there are such numerous species of useful and curious trees are enriched each day, and which, transported from North America, are beginning to multiply, in the royal nursery [Pépinieres du Roy], as in the new plantations at Rambouillet, under the eyes of His Majesty [Louis XVI]."[34] Marshall fielded orders from French officials posted in the United States but also catered to private clients. He received via Philadelphia merchant John Vaughan an extensive order from Louis-Philippe-Joseph, the Duc d'Orléans, for different species of trees, including oaks, magnolias, and viburnum, all nearly requisite in European orders from America.[35] In 1787 he received an equally large order from Adrienne Catherine, Comtesse de Noailles de Tessé, a Parisian *salonnière,* aunt of the Marquis de Lafayette, and passionate gardener.[36] Orders continued into the French revolutionary period: in 1791, he received a letter from Stephen Girard, a Frenchman living in Philadelphia, who wrote on behalf of a "Gentleman in Paris" to request specimens of magnolia, kalmia, franklinia, and azaleas, the American species regarded as essential in the eighteenth-century English-style landscape garden.[37]

While Marshall sought to take advantage of growing French taste for American flowering trees and shrubs, some of his American compatriots sought to exploit the French interest in American specimens for their own botanical gain. Richard Cary of Warwick, Virginia, judge of the Admiralty of Virginia and member of the Virginia Supreme Court, became aware of French interest in American plants through Martin Oster, French vice consul in Richmond, Virginia.[38] As part of the French government's systematic effort to gather American botanical specimens, diplomats such as Louis Guillaume Otto were instructed to seek out landed Americans who might have improved their estates with gardens and who, therefore, would have knowledge of American plants and trees.[39] Martin Oster may have received similar instruction and, seemingly, reached out to Richard Cary. On May 19, 1786, Oster wrote to d'Angiviller expressing regret that many of the specimens he had gathered had perished in the hot summer.[40] Oster, then, had been gathering specimens to send to France. He continued in the letter, however, to describe the fruits born of his interaction with Cary. Cary inherited Peartree Hall, his father's plantation in Warwick, Virginia, on Potash Creek, which flowed into the James River.[41] Little information survives about his garden, though one account suggests that the grounds were terraced to the river.[42] What is clear, however, is that Cary was enterprising and engaging in botanical reciprocity through his attempts to acquire plants to furnish his garden. It was Cary who assembled a collection of specimens for Oster to send to France. Oster wrote, "The seeds that I was able to collect last year (with the help of Mr. Cary of Warwick, honorable judge of the Admiralty and of the state of Virginia and great botanist) number 51 species and are most curious. You will find the historic list enclosed."[43] In addition to assembling the plants, Oster was able to supply a translation of the English plant names into French, thanks to the efforts of Thomas Jefferson, who engaged Mr. Mazzei to translate.[44]

Oster, then, had succeeded in finding a landed American gentleman who proved helpful in sending specimens back to France. The American Cary, however, felt emboldened to ask for botanical reciprocity. He wrote first to express pleasure in the possibility of exchanging botanical information: "If, in another year, you find yourself in need of other items . . . I would with very great pleasure be obliged for you to depend upon me; and nothing would add more to my satisfaction than to maintain a correspondence with some amateurs in France, I flatter myself that this would be the means to procure such a great pleasure."[45]

But beyond that, he also wished for a more material reciprocity:

> By a reciprocal exchange of the productions of nature, the inhabitants of the two countries can not only receive pleasure, but also great advantage; and I know not of two other countries, as France and America, who would more appropriately secure such advantages: there is little vegetation in France, which could not be cultivated in one or another or the thirteen states; and few [plants] in America which could not be cultivated in France. Thus here is a vast field for experiment.[46]

Cary, then, saw the exchange of plants as mutually beneficial to France and America, but also to himself: "It would be a pleasure to send to me from France some things of the same genre, I have taken the liberty of requesting [some] following the enclosed list."[47] Oster then included the list of twenty-one items, enumerated in English and French. The list itself offers a picture of what plants Cary desired for his garden and what plants he believed he could and should acquire from French sources. Cary's request came with a gentle reminder that Oster had presumably promised specimens for him:

> M. Oster having been so kind as to tell Rich[d] Cary, he would procure for him some Roots & c. from France." Rich[d] Cary takes the Liberty to request the following:
>
> 1. Tulips a few Roots of the good kinds, in french tulipe.
> 2. Hyacinths a few Roots of the good kinds, in French Jacinte.
> 3. Ranunculus, in french Renoncule, some roots of the good Persian kinds & some seeds of the same.
> 5. [*sic*] L'Anemone Roots of the good kinds & some Seeds of the Same.
> 6. Dianthus, caryophillus, in french Oeillet, some good Seeds.
> 7. Auricula ursi, in french Oreille d'ours, Some Seeds.
> 8. Primula veris, in french Primavere, Some Seeds.
> 9. Franxinella, in french fraxinelle, Some Seeds.
> 10. Fritillaria, in french fritillaire, Some Roots.
> 11. Amaryllis (Sarncensis) Spatha multiflora, corollis revolutis genitatibus strielis, commonly called guernsey Lilly; some Roots.
> 12. Amaryllis (Belladonna) Spatha multiflora, corollis campanulatis aqualibus, genitalibus declinatis, commonly Belladonna Lilly, Some Roots.
> 13. A few good annuals, the seeds.
> 14. A few colly flower & Broccoli Seeds.
> 15. A few good cantaloupe musk melon Seeds.
> 16. A few good fruit trees would be a great treat, but I am afraid they will perish on the passage, perhaps the seeds would answer.
> 17. A few roots of the polianthes, Len. Gen. plant. 384. Called in England tuberose, would be greatly acceptable.

18. Bellis, in french Paquerete, Eng. Daisy Some Seeds of the garden cultivated kinds.
19. Pulsatitla, in french Coquelourde, Some Seeds.
20. Sorbus, in french Sorbier, in Engl. Service Tree. Some Seeds of the good kinds.
21. Narcissus a few Roots of the good Kinds.[48]

While Marshall's records reveal what French gardeners desired from North America, Cary's list exposes the wants and wishes of American gardeners. It is notable in that it contains the most fashionable and highly collected flowers and flowering bulbs—the tulips, hyacinths, ranunculi, anemones, and dianthus that were requisite in a formal flower parterre. That Cary specifically requested examples "of the good kinds" of tulips and hyacinths, for example, demonstrates his awareness that the French royal gardens were unequalled in their flower collections.[49] He, like Manasseh Cutler, equated French gardens with beauty and quality.

Cary's request was fulfilled, though many specimens perished in transit.[50] But that did not stop Cary from making a further request. On March 21, 1787 he wrote,

> Permit me to tell you, Monsieur, that I regard it as one of the happiest circumstances of my life to find myself engaged in a liaison so flattering, and to be able to be of such usefulness to your great country. My heart finds proof of its movement in the satisfaction . . . by the certitude that that which I can send is destined for the gardens of the best and greatest of monarchs, our powerful ally and protector that I regard as our savior on earth.[51]

Cary expressed delight in helping the French, but he also asked for more:

> Some flowering bulbs, like those which have been sent, if it is easy otherwise I do not desire them . . .
> Some cyclamens
> Some seeds of bears' ears
> Cary [in a note presumably inserted by Oster] has never seen a true auricula, he would be very curious to see one.
> Some seeds of pulsatille.
> Colchicum for fall and spring
> Iris variegated Xyphien.
> Some seeds of *datura fabrosa* or pomme épinente d'Egypte . . .
> Different species of hepaticas.

> Seeds of the different species of marguerites.
> Fruit trees:
> The stones of peaches, de "pavies," of plums, apricots, pistachios, almonds, walnuts, I would be well pleased to have the best species[52]

Cary's requests are the words of a botanically curious American who sought both to improve his garden with the finest French specimens and engage his French botanical peers in a trans-Atlantic conversation. While the French were willing to reciprocate Cary's generosity by sharing their national botanical wealth, it is less clear that they were as desirous of his epistolary company as he of theirs. But the exchange between Cary and the French reveals that d'Angiviller's instincts were correct: landed American gentlemen were interested in botany and gardening, were motivated to improve their estates, and were cognizant of French botanical superiority.

Cary also reveals the networks of exchange that spread like tentacles among the botanically curious on both sides of the Atlantic. While Thomas Jefferson served in Paris as United States ambassador to France, among the Americans to whom he wrote was Richard Cary. In a letter Jefferson sent from Paris in 1786 he wrote, "Knowing your fondness for Botany, and meeting with a new edition of Linnaeus's *systema vegetabilium* in English, with many additions furnished the editors by young Linneaus which have never yet been in print, I procurred one for you."[53] Jefferson continued, "I saw in the hands of mr Mazzei a list of flower roots & seeds which you had desired him to send you. I have taken a copy of it, and will endeavor to find an opportunity of sending them."[54]

Cary and Jefferson continued to exchange letters and plants. In August 1786 Jefferson wrote to Cary to request that Cary send him American azaleas, magnolias, kalmias, and rhododendrons, which "are desired in greater quantities," which he presumably wished to share among his French acquaintances.[55] In the same letter, Jefferson continued, "I send you seeds of Ranunculus, Broccoli & Cauliflower, bulbs of the tulip," though he failed in procuring carnations, auriculas, tuberoses, hyacinths, and lilies in time for the shipment. He also indicated the necessarily bookish nature of trans-Atlantic botanical exchange writing: "I do not know what the Nutberry pine is. I have no Miller's Dictionary here. You must therefore always give the Linnaean names."[56]

Jefferson also engaged in a long-term exchange of plants with the aforementioned Comtesse de Tessé. In 1787 he reported to her that he had learned that "our box of Magnolia & Dionaea" were safely in the hands of Mr. Berard in L'Orient and would be sent to Paris "by the first Diligence."[57] He was still exchanging plants with her as late as 1803.

In addition to facilitating trade in French and American plants, Jefferson also sent French plants back to America for himself. He was particularly pleased with a fig he acquired in Marseilles. In 1794, years after his return from France, he wrote to George Wythe, "knowing your fondness for figs, I have daily wished you could have partaken of ours this year. . . . Of three kinds which I brought from France, there is one, of which I have a single bush, superior to any fig I ever tasted anywhere."[58] in 1796 he wrote again of his French figs and was still doing so in 1809, writing to William Thornton, "I will take some occasion of sending you some cuttings of the Marseilles fig, which I brought from France with me, & is incomparably superior to any fig I have ever seen."[59] Strikingly, even after twenty years growing at Monticello, the fig retained its French identity in *Jefferson's* botanical memory.

While in France, Jefferson absorbed, wrote about, and shared what he observed about French gardening, agriculture, and viticulture. Though he seems to have not recorded his impressions of the royal gardens, his account books reveal that he visited Versailles on multiple occasions.[60] And he made critical judgments comparing French and American specimens: though many Americans imported English and Continental fruit trees, to James Madison, for example, he wrote, "They have no apples here to compare with our *Redtown* pippin. They have nothing which deserves the name of a peach; there being not sun enough to ripen the plum-peach and the best of their soft peaches being like our autumn peaches. Their cherries and strawberries are fair, but I think lack flavor. Their plums I think are better; so also their gooseberries, and the pears infinitely beyond any thing we possess."[61] And just as the French were seeking North American trees to enhance the French geopolitical stature, so Jefferson was on the lookout for plants that might contribute to the American agricultural and political economy. He was particularly hopeful that his efforts would introduce both European varieties of rice (that could be grown in much healthier conditions in the highlands) and olives to North America.[62]

For Thomas Jefferson, then, the republican soil of America could benefit greatly from the plants that had originated in the monarchical climate of France. He, as with other Americans, understood botanical exchange between the two countries could be a valuable and rewarding enterprise. Indeed, the spirit of botanical exchange between the two, initiated by the French in the 1780s, proved the most significant aspect of French influence on American gardens. Later in his life, Jefferson maintained a correspondence—and a regular botanical exchange—with André Thouin, botanist at the Muséum national d'histoire naturelle in Paris who, with d'Angiviller, had initiated Michaux's mission to North America in the mid-1780s. In 1808 Jefferson wrote to his daughter Martha (Jefferson) Randolph, "tell Anne that my old friend Thouin of the National garden at Paris has sent me 700 species of seeds. I suppose they will contain all the fine flowers of France and fill all the space we have for them."[63] The French reputation for fine flowers had survived the French Revolution. But so had the spirit for botanical exchange for the mutual benefit of both countries. In 1821, Jefferson wrote to Jonathan Thompson to thank him for notification of the arrival of a box of seeds: "This comes from the King's garden at Paris. They send me a box annually, depending on my applying it for the public benefit. I have generally had them delivered for a public garden at Philadelphia or to Dr. Hosack for the Botanical Garden at N.York."[64] Thouin, therefore, willingly sent plants to Jefferson, provided that Jefferson distribute them in a manner consistent with the spirit of botanical exchange. Jefferson returned the favor by doing just that, sending the specimens to botanical gardens in the United States. Jefferson most likely sent the seeds to Bernard McMahon, the Irishman who had established a nursery in Philadelphia where Jefferson sent the specimens gathered in the western United States by Lewis and Clark, in addition to David Hosack, a professor of medicine at Columbia University, who established a botanical garden in New York City.

The eighteenth-century roots of French and American botanical exchange initiated by French and American diplomats and gardeners would go on to bear much fruit in American gardens of the nineteenth century. David Hosack's botanical garden in New York City would not thrive for long, but he created a new one on the Hyde Park estate he purchased from Samuel Bard, which eventually would be purchased and improved by John Jacob Astor and then Frederick William Vanderbilt, who constructed a Beaux-Arts mansion on the property and hired James Greenleaf to refine the gardens.[65] The efforts of André Michaux lived on, too: Michaux's history of North American oaks and his son's *North American Sylva* became defining works in the history of American botany.[66] Meanwhile Michaux's gardener Paul Saunier, who accompanied Michaux from France to North America, remained on the New Jersey garden for the rest of his life, facilitating French-American plant exchange with E. I. DuPont, who established his own French-American garden legacy.[67] More importantly, these French ventures and exchanges launched a lasting American effort to grow botanical knowledge and collections in America. If the French had been unable to persuade American governments to establish their own botanic gardens during the Revolution, the notion that such a project was worthy and important was revived in the Early Republic. In 1796, George Washington entertained proposals that the planned capital city include a botanic garden.[68] Therese O'Malley has shown that the botanic garden "was particularly useful during the formative decades of American nationality, when the ruling elite was trying to establish superiority over Europe and to create a national identity celebrating the natural richness of the new continent."[69] That identity was, however, consciously constructed in the context of European precedents. It would take several decades for initial proposals for a national botanic garden to be implemented and the United States Botanic Garden established. The Columbian Institute for the Promotion of Arts and Sciences succeeded in pushing a bill through Congress, and signed by President Monroe in 1820, granting them a plot of land for such purposes. Serious plant collecting would not get under way for several years, but subsequent debate would continue to hinge on American botanical stature in the wake of foreign collections. William Darlington, American botanist and physician, argued in 1841 that the Smithson bequest to create the Smithsonian Institution include a botanic garden:

> But [I] will look forward with confidence to the day, when the citizens of this Republic shall possess all the means, and enjoy all the advantages of Intellectual culture, which have been hitherto monopolized by the subjects of European monarchies.
>
> Let us, then, never falter in our efforts . . . until our Temples of Science shall vie with the noblest of those beyond the Atlantic: And while the Frenchman justly glories in the Jardin des Plantes, while the Briton boasts with reason, of the royal Garden at Kew,—and even the Russian, in his frozen clime is warmed in admiration of the Imperial Conservatory of the Czars,—let American freemen, in their turn be enabled to point with patriotic pride, to a *National Institution* of no less beauty and value, at the Metropolis of their own favored land.[70]

In the first decades of the nineteenth century, then, both French plants and French notions of botanical exchange informed American efforts to create American botanic gardens. While Manasseh Cutler had not been impressed by what he saw at Michaux's garden, the spirit that was taking root proved a lasting influence on American soil.

Notes

1. William Parker Cutler and Julia Perkins Cutler, eds., *Life, Journals and Correspondence of Rev. Manasseh Cutler, LLD* (Cincinnati, OH: Robert Clarke, 1888), 1:239.

2. Ibid., 1:228–29.

3. For a review of the botanic garden in America and the usage of the term, see Therese O'Malley, *Keywords in American Landscape Design* (Washington, DC: National Gallery of Art, 2010), "Botanic Garden," 146–55.

4. Cutler, *Life, Journals and Correspondence,* 1:238.

5. Cutler also recorded a dinner, at the home of General Knox, as "served in high style—much in the French taste," while at the home of Sir John Temple, "Our dinner was in the English style, plain, but plentiful." Ibid., 1:231, 235.

6. Ibid., 1:291–93.

7. See Elizabeth Hyde, "André Michaux and French Botanical Diplomacy in the Cultural Construction of Natural History in the Atlantic World," in *Of Pictures & Specimens: Natural History in Post-Revolutionary and Restoration France,* ed. Sue Ann Prince (Philadelphia: American Philosophical Society, 2013), 89–100.

8. Some plants survived the journey better in plant form, others as seeds. Shipments needed to be timed according to season to coincide with periods of a plant's dormancy or its seeds' viability.

9. See William Livingston, *Philosophic Solitude: or, the Choice of a Rural Life. A Poem. By a Gentleman educated at Yale College* (New York: James Parker, 1747).

10. For more on Livingston and his trees, see Elizabeth Hyde, "Arboreal Negotiations, or William Livingston's American Perspective on the Cultural Politics of Trees in the Atlantic World," in *Invaluable Trees: Cultures of Nature, 1660–1830,* ed. Laura Auricchio, Elizabeth Heckendorn Cook, and Giulia Pacini (Oxford: Voltaire Foundation, 2012), 185–99.

11. William Livingston to François, Marquis de Barbé-Marbois, September 24, 1783, *William Livingston Papers* (Ann Arbor, MI: University Microfilms, 1986).

12. Ibid.

13. *New-Jersey Gazette,* April 3, 1786. Isaac Collins, publisher of the newspaper, included on the masthead of the paper that he was "Printer to the State."

14. *Political Intelligencer and New Jersey-Advertiser* 3, no. 129 (April 5, 1786).

15. Ibid., 3,no. 131 (April 19, 1786).

16. *New-Jersey Journal, and Political Intelligencer,* no. 193, (June 27, 1787).

17. The paper was printed and published by Shephard Kollock in Elizabeth Town, New Jersey.

18. The term *French style,* however, was not widely used in America until the nineteenth century. See "French style" in O'Malley, *Keywords in American Landscape Design,* 290–94.

19. Within this volume, see Raffaella Fabiani Giannetto, "The American Colonial Garden and the Garden of the Country Place Era: The Role of Ancient and Early Modern Italy," and Emily T. Cooperman and John Dixon Hunt, "The American Translation of the Picturesque." Abbott Lowell Cummings's review of surviving images of eighteenth-

century gardens demonstrates the dominance of the geometric style in New England. See Abbott Lowell Cummings, "Eighteenth-Century New England Garden Design: The Pictorial Evidence," in *British and American Gardens in the Eighteenth Century: Eighteen Illustrated Essays on Garden History,* ed. Robert P. Maccubbin and Peter Martin (Williamsburg, VA: Colonial Williamsburg Foundation, 1984), 130–35. Meanwhile, surviving plans and maps of Claude Joseph Sauthier, a French cartographer and garden designer who worked in North Carolina in the 1760s and 1770s, are in keeping with French garden design principles. See John Flowers, "People and Plants: North Carolina's Garden History Revisited," in Maccubbin and Martin, *British and American Gardens,* 121–24. For elements of the picturesque, see James D. Kornwulf, "The Picturesque in the American Garden before 1800," in Maccubbin and Martin, *British and American Gardens,* 93–106, esp. 98–99.

20. "A List of Books," *William Livingston Papers, 1695–1839,* Massachusetts Historical Society, Boston, Ms. N-1579.1, Box 2, 1783.

21. Robert R. Livingston, *Catalogue of Books in the Library of the Hon. Robert R. Livingston* (Poughkeepsie, NY: James Woods, 1800).

22. For Thomas Jefferson's own list of his book collection, see Jefferson, *Thomas Jefferson's Library: A Catalog with the Entries in His Own Order,* ed. James Gilreath and Douglas L. Wilson (Washington, DC: Library of Congress, 1989; rpt., 2001). This text is available electronically at http://catdir.loc.gov/catdir/toc/becites/main/jefferson/88607928.toc.html.

23. See Andrea Wulf, *Founding Gardeners: The Revolutionary Generation, Nature, and the Shaping of the American Nation* (New York: Alfred A. Knopf, 2011), 38–45.

24. Livingston, *Philosophic Solitude,* lines 11–15.

25. Ibid., lines 25–28.

26. Ibid., lines 68–74.

27. André Michaux to Charles-Claude Flahaut de la Billarderie, Comte d'Angiviller, January 18, 1786, New York, Série O[1]2113, Archives Nationales de France (hereafter AN), via microfilm copy at American Philosophical Society (hereafter APS), Philadelphia.

28. Thomas Bond to Humphry Marshall, August 7, 1779, in William Darlington and Peter Collinson, *Memorials of John Bartram and Humphry Marshall with Notices of Their Botanical Contemporaries* (Philadelphia: Lindsay & Blakiston, 1849), 536–37. He continued, "This is, therefore, to request you would come forth with me, to make an offer of mutual good offices; and to furnish me with a list of such seeds, vegetables, plants, trees, & c, as this country wants, and what we could give him."

29. Bond to Marshall, December 2, 1780, in ibid., 539. "As the other [formal request made by Marbois] is a very large affair, and will cost you [Humphry Marshall] much trouble, you ought to be well paid for it."

30. William Livingston to Hector St. John de Crevecoeur, December 11, 1783, Trenton, NJ, *William Livingston Papers.*

31. "The Petition of M. André Michaux Botanist to the King of France to the honourable the Chairman, and the Members of the Assembly, of the State of New Jersey," 1786, *William Livingston Papers.*

32. "L'Empereur nous a deja devancé dans cette mesure, il y a environ deux ans qu'il envoya en Amerique un botaniste chargé de parcourir toutes les partiens cultivées des

Etats unis et de faire passer à sa Cour les graines et les plantes des differens arbres qu'ils y trouveroit." Louis Guillaume Otto to d'Angiviller, October 27, 1785, New York, Série O^{1}2113, AN at APS.

33. Humphry Marshall, *Arbustrum Americanum: The American Grove, or, An Alphabetical Catalogue of Forest Trees and Shrubs, Natives of the American United States, Arranged According to the Linnaean System* (Philadelphia: Joseph Crukshank, 1785), emphasis in the original.

34. *Catalogue alphabetique des arbres et abrisseaux, qui croissent naturellement dans les Etats-Unis de l'Amérique Septentrionale, arrangés selon le Systême de Linne* (Paris: Chez Cuchet, 1788), n.p. He wrote, "C'est à vos soins que sont dues les nombreuses espèces d'Arbres utiles & curieux dont elle s'enrichit chaque jour, & qui, transportés des l'Amérique Septentrionale, commencent à se multiplier, tant dans les Pépinieres du Roy, que dans les nouvelles Plantations de Rambouillet, & sous les yeux de Sa Majesté."

35. Louis-Philippe-Joseph, Duc d'Orléans, to John Vaughan and Humphry Marshall, c. 1785, in Marshall Papers, William L. Clements Library, University of Michigan, Ann Arbor.

36. Adrienne Catherine, Comtesse de Noailles de Tessé to Humphry Marshall, December 6, 1787, Marshall Papers.

37. Stephen Girard to Humphry Marshall, Philadelphia, August 11, 1791, Marshall papers.

38. For more on Martin Oster, see J. Rives Childs, "French Consul Martin Oster Reports on Virginia, 1784–1796," *Virginia Magazine of History and Biography* 76, no. 1 (January 1968): 27–40; and Peter P. Hill, *French Perceptions of the Early American Republic, 1783–1793* (Philadelphia: American Philosophical Society, 1988).

39. On October 27, 1785, Otto wrote, "J'ai suivre vos instructions en m'adressant à de grands possessieurs de terre et en leur faisant l'offre de leur faire parvenir aux depens du choix tous les arbres fruitiers et autres objets quils pouvroient desirer de France." Otto continued, "J'en ai ecrit entre autres à W. Livingston, un des proprietaires les plus considerables. . . . Le jardinage est ici [in the United States] dans son enfance, ou est très indifferent pour toutes les ameliorations de ce genre et les devreér conumerables absorbest tellement toute l'attention des Americains qu'ils ne s'occupaient de leurs jardins que pour avoir quelques mauvais fruits et des legumes." Otto to d'Angiviller, October 27, 1785, New York, Série O^{1}2113, AN at APS.

40. Martin Oster, Williamsburg, Virginia, to Monsieur Le Comte [d'Angiviller], May 19, 1786, Série O^{1}2113, AN at APS.

41. Fairfax Harrison, *The Virginia Carys: An Essay in Genealogy* (New York: De Vinne Press, 1919), 54.

42. Mary Selden Kennedy, *Seldens of Virginia* (New York: Frank Allaben Genealogical Company, 1911).

43. Martin Oster to d'Angiviller, Série O^{1}2113, AN at APS. "Les graines qu'il m'a reussi de rassembler l'annee derniere (avec le Secours de Mr. Cary de Warwick, honnorable juge de l'amiraute de l'etat de Virginie et grand botaniste) sont au nombre de 51 especes et des plus curieuses. Vous en trouverez la liste historique ci incluse."

44. Ibid. "Si dans une autre année, ou en tel tems que ce puisse etre, vous a vien besoin d'autres articles, soit pour vouer ou quelqu'un de vôtre connoissance en france,

je serai avec la plus grand plaisir, tout ce qui dépendera de moi pour vouer obliger; et comme rien n'a jouteroit plus à ma satisfaction, que d'entretenir une correspondance avec quelques Amateurs en France, je me flatte que ce seroit le moyen de me procurer ce grand plaisir."

45. Richard Cary to Oster, March 21, 1787 Série O¹2113, AN at APS.

46. Ibid. Cary wrote, "Par un échange réciproque des producions naturelles, les Habitans de deux païs éloignér peuvent non seulement en recevoir du plaisir, mais peut être aussi beaucoup d'avantager; et je ne connois pas deux autres contrees, comme la France et l'Amérique, qui soient plus propres à procurer ces avantages: il y a peu de végétaux en France, qui ne puissent être cultivér dans l'une , ou l'autre des 13 provinces; & peu en Amérique, qui ne puissent de même être cultivér en France. Voila donc un champ vaste pour les expériences."

47. Ibid. "Vous cuter [illegible] la Bonté de m'informer que le Gentilhomme pour qui les sémences sont destinées, se seroit un plaisir de m'énvoyer de France quelque chose dans la même genre, j'ai pris la liberté d'en demander, suivant la liste incluse, pour vue cependant, que cela ne vous Causal [?] point à l'un, où a l'autre, trop d'embarras."

48. Cary to Oster, March 21, 1787 (enclosed with Oster to d'Angiviller), ibid.

49. For more on flowers in French gardens and culture in the early modern period, see Elizabeth Hyde, *Cultivated Power: Flowers, Culture, and Politics in the Reign of Louis XIV* (Philadelphia: University of Pennsylvania Press, 2005).

50. Cary to l'Abbé Nolin, March 21, 1787. Série O¹2113, AN at APS.

51. Cary to d'Angiviller via Oster, March 21, 1787. Série O¹2113, AN at APS. "Permettez moi, M, de vous dire que je regarde comme une des plus heureuse circonstances de ma vie de me trouver engagé dans une liaison aussi flatterise, et de pouvoir être de quelque utilité à votre bonne patrie. Mon cœur reconnoissance éprouver les mouvements de la satisfaction la plus vive par la certitude que ce que je puis envoyer en destiné pour les jardins du meilleur et du plus grand des monarques, notre allié puissant et protecteur que je regarde comme notre saveur sur la terre."

52. Ibid. His list included the following: Quelques oignons de fleurs, sela que ceux qui ont été envoyés, si cela est facile autrement je n'en désire pas } Ils devroiens arriver en virginie vers le milieu ou la fin d'8bre

Quelques ciclamens

Quelques graines d'oreilles d'ours

Cary [in a note presumably inserted by Oster] n'a jamais en la véritable auricule, il seroit très curieux de la voir.

Quelques graines de pulsatille

Colchique d'automne et de printems

L'Iris Xyphien panaché } [the preceding] en même tems

Quelques graines du *datura farbosa* ou pomme épinente d'Egypte } [the preceding] même tems ou plutard puisque cette plante en annuelle

Les différentes espéces d'hépatiques [}] le millieu ou la fin d'avril

Des graines de différentes espéces des Marguerite [}] même tems

Arbres fruitiers

Des noyau de pêches, de pavies, des prunes, abricots, pistaaches, amandes, noix, dom je serois bienaise d'avoir les bonnes espéces } Ils doivent arriver en même tems ou plutard.

53. Jefferson to Cary, 1786, in Thomas Jefferson, Edwin Morris Betts, and Peter J. Hatch, *Thomas Jefferson's Garden Book, 1766–1824, with Relevant Extracts from His Other Writings* (Charlottesville, VA: Thomas Jefferson Foundation, 2008), 115.

54. Jefferson to Cary, May 4, 1786, in ibid., 115.

55. Jefferson to Cary, August 12, 1786, in ibid., 116.

56. Jefferson to Cary, August 12, 1786, in ibid., 117.

57. Jefferson to Comtesse de Tessé, February 22, 1787, in ibid., 122.

58. Jefferson to George Wythe, 1794, in ibid., 223–24.

59. Jefferson to Benjamin Hawkins, March 22, 1796, in ibid., 249; Jefferson to William Thornton, October 11, 1809, in ibid., 416.

60. Jefferson's account books, covering 1785 in ibid., 105–6.

61. Jefferson to the Reverend James Madison, October 28, 1785, ibid., 106.

62. Jefferson wrote to John Jay, John Adams, and William Drayton, among others, in 1787 about the cultivation of and trade in rice. Ibid., 122–29.

63. Jefferson to Martha (Jefferson) Randolph, October 18, 1808, in ibid., 378.

64. Jefferson to Jonathan Thompson, June 25, 1821, in ibid., 596–97.

65. For a history of the site, see Peggy Albee, Molly Berger, H. Elliot Foulds, Nina Gray, and Pamela Herrick, *Vanderbilt Mansion: A Gilded-Age Country Place* (Boston: National Park Service, 2008).

66. Lisa Ford, "The 'Naturalisation' of François André Michaux's North American Sylva: Patriotism in Early American Natural History," in Auricchio, Cook, and Pacini, *Invaluable Trees*, 201–18.

67. Norman Wilkinson, *E. I. DuPont, Botaniste: The Beginning of a Tradition* (Charlottesville: University Press of Virginia for the Eleutherian Mills-Hagley Foundation, 1972).

68. Richard Rathbun, *The Columbian Institute for the Promotion of Arts and Sciences: A Washington Society of 1816–1838, Which Established a Museum and Botanic Garden under Government Patronage* (Washington, DC: Government Printing Office, 1917), 37.

69. Therese O'Malley, "'Your garden must be a museum to you': Early American Botanic Gardens," *Huntington Library Quarterly* 59, no. 2/3 (1996): 207.

70. William Darlington, *A Plea for a National Museum and Botanic Garden to Be Founded at the Smithsonian Institution at the City of Washington* (Westchester, PA, 1841), 12.

PART 3

The Reception of the Italian Garden in America

The American Colonial Garden and the Garden of the Country Place Era

The Role of Ancient and Early Modern Italy

RAFFAELLA FABIANI GIANNETTO

As the birthplace of classical gardens and home of Renaissance villas, Italy occupies a prominent role among the many foreign countries whose garden design traditions contributed to shape American landscape architecture. The assimilation of the Italian garden tradition, however, occurred slowly over the course of three centuries and gave rise to American gardens that were different from each other according to their degree of translation and imitation of their Italian sources.[1] The application of Italian garden forms was piecemeal during colonial times when plantation owners perceived themselves as the American equivalent of learned and virtuous Roman farmers, and it was the meaning of Italian classical gardens, more than their layouts, that Americans sought to translate.

By contrast, at the turn of the twentieth century the design of Italian gardens had been understood, spelled out, and made available to American garden enthusiasts eager to imitate their forms, which were appreciated especially for their geometric rigor. This, however, the Italian garden shared with other European traditions, such as the French, Dutch, and Elizabethan English—whose gardens were all lumped together as formal—along with another fundamental characteristic associated with their appearance: their being symbols of family worthiness and prestige.

By the time Frank A. Waugh elaborated on the principles of formal gardens in relation to their use in America in 1927, most wealthy Americans had been choosing the formal style for their gardens and for the representation of their social status for more than two decades.[2] In this they were facilitated by a considerable number of architects and landscape architects who were ready to help their clients spend their wealth by experimenting with one of the most expensive forms of garden design. Later, the professional literature contributed to the popularization of the style by making a case for its appropriateness to the pockets of more modest citizens. And by the end of the first quarter of the twentieth century, glistening images of balustraded terraces, symmetric pools, and pergolas provided dignifying backgrounds for the most disparate of commercial products—from cement to hand-wrought iron gates and fences, to automobiles and refrigerators (fig. 1). So the style became a passe-partout as useful as a black tie to be worn on those social occasions demanding (or pretending) a certain degree of formality.

Beatrix Farrand wrote in *Garden and Forest* that a formal garden was needed, and indeed required, "when an imposing or somewhat pretentious building is at the end of it," because "formal work" alone can confer "dignified and quiet delight" to the whole.[3] Also in an editorial in the same journal about the appropriateness of the formal garden for the "large and dignified" houses of Newport, the author claimed that even if their grounds are small, "the self-assertion of the house[s]" requires a formal layout for the gardens. As for why that is the case, the following lines provide the answer: "green little lawns, cut by one or two lines of gravel and encircled by naturalistic groups of trees and shrubs . . . are pretty in themselves, but not dignified enough, not consciously artistic enough, to befit their place as adjuncts to a big, costly house." The gardens of Newport, according to the author, suffered from "lack of design" and from the "perpetual repetition of the same small list of showy plants and flowers."[4] Design, or man's ordering hand over nature, was in itself a sign of civilization, especially when visually perceptible, and therefore any evidence of it was already an indication of distinction. Such was not the case with naturalistic gardens, due to their apparent, though studied, artlessness. Therefore, because "formal gardens alone show anything like design,"[5] they were the obvious choice in most circumstances demanding a "formal" character.

Now, how this formality was achieved, in fact, depended on the foreign source adopted. For Inigo Thomas, who illustrated Reginald Blomfield's *The Formal Garden in England,* a popular book in the United States, the source of inspiration was the old and relatively small "gardens of Italy, of Scotland and of England";[6] for others like Thomas Hastings of Carrère and Hastings—a firm often commissioned for large-scale projects—inspiration could came from France in the work of André Le Nôtre. In many cases, one single project could display multiple foreign influences, as in Thomas Hastings's Indian Harbor, designed for Elias Cornelius Benedict in Greenwich, Connecticut. About this project Hastings wrote that "the architecture and landscape work are somewhat Italian in character,"[7] and indeed the pergola linking the main house to the guesthouse was a replica of a famous trellis-

Fig. 1. Detail of Vizcaya, residence of James Deering in Miami, Florida, used for the advertisement of Lorillard Refrigerator Co., *Arts and Decoration* 13, no. 2 (1920): 135.

work the architect had seen at Amalfi, Italy. The design of the house's main axis of symmetry, on the other hand, was inspired by Versailles, where "the axis of the Château, being an extended vista" allowed the eye to glance "first over entirely formal surroundings, and gradually, through a less formal garden, until it reaches the natural landscape beyond."[8]

In other cases, the formal garden was a concoction of Italian and Arts and Crafts or even colonial revival elements, as in the gardens designed respectively by Beatrix Farrand and in those of Cornish colony residents Charles Platt and Ellen Biddle Shipman. Thus, at the turn of the new century, Italy, like other European countries, represented an example of good taste, a great resource from which to borrow ideas and a design vocabulary of forms and principles suitable for the representation of Americans' idea of the formal.[9]

But if the Italian garden offered one of the plausible answers to a country in search of stylistic identity, it was also not the only one it ever provided for the American people. Two centuries earlier, in fact, Italian garden ideas had been adopted in the British colonies of the eastern shore for entirely different purposes. Unlike most of the Italianate gardens that followed, those of the British colonies of the eastern shore were not intended as formal; rather, they were meant to be classical by calling to mind the ideals of villa life made known through Roman literature and its Renaissance revival. Moreover, colonial gardens were not laid out by professional designers but contrived by their very owners, who were knowledgeable in the arts of architecture and gardening. These men were learned virtuosi, described by Thomas Jefferson as "the only farmers who can read Homer."[10] One of them was William Byrd II, a colonial government official who inherited his father's plantation at Westover, on the north bank of the James River in Virginia in 1705.

One of the most celebrated among the colonial gardens, Westover was implemented from the 1720s onward. The earliest surviving drawing (fig. 2) of the property shows the grounds symmetrically laid out around the house with equally spaced trees planted along symmetrical curved lines. A written description accompanying the drawing mentions a "very large and exceedingly beautiful garden" and "a pretty grove neatly kept."[11] While the drawing is too schematic to allow us to claim Italian descent, there are a number of other sources, including travelers' diaries and correspondence, pointing to the fact that Westover contributed to the burgeoning villa culture of eighteenth-century Virginia. "The garden of Virginia,"[12] as the Marquis de Chastellux called the landscape along the river James, pullulated with plantations and terraced gardens, and their owners led a life of retirement and self-improvement that is comparable to that of classical Roman writers.

The view is generally held that the cultural landscape along the rivers of Virginia conjured up, in the minds of British visitors, memories of "the villa gardens bordering the banks of the Thames."[13] In 1732, for example, the English gentleman William Hugh Grove wrote about one such river landscape that it was "thick seated with gentry on its banks within a mile or at most two miles from each other . . . most of these have pleasant gardens and the

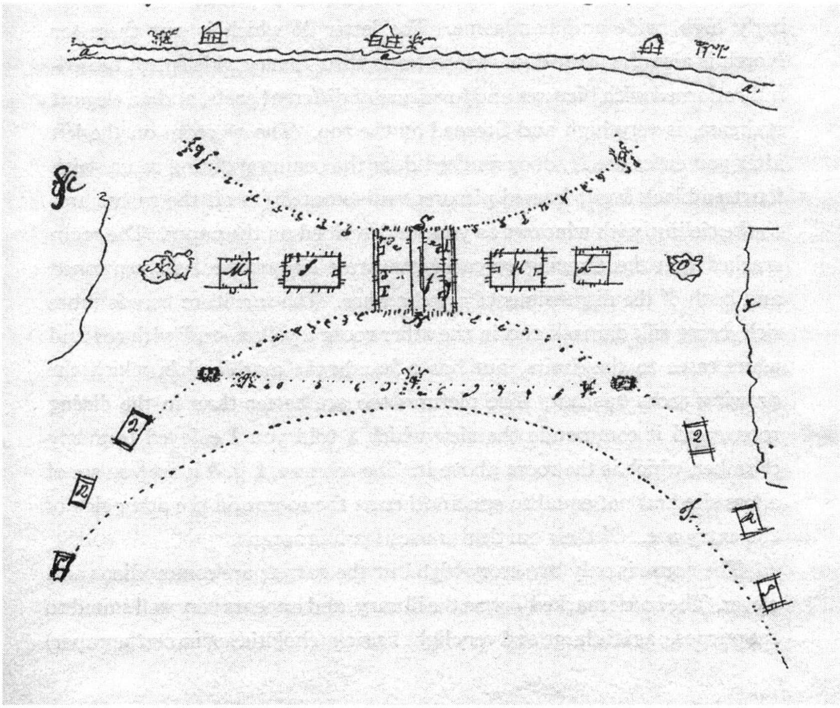

Fig. 2. Sketch from letter by Thomas Lee Shippen of the grounds at Westover, Virginia, 1783. (Shippen Family Papers, Library of Congress)

prospect of the river render them very pleasant and equall to the Thames from London to Richmond, supposing the towns omitted."[14]

The absence of the urban environment accentuates the atmosphere of country retreat as exemplified by the words of another visitor to Virginia writing in 1710. He finds the gentry enjoying "a perfect retir'd country life; for here is not in the whole colony a place that may be compared to a British village; every one living disperst up & down at their plantations."[15] The perfection of the former (retired country life) seems to be made possible by the lack of the latter (villages). This remark implicitly recalls the classical dichotomy of virtuous rural retirement and enticing urban living articulated by Roman writers from the late Republic to the Empire and revived in early modern Italy by Petrarch.[16]

When Roman society was largely agricultural and characterized by the "libertarian spirit of the independent farmer and patriotic public servant,"[17] Roman writers, such as Cato, Varro, Cicero, and Pliny the Elder idealized the traditional husbandman, who enjoyed a simple and frugal lifestyle. Self-denial and virtue to be achieved through the toil of farming the land became less of an imperative when wealthy Roman landowners residing in the city started to use the villa as a secondary residence and employed slave labor for the cultivation of their fields. At this time, villa life was praised in literature for its informality, simplicity, healthfulness, and the possibility of engaging in undisturbed intellectual activities. The tradition of a leisurely rustic retirement, or *otium,* was sustained by the Roman poets Lucretius, Catullus, and Horace as early as the first century BC and continued later on as the writings of the younger Pliny indicate.[18]

Horace's opening verses from his *Epode* II, "Happy the man who, far away from business cares, like the pristine race of mortals, works his ancestral acres,"[19] became very popular with later villa enthusiasts. In England, Alexander Pope paraphrased Horace in his *Ode on Solitude,* and Thomas Jefferson in colonial Virginia wished to inscribe Horace's verses on a plate to be fastened to a tree in a grove of aspen and beech.[20] But if Pope "subscribed to the tradition of classical husbandry" in words,[21] in that he could only rent his villa at Twickenham, Jefferson not only let Horace inspire him but also set out to realize the ideal of georgic self-sufficiency that had been extolled by Cato and Varro. Jefferson echoed the latter's belief that farming keep "men honest, vigorous and independent. The goal of his life at Monticello was . . . to affirm his belief that labor in the earth gives health and moral strength," which are indispensable qualities for a new democracy.[22]

In spite of his georgic efforts, however, Jefferson was a more expert horticulturist than he was a farmer, and he was constantly in debt because of the poor yield of his plantations, which he himself attributed to his lack of experience. Yet, his determination to carry out the wisdom of the ancients is apparent not only from the meaning he bestowed upon living in the country, but also from the forms he chose as a vessel of that meaning. His early designs for Monticello recall the descriptions of Roman villas by classical authors. In particular, his terrace plan, shaped as a hippodrome, brings to mind Pliny the Younger's description of his Tusci villa and was perhaps inspired by Robert Castell's rendering of it in his book *The Villas of the Ancients Illustrated* (1728), which Jefferson owned (fig. 3). Other details of the early design were classically inspired. For other Virginia planters, "their vision of their world was as a Virgilian Virginia," as the diary of Colonel Landon Carter indicates.[23] Sabine Hall, for example, Carter's plantation property close to the Rappahannock River, directly evoked the memory of Horace's villa.

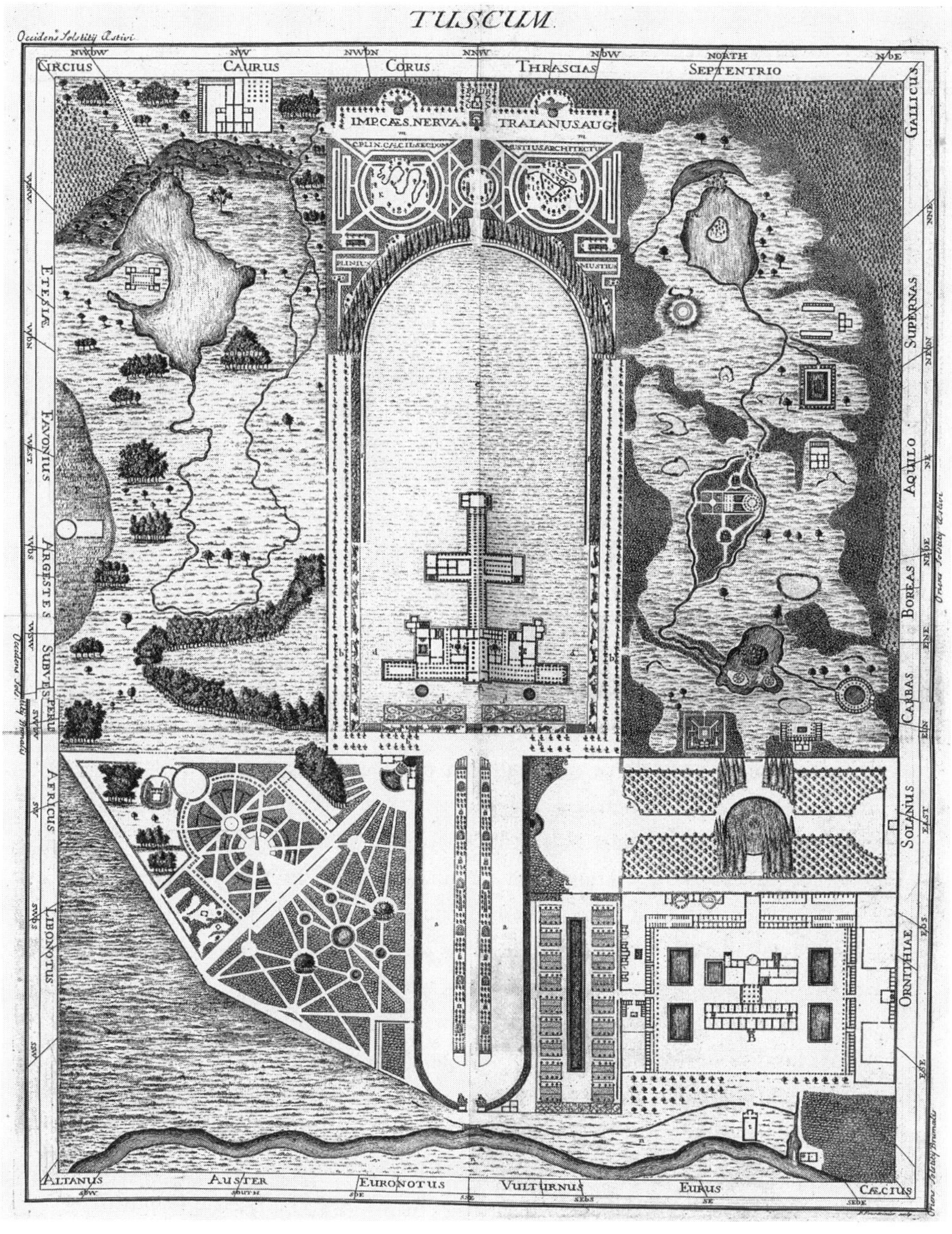

Fig. 3. "Tuscum" (1728) in Robert Castell, *Villas of the Ancients Illustrated,* 1729. Printmaker: Pierre Fourdrinier, 1758, French. (Photograph courtesy of Catena Historic Gardens and Landscapes Archive, Bard Graduate Center)

The reason for such idealization of country living is obvious. America was a relatively unspoiled land; it represented the "oasis of harmony" where the realization of Virgil's dream, the withdrawal from the great world of Western society and the start of a new life, would have been possible.[24] This explains the enthusiasm of many planters for classical literature and classical forms, as in the case of Jefferson's early project for Monticello, though the latter was more an exception rather than the rule. In fact, classical forms, as the English had learned since the Elizabethan era, were difficult to reconstruct, due to the lack of visual sources, and the best efforts in plastically rendering the convoluted and lengthy descriptions of Roman authors were credited to the garden makers of the Italian Renaissance, in particular those of central Italy. The gardens of the Lazio and Tuscany regions were among the most sought after by Englishmen embarking on the Grand Tour.

In their travel journals and other writings, English gardenists described the experience of visiting Italian gardens. Among the latter's most admired characteristics were the gardens' changing topography, the heterogeneity of waterworks, the diversity of their prospects, and the juxtaposition of orderly garden layouts and wilder groves. All of these were summed up with one word: variety.[25] "Variety, in all its aspects was certainly one criterion by which gardenists like Evelyn judged the success of contemporary gardening,"[26] as John Dixon Hunt has pointed out, and the success, I would add, of the gardening efforts of other Italian regions. Thus, for example, if the British were fond of Palladio's architecture, they did not speak enthusiastically (when they did at all) of his old-fashioned gardens, which displayed a conspicuous lack of the characteristic variety found in other Italian pleasances.[27] At any rate, on English soil the application of Italian garden forms usually took place in a piecemeal fashion due to the difficulty of transforming already existing gardens. In addition, when the taste for Palladian architecture became mainstream, English gardenists not only used selectively the more classical forms of central Italian gardens to compensate for the lack of a "Palladian" garden, but also supplied their villas with their own garden inventions. One of these is the turf terrace to be found, for example, at Henrietta Howard's Marble Hill at Twickenham (fig. 4) and at several American plantation gardens. While it is true that the terrace is a typical Italian feature, it is also important to remember that shallow terraces such as the ones found in the Chesapeake region also characterized French gardens. Moreover, a possible source for it may derive from an early-seventeenth-century British work called *A New Orchard and Garden* (fig. 5) in which the author, William Lawson, depicts a simple plan of three garden terraces symmetri-

Fig. 4. Marble Hill, Twickenham; view of the south from the Thames. Engraving by James Mason, after Augustin Heckell, 1749. (London Metropolitan Archives, City of London)

cally arranged along the main axis of the house and variously planted as orchards, parterres, and probably kitchen gardens.

Sloping falls gardens, as these terraced gardens were usually called, were built along the Atlantic coast throughout the eighteenth century. In some cases the terraces were laid out independently of the position of the house, as in the case of Charles Carroll's gardens in Annapolis (1770s), and in other cases the terraces and the house shared the same axis of symmetry, as is the case at Carter's Grove, near Williamsburg, built by Carter Burwell in 1751.[28] In Maryland, falls were usually connected by grass ramps, whereas in Virginia, stone steps were more common.[29] Despite these differences, falls gardens were fairly ubiquitous. A reason for their popularity may be functional, in that falls diverted water drainage and thus slowed down soil erosion while also facilitating access to the house when the latter was constructed atop a sloping site. But falls may have served an aesthetic purpose, too, as "platforms for viewing the landscape."[30] The practical and aesthetic function of the falls is evident also from the uses to which they were put, that is, both for the cultivation of ornamental plants and fruit trees or vegetables, the latter usually grown on the lower terraces, farther away from the house and from sight, as was the case at Sabine Hall. The uppermost terrace, or bowling green (fig. 6), was usually seeded with grass and derived its name from the game often played on it.[31]

That sloping falls gardens owed their structure to the shallow terraces of

English Thames side villas does not exclude the possibility that other elements in colonial gardens may derive from the Italian garden tradition. The custom of embellishing gardens with statues, for example, dates to classical Rome. Sculptures of Roman deities were particularly popular among colonial gardenists. They could be made in the colonies or imported from Europe and could be set in turfed garden squares, within groves, on the grassy terrace closest to the house, and even in orchards (fig. 7). Statuary could also be found in city gardens, such as that of Virginia Governor's Council member John Custis in Williamsburg, which displayed statues of Venus, Apollo, and Bacchus in the early eighteenth century, and that of Joseph Barrell's Boston estate, which was decorated with "marble figures as large as life," according to a description from 1791.[32] The future president of Yale College, Ezra Stiles, also counted "seven statues in fine Italian marble curiously wrot," ornamenting Governor Hamlinton's "very elegant garden" in Philadelphia.[33]

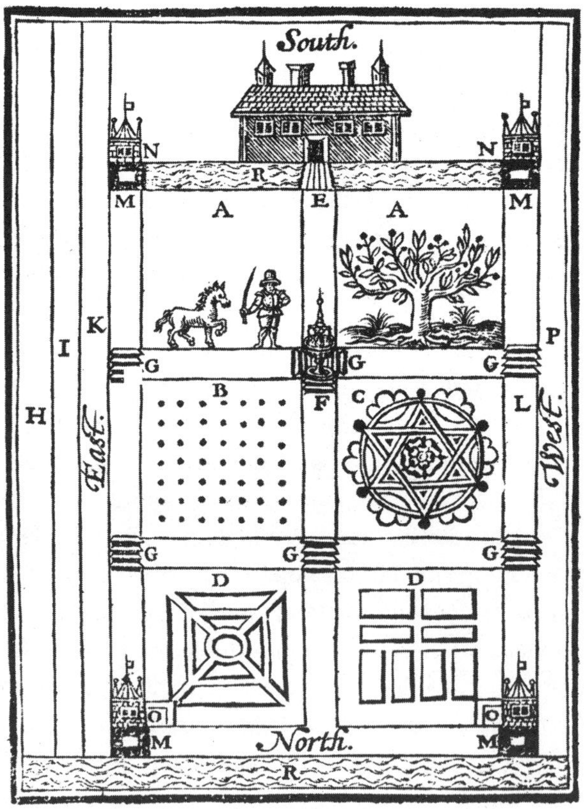

Fig. 5. Plan of a terraced garden from William Lawson's *A New Orchard and Garden* (London, 1618).

Fig. 6. Mount Airy, Virginia; southwest front as viewed from the bowling green, 1827. Watercolor by Anthony St. John Baker from *Mémoires d'un voyageur qui se repose,* London, 1850. (This item is reproduced by permission of The Huntington Library, San Marino, California)

The presence of other Italian ornaments or ornamental and functional structures was not uncommon in colonial gardens. In 1705, "Robert Beverly remarked that Virginians sought relief from the sun in 'Summer-Houses, Arbors and Grottoes' in their gardens."[34] A record of William Byrd's wife ordering shells from Barbados suggests that a grotto may have been created at Westover.[35] Also, Jefferson made plans to build a grotto at Monticello, which seems to have been inspired by Pope's grotto at Twickenham, but this was never realized.[36] Topiary, so characteristic of classical gardens, was also particularly common. Custis wrote in a letter to Quaker botanist and draper Peter Collinson in England that his garden displayed "very fine yews balls and pyramids . . . established for more than twenty years."[37] And merchant Israel Pemberton's garden in Philadelphia was apparently "decorated with a number of evergreens, carefully clipped into pyramidal and conical forms," as was William Penn's Springettsbury, an estate along the Schuylkill River just outside Philadelphia, which was described by Ezra Stiles as having "spruce hedges cut into beautiful figures."[38] After a brief mention of the gardens' "agreeable variety" and "regular confusion and disorder," Stiles goes on to describe the "wood behind & adjoining to the gar-

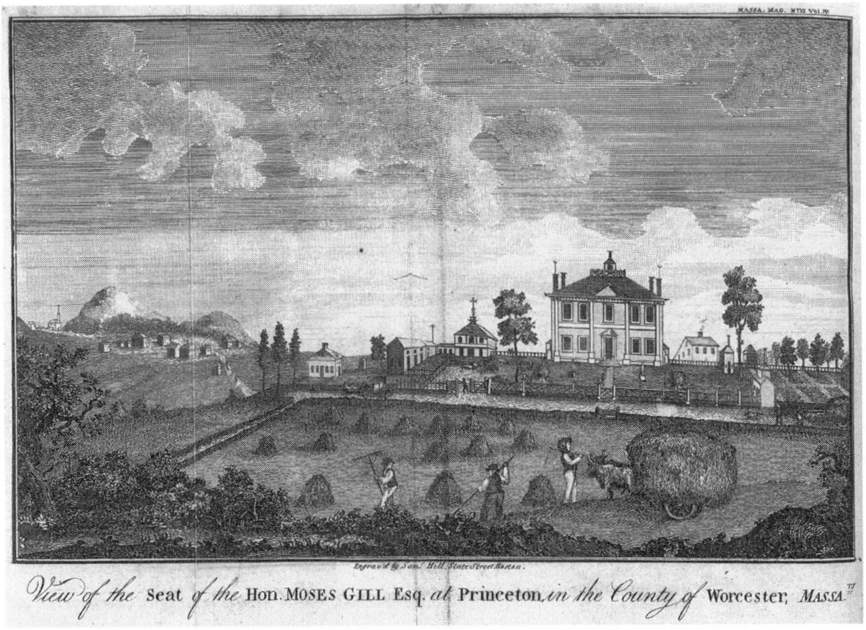

Fig. 7. View of the seat of the Hon. Moses Gill Esq. at Princeton, in the County of Worcester, Massa.ts. Detail of engraving in *Massachusetts Magazine* 4 (November 1792). (Courtesy of the John Carter Brown Library at Brown University)

dens, the whole scene most happily accommodated for solitude and rural contemplation."[39]

The fact that travelers and planters described colonial grounds in terms of gardens and groves—the juxtaposition of which, in addition to their characteristic variety, was a hallmark of central Italian gardens according to English travelers—indicates that a love for things Italian may have been imported from England. This affinity between England and the colonies, however, may be due to the latter's borrowing of British gardenist rhetoric more than to the actual Italianate configuration of their villas. In fact, the application of Italian forms or classical features was more gradual on American gardens than it had ever been on English soil. Moreover, the presence of regular layouts with straight and axial paths, square or rectangular parterres, and beds cultivated with flowers, herbs, or vegetables may have been motivated by functional convenience more than, or in addition to, a deliberate aesthetic choice.

Arguing against the old claim that the colonies lagged behind England with regard to the introduction of the naturalistic landscape style, Peter

Martin has noted that "Not as many people were designing decorative gardens in the colonies. . . . There was simply not enough money, nor were there enough individuals with sufficient land and time to indulge in this sort of deliberate landscaping."[40] According to Abbott Lowell Cummings, "Not until the 1790s, and then especially in the planning of country estates, are there important excursions into the long-popular cult of English naturalism," the reason being that "formality in landscape design and the layout of gardens . . . seems to have been the prevailing taste in America during much of the eighteenth century."[41] To take these arguments a step further one could say that the predominance of regular layouts, especially in the eighteenth century, does not mean that American gardens lagged behind contemporary British practice because they chose to perpetrate the older style. Rather, the ubiquity of the regular model may have several motives. A note accompanying a late-eighteenth-century painting of a Princeton estate (fig. 7) says, "Foreigners must have an high idea of the rapid progress of improvement in America, when they are told that the ground which these buildings now cover . . . [was], in the year 1766, as perfectly wild as the deepest forest of our country. The honourable proprietor must have great satisfaction on seeing *improvements* so extensive, made under his own eye, under his own direction, and by his own active industry."[42]

Of course, "improvements" on American soil were very different from the landscapers' improvements at home. The native landscape was already "natural," with a lush tangle of trees and underbrush that stood in the way of creating settlements and clearing fields for agriculture. Not surprisingly the Princeton painting shows a clearly marked ornamental garden in front of the house adjacent to which are men at work in the fields. As in one of the many miniatures illustrating Pier de Crescenzi's fourteenth-century work on agriculture, the emphasis is on labor more than on style. And just as early Renaissance gardens develop the forms of earlier productive fields with their rectilinear ridges and furrows, and orderly subdivisions motivated by sharecropping methods, the geometrical rigidity of many colonial gardens is directly related to coexisting agricultural practices and functional exigencies calling for straight paths and irrigation ditches, fruit trees planted in rows and rectangular planting beds. However, practical considerations did not exclude the aesthetic enjoyment of gardens and their use as venues for social gatherings and private encounters.[43]

The gardens of such colonists as Byrd, Colonel Carter, Custis, and others, with their additional ornamental bend represented by their collections of topiary and statues, were, of course, exceptional, unlike their orderly layouts. These the gentry may have derived not only from agricultural practices but also from their interpretation of the same classical authors who provided them with the rhetorical tools to express the meaning of their country living. Just as popular as the Romans' works on ethics and moral philosophy were their books on gardening and farming, such as Cato's *De agricultura,* Varro's *Rerum rusticarum libri tres,* and Columella's *De re rustica.* "These writings satisfied the yen for precedent, order, and restraint that appealed to a people carving a pure, new nation out of a 'howling' wilderness and toiling to establish an orderly new government."[44] Thus, for some colonists the orderliness of their gardens derived from the Roman classical tradition, which had, in Jefferson's words, "the approbation of thousands of years."[45] But while the orderly layouts of the colonists' gardens, as well as their meaning, may be said to be classical, some of their parts, such as the grotto and the terrace, were indebted as much to classical Italy as they were to England, where they blended with local garden elements and traditions.

We have to wait until the end of the nineteenth century and the beginning of the twentieth to see a less rhetorical and more thorough application of Italian garden design principles to American grounds. These gardens, however, will have lost the classical meaning that was attributed to the gardens of the British colonies along with their only Palladian characteristic, that is, their function as economically self-sufficient centers for agricultural production. In fact, in the period of American architectural history that is commonly known as the Country Place Era, hardly any garden owners were also gardenists as William Byrd and Jefferson used to be, and for those who were, it was the aesthetic value associated with gardens more than the moral underpinnings of country life that stimulated their interest.

"What I want to build is an Italian villa 3 sides of a court with a collonade in the middle. . . . Haven't you got some photo or something that would help me in regard to detail?" a young Charles Platt asked Stanford White right before building High Court, one of his earliest commissions in Cornish (completed in 1891).[46] The New England setting opposite the peaks of Mount Ascutney, along the Connecticut River, attracted numerous American artists precisely because of its strong resemblance to the hilly Italian landscape. Both Rose Standish Nichols, author of the book *Italian Pleasure Gardens,* and her uncle, famed sculptor Augustus Saint-Gaudens (who had trained in Italy for years before settling in Cornish), noted this similarity.[47] The artists' designed properties in Cornish, with their studied views of Mount Ascutney and masterful adaptation to the existing topography, responded to the local landscape just as cleverly as an Italian Renaissance villa. About Dingleton

House, for example, the last property Platt designed in the colony in 1904, neighbor Herbert Croly wrote: "when this garden is fully grown, it will be one of the most beautiful in the country; and its beauty will consist precisely of the admirable manner in which it has fitted to the plan of the house, and to the layout and the planting of the surrounding land."[48] But while Dingleton House may have resembled a Renaissance villa, it carried none of the meanings associated with life in classical Italy that colonial gardenists deemed so important. Cornish villas were also different from other Italian-inspired residences that contemporary wealthy patrons were commissioning elsewhere in the country. Unlike these, the ones in Cornish tended to be unpretentious: Italianate in conception but without Italian quotes, and certainly not "formal." Cornish artists used hardy plants such as poplars instead of Italian cypress, and white pine for hedges in place of boxwood, to adapt to local weather and soil conditions. In addition to these mandatory acts of translation that had also appeared elsewhere, they deliberately adapted the syntax of early American gardens, such as the vernacular planting tradition of New England and the turf terrace or sloping fall of colonial origin that is visible in the gardens of Saint-Gaudens, Maxfield Parrish, and Annie Lazarus (figs. 8 and 9). Moreover, Cornish artist-gardeners relied on layers of abundant plants and leafy boughs that spilled over and softened the

Fig. 8. Aspet, residence of Augustus Saint-Gaudens, Cornish, New Hampshire, the middle terrace. (Photograph by Elizabeth Jones)

Fig. 9. The South Garden at High Court, Cornish, New Hampshire. From *House and Garden* 8, no. 1 (July 1905): 19.

rectilinear shapes of paths and planting beds. Although reminiscent of the English cottage garden tradition as theorized by Gertrude Jekyll, this practice was also rooted in the local New England past and was artfully mastered by many residents, some of whom, like Ellen Biddle Shipman, would eventually become professional landscape architects.[49] About Cornish gardens, Shipman remarked that they represented "the renaissance of gardening in America, the first effort in this country to return to early traditional gardening."[50] The revival of the American tradition was a mixture of British precedents and Italian principles among other foreign influences, which were seamlessly combined in a truly unique, original, and expressive form.

Outside of the Cornish colony, however, the Italian garden tradition was often imitated in a more pronounced and rigorous manner and at times also directly quoted. In particular, Italianate gardens were commissioned by a new class of citizens including a few American landowners as foils to their sumptuous country residences, which were usually not the only ones they possessed. The new clients, in addition, were mostly town-bred people, who used their country residences for a few months during the summer or occasionally for weekend parties during the winter. But, as architectural critic and Cornish resident Croly pointed out in an editorial of 1905, "their relation to the country remains essentially casual and artificial. . . . The well-to-do American . . . may take a genuine interest in certain country sports; but beyond that in 'returning to the country' he is merely adapting himself to a tradition, which his common sense tells him is a good thing for himself and his children. The country means to him a country house within an hour or two of New York."[51]

The reason for the change in meaning and in function of these new American gardens follows a change in the cultural, social, and economic life of the United States in the years following the Civil War. By the late 1870s a northeast driven market economy had replaced an older one based largely on agriculture, and on commerce and manufacturing to a lesser extent. Private investment bankers began to promote intercorporate cooperation in financing large-scale private ventures. Among them, the improvement of transportation systems, such as the restructuring and formation of the national railroad, facilitated the expansion of business enterprises and permitted an unprecedented accumulation of wealth in the hands of few self-made Americans.[52] With the exception of J. P. Morgan and a few others, most of the so-called robber barons were individuals of humble origins who climbed up the social ladder with intuitive skill and forceful determination. The offspring of the new capitalists were fortunate children, who had the resources to attend the universities of New England and the means and the leisure to travel around the world. But they were a lot less motivated than their fathers had been and also uncertain about their identity and their place in American society.[53] Unlike their fathers, most of whom contented themselves with frugal lifestyles, the progeny spent lavishly, particularly in the construction of luxurious homes that represented an image of how they perceived themselves and how they wanted others to perceive them.

In a rather cynical depiction of the American millionaire published in 1902, Croly writes,

> The millionaire . . . confines his enterprise to his business. In intellectual, artistic and moral affairs he lives by tradition alone. His attitude is a curious compound of somewhat contradictory motives. His very deep-seated desire for excellence in whatever he does or has, is diverted by his lack of social self-confidence into these traditional and conventional channels. . . . He prefers to remain a business man. But he does wish to emancipate his children and his fellow countrymen from the reproach of being raw and new; and consequently he tries in every way to bring to bear upon them

> historical and traditional influences. He wants them to acquire and to realize more of a past than a few hundred years on a new continent can afford; and he wants to make that past something to be seen and felt . . . what he seems to like are almost exclusively things rich in historical associations . . . he often becomes an ambitious collector of pictures and "objets d'art"; particularly in all aesthetic matters, he wants things with a European reputation.[54]

The American fascination with objets d'art that speak of a long and usually foreign cultural tradition drove designers and clients alike to choose from more than one possible European formal style, and, in fact, French Baroque gardens were imitated just as much as Italian Renaissance models.[55]

As French novelist and critic Paul Bourget observed at the turn of the century, one must "recognize the sincerity, almost the pathos of this love of Americans for things about which there is an atmosphere of time and stability. In this country, where everything is of yesterday, they hunger and thirst for the long ago, and under such surroundings, it is almost a physical satisfaction, as I felt myself, to meet the faded colors of an ancient painting or the softened shades of a mediaeval tapestry."[56] It is the same appreciation of the effects of time on a work of art from a distant and glorious past that pervades the rhetoric of the Americans who describe for their fellow citizens the old gardens of Italy at the turn of the twentieth century and who will find them overgrown and sometimes even crumbling, but still exuding a magical atmosphere.

Charles Platt, for example, writes his *Italian Gardens* in 1894 because he finds that the work of his predecessors, such as Perciere and Fontaine, "fails to give a fair idea of the existing state of the villas . . . [which] have all passed through a variety of changes. . . . However, in almost all of them there is something of their best time which, either by reason of the great difficulty of alteration or from some other cause, has been allowed to remain."[57] Thus, Platt notes that the stone steps of the old racecourse at the Villa Borghese in Rome are "now greatly overgrown with grass" and adds that it is "so delightful now that one does not care to be too curious about its past,"[58] meaning that what matters most is not so much to know the history of the racecourse, but to simply appreciate the effects that the passing of time produced on it and to just delight in the way it is currently used. Similarly, the Giusti garden (fig. 10) leaves Platt with an impression of a "great tangle, and of a profusion of growing things mixed with the most charming garden statuary."[59] Like Platt, Edith Wharton notes in her famous account of Italian villas the gardens' ruinous conditions, which, however, contribute to their charm:

Fig. 10. The Giusti Garden, Italy, photographed by Charles Platt. From *Italian Gardens* (1894). (Avery Architectural and Fine Arts Library, Columbia University)

"It is the glory of the Italian garden-architects that neglect and disintegration cannot wholly mar the effects they were skilled in creating . . . [so that] while a trace of their plan remains one feels the spell of the whole."[60]

Platt's sensitivity toward the "atmosphere of time" that distinguished the gardens he visited in Italy derives from his training as a painter and etcher, used to observe landscapes through the lens of a Romantic aesthetic. This aspect was criticized by some of his contemporaries, who reacted to his essays and photographs of old Italian gardens published earlier in the *Harper's New Monthly Magazine:* "much of the interest which invests these pictures . . . is derived from the fact that [the gardens] are, in a measure, ruined."[61]

But it was precisely for their ability to re-create in a new design the atmosphere of a long-lived garden that the approach of designers partial to the Italian style appealed to so many of their wealthy clients. These designers also advocated a design unity of house and grounds, facilitated by functional relationships among spaces and achieved by axial and interlocking layouts, which they considered as the salient characteristic of Italian villas.[62] This characteristic is to be found not only in Platt's projects—from the relatively small Faulkner Farm to the larger lakeside estates like Gwinn and Villa Turicum—but also in those of later landscape architects who had been influenced by both Platt's writings and Wharton's. We find the same principles reiterated by James Sturgis Pray at Harvard during his long tenure as chairman of the Program in Landscape Architecture (1908–1928),[63] and in the projects of his students, among whom Richard Webel, who was also a landscape architecture fellow at the American Academy in Rome in the late 1920s. Incidentally, the establishment of the fellowship in landscape architecture at the American Academy in 1915 contributed even more to a thorough understanding of the Italian garden and to the systematization of its design principles.[64] In an effort to learn "the secret of the subtle refinement of the Renaissance," which produced the best interpretation of Roman classical architecture and gardens, fellows like Webel were in fact required to analyze, measure, and draw the most important of the Renaissance villas throughout Italy (fig. 11), so as "not to learn to copy what . . . [they] inspired, but to put the same culture and grace into new things at home."[65] Back in the United States, Webel eventually acquired a reputation for his ability to interpret the Italian garden style and to adapt it to American tastes. In partnership with an Italian gardener from Fiesole, Umberto Innocenti, Webel's designs (fig. 12) were known for his use of mature plantings of large trees and understory plants that captured the atmosphere of fleeting time so magically embodied by Italian gardens.[66]

The turn-of-the-century interpretation of Italian gardens as vestiges of Renaissance culture veiled by the great tangle of their luxuriant vegetation contrasts greatly with an earlier one formulated during the colonial era. The direct study of Italian models by the pioneers of American landscape

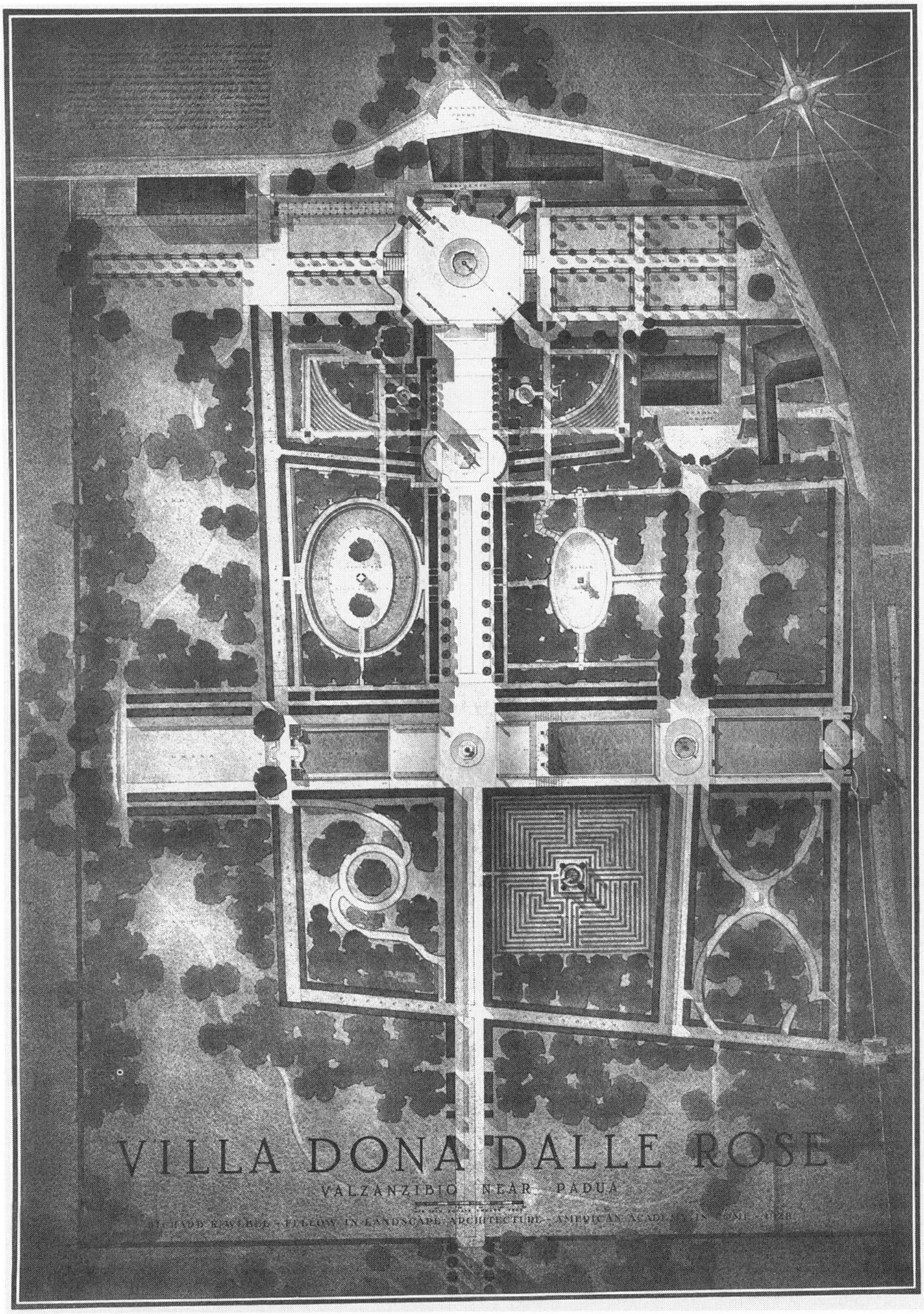

Fig. 11. Plan of Villa Donà dalle Rose, Valsanzibio, Italy, by Richard K. Webel, 1928. (American Academy in Rome, Photographic Archive)

Fig. 12. Evelyn Marshall Field House, Long Island, by Innocenti & Webel (1932). (Library of Congress)

architecture, among them Platt, Wharton, Farrand, and the fellows of the American Academy in Rome, allowed for a more accurate understanding of the design principles of Renaissance gardens.[67] But if the forms of the Italian garden could be easily re-created on American soil and adapted to the wants and needs of the American upper class, the earlier moral message, once associated with the notion of the classical villa and the idyll of rustic retirement that the colonists imported from England and learned from classical sources, had vanished. In 1893, the editors of *Garden and Forest* thought that Italianate gardens "only appeal to the aesthetic sense; they delight the eye and satisfy the cultivated taste as a beautiful piece of tapestry or pottery does. It is beauty for its own sake. It expresses no sentiment and carries no inner meaning; it does not address itself to the nobler part of our nature as simple natural scenery does."[68] Indeed, the Italian garden and the idea of Italy appealed not only to those wealthy Americans who wished to give a formal expression to their social status, but also to those aesthetes whose sole interest was the pursuit of beauty. The outcome of their learned experimentations with the Italian model resulted in something that ultimately appeared more American and more local than anything that had been done before.

Notes

1. On the meaning of *translation* and *imitation* in this context, see David Leatherbarrow, John Dixon Hunt, and Laurie Olin, "Some Terms for the Transposition of Gardens between Countries," *Studies in the History of Gardens and Designed Landscapes* 31, no. 4 (2011): 355–56.

2. Frank A. Waugh, *Formal Design in Landscape Architecture: A Statement of Principles with Special Reference to Their Present Use in America* (New York: Orange Judd; London: Kegan Paul, Trench, Trübner, 1927), 11.

3. Beatrix Jones [Farrand], "The Garden in Relation to the House," *Garden and Forest* 10, no. 476 (April 1897): 132–33.

4. E. N. Plank, "Some Uses of Formal Gardening," *Garden and Forest* 6, no. 268 (April 1893): 161.

5. Editorial article, "Garden Design," *Garden and Forest* 10, no. 475 (March 1897): 121.

6. Ibid.

7. Thomas Hastings, "An Architectural Garden," *Garden and Forest* 9, no. 434 (June 1896): 241.

8. Ibid.

9. Rebecca Warren Davidson, "Images and Ideas of the Italian Garden in American Landscape Architecture" (PhD diss., Cornell University, 1994).

10. C. Allan Brown, "Eighteenth-Century Virginia Plantation Gardens: Translating an Ancient Idyll," in *Regional Garden Design in the United States,* ed. Therese O'Malley and Marc Treib (Washington, DC: Dumbarton Oaks Research Library and Collection, 1995), 159.

11. Thomas Lee Shippen, letter, 1783, in *Garden of Colony and State: Gardens and Gardeners of the American Colonies and of the Republic before 1840,* ed. Alice Lockwood (New York: Charles Scribner's Sons, 1934), 2:98.

12. François Jean Marquis de Chastellux, *Travels in North America in the Years 1780, 1781, and 1782,* trans. and ed. Howard C. Rice Jr. (Chapel Hill, NC: Published for the Institute of Early American History and Culture at Williamsburg, VA, 1963), 2:430.

13. Brown, "Eighteenth-Century Virginia Plantation Gardens," 139. Also Peter Martin, "'Long and Assiduous Endeavours': Gardening in Early Eighteenth-Century Virginia," in *British and American Gardens in the Eighteenth Century,* ed. Robert Maccubbin and Peter Martin (Williamsburg, VA: Colonial Williamsburg Foundation, 1984), 113.

14. Gregory A. Stiverson and Patrick H. Butler III, eds., "Virginia in 1732: The Travel Journal of William Hugh Grove," *Virginia Magazine of History and Biography* 85 (January 1977): 18–44.

15. Brown, "Eighteenth-Century Virginia Plantation Gardens," 134.

16. The dichotomy of country and town, however, may have been a cliché affecting the rhetoric of foreign visitors more than the planters' lives. Although some colonists described their country living in terms that evoked the classics' idyllic retirement, they did not alienate themselves completely from towns and cities and did not perceive the latter as menacing as they appeared in the old world. See Martin, "'Long and Assiduous Endeavours,'" 113–14, and Elizabeth McLean, "Town and Country Gardens in Eighteenth-Century Philadelphia," 140, in Maccubbin and Martin, *British and American Gardens.*

On the evolving relationship between city and country in America, see Donald Simon, "Green-Wood Cemetery and the American Park Movement," in *Essays in the History of New York City: A Memorial to Sidney Pomerantz,* ed. Irwin Yellowitz (Port Washington, NY: Kennikat Press), 61–77.

17. James Ackerman, *The Villa: Form and Ideology of Country Houses* (Princeton, NJ: Princeton University Press, 1990), 37.

18. The wealthy Romans' pursuit of *otium,* however, did not exclude their quest for profit from sources other than the traditional agricultural ones, such as pasturage and "investment in the rearing of luxury foodstuffs." Nicholas Purcell, "The Roman Villa and the Landscape of Production," in *Urban Society in Roman Italy,* ed. Tim Cornell and Kathryn Lomas (New York: St. Martin's Press, 1995), 152.

19. Beatus ille qui procul negotiis / ut prisca gens mortalium / paterna rura exercet.

20. William Beiswanger, "The Temple in the Garden: Thomas Jefferson's Vision of the Monticello Landscape," in Maccubbin and Martin, *British and American Gardens,* 174.

21. John Dixon Hunt, *Garden and Grove: The Italian Renaissance Garden in the English Imagination, 1600–1750* (Philadelphia: University of Pennsylvania Press, 1996), 200.

22. Jefferson's convictions were shared by many of his contemporaries. George Washington, for example, embodied the ideal of the soldier/farmer who retired to Mount Vernon to farm the land. See Brown, "Eighteenth-Century Virginia Plantation Gardens," 154–55.

23. Ibid., 159.

24. Leo Marx, *The Machine in the Garden: Technology and the Pastoral Ideal in America* (Oxford: Oxford University Press, 2000), 3.

25. Hunt, *Garden and Grove,* 83, 130, 162.

26. Ibid., 162.

27. Some authors consider Veneto gardens and Palladio's villas as models for British Thames-side villa gardens and American plantations. According to Barbara Wells Sarudy, Palladio's influence on American colonial gardens was due to the circulation in the Chesapeake region of the English edition of Palladio's *Four Books on Architecture.* Barbara Wells Sarudy, *Gardens and Gardening in the Chesapeake, 1700–1805* (Baltimore: Johns Hopkins University Press, 1998), 98, 188n23. See also Brown, "Eighteenth-Century Virginia Plantation Gardens," 131–32. In my forthcoming study of the reception of the Palladian villa outside of Italy, I explain why Veneto and Palladio's gardens were never used as a design model for the grounds of later British and American villas.

28. Terraces were also built in New England, as some written sources testify. See, in particular, Thomas Hancock's 1736 description of his Boston estate of Beacon Hill in Abbott Lowell Cummings, "Eighteenth-Century New England Garden Design: The Pictorial Evidence," in Maccubbin and Martin, *British and American Gardens,* 131.

29. One exception in Virginia is Sabine Hall, where grass ramps connected the terraces instead of steps.

30. Brown, "Eighteenth-Century Virginia Plantation Gardens," 142. Not all plantation gardens afforded a view over the surrounding landscape. Some of them may have been walled, too, especially if belonging to the gentry. Brick walls were particularly expensive, and only persons of means could afford to build them. In some cases only a portion of

the property, the kitchen garden, was walled. An alternative to the brick wall was the more affordable picket fence.

31. William M. S. Rasmussen, "For Profit and Pleasure: The Art of Gardening in Colonial Virginia," *Arts in Virginia* 21 (Fall 1980): 23.

32. The record of statues at Custis's garden is in a note by Robert Bolling (1772) cited by Martin, "'Long and Assiduous Endeavours,'" 115n17. The description of Barrell's estate by Reverend William Bentley is cited by Cummings, "Eighteenth-Century New England Garden Design," 133.

33. "Ezra Stiles in Philadelphia, 1754," *Pennsylvania Magazine of History and Biography* 16, no. 3 (October 1892): 375.

34. Brown, "Eighteenth-Century Virginia Plantation Gardens," 145.

35. The crushed fossilized seashells also may have been used for paths in place of gravel. See M. Kent Brinkley, "Interpreting Colonial Revival Gardens in Changing Times," in *Breaking Ground: Examining the Vision and Practice of Historical Landscape Restoration,* Proceedings of the 11th Conference on Restoring Southern Gardens and Landscapes, October 2–4, 1997 (Winston-Salem, N.C.: Old Salem, 1999), 68.

36. For a description of Jefferson's project for a grotto see Beiswanger, "The Temple in the Garden," 172.

37. John Custis to Peter Collinson, cited by Martin, "'Long and Assiduous Endeavours,'" 111.

38. Alexander Graydon, *Memoirs of a Life, Chiefly Passed in Pennsylvania, within the Last Sixty Years* (Harrisburgh, PA: John Wyeth, 1811), 34–35, cited by McLean, "Town and Country Gardens in Eighteenth-Century Philadelphia," 137; "Ezra Stiles in Philadelphia, 1754," *Pennsylvania Magazine of History and Biography* 16, no. 3 (October 1892): 375.

39. "Ezra Stiles in Philadelphia."

40. Martin, "'Long and Assiduous Endeavors,'" 110. On life in the colonies and the economy of the early plantations, see Cary Carson, Norman F. Barka, William M. Kelso, Garry Wheller Stone, and Dell Upton, "Impermanent Architecture in the Southern American Colonies," *Winterthur Portfolio* 16, no. 2/3 (Summer–Autumn, 1981), esp. 140–78.

41. Cummings, "Eighteenth-Century New England Garden Design," 130.

42. Qtd. by Cummings in ibid., 133, emphasis added.

43. On this topic see Sarudy, *Gardens and Gardening in the Chesapeake,* 103–14.

44. Ibid., 98.

45. H. M. Kallen, "The Arts and Thomas Jefferson," *Ethics* 53 (July 1943): 274. Jefferson eventually moved away from classical forms and speculated about an American equivalent of the English landscape garden, acknowledging that it is to England "without doubt [that] we are to go for models in this art." See Beiswanger, "The Temple in the Garden," 182.

46. Platt's remark is in Alma Gilbert-Smith and Judith B. Tankard, eds., *A Place of Beauty: The Artists and Gardens of the Cornish Colony* (Berkeley, CA: Ten Speed Press, 2000), 79.

47. Ibid., 89.

48. Herbert Croly, qtd. in ibid., 122.

49. Shipman often collaborated with Platt for the planting schemes of his gardens as he neither selected the plants himself nor indicated them on his plans, but rather showed the effect of them on his paintings and sketches. See Charles Downing Lay, "An Interview with Charles Platt," *Landscape Architecture* 2, no. 3 (April 1912): 127–31.

50. Ellen Biddle Shipman, qtd. in Gilbert and Tankard, *A Place of Beauty,* 51.

51. Herbert Croly, "The American Country Estate," *Architectural Record* 18, no. 1 (July 1905): 2.

52. Exemplary are the lives of Cornelius Vanderbilt, John D. Rockefeller, Charles Lang Freer, Andrew Carnegie, Frank Winfield Woolworth, and Cyrus McCormick.

53. Typical examples are George Washington Vanderbilt II, John D. Rockefeller Jr., Edith Rockefeller McCormick, and Barbara Woolworth Hutton.

54. Herbert Croly, "Rich Men and Their Houses," *Architectural Record* 12, no. 1 (May 1902): 29.

55. Few among the wealthy industrialists did not express an interest in foreign cultures. William Robertson Coe represented one such exception. His passion was the history of the American West, and his "Planting Fields" estate on Long Island's North Shore was designed by the Olmsted Brothers.

56. Paul Bourget, qtd. in Croly, "Rich Men and Their Houses," 29.

57. Charles A. Platt, *Italian Gardens* (1894; rpt., Portland, OR: Sagapress/Timber Press, 1993), 13–15.

58. Ibid., 27.

59. Ibid., 89.

60. Edith Wharton, *Italian Villas and Their Gardens* (1904; rpt., New York: Rizzoli, 2008), 175–76.

61. Editorial article, *Garden and Forest* 6, no. 284 (August 2, 1893): 322. The editorial was likely written by Charles Eliot. See also Charles Platt, "Italian Gardens," *Harper New Monthly Magazine* 87 (July 1893): 164–80, and (August 1893): 393–406.

62. In Platt's projects, the relationship between architecture and gardens, when not axial, was guided by the principle of interlocking units, as is the case at his Faulkner Farm, which seems to have been inspired by the design of Villa Gamberaia. See Rebecca Warren Davidson, "Charles A. Platt and the Fine Art of Landscape Design," in *Shaping an American Landscape: The Art and Architecture of Charles A. Platt* (Hanover, NH: Hood Museum of Art, Dartmouth College, and University Press of New England, 1995), 85.

63. James Sturgis Pray is the author of a four-part article, "The Italian Garden," *American Architect and Building News* 67 (February 10, 1900): 43–45, (February 17, 1900): 51–52, (March 17, 1900): 83–85, and March 24, 1900): 91–92, which "remained required reading for decades in the department's introductory course in landscape architecture." Melanie Simo, *The Coalescing of Different Forces and Ideas: A History of Landscape Architecture at Harvard, 1900–1999* (Cambridge, MA: Harvard University Graduate School of Design, 2000), 15.

64. The Academy had been founded in 1894 in response to "the generally increasing demand in America for evidences of higher culture and taste in all the arts, and particularly in architecture," and with the purpose of providing young American artists and architects with an opportunity to "study thoroughly the monuments of antiq-

uity . . . before they start upon independent professional careers," Charles Henry Cheney, "The American Academy in Rome," *Architectural Record* 31, no. 3 (March 1912): 244. Edward G. Lawson was the first American to win a three-year fellowship at the American Academy in 1915–18. Laurie Olin, "L'architettura del paesaggio presso l'Accademia Americana a Roma (1915–1940)," in *Ville e Giardini Italiani: I disegni di architetti e paesaggisti dell'American Academy in Rome,* ed. Vincenzo Cazzato (Rome: Istituto poligrafico e Zecca dello Stato, 2004), 197–210.

65. Cheney, "The American Academy in Rome," 251.

66. Webel had learned the technique of moving large trees while working as an intern at the office of Ferruccio Vitale. The latter had devised a method to protect the roots of large trees by lifting with them large amounts of soil. Before Vitale implemented his method, the Olmsted Brothers had been able to move large bare-root trees, but because most of them didn't survive, they were forced to plant them in groves to minimize the impact of the losses. See Gary Hilderbrand, ed., *Making a Landscape of Continuity: The Practice of Innocenti and Webel* (Cambridge, MA: Harvard Graduate School of Design, 1997), 12–13. Carrère and Hastings were also well known for their use of mature trees. Their planting technique is mentioned in an article on their Indian Harbor project in Connecticut: "holes were blasted in the rock, which is naturally full of fissures, and were filled with soil, in which [masses of large trees] have been planted." Thomas Hastings, "An Architectural Garden," *Garden and Forest* 9, no. 434 (June 1896): 242.

67. The use of photography in the twentieth-century study of Italian gardens facilitated a deeper understanding of their design principles, as Rebecca Warren Davidson explains in this volume.

68. Editorial article, *Garden and Forest* 6, no. 284 (August 2, 1893): 322.

Camera Bella

The Printed Photograph and the Perception of the Italian Garden in America

REBECCA WARREN DAVIDSON

Photography as a tool for studying and documenting gardens, and the garden as a favorite subject of photographs, are both so commonplace in our culture that their effects on each other, especially from a design standpoint, have been relatively overlooked.[1] In this essay, I focus on a specific instance of their interrelationships: the influence of photographs of Italian gardens on early-twentieth-century American landscape design. Beginning with the refinement of the halftone process in the late nineteenth century, the reading and viewing public has been inundated with photographic reproductions. During this same time span, that is, from about 1890 to the beginning of the Great Depression in 1929, American designers looked to the Italian garden, specifically, as a model, both in response to requests from their clients and—even more significantly—as a source from which to learn the basic principles of landscape design. This essay thus seeks to investigate the connections between these two phenomena as a new way of understanding how garden design knowledge is acquired, transmitted, and transformed, with specific reference to certain kinds of visual knowledge by which we create environments and shape our surroundings.[2]

The influence of Italian gardens on Western landscape design is well known; however, in this context, a brief summary is useful.[3] The gardens of Italy, famed for their classical pedigree, their Renaissance and Baroque splendor, and their subsequent decline into picturesque ruins, have been variously invoked as a theoretical ideal and used as a working model for American gardens since the seventeenth century. Although with some exceptions the majority of gardens created by the colonists were for necessity rather than display, their debt to European Renaissance gardens is clear in their geometrical arrangements within enclosed spaces. By contrast, American garden design in the nineteenth century was dominated by the influence of the English landscape garden, as reinterpreted for a democratic society in both American public parks and private gardens by such notable practitioners as Frederick Law Olmsted.

The first American gardens actually identified as "Italian" were created as early as the mid-nineteenth century although, in reality, they owed a greater debt to the so-called Italianate gardens of England than to those of Italy itself.[4] The most notable American example of this hybrid style is the garden of Hollis Hunnewell, created in Wellesley, Massachusetts, in the 1850s. Its defining characteristics, like those of its English models, were magnificent terraces of evergreens overlooked by a balustraded walk ornamented with urns. Hunnewell's own interest in the terraced arrangement was horticultural as well as aesthetic. While his professed aim was to plant every species of evergreen that could survive the harsh New England climate, he apparently could not resist the lure of the topiary arts. The result is a forest of sheared and shaped trees, including some modeled on the *estrade* seen in medieval paintings. Ranged on multiple levels bordering Lake Waban, Hunnewell's literally fantastic creation was—and is—one of the most celebrated and photographed of nineteenth- and early-twentieth-century American gardens with Italian references.[5]

As Americans gained more information about Italian gardens directly from the source—through their travels abroad as well as via texts and images—their interest in and ability to fashion reproductions that more accurately represented those in Italy increased. The Villa Vizcaya, for example, built in Miami, Florida, beginning in 1914, displays many specific quotations from well-known Italian gardens: a cascade modeled on one at the Villa Corsini in Rome, a "secret garden" based on the *limonaia* at the Villa Gamberaia in Settignano, a stone barge recalling Isola Bella, and numerous other more diffuse references. It is one of the most faithful reproductions of an Italian house and garden ever created in America, yet its combination of these motifs with the native tropical vegetation makes it a unique and compelling ensemble.[6]

Estates such as Vizcaya were built by a class of newly wealthy individuals who had made fortunes exploiting the riches of the American continent. From about 1890 until the economic Depression of the 1930s, Italian-style gardens were a nationwide phenomenon, built from Boston to Miami, and from Chicago to Los Angeles, seemingly without regard for the suitability—or more often the unsuitability—of the terrain, climate, and native vegetation. In other words, the impetus for building "Italian Gardens in America" was initially social and cultural, rather than suggested by the surrounding landscape itself. As an example, one could hardly imagine a more inhospitable location for building an Italian garden than the one at Vizcaya. The original site was a forbidding tangle of dense forest and mangrove swamp at the edge of Biscayne Bay. The enchanting changes of level in the gardens of Vizcaya are entirely man-made, the result of a great expenditure of money and vast (re)arrangements of earth, water, and vegetation.[7] Other examples range from the singular beauty of Arcady, the Knapp Estate in Montecito, California, to others that make the case that the epithet "Italian Garden" had more cachet than authenticity in early-twentieth-century America.[8] In spite of the popularity of the Italian garden with the public, however, a vigorous debate was being conducted in the professional literature of the time regarding the appropriateness of American designers' "imitating" the art of another culture instead of creating a "native" garden style.[9]

A parallel—but less widely known or acknowledged—phenomenon during the same era was the use made by American designers of the basic principles of the Italian garden as a model, not only for the estates of the wealthy, but also for gardens associated with middle-class suburban dwellings. Imagery of the Italian garden had so permeated American popular culture by the 1920s that it was being widely used in advertising—Kodak cameras, for example, appeared surrounded by Italian cypress—as well as informing the décor of theaters, restaurants, and the rooftop gardens of urban hotels.[10] The ideas associated with an Italian garden clearly appealed not only to members of the elite class who could afford to actually create one on their private estates, but also to the bourgeoning middle class. For the latter, the Italian garden was viewed as the paradigm of all gardens with aspirations to gentility: its axial paths, hedges, and connections to the house bringing order to the exuberant plantings of native and naturalized vegetation, while views of the surrounding landscape contrasted with the intimacy of its private garden rooms through which one passed in anticipation of continual variety and delightful surprise.

Coincidence does not imply causation; yet the temporal juxtaposition of these two phenomena, namely, the rise in popularity of the Italian garden itself—in both elite and popular American culture—and the sharp increase in availability of printed images of the Italian garden, suggests an investigation into their mutual influence. As noted above, the turn of the twentieth century witnessed a number of advances in the printing of photographic images, most notably the halftone, which simulates the continuous tone imagery of a photograph by re-creating it as a multitude of dots, varying in size, shape, or spacing. The halftone process had been used to print photographs as early as the 1850s; it was not until 1881, however, that a commercially successful method was patented, and not until the 1890s that the use of halftone blocks to reproduce photographs in popular publications became commonplace.[11] Figures 1 and 2 show two halftone reproductions from popular books of the time, comparing the garden of Weld, designed by Charles Adams Platt for Isabel and Larz Anderson in Brookline, Massachusetts, around 1900, with what was clearly its model, the flower garden of the Villa Pamphili in Rome.[12] Before he embarked on a career as an architect and landscape designer, Charles Platt was an etcher, who—typically for this

Fig. 1. "The Garden of Weld," photograph by Thomas Marr and Sons as printed in Louise Shelton, *Beautiful Gardens in America*, 1915.

Fig. 2. "Villa Pamphili, Rome, Stairway Leading to Casino," photograph by Mrs. Aubrey Le Blond [Elizabeth Hawkins-Whitshed], one of the prints making up Plate 84 in H. Inigo Triggs, *The Art of Garden Design in Italy,* 1906.

period—had gone to Europe to complete his artistic training. On a visit to Italy in 1892 Platt made photographic studies of a number of gardens. These, along with his brief text, were published in 1894 as *Italian Gardens,* the first book-length treatment of the subject in English.[13] In his introductory remarks, Platt notes that "the art of photography has been perfected . . . and the object of the present writer has been by its means to illustrate, as far as possible, the existing state of the more important gardens in Italy, leaving out the matter of research altogether, since a more profitable study of the subject can be made as the result of these *reproductions of nature.*"[14]

Platt was concerned, with some justification, that earlier European works on the Italian garden—the example he cites is a book of engravings by Charles Percier and Pierre Fontaine originally published in 1809—were, in fact, works of what he called "restoration," in which the images provided by the artist portray the gardens as he imagined they might have been rather than as an actual rendering of the site.[15] Platt's stated aim in writing his own book was to enable his readers (among whom, undoubtedly, he hoped would be his future clients) to understand the "fundamental principles which guided the original designers" of Italian gardens.[16] He believed that photography was the way to best achieve this understanding, although he allegedly also made measured drawings of the gardens, the latter not published, nor apparently saved for posterity. The fact that Platt used both drawing and photography to study gardens, although commonplace now, was then new. There is also a significant link between the two activities. Although photography—especially as practiced by amateurs with "point and shoot" cameras—is a more passive activity than drawing, both provide personally derived knowledge of a subject, in contrast to impressions gained from merely gazing upon an object. Zola's assertion that one cannot claim to have really seen something until one has photographed it is reminiscent of the architect's assertion that one can never really understand a building until one has measured and drawn it.[17] There is unquestionably a different kind of knowledge that comes through the hand and the pencil, and to some degree that is also true of taking a photograph. To photograph something is to select it, to possess it, and to "take" it with you, albeit in miniature form.

In addition to collecting photographs of gardens, Americans of this period famously collected the actual gardens themselves. Depending on the owner's resources, these collections ranged from modest to elaborate living museums of garden history. One extant example is Sonnenberg, in Canandaigua, New York, begun in 1902 by owner Mary Clark Thompson and architect Ernest Bowditch.[18] This ensemble originally included gardens in the Italian, French, and Japanese styles, as well as special garden rooms devoted to roses, lilies, and pansies. Other themes were a Blue and White Garden, Moonlight Garden, Old-Fashioned Garden, Rock Garden, a "Sub-Rosa" (by which they meant "secret") Garden, and a swimming pool called "The Roman Bath." What to make of this? It is reminiscent of the cabinets of curiosity in which Renaissance princes sought to create a microcosm of the known world.[19] Moreover, tourists often likened the Italian peninsula itself to a cabinet of curiosities, in which nature and art were collected and displayed in admirable harmony. Just so, photographs "give us the sense that we can hold the whole world in our heads—as an anthology of images."[20] From the very earliest days of photography, Louis Daguerre predicted that his invention would encourage and enable ordinary people to "form collections of all kinds, which will be the more precious because art cannot imitate their accuracy and perfection of detail."[21]

To photograph something is to allow for the possibility of manipulating it in ways not previously possible, both in photographic form and as a model for re-creating it in another environment, as here, specifically, the Italian garden in America. Charles Platt did both for his American audience: first, by retouching many of the photographs in his book, some quite dramatically, and then by re-creating specific features of the gardens for his clients. In addition to the garden of Weld, mentioned earlier, Platt also invoked Italian gardens in most of the other estates he designed in the early years of his career, most notably those at his own house in Cornish, New Hampshire, at Faulkner Farm in Brookline, Massachusetts, and at the Villa Turicum in Lake Forest, Illinois.[22] As to the former, in light of Platt's seemingly naive assertion that his photographs would stand as "reproductions of nature," it is instructive to compare his original glass plate negatives with the images actually published in his book.[23] As shown in figures 3 and 4, for example, Platt has edited his photograph for publication by removing the entire town of Bagnaia in this view from the fountain garden of the Villa Lante. Figure 3 is a print from his original negative; the image as published in *Italian Gardens* is shown in figure 4.[24] Clearly, Platt wanted to preserve the view of the garden features in the foreground without the distraction of the townscape beyond.

The changes made by Platt in his own photographs are revealing, however, of what he—and the contemporary reader of his book—understood as "reproductions of nature." There is a sense in which Platt, like many visual artists, may not have seen any inconsistency in presenting an image as a true representation of nature, while at the same time adding or removing details to "improve" it. Today, after nearly two centuries of critical analysis and commentary on photography, most observers would view these as different investigations of the subject. The camera was—and, in some contexts, still is—believed to record the "truth." At the same time, the art of landscape design—including the so-called natural garden style—is predicated on the notion that nature is even more "natural" when perfected and revealed by man's artistry. Thus Platt's retouching was—if not by our standards a reproduction of nature—then certainly a calling out in some way of its essential being. In our own time, we are consciously aware that the camera—and the resulting photograph—is interposed between photographer/viewer and the subject. Photographs—at least those under consideration in this essay—are reassuringly neutral and objective. Like other artists, however,

Fig. 3. "Fountain and flower-garden, Villa Lante," printed from the original glass plate negative by Charles Adams Platt, 1892. (Avery Architectural and Fine Arts Library, Columbia University)

Fig. 4. "Fountain and flower-garden, Villa Lante," retouched photograph by Charles Adams Platt, as printed in his *Italian Gardens*, 1894.

photographers choose their stance in the garden, altering or omitting features and deceiving the eye as they deem necessary. At the same time there are important differences between photography and the other arts. One has to do with the kind of information photographs contain, which includes the appearance of real objects, in space, at a given moment in time. The other arises from the attitude of the viewer, who wants to believe that a photograph portrays—at least at some basic level—an inescapable, inevitable "truth."

Before the photograph, the most significant medium documenting the appearance of gardens was the print. The inclusion of any kind of images with text was relatively rare, however, before the late nineteenth century because it was such a painstaking process to print them together—when both were created as relief images—or to print them separately and bind them together—if the image was made by an intaglio process. Others have written eloquently on the history of including text with images on the printed page.[25] Here, suffice it to say that the remarkable rise in the number of printed photographs in the popular press at the turn of the twentieth century was a phenomenon whose effects may be difficult for us to imagine today, surrounded as we are with a world of digital images. But the ubiquity of the images is only part of the story. To compare a print—no matter how beautiful or detailed—to a photograph of a garden scene is to be drawn to the fact that the photograph gives the viewer the impression of both *immediacy* and *verisimilitude.* In spite of the fact that both printmaker and photographer have omitted or included certain features, have established a point of view, and have, as we say, "framed" the subject, a photograph is still believed to be more reliable than a print. But it is more than just its resemblance to the "reality" we see around us. The photograph adds meaning to its subject in a way that differs from a print or a painting. I would characterize this meaning as a form of personalization—or even equation—of subject and viewer. When we look at a photograph we experience a *frisson* of recognition, telling us that "this could be a record of *my* visit to this garden," or "this image could have been created by *me.*" Unless we are artists, we don't feel that way about a print or a painting. The photograph personalizes the experience of the garden in a way that a more elite work of art does not, allowing us to feel present in the scene. It provides us with our own—albeit virtual and miniaturized—Grand Tour of Italian Gardens. Thus the "other" of the print is transformed into the "self" of the photograph. A photograph narrows the world down into a finite and, perhaps, desirably manageable space, inhabited only by the viewer and what is pictured in the image.

Looking at photographs is in some ways always a private, intimate, and delicious experience, whether or not others are present in the image. In fact, the absence of people in a garden photograph might be said to enhance its exclusiveness. Indeed, of all the photographs of Italian gardens published in the most well-known books of this period, almost none contain any people.[26] While the lack of a human presence in photographs from this period is no doubt in part due to technical reasons—specifically the long exposure necessary to make an 8" × 10" negative—it was also an aesthetic choice, and one with which many of us can still identify as we go about making individualized and personalized records of our interactions with the world. In a very real sense, these early-twentieth-century photographs of Italian gardens are stage sets, captured at a given moment, whether at their inception, prime, or decline.

Moreover, even if human beings are present, as in figure 5, an example from Platt's work showing two people at the Villa Borghese, their relationship to the viewer is not personal. They do not interfere with one's private visual experience of the garden; rather, they might almost be part of the garden furnishings. In this image two close friends or relatives are so absorbed in each other that they seem unaware they are being observed. At the same time, it is a scene—both timeless and particularized—to which many viewers can relate: nostalgic, romantic, slightly unkempt, with a reference to the classical past in the oval shape of the overgrown amphitheater where they are seated, the so-called Piazza di Siena, actually constructed in the late eighteenth century.

Indeed, for Americans, the link with the classical and Renaissance heritage of Italy was one of its chief attractions, imbued with the sense that this landscape had been the setting of the actions of a great civilization, now past its prime, whose mantle had been the destiny of Americans to assume. In the case of the Italian garden photograph and the American viewer, it is my contention that the ubiquitous and inexpensive photographic images available beginning in the 1890s—not just those in books and magazines, but also as picture postcards, stereographs, and *vedute* available for purchase from commercial photographers such as Alinari—contributed to a change in Americans' *thinking* about the Italian garden, altering the perception that it was one of the trappings of wealth and privilege; it became instead an amenity attainable by the middle class.[27]

Why the link of photography to the Italian garden, specifically, when photographs of every other kind of garden were available as well? The answer to this question is complex but—briefly and in my view—it has to do

Fig. 5. "Piazza di Siena, Villa Borghese," photograph by Charles Adams Platt, as printed in his *Italian Gardens,* 1894.

with the *mythos* of Italy: the appropriation of an older culture that seemed to answer many of the needs of a younger one in terms of a balance between art and nature, between the weight of history and the demands of modernity. In addition, it is not irrelevant that the Italian garden photographs well, much better than the expansive English garden, for example. It has the angles. The camera loves it. It *is* the *camera bella,* the beautiful room, with whose subject we (desire to) identify.

A decade after Platt's *Italian Gardens* appeared, Edith Wharton published the book frequently claimed to be the most influential for American readers on this subject. Her *Italian Villas and Their Gardens* was first issued as a series of periodical articles, in this case in the *Century* magazine, 1903–4, and then in book form by the same publisher.[28] Wharton was not yet the internationally famous novelist she was to become, but her 1902 novel set in Italy, *The Valley of Decision,* had met with unexpected success.[29] In addition, she had shown herself to be an arbiter of taste in *The Decoration of Houses,* a book credited as one of the founding documents of the so-called American Renaissance with its advocacy of a return to classical principles of architecture and interior design.[30] Thus the editors of the *Century* deemed Wharton an ideal choice to undertake a series of descriptions of Italian gardens for the popular press, to be illustrated with paintings by the well-known artist Maxfield Parrish, the latter commissioned separately.[31]

It seems that at first Wharton planned for *Italian Villas and Their Gardens* to be primarily a travel account, but as she became more involved in the work—and realized how little had previously been published on the subject—she changed the focus, providing more historical details and cultural context. She also began to see herself as an advocate for the Italian garden as a model for the American garden, if properly understood and adapted. A letter to her publisher requesting additional funds midway through her sojourn in Italy is revealing of the widening scope of Wharton's project. She was visiting many more villas than she had originally planned, she claimed, and taking "innumerable photographs, [which] I have developed on the spot in order to classify them."[32] Although the paintings by Parrish garnered the lion's share of the public's attention, both then and now, Wharton's book eventually included nineteen photographs (in comparison to twenty-six paintings by Parrish). There are also seven sketches of details, six of which are identified in Wharton's "List of Illustrations" as being "drawn from" photographs. Whether Wharton took all these photographs herself is unknown and perhaps irrelevant.[33] In the text of *Italian Villas and Their Gardens,* Wharton mentions photography only once, while describing Alessi's two villas at San Francesco d'Albaro: "At . . . [the villa] higher up the hill . . . a more hospitable welcome awaits the sight-seer. Here admission is easily obtained, and it is possible to study and photograph at leisure."[34] It seems reasonable to assume that she must at the very least have had a hand in selecting the illustrations for *Italian Villas*—except those by Parrish—based on the meticulous care with which she is known to have supervised every other aspect of the printing of her works.[35]

The photographs used to illustrate Wharton's book emphasize, with few exceptions, the architectural and sculptural features of the villas. There is a predominance of grand entrances, impressive gates, and facades, in contrast to Platt's frequent choice of "a secluded corner" for many of his images. Wharton's photographs are illustrative of the constant tension in her text between her dual—and not always compatible—aims in writing the book. On the one hand, she was determined to produce a scholarly work, which would be a definitive source of information on Italian villas and gardens. On the other, she wanted to direct the cultural aspirations of the reading public toward a greater appreciation of the Italian model by writing an entertaining and informative—but at the same time clearly didactic—account, one that warned Americans not to merely copy the details but to understand the principles, uses, and informing spirit of Italian gardens. At the first aim she clearly succeeded; nearly every subsequent major writer on the Italian garden has quoted or cited Wharton's book as a valuable resource (by contrast, almost no one mentioned Platt's book in the first eighty years or so of its existence). At the second she was also successful, but almost in spite of her weighty text and her photographs, which are for the most part poorly framed, incorrectly exposed, dark, and generally unappealing. Moreover, the photographs are actually at odds with her text in some ways. Wharton writes persuasively, for example, of the importance of understanding the purposes and uses of the Italian garden, which she considers essential to its transfer to an American setting. Yet her photographs do not provide examples of these uses. In sharp contrast to earlier prints of Italian gardens, which often show a great variety of visitors, from a range of social classes and engaged in numerous activities,[36] the Italian gardens portrayed in Wharton's photographs leave such activities to the imagination. Again, the iconic and idealized nature of late-nineteenth- and early-twentieth-century photographs of Italian gardens dominates, belying the discussion of "use" in the text.

In spite of these drawbacks, however, Wharton's photographs are more than just documentation of her architectural criticism. They are, for example, in spite of their monumentality, still a private and personalized experience of these spaces. As such, they are in some ways the perfect vehicle for negotiating our modern experience of the garden. As Sontag noted, "To see something in the form of a photograph is to encounter a potential object of fascination. Photographs, which cannot themselves explain anything, are inexhaustible invitations to deduction, speculation and fantasy."[37] There is also a sense in which Wharton's photographs perform the same function as

Parrish's paintings, which have an otherworldly, almost dream-like quality, suffused with light and saturated with color. Figure 6 shows an image of the reservoir at the Villa Falconieri, this one from the drawing by Parrish, which Wharton used, significantly, as the frontispiece for her introductory chapter entitled "Italian Garden-Magic."[38] Here Parrish has chosen to portray a part of the villa Wharton hardly mentions in her text. His painting depicts a mirror-like sheet of water whose calm surface reflects the ancient cypress trees in the background. The tiny ball-topped finial beneath the trees is the only suggestion of the massive retaining walls that, in a different kind of contrast, so interested Charles Platt in the latter's *Italian Gardens* (fig. 7).[39] Parrish's brimming water and seemingly infinite vista, combined with the carefully shaped and arranged trees, are reminiscent of Hunnewell's Italian garden. Both are enchanted worlds where water, sky, and vegetation combine into a landscape of infinite possibility, thereby increasing both its desirability and its promise.

In this context it is significant that both Platt and Parrish—as hundreds of artists have done before and since—used photographs as aide-mémoire from which to compose their finished works. However, when Platt painted out Bagnaia—and made his other "improvements" of one art with another—he generally did not bring this change to our attention. Parrish, on the other hand, readily admitted that in some ways painting from a photograph after the fact is better than painting at the scene, "for a *literal rendering* of the material facts can be avoided, and *the part that stays in the mind* can the better be brought out, the spirit and atmosphere of the place."[40] Though a superb draftsman, Parrish eventually decided to use the camera to "sketch" time-consuming aspects of his paintings such as landscape backgrounds and drapery. He apparently felt that their skills in this regard (his and the camera's, that is) were equally matched.

George Eastman's development of the first practicable roll film in 1884 and his patent of the Kodak camera in 1888 enabled millions of middle-class people to make their own photographs. American students of landscape architecture were no exception, and they increasingly began to use photographs to study and document gardens. One notable example is Edward Lawson (1884–1968), a 1913 graduate of Cornell, who was awarded the first Fellowship in Landscape Architecture at the American Academy in Rome. His extensive stay in Italy, prolonged by World War I, is partially recorded in his sketchbook, now in the Rare and Manuscript Collections of Cornell University Library.[41] This record of Lawson's studies differs markedly from eighteenth- and nineteenth-century artists' sketchbooks by his inclusion of

Fig. 6. “The Reservoir, Villa Falconieri,” Frascati, drawn by Maxfield Parrish, as printed in Edith Wharton, *Italian Villas and Their Gardens,* 1904.

Fig. 7. "A Frascati Reservoir" [Villa Falconieri], photograph by Charles Adams Platt, printed from the original glass plate negative and used in *Italian Gardens,* 1894. (Avery Architectural and Fine Arts Library, Columbia University)

photographs on almost every page, many taken by him with an inexpensive camera, others purchased from commercial vendors. The photographs he and other academy fellows selected for the records of their garden experiences served a specific didactic purpose. They were placed side by side with their sketches and measured drawings of the same garden feature, enhancing the student's ability to prepare finished drawings in the studio as well as to re-create these features for future clients. Although the primary subject of Lawson's studies was the Villa Gamberaia—for which he made an impressive wash drawing of the plan, also in the Cornell collections—Lawson visited, sketched, and photographed many other Italian gardens as well. For Lawson and other students, the photograph was an important method of organizing experience and thus reordering and reimagining it.[42]

Another landscape architect who took her own photographs for educational and didactic purposes was Martha Brookes Hutcheson (1871–1959). In her book *The Spirit of the Garden,* published in 1923, she cites numerous examples of how the principles of Italian gardens could inform middle-class American gardens.[43] It is clear from a study of her book that Hutcheson derived her basic architectural ideas about garden design from her study and knowledge of Italian gardens, which she translated and simplified for her American audience. For example, she contrasts a classical Italian stone grape arbor with a structure of her own design made of inexpensive materials—upright posts of natural wood with rough fence rails as beams, covered with grapes, roses, and gourds, plants native to America—to make the point that the *principles* of their design, placement, and use are identical.

The work of professional photographer Frances Benjamin Johnston (1864–1952) appeared in countless articles about gardens in popular magazines during the 1920s and 1930s, notably *Country Life in America, House Beautiful,* and *House & Garden.* She and her sometime partner Mattie Edwards Hewitt (d. 1956) were also commissioned to document many private gardens and estates, including the Villa Vizcaya mentioned earlier in this essay. They also made some of the earliest color photographs of American gardens. Johnston's 1926 exhibition of her photographs featured many Italian gardens, including an image of the Villa Falconieri at Frascati used as the cover of her exhibition catalog.[44] Johnston and her work have always been undervalued because so much of it was considered primarily documentary in nature.[45] But even if that is the case, it increases the relevance of her work in this particular instance. As the examples used throughout this essay have shown, most of our recent understanding of all types of gardens derives from our experience of them as photographs, thus blurring traditional distinctions between elite and bourgeois art and design.

The photograph is the emblem of its time, and time is an important dimension of garden making. A photograph captures the ever-changing garden at a certain moment to which it—and we—can never return except by means of the photograph itself. Consequently, photographic images set up a powerful personal relationship between subject and viewer, engendering in the latter both desire for the subject and belief in its attainability. In the specific examples discussed here, widely disseminated images of Italian gardens influenced the course of American garden design in the early twentieth century, not only in the creation of the desire for "Italian" gardens at elite country estates, but also affecting the work of many professional garden designers and informing the aspirations of the middle-class garden builder and consumer. In the end, designers—professional and amateur alike—are influenced by a myriad of factors in the choices they make: cultural, personal, aesthetic, emotional, topographical, often even political. The late nineteenth and early twentieth centuries were a period of exploration into a number of different design modalities in the United States, most of them readily available in photographic images. Yet of all the possibilities pictured in photographs and discussed in the literature, it was the Italian garden, specifically, that became most influential, and for two primary reasons. The first was the importance of the larger cultural and political connections between Italy and America. The second was unquestionably the seductive nature of its reproduced image. The Italian garden, Americans were persuaded to believe, embodied the perfect balance of art and nature, of classical and romantic, of public pomp and private delight. Thus through the medium of photography the Italian garden was made accessible, collectible, and transformable in the American landscape.

Notes

I would like to thank Raffaella Fabiani Giannetto for inviting me to participate in the "Foreign Trends on American Soil" conference at the University of Pennsylvania, where this paper was originally presented, and for a number of stimulating and useful conversations about our mutual interest in the re-creation of Italian gardens in America. I would also like to thank Diane Brown for her close reading and cogent suggestions on an earlier version of this paper.

1. Marc Treib's review essay, "Frame, Moment and Sequence: The Photographic Book and the Designed Landscape," *Journal of Garden History* 15 (Summer 1995): 126–34, raises some of the issues I discuss here—for example, our continuing belief in the objectivity of photographs, as well as their selection, framing, and relationship to text—but primarily within the context of their assemblage in book form.

2. Susan Sontag prepared the way for such an investigation more than three decades ago in her series of essays *On Photography* (New York: Farrar, Straus & Giroux, 1977). While my thinking in the present essay has been informed by her work, particularly in the matter of using photography as a tool of appropriation of the object photographed, I am seeking here to extend such concepts—and others—to understanding gardens as a form of cultural transmission.

3. For specific aspects of the influence of the Italian garden on the profession of land-

scape architecture in the United States, as well as a general overview, see Rebecca Warren Davidson, "Images and Ideas of the Italian Garden in American Landscape Architecture" (PhD diss., Cornell University, 1994).

4. For images of some of these "Italianate" gardens, see the remarkable series of chromolithographs by E. Adveno Brooke in *The Gardens of England* (London: T. McLean, 1856).

5. The Hunnewell garden is extant and remains privately owned. For further information, see Alan Emmet, *So Fine a Prospect: Historic New England Gardens* (Hanover, NH: University Press of New England, 1996), 84–100.

6. The cascade at the Villa Corsini was well known to American designers. Although Vizcaya's builder James Deering and his architects probably saw it on one of their visits to Rome, it was also the subject of many subsequent drawings, photographs, and quotations, notably in the gardens of the Swan House in Atlanta, designed by American Academy in Rome fellowship in architecture winner Philip Trammell Schutze. See also R. H. Wilcox, "Villa Corsini—Rome: Cascade," *Landscape Architecture* 11 (April 1921): 119–23, reprinted in *Architectural Record* 49 (May 1921): 392–97, which includes the author's text, his measured drawings, and—significantly in this context—his photographs. For an admiring account of the Villa Gamberaia in an early-twentieth-century American publication, see B. C. Jennings-Bramly, "The Gardens of the Villa Gamberaia," *House and Garden* 5 (February 1904): 49–56. Gamberaia was also praised by Edith Wharton as having "almost every typical excellence of the old Italian garden" in her influential *Italian Villas and Their Gardens,* illustrated with pictures by Maxfield Parrish (New York: Century, 1904), 46. In the same volume she provides a lengthy discussion and description of Isola Bella (197–206).

7. The estate was saved from destruction in 1952 when it was purchased by Dade County; it is now a public museum. For more details about Vizcaya, see Rebecca Warren Davidson, "Past as Present: Villa Vizcaya and the 'Italian Garden' in the United States," *Journal of Garden History* 12 (January–March 1992): 1–28; and Witold Rybczynski, Laurie Olin, and Steven Brooke, *Vizcaya: An American Villa and Its Makers* (Philadelphia: University of Pennsylvania Press, 2007).

8. Many—both appropriately and inappropriately designated by their owners or designers as "Italian" gardens—are pictured and described in Mac Griswold and Eleanor Weller, *The Golden Age of American Gardens: Proud Owners, Private Estates, 1890–1940* (New York: Abrams, 1991).

9. The contrasting viewpoints are exemplified, on the one hand, in James Sturgis Pray's series of articles, "The Italian Garden," *American Architect and Building News* 67 (February 10, 1900): 43–45, (February 17, 1900): 51–52, (March 17, 1900): 83–85, and (March 24, 1900): 91–92, in which Italian garden design is praised as a model worthy of emulation by American designers; and on the other, by the anonymous author of the "Books and Papers" column in volume 78 of the same journal (December 20, 1902), 95, who insisted that "all the machinery of exedras, pergolas, terraces, well-curbs and architectural gewgaws generally are sheer make-believes, an impertinent affront flung by the uneducated in the very face of the genius of the country."

10. The Venetian Pool in Coral Gables, Florida, and the Venetian Theatre in Milwaukee, Wisconsin, both built in the 1920s, are among countless places of leisure and

recreation in the United States designed to resemble Italian gardens. See also the interior of the Capitol Theatre in Chicago designed as an "Italian Garden" in G. H. Edgell, *The American Architecture of Today* (New York: Charles Scribner's Sons, 1928), 329, 331.

11. For a basic explanation that mentions the importance of the halftone process to the publishing industry, see Brian Coe and Mark Haworth-Booth, *A Guide to Early Photographic Processes* (London: Victoria & Albert Museum/Hurtwood Press, 1983), 23, 102; and Michael Twyman, *Printing, 1770–1970: An Illustrated History of Its Development and Uses in England* (London: British Library/Reading University Press, 1998), 31–32.

12. This image of the Villa Pamphili was made by one of the most notable early women photographers of Italian gardens, Mrs. Aubrey Le Blond. Née Elizabeth Hawkins-Whitshed, she was also an expert mountain climber and allegedly the first person to make films of mountaineering subjects. Her own book, *The Old Gardens of Italy: How to Visit Them* (London: John Lane, 1912), is illustrated entirely with her own photographs.

13. Charles A. Platt, *Italian Gardens* (New York: Harper & Bros., 1894); first issued as two articles in *Harper's New Monthly Magazine* 87 (July 1893): 164–80, (August 1893): 393–406. The definitive reference on Platt is Keith N. Morgan, *Charles A. Platt: The Artist as Architect* (New York: Architectural History Foundation; Cambridge, MA: MIT Press, 1985). Morgan also edited the reprint edition of Platt's *Italian Gardens* (Portland, OR: Sagapress/Timber Press, 1993).

14. Platt, *Italian Gardens,* 15, emphasis added.

15. Charles Percier and Pierre Fontaine, *Choix des plus célèbres maisons de plaisance de Rome et de ses environs* (Paris: P. Didot, 1809).

16. Platt, *Italian Gardens,* 15.

17. "À mon avis, vous ne pouvez pas dire que vous avez vu quelque chose à fond si vous n'en avez pas pris une photographie révélant un tas de détails qui, autrement, ne pourraient même pas être discernés." Zola allegedly said this in an interview he gave in 1901, subsequently published in the English review the *King,* but while it is frequently quoted, a written citation remains elusive.

18. For Sonnenberg, see Griswold and Weller, *Golden Age of American Gardens,* 88–89, and Lynn Lewis Monroe, *Sonnenberg Gardens, Canandaigua, N.Y.: A Splendid Collection of Gardens* (Alfred, NY: 1985).

19. Giuseppe Olmi, "Science-Honour-Metaphor: Italian Cabinets of the Sixteenth and Seventeenth Centuries," in *Grasping the World: The Idea of the Museum,* ed. Donald Preziosi and Claire Farago (Aldershot, UK: Ashgate, 2004), 129–43.

20. Sontag, *On Photography,* 3.

21. Louis-Jacques-Mandé Daguerre, "Daguerreotype," in *Classic Essays on Photography,* ed. Alan Trachtenberg (New Haven: Leete's Island Books, 1980), 12.

22. For Charles Platt's work in landscape architecture, see Rebecca Warren Davidson, "Charles A. Platt and the Fine Art of Landscape Design," in *Shaping an American Landscape: The Art and Architecture of Charles A. Platt,* ed. Keith N. Morgan (Hanover, NH: University Press of New England, 1995), 74–95.

23. For Platt's quote see Platt, *Italian Gardens,* 15. The negatives are now part of the Charles Adams Platt Architectural Records and Papers, 1879–1981, Department of Drawings & Archives, Avery Architectural & Fine Arts Library, Columbia University.

24. The reprint edition of *Italian Gardens,* published in 1993, did not for the most part

use the photographs as they were published in the original articles and book, including this one of the Villa Lante. Instead, they were specially reprinted from Platt's glass plate negatives. One may speculate why this was done by those in charge of the reprint—especially as it purports in other ways to be a facsimile—but the unfortunate result is to leave today's uninitiated reader in the dark about Platt's "retouching." Only by comparing the photographs as printed in the original book with the glass plate negatives can these changes be seen and understood.

25. In particular, William M. Ivins, *Prints and Visual Communication* (New York: Da Capo Press, 1969) and, more recently, Richard Benson, *The Printed Picture* (New York: Museum of Modern Art, 2008).

26. In addition to Platt, notable early-twentieth-century works on the Italian garden containing primarily photographs include those by Charles Latham, *The Gardens of Italy* (London: Country Life/G. Newnes, 1905); H. Inigo Triggs, *The Art of Garden Design in Italy* (London: Longmans, Green, 1906) and Luigi Dami, *Il giardino italiano* (Milan, 1924), *The Italian Garden* (New York: Brentano's, 1925).

27. *Una storia della fotografia italiana nelle collezioni Alinari: 1841–1941* (Florence: Alinari, 2006).

28. Edith Wharton, "Italian Villas and Their Gardens," *Century* 67 (November 1903): 21–33, (December 1903): 162–64, (February 1904): 562–72, (April 1904): 860–74), and 68 (August 1904): 540–54, (October 1904): 884–902; Wharton, *Italian Villas and Their Gardens.*

29. Edith Wharton, *The Valley of Decision* (New York: Charles Scribner's Sons, 1902). *The House of Mirth,* which forged her reputation—and incidentally provided the funds to augment her own estate, The Mount, in Lenox, Massachusetts, with an Italian garden—appeared in 1905.

30. Edith Wharton and Ogden Codman Jr. *The Decoration of Houses* (New York: Charles Scribner's Sons, 1897).

31. For more details on the genesis of *Italian Villas and Their Gardens,* see Rebecca Warren Davidson, "Opposites Attract: The Garden Art of Charles Platt, Maxfield Parrish, and Edith Wharton," in *Edith Wharton and the American Garden* (Lenox, MA: The Mount, 2010).

32. Wharton to Richard Watson Gilder, March 18, 1903, reproduced in *The Letters of Edith Wharton,* ed. R. W. B. Lewis and Nancy Lewis (New York: Charles Scribner's Sons, 1988), 82.

33. Research in the archives of the Century company at the New York Public Library and in Wharton's letters has so far not resulted in a definitive answer to this question. She probably took some of the photographs herself and may have also hired a photographer. It seems unlikely the photographs used in the book were purchased from commercial firms, since even in the early twentieth century Fratelli Alinari, for example, would not have permitted publication of their work without attribution.

34. Wharton, *Italian Villas and Their Gardens,* 189.

35. The photographs were important enough to Wharton that she even included their mention on the title page: "Illustrated with pictures by Maxfield Parrish, and by photographs."

36. See, in particular, those by Giovanni Battista Falda published in *Li giardini di Roma* (Rome: Giovanni Giacomo de'Rossi, after 1677).

37. Sontag, *On Photography,* 23.

38. Wharton, *Italian Villas and Their Gardens,* 4.

39. For unknown reasons, Platt did not identify this photograph specifically as the Villa Falconieri, although it clearly shows the walls of that villa's reservoir.

40. Maxfield Parrish to Spencer Penrose, September 15, 1919, emphasis added. For a detailed description of how Parrish used photography to create his paintings, quoting from his own unpublished manuscript, "Maxfield Parrish's Technique," see Coy Ludwig, *Maxfield Parrish* (New York: Watson-Guptill, 1973), 198–200.

41. Edward G. Lawson Papers, #4237, Division of Rare and Manuscript Collections, Cornell University Library.

42. Among other early Cornell winners of the Rome Prize in Landscape Architecture were Ralph E. Griswold (1923), Norman T. Newton (1926), and Michael Rapuano (1930). All three men—under the editorial direction of Lawson, who taught landscape architecture at Cornell from 1922 to 1940—compiled albums of photographs of Italian gardens, as well as photographs of their own measured drawings of the villas. These were used as teaching materials by the department for many years and are now part of the Rare and Manuscript Collections of Cornell University Library.

43. Martha Brookes Hutcheson, *The Spirit of the Garden* (Boston: Atlantic Monthly Press, 1923), reprinted with a new introduction by Rebecca Warren Davidson (Amherst: University of Massachusetts Press, 2001).

44. Hewitt made the photographs for the first major documentation of Vizcaya, which appeared in "Vizcaya: The Villa and Grounds, A House in Miami, Florida," *Architectural Review* 5 (old series 22), no. 7 (July 1917): 121–67. For examples of Johnston's and Hewitt's color photography, see Louise Shelton, *Beautiful Gardens in America* (New York: Charles Scribner's Sons, 1915). The catalog of Johnston's exhibit was entitled *In Old World Gardens* (New York: Ferargil Galleries, 1926).

45. See Maria Elizabeth Ausherman, *The Photographic Legacy of Frances Benjamin Johnston* (Gainesville: University Press of Florida, 2009) for a more recent and appreciative assessment of Johnston's work.

PART 4

The American Identity as Perceived by the Americans and the Foreigners

Considering Fitness and Fairness

The Search for American Identity in *Garden and Forest*

ERIC MACDONALD

After enduring nearly three months of cold and blustery weather, the winter-weary residents of New York City greeted the clear skies and mild temperatures of Saturday, March 28, 1896, as a sign that "the budding time of year" had arrived at last. Bicyclists flooded the city's parks and boulevards, weekend vacationers flocked to New Jersey's seaside resorts, and gardeners prepared the soil for spring vegetables and flowers.[1] For one New Yorker, however, the day brought a different kind of springtime satisfaction: William A. Stiles, himself an enthusiastic horticulturist and promoter of public parks and outdoor recreation, had just completed his work on the 423rd issue of *Garden and Forest,* the weekly horticultural periodical for which he was managing editor (fig. 1). Stiles was especially pleased because, in addition to the periodical's typical content of horticultural news, botanical information, and gardening advice, this edition of *Garden and Forest* was to feature an editorial article that eloquently presented a rational argument for how Americans ought to view and design their surroundings—a vision of future American landscapes that Stiles and his collaborators had struggled to articulate for nearly nine years. While his fellow New Yorkers reveled in "the pleasantest day of spring," Stiles took a few moments to compose a letter to Charles Eliot, the young landscape architect who had authored the article. Eliot's essay, Stiles wrote, was "one of the most discriminating and useful articles that has ever been published in 'Garden and Forest,' that is, it states principles which have never before been stated, or, at least, which have not been defined and separated from other matters so cleanly and clearly." Two days later, Stiles offered a further compliment: "If it teaches all of our readers as much as it has taught me, you ought to feel gratified as an educator."[2]

Entitled, "What Would Be Fair Must First Be Fit," Eliot's essay ostensibly addressed the increasingly heated disputes that had surfaced in the horti-

Fig. 1. Portrait of William A. Stiles from *Garden and Forest* 10, no. 503 (1897): 401.

cultural press regarding the proper place of architectural elements, ornamental details, and horticultural novelties in American landscape design. Beyond merely adjudicating the current quarrel about the relative merits of "formal" versus "informal" design, however, Eliot's editorial expounded on the essential meaning and core purpose of landscape design. Significantly, it also crystallized the logic that *Garden and Forest* writers had devised for assimilating foreign plants and garden styles to North American environments, while also fostering the evolution of a modern and distinctively "American" mode of landscape design. Like many of their contemporaries, Eliot, Stiles, and other *Garden and Forest* contributors sought to understand how a steady influx of people, plants, and ideas from foreign lands might shape future American landscapes. Which foreigners should be admitted? Which should be turned away? How should such decisions be made? And once newcomers were admitted, how might they be assimilated into a unified, harmonious, and beautiful whole? The strategy articulated in *Garden and Forest*—and the one proposed by Eliot and endorsed by Stiles—was rooted in an appeal to Anglo-American gardening culture, Darwinian evolution, and pragmatic logic: "what would be fair, must first be fit."

Garden and Forest

The first issue of *Garden and Forest* appeared on February 29, 1888, a venture initiated during the previous year by Charles Sprague Sargent, the first director of Harvard University's Arnold Arboretum and a leading authority on North American forests and woody plants (fig. 2). Sargent's interest in creating *Garden and Forest* initially stemmed from his desire to bridge what he perceived to be a widening gap between scientific and popular discourse

Fig. 2. Portrait of Charles Sprague Sargent, ca. 1890, by George Collins Cox. (Photograph courtesy of the Arnold Arboretum Horticultural Library of Harvard University, © President and Fellows of Harvard College. Arnold Arboretum Archives)

in the United States. In his 1888 report to the president of Harvard, Sargent noted that while botanical and horticultural research sponsored by institutions like the Arnold Arboretum had produced an ever-expanding "mass of facts about plants," there was no effective way to communicate this knowledge to the many people who had become interested in these topics.[3]

Wishing to make scientific and other expert knowledge more widely available to the public, Sargent recruited the aid of several collaborators, including Frederick Law Olmsted Sr., who viewed *Garden and Forest* as a vehicle for advancing the nascent profession of landscape architecture—a motive that Sargent also supported.[4] From his previous work as a journalist and editor, Olmsted contributed valuable experience and knowledge about the business of periodical publishing. The success of *Garden and Forest,* however, hinged even more critically on the expertise brought by William A. Stiles (1837–1987), who became the journal's managing editor. During the previous three decades, Stiles had built a distinguished career as a newspaper writer and editor, serving as a member of the editorial staff of the *New-York Tribune* and as the agricultural correspondent for the *Philadelphia Press.* An avid horticulturist and a member of the New York City Park Commission, he had become one of Olmsted's staunchest allies in defending the integrity of New York's Central Park and advocating the preservation of Niagara Falls.[5] With additional financial backing from several investors, Sargent, Olmsted, and Stiles conceived *Garden and Forest* as a weekly journal of "horticulture, landscape art, and forestry"[6] (fig. 3). As Olmsted had hoped, the cause of advancing landscape architecture fell squarely within *Garden and Forest*'s mission.[7] For Sargent and his collaborators, however, the *means* by which *Garden and Forest* would fulfill its mission were as important as the journal's content and scope: the journal's first issue informed readers that *Garden and Forest* intended to promote these fields by placing "scientific information clearly and simply before the public" and presenting "the conclusions reached by the most trustworthy investigators."[8] *Garden and Forest* was to be, first and foremost, a popular publication devoted to upholding the integrity and practical merit of scientific investigation.

With Stiles as its managing editor and Sargent as the journal's "conductor," *Garden and Forest* set out to accomplish its mission by publishing contributions from a diverse community of distinguished professionals.[9] The publication's network of "trusty investigators" included botanists, horticulturists, foresters, landscape designers, nature writers, and art critics, and it spread across the North American continent as well as overseas.[10] While writers with elite pedigrees enjoyed prominence in *Garden and Forest,* Sar-

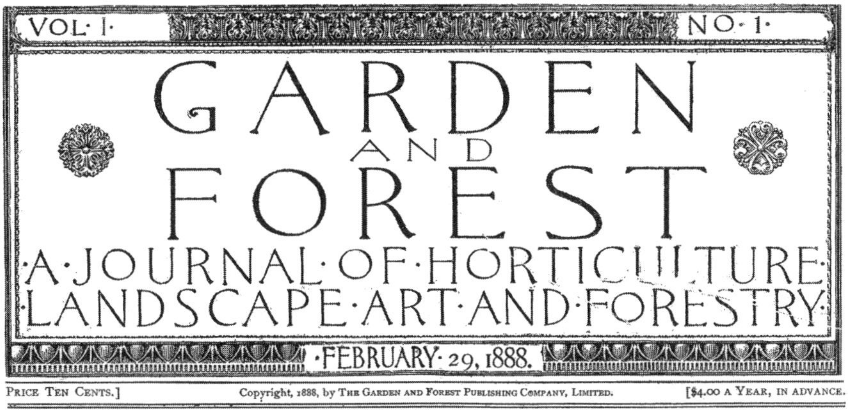
VOL. I. NO. I.
GARDEN AND FOREST
A·JOURNAL·OF·HORTICULTURE·LANDSCAPE·ART·AND·FORESTRY·
·FEBRUARY·29, 1888.
PRICE TEN CENTS.] Copyright, 1888, by THE GARDEN AND FOREST PUBLISHING COMPANY, LIMITED. [$4.00 A YEAR, IN ADVANCE.

Fig. 3. Masthead from the first issue of *Garden and Forest* 1, no. 1 (February 29, 1888).

gent and his colleagues intended to create a popular periodical, not an elitist one. They encouraged readers to submit letters and articles, and much of the dialogue that consequently emerged within its pages evoked a spirit of collaboration that spanned social distinctions based on gender, vocation, and education. Frequent contributors to *Garden and Forest* included journalists, schoolteachers, businessmen, farmers, and amateur gardeners, as well as scientists and professional landscape designers, horticulturists and foresters. Indeed, the journal might be appropriately characterized as a discourse community—an assemblage of writers and readers who coalesced around discussions about the interrelations of people, plants, and the environment.[11]

For these discussions to occur, participants had to employ a common language capable of spanning disciplinary boundaries, as well as the social distinctions among academics, professionals, and laypersons. In *Garden and Forest,* this language was rooted foremost in botanical science and popular nature study. Writers discussed "right" and "wrong" ways to investigate nature throughout the journal's ten-year run, and most authors steadfastly upheld the premise that amateur nature study should closely model professional scientific practices. In letters to the editor, readers signaled their concurrence with this imperative, for example, by insisting that discussions about plants should employ Latin terms and the Linnaean system of taxonomy rather than "common" or vernacular terminology.[12] On the surface, such conversations were about the relationship between science and popular nature study practices. However, debates about vocabulary also functioned as a tacit community self-policing activity, as well as a way to let readers know they belonged to a distinct community: *Garden and Forest* contributors and their readers shared a unique language that was set apart from the "common" vernacular of the general public.

In addition to upholding principles of scientific inquiry and discourse, contributors to *Garden and Forest* also widely endorsed Charles Darwin's theory of evolution by natural selection. Many writers implicitly accepted a Darwinian view of nature, suggesting that—within this community at least—evolution was regarded not as a contestable theory but as a taken-for-granted "law" of nature.[13] Thus, in addition to conveying useful botanical and horticultural information, writers also constructed their texts to model good scientific practices, demonstrate the practical value of scientific inquiry, and uphold the modern theory of evolution.

While professional science served as a foundation for conversations about plants and landscapes in *Garden and Forest,* both scientists and amateur gardeners also borrowed liberally from the vocabulary of art and aesthetics. Authors regarded both empirical description and aesthetic evaluation to be necessary to a holistic understanding of the significance of plants. Academic botanists frequently commented on the aesthetic qualities of plants and landscapes, while writers who focused on aesthetic concerns often presented their evaluations interwoven with descriptive botanical information. In language that was sometimes explicit but often subtle and nuanced, writers posited that the practices of the artist and those of the scientist complemented one another.[14]

Art, Science, and the Nature of Landscape Design

In *Garden and Forest* the premise that science and art offered complementary modes of enquiry became fundamental to discussions about gardening and landscape design. Indeed, a lively discussion about the relation between art and technique in design emerged within the journal's inaugural issue, sparked by the first installment of Mariana Van Rensselaer's four-part essay on the evolution of modern landscape gardening.[15] Van Rensselaer proclaimed the English landscape garden to be the foundation of "modern" landscape design. She suggested that the development of naturalistic design in England during the eighteenth and early nineteenth centuries heralded a more sophisticated manipulation of nature's own materials, and that it constituted a significant artistic advancement because the gardener's work came closer to producing "effects which under fortunate conditions nature might produce without man's aid."[16] While the true artist of landscape never produced exact copies of nature, she insisted, the artist nonetheless conceived "his general idea in deference to the local prescriptions of Nature" and developed "his general scheme as artistic fitness may seem to counsel." Subservience to "local prescriptions" required the artist to "discover the special features and details which are needed to perfect [his idea] (considering which Nature will permit among those he might desire); and then, half consciously perhaps, search for memories of natural results which may teach him how to achieve his own."[17]

Van Rensselaer's definition of landscape gardening maintained artistic "imagination" as the essence of art, relying on Romantic ideals such as *genius loci* and the "perfection" of Nature's forms through divine inspiration or intuition.[18] Her evocation of "artistic fitness" and "the local prescriptions of nature," however, were seeds for rooting the practice of garden art within the fertile soil of contemporary science—seeds that were readily taken up and sown by other *Garden and Forest* writers.[19] In subsequent discussions about gardening, numerous authors recast *genius loci* as a notion that referred not to abstract, ideal forms of beauty, but to the perfection of real, local nature—site-specific phenomena that could be described and understood via scientific investigation. Indeed, in *Garden and Forest* conversations about horticulture and gardening often explored the possibility that beautiful landscapes might result less from "half-conscious" discovery, as Van Rensselaer had suggested, and more from systematic, empirical study. The scientific discourses that populated the journal offered new possibilities for thinking about foundational principles of art, such as composition, unity, harmony, variety, and fitness, and thus provided writers with new perspectives on the relationship between form and function in landscape design. For many *Garden and Forest* writers the chief aim of landscape design extended well beyond simply creating ideal scenery. While not divorced from aesthetic concerns, design was about attaining an optimal "fit" between human needs and the natural conditions of a place, a kind of ideal relationship that served human purposes while also conserving and perfecting the natural beauty inherent in situ.

Aside from establishing a framework for discussing landscape design in terms of both contemporary aesthetics and science, Van Rensselaer's essay also initiated inquiry into the relation between gardening traditions and national identity. In characterizing the English landscape garden as the root of the "modern" art form—and, indeed, as a significant advance over previous gardening traditions—Van Rensselaer implied that a process of cultural evolution was at work.[20] Other writers similarly proposed that each culture evolved its own "imaginative charm," which was woven into its garden traditions. One editorial, for example, suggested that the "formality" of Italian gardens was an expression of the "stateliness, of mystery, or classic grace" that characterized Italian culture. French gardens likewise displayed "the restraints of that Gallic taste," while the gardens of the Netherlands reflected the "orderliness, practicality, straightforwardness and simplicity" of the Dutch.[21] Such resonances between garden traditions and broader cultural dispositions were thought to emerge from a civilization's slow attunement to the unique climate and geology bestowed upon it by nature. Distinctive forms of garden art were believed to coalesce organically as human communities learned, through the labors of multiple generations, how to interpret and harmonize with local nature.[22]

Contributors to *Garden and Forest* surmised that a truly American garden art would be borne through a similar evolutionary process. Once Americans had evolved a garden style that differed from those of their predecessors and neighbors, its perfection was "but a matter of time and study and adaptation to our changing circumstances," wrote Mary Caroline Robbins in an 1894 editorial.[23] Similar sentiments resounded through the pages of *Garden and Forest,* and they were often infused with a sense of anticipation. The United States seemed poised to usher in a new phase of sophistication in landscape design. For example, New York City's Central Park was frequently acclaimed as a landmark achievement in design, as well as a distinctly American work. In 1897 the editors characterized the development of public parks in the United States as a "national art"—works that were unparalleled artistic expressions of American culture, as well as a force for unifying an increasingly diverse and geographically dispersed population.[24]

The Quest for an American Style

While the editors and other *Garden and Forest* writers looked forward to a time when the United States would evolve a mode of landscape design that surpassed its European antecedents, many observers admitted that an authentic American style had yet to emerge.[25] Writers attributed the immaturity of American gardening culture to several factors, particularly the nation's status as a "new country" that had been settled only recently by European immigrants. Rather than adapting to the natural conditions they encountered in the New World, these settlers had attempted to impose foreign plants and garden traditions on the land. Although some of their efforts had been successful, many horticultural endeavors had utterly failed or proven to be poorly suited to North American climate and geology. Moreover, in focusing on transplanting European flora and gardens to New World environments, immigrants had too often overlooked the beauty and usefulness of indigenous plants. The editors speculated that American enthusiasm for "so-called 'decorative gardening'" represented a lingering desire to create "something trim and prim, ornate and artificial" in the landscape "as a sign that nature has been subjugated."[26]

Other cultural dispositions—particularly the tendency of Americans to abandon their home places in pursuit of fortune and adventure in some far-off frontier—seemed to impede the development of a true national style of gardening. Because of the nation's relative youth and its notoriously restless, "shifting population," American landscapes lacked "the interest which accompanies long continued human association," declared one *Garden and Forest* editorial. In most parts of the country, nature had yet to be "subdued into that tranquil and home-like aspect which is worn only where generation has succeeded generation, each impelled by a strong local attachment to its birthplace to conserve and develop its native beauties with affection and intelligence."[27] In essence, the status of American garden art was explained in terms of the larger narrative of cultural adaptation and evolution embraced by *Garden and Forest* contributors: an American style had yet to mature because Americans had not developed an intimate knowledge of, and affinity for, the nature that graced the places they called home.

This "frontier thesis" of American horticultural history implied two challenges for those who wished to hasten the birth of a true American style.[28] First, they would have to loosen the hold of Old World traditions on American gardening and landscape practices. Second, they would have to nurture a greater knowledge of local nature and a deeper attachment to home and place. On both accounts, foreign influences were cause for concern. Indeed, by the close of the nineteenth century, American gardens seemed increasingly populated by plants whose ancestors had originated in other places. To the eyes of many *Garden and Forest* contributors, these exotic species appeared glaringly out of place.[29] Modern horticulturists also had contributed to this dilemma through plant breeding and propagation efforts that one editorial characterized as "efforts to perpetuate freaks of nature, which, had she been left to herself, would never have multiplied in any appreciable extent."[30] The editors suggested that when American gardeners introduced such artificial novelties into the landscape, they were eschewing "nature's essential scheme" and "weaving in materials foreign to her local ideal."[31]

Exotic plants were not the only foreign elements being woven into the landscape tapestry, however, nor were commercial nurserymen the only agents easing their passage to American shores. Importers and manufacturers provided American gardeners with an abundance of statuary, urns, sundials, and other ornamental elements modeled on neoclassical garden art, while books and popular magazines celebrated the romance of old European gardens and generated interest in the history and gardening traditions of other parts of the world. In the United States and abroad, popular writers revived interest in Old World garden design practices, while a profusion of photographs, commercial lithographs, postcards, and other visual materials provided the American public with seductive glimpses of these faraway places. A growing number of Americans also gained firsthand familiarity with European gardening traditions through travel abroad, while aspiring architects increasingly sought training at European academies such as the Ecole des Beaux Arts in Paris. Moreover, a casual glance through the pages of *Garden and Forest* reveals that each week the journal itself delivered a steady stream of foreign influences to sway the imaginations of its readers away from "nature's local ideal." These circulated through descriptions of historic and contemporary gardens in foreign countries, accounts of exotic and strange plants from other regions of the world, and reports of new ornamental hybrids and cultivars—not to mention numerous commercial advertisements[32] (fig. 4). Thus, while the editors and other contributors to *Garden and Forest* cautioned against the use of foreign elements in American landscapes, advertisers and other contributors extolled their virtues.

The commingling of seemingly contradictory messages about the value of foreign garden elements was not a sign of duplicity on the part of *Garden and Forest*'s publishers, nor was it necessarily troubling for the journal's readers. Indeed, a liberal and cosmopolitan attitude was integral to the journal's mission of broadly disseminating the "mass of facts about plants" that was accumulating throughout the world, and *Garden and Forest*'s pages accordingly featured descriptions of gardening and horticultural developments in other countries. These appeared in reports on forest management practices in Europe and Asia, accounts of botanical expeditions and new plant discoveries from far-flung corners of the world, letters from institutions such as the Royal Botanic Gardens at Kew, and excerpts from foreign papers such as England's *Gardener's Chronicle,* France's *Revue Horticole,* and Germany's *Gartenflora.* Such editorial practices aligned with the ecumenical and progressive attitudes that the editors and other contributors associated with American civilization. Moreover, faith in modern science and

February 3, 1892.] Garden and Forest. v

MISS FLORA CULTURE: "What is that strikingly bold flower?"
JOHNSON & STOKES: "That is the Single-Flowered Tuberous Begonia. The new floral sensation."
MISS FLORA: "Can I raise them as large as that, and will they grow for me? I don't know much about Begonias."
J. & S.: "Most certainly you can! They require no special skill, but will repay any care you give them. Pot them early, and set out in the open ground when warm enough. If you have a place where they will be shaded part of the day, save that for the Begonias, though this is not essential. Water well in dry weather."
MISS FLORA: "What colors do they come in?"
J. & S.: "It would take less time to tell what colors they *don't* come in! But their flowers run from Pure White through all shades of Yellow, Pink, Rose, Orange-Scarlet to fiery Crimson."
MISS FLORA: "What about the Double Varieties?"
J. & S.: "They are exquisitely beautiful, many of them rivaling the rose in form and coloring. You will find them described, with many other Floral Beauties, in our **Money Growers' Manual**, sent free, provided you send 4 cents in stamps, to pay postage, and mention Garden and Forest."
MISS FLORA: "How much does it cost to enjoy these beautiful Begonias?"
J. & S.: "Our prices are—

FOR STRONG BLOOMING BULBS.

Single Varieties, in Finest Mixture, 15 cents each; $1.50 per dozen, post-paid. $10.00 per 100 by Express.
Single Varieties, in Separate Colors: Crimson, Pink, White, Yellow and Orange, 20 cents each; $2.00 per dozen, post-paid. $14.00 per 100 by Express.
Double-flowering kinds, Splendid Mixed, 40 cents each, $4.00 per dozen, post-paid.

FOR SEED.

Single Mixed, all Colors, 25 cents per packet.
Double " " " 25 cents " "

JOHNSON & STOKES,
217 and 219 Market Street, PHILADELPHIA, PA.

EVERGREENS 6 inches to 8 feet. Shade Trees, etc.
R. DOUGLAS & SON,
751 Genesee Street, Waukegan, Ill.

MEN OF REFINEMENT, who love the Rare and Beautiful, should send for our list of three hundred varieties of BEAUTIFUL EVERGREENS Natives of all lands.
EVERGREEN NURSERIES, Evergreen, Wis.

EVERGREENS
AND FOREST TREES.
Catalogue Free. Send for it.
For Wind-breaks, Ornament, etc., Hardiest Varieties, Nursery grown Scotch Pine, 2 to 3 feet, $10 per 100. Scotch and Austrian Pine seedlings, 12 to 15 inches, $10 per 1000. Other sizes and varieties in proportion. Over 10 million for sale.
Good local Agents Wanted.
D. HILL, Evergreen Specialist, Dundee, Illinois.

Readers of Garden and Forest are requested to mention that paper in corresponding with advertisers.

INCUBATORS & BROODERS
Brooders only $5. Best and Latest Invention on raising Poultry. Address, Geo. S. Singer, Cardington, O

HATCH CHICKENS BY STEAM.
IMPROVED EXCELSIOR Incubator
Will do it. Thousands in Successful Operation.
SIMPLE, PERFECT, and SELF-REGULATING.
Guaranteed to hatch a larger percentage of fertile eggs, at less cost, than any other Incubator.
Send 6c. for Illus. Catalog.
Circulars free.
Lowest priced first-class Hatcher made.
GEO. H. STAHL, Pat. & Sole Mfr., Quincy, Ill.

Tickle The Earth
With a Hoe, SOW FERRY'S SEEDS and nature will do the rest.
Seeds largely determine the harvest—always plant the best—FERRY'S.
A book full of information about Gardens—how and what to raise, etc., sent free to all who ask for it. Ask to-day.
D. M. FERRY & CO., P. O. Box 1233 DETROIT, MICH.

Costs only a Cent.
Send us your address on a postal card; by next mail we will send you a Buck-Thorn fence circular full of good points and suggestions about Fence Building; cheap at a dollar to any fence builder. If the Buck-Thorn Solid Steel Barb Fence is not sold in your neighborhood we will ship it to you from the mill, *all freight paid.*
The Buck-Thorn Fence Co., Trenton, N.J.

Barb Wire Nowhere.
Where parties are well acquainted with the Buck-Thorn, I can get one cent a pound more for it than for any other wire, and can just "knock the stuffing" out of barb wire at half a cent more.
O. P. Griffith, Connersville, Ind.

Parsons & Sons Co.
Limited.
Kissena Nurseries, Flushing, N. Y., offer
Rhododendrons
of American grown hardy sorts.
Hardy Azaleas.
For other rare and old plants, see Catalogue.

OUR TREES GROW!
Because like a GOOD BOY they are properly raised. Our Catalogue for 1892 is just what you want if you are going to plant Trees, Plants, Evergreens or Shrubs, and want to buy at PRICES that are RIGHT. How can you afford to do without our Catalogue? It is sent FREE TO ALL WHO APPLY.
FREEPORT NURSERIES, Freeport, Ill.

FIRE! FIRE! FIRE!
A. H. HEWS & CO.
Wish to inform their customers that, notwithstanding the recent disastrous FIRE in their Factory, through the kindness of their friends in the trade they will be able to fill all orders which they may receive with an excellent quality of
STANDARD FLOWER POTS.
All orders will receive prompt attention.

Fig. 4. Advertisements for exotic and "showy" plants of the type criticized by many *Garden and Forest* authors, from *Garden and Forest* 5, no. 206 (February 3, 1892).

professional expertise, which constituted core values of the *Garden and Forest* community, provided writers with the means to embrace foreign plants and garden ideals while at the same time restricting the extent to which they might impede the achievement of an American style. By grounding landscape design in modern science and placing more of this work in the hands of competent professionals, Americans could ensure that their art would develop in harmony with nature.

Assimilating "Vegetable Immigrants" and Other Foreigners

Garden and Forest writers sought to contain foreign influences by appealing to contemporary evolutionary theory and pragmatic logic. In place of horticultural novelties, the editors of *Garden and Forest* worked tirelessly to promote the use of native American species in both public and private landscapes, an effort that many *Garden and Forest* contributors eagerly embraced. Botanists, horticulturists, amateur naturalists, and gardeners collaborated to discover the horticultural potential of wild North American plants and to advocate their cultivation in gardens and landscapes (fig. 5). While *Garden and Forest* writers often noted that native American plants were generally hardier than exotics, they also extolled their aesthetic virtues. "If, in ornamental planting, we used only the materials which nature supplies in the neighborhood of our homes," the editors argued in one of many articles that addressed the subject, American planters could be assured that their landscape compositions would never be discordant in terms of form, texture, or color.[33] In contrast to foreign plants or "showy garden specimens" purchased from commercial nurserymen, "species brought in from the native forest" would necessarily harmonize with the local scenery[34] (fig. 6). By limiting themselves to a palette of indigenous materials, American gardeners could hardly go wrong.

Aside from their presumed hardiness, native plants were considered to be essential to American landscape gardening because only local materials could cultivate the sympathy for nature required to produce authentic works of art.[35] Unlike "showy" exotics or "foreign" specimens, native plants could engender affective bonds to place, thereby turning a mere habitation site into a true home. Artificially produced cultivars and "foreign" plants were unable to nurture a "love for Nature in her loveliest forms" or develop "united, home-keeping, truly domestic habits of life."[36] For this reason, the use of exotic plants in public parks was of special concern. Many *Garden and Forest* writers hoped public parks would provide American citizens with appropriate models for developing private residential grounds.[37]

Public parks thus performed a double function: while serving as examples of modern and distinctively American works of landscape gardening, they also were vehicles for inspiring popular interest in nature study, a trend that *Garden and Forest* contributors hoped would contribute to the eventual perfection of American gardening. The capacity of public parks to perform these functions, however, hinged upon how civic leaders conceived, constructed, and maintained these landscapes. An approach based

Fig. 5. Illustration of *Rhododendron (Azalea) arborescens,* typical of the numerous botanical drawings that appeared in *Garden and Forest.* From Charles Sprague Sargent, "Rhododendron (Azalea) arborescens," *Garden and Forest* 1, no. 34 (October 17, 1888).

on the preservation of native vegetation and the exclusion of large ornate buildings, gardenesque features, and other costly details was essential to optimize the educational influence of public grounds.[38] Parks thus joined native plants as crucial resources for cultivating affective bonds to place and thereby advancing American garden art.

Although *Garden and Forest* editors heartily endorsed the use of native plants, they stopped short of categorically prohibiting foreign species

Fig. 6. "Rhododendrons in a Natural Wood, at Westbrook, Long Island," from *Garden and Forest* 8, no. 383 (June 26, 1895).

in American landscapes. An 1891 editorial, for example, noted that exotic plants might be "mingled" among natives in order to "give variety, interest and a true garden-like air and charm," as long as the foreigners were chosen to "harmonize with the other plants about them." For this reason, the editors urged gardeners to carefully select plants that originated "from lands with climate akin to our own." This advice was suggested by "Nature's own example," the editors added, since "Nature chooses which exotics she will grow for what we may call scientific reasons, but the artistic effect of her results is invariably good." Nature's example also seemed to support the democratic ideals, entrepreneurial spirit, and cosmopolitan potential of American culture, for the editors noted that American society itself was not made up only of people who were "originally American." Nature "takes up vegetable immigrants as hospitably as our civilization takes in human immigrants, and assimilates them as quickly and as naturally," the editors observed.[39] The most important question for American landscape designers was therefore not so much whether to admit immigrants, but how to choose among them and how to settle the chosen ones comfortably into the American scene.

Like human immigrants, "vegetable immigrants" could be welcomed to American soil as long as they were not allowed to take up residence indiscriminately and could prove themselves capable of living in harmony with their new neighbors.[40] Indeed, even the most exotic and "conspicuous" plants might find homes in American gardens if they were restricted to "locations specially set apart for them where they will not injure the main picture formed by the general environment of the house and the encircling landscape."[41] This imperative arrayed garden plants in a kind of natural hierarchy of fitness; it was the gardener's responsibility to respect this order in the designed landscape. Of first rank were species that grew naturally in the forests, meadows, and wetlands just beyond the gardener's dooryard. By restricting themselves to only these plants, and by arranging them in ways that followed nature's example, American gardeners were almost nearly assured success in their efforts to perfect the landscape picture suggested by nature (fig. 7). Of subordinate rank were plants imported from foreign lands that approximated the geologic and climatic conditions of North American environs. These species were assumed to be naturally well adapted to growing in similar American environments; the gardener might therefore carefully select and integrate them into the landscape for added artistic effect. The lowest stratum of the horticultural hierarchy was occupied by exotic plants that had "developed under other climatic conditions," along with the artificial inventions of modern horticulturists.[42] The latter, like exotic specimens imported from far-off lands, were poorly adapted to American conditions. Gardeners were therefore advised to use these plants sparingly and to restrict them to special settings.[43]

In addressing how elements of formal garden art ought to be incorporated into the American landscape, *Garden and Forest* writers devised a rationale that mirrored their hierarchical ordering of native and nonnative plants: if the beauty of all naturally evolved plants derived from the way in which nature had adapted them to their home environments, true garden art likewise might be assumed to be the natural result of cultural practices that evolved in harmony with the natural environment. This line of reasoning implied that legitimate forms of garden art might be as numerous as the varied environments found throughout the world. "There is no reason why one kind of gardening only should be used; indeed, there is every reason why different styles should be employed for different purposes in different places," advised an editorial published in the May 4, 1892, issue of *Garden*

Fig. 7. "A Group of Staghorn Sumachs on the Border of a Lawn," from *Garden and Forest* 2, no. 73 (July 17, 1889).

and Forest.[44] Hence, rather than categorically excluding a garden tradition that had originated in a foreign land, the matter had to be resolved in terms of its ability to be assimilated to the surrounding environment and its intended function. An 1893 article concisely summarized the editors' position: "each system of design is right in its own place."[45]

Although this view gave gardeners permission to accommodate foreign garden styles in American landscapes, it also effectively restricted them to specific situations—the use of formal design elements was to be sanctioned only by "some natural or architectural peculiarity."[46] With respect to natural "peculiarities," the editors hypothesized that American environments themselves would impede the widespread adoption of formal gardens modeled on European precedents. For example, the editors believed that the severe cold of North American winters would ruin sculptures and other decorative stonework that were essential elements of Italian gardens, while frost would make the construction of extensive terraces and architectural details impractical. In the South, where winters were more moderate, American gardeners confronted humid summers, tropical storms, and heavy soils that dramatically contrasted with the salubrious climate and terrain of the northern Mediterranean.[47]

Aside from environmental constraints, *Garden and Forest* writers assumed that social and economic factors as well as racial dispositions would further limit the current fashion for "geometrical" gardens. "Our Teutonic blood predisposes us to a more spontaneous and general love for Nature than for art, and thus to an instinctive preference for naturalistic rather than architectonic ideals in gardening," the editors stated in 1893. "We are not likely ever to become so enamored of formal gardening that we shall turn to it in cases where landscape-gardening would serve us better," they reassured readers. Given this deep-seated inclination, the editors reasoned that greater knowledge of formal garden design might even prove beneficial if it better prepared Americans to recognize when formal elements were useful and when they were merely "needless and, therefore, inharmonious and inartistic."[48] As with exotic plants, foreign architectural elements were not to be categorically banned from American landscapes, but rather carefully adapted with respect to environmental and cultural imperatives.

While such reasoning may have reassured *Garden and Forest* readers that American gardens would evolve in the naturalistic mode, many writers also admitted that an authentic American style of naturalistic design could not be derived simply by appropriating forms and techniques from the English landscape garden.[49] Landscape architect Charles Eliot effectively argued this view in the journal's first volume. In an article entitled "Anglomania in Park Making," Eliot attacked American attempts to create "English smoothness" everywhere, while disregarding environmental constraints and the distinctive aesthetic qualities of the locality. He advised Americans to forgo "futile striving after the loveliness of England or any other foreign land." Instead, he urged his readers to appreciate the diversity of natural scenery found on the continent, and "try to perfect each type in its own place."[50] The trouble with "Anglomania," then, was not so very different from attempts to emulate the formal gardens of Europe: in imposing a foreign garden style on the landscape, Americans spurned the *genius loci* that was the true source of authentic works of landscape art. As a path toward greater understanding of nature, scientific study of local environments provided a way for Americans to neutralize "Anglomania" and other foreign influences, thus furthering the evolution of an incipient American style.

Considering the Fit and the Fair

While writers like Eliot continued to frame discussions about landscape gardening in terms of artistic composition, their insistence that aesthetic principles ultimately derived from nature also suggested how this art might incorporate the techniques of natural science. Aesthetic concepts such as "composition," "harmony," and "fitness" were easily recast into the lexicon of science that circulated so prominently within the pages of *Garden and Forest.* The notion of composition, for example, acquired new connotations when published amid numerous accounts by professional botanists and amateur naturalists that cataloged the array (or "composition") of native species found growing in particular North American locales. Likewise, the concept of harmony suggested a fortuitous association of species in a particular place—a set of ecological relations that *Garden and Forest* writers often described as "nature's arrangements"—while the concept of fitness implied a view of interspecies relations that had obvious resonance with Darwin's concept of natural selection.[51] Such semantic resonances helped *Garden and Forest* writers envision how American landscape design might become more systematic and empirical, relying less on intuition, and more on scientific observation and exacting imitation of nature's own methods.

Several contributors to *Garden and Forest* worked to reframe prevailing naturalistic design methodology to incorporate systematic inventories of natural systems, using knowledge borrowed from modern geology and biogeography. The clearest expression of the shift toward science surfaced in discussions about parks and regional park systems, particularly those addressing the writings and work of Charles Eliot (fig. 8). While certainly concerned with beauty, Eliot regarded landscape design as fundamentally a problem-solving profession, addressing regional-scale questions "and many other problems" of urban development that were "equally difficult of solution." Moreover, this art was conservative, centering on practical questions such as how to add roads and buildings to a landscape without destroying nature.[52] During the winter of 1890, *Garden and Forest* began promoting Eliot's efforts to establish a system of "metropolitan reservations" in the region surrounding Boston. Eliot characterized his metropolitan work as a "scientific Park System" that was to include examples of the region's most distinctive and typical landscapes, including stretches of shoreline and islands, tidal estuaries, bogs, forests, and small urban parks.[53]

In 1896, Eliot outlined the underlying premises of a scientific mode of landscape design practice in an essay entitled "What Would Be Fair Must First Be Fit"—the essay that had impressed William A. Stiles as one of the most important articles ever published in *Garden and Forest.* Eliot began by addressing the increasingly acrimonious debate raging among those who promoted unrestrained ornament and novelty in both public and private gardens, those who insisted that all landscapes should be molded in an image of ideal nature, and those who demanded a strictly architectural ap-

Fig. 8. Portrait of Charles Eliot, from Charles William Eliot, *Charles Eliot, Landscape Architect* (Boston: Houghton Mifflin, 1902).

proach to design. Faced with a cacophony of voices, average Americans were understandably bewildered by the confusing and "strange conflict of modern doctrine concerning beauty in the surroundings of daily life," as Eliot suggested. Yet all of the confusion and quarrelling was really quite absurd, Eliot argued—for lost in these clashes of modern dogma was an acknowledgment of one true, universal principle: "The cause of the failure to attain to beauty in these and all similar cases is doubtless the same; it is (is it not?) the common lack of rationality at the foundation." *Reason,* Eliot suggested, was the key to achieving true beauty in the surroundings of everyday life.[54]

The path to true beauty, Eliot asserted, could be deduced from carefully observing the general laws that governed all of nature. "How is it that so much of the natural scenery of the world is beautiful and that so many myriad kinds of living things are lovely?" Eliot asked. Echoing Darwin's evocation of nature's wonderfully "entangled bank," Eliot reminded readers that it was "one of the commonplaces of science that the form which every vital product takes has been shaped for it by natural selection through a million ages, with a view to its use, advantage or convenience, and that beauty has resulted from that evolution."[55] Taking this analogy further, Eliot inferred the "same natural law" of evolutionary beauty at work in "the humanized landscape of the world." In the rural, vernacular landscapes of New England, which had evolved in accord with humble commonsense, Eliot discerned a lesson that he urged his modern contemporaries to heed: they would succeed only when their work deferred to "the law of nature"—that is, when it achieved an optimal state of evolutionary "fitness." While Eliot conceded that "beauty does not consist in fitness," he nevertheless insisted that "all that would be fair must first be fit."[56]

In seeking an optimal fit between human purposes and the restraints imposed by nature, Eliot concluded that humanized landscapes, in most cases, would be "generally and fittingly informal" and geometric and symmetrical "only occasionally and for good reasons." Eliot thus maintained the superiority of naturalistic design, without categorically dismissing the forms of garden art admired by architects and ornamental horticulturists. In appropriating the evolutionary principle of fitness, Eliot's appeal to reason also suggested that modern landscape designers merely needed to return to the prescient "good sense" of landscape gardeners like Humphry Repton. If the "quarreling faddists" were to do this, Eliot suggested, they might once again resume "the advancement of Repton's real and much needed art of arranging land, vegetation, buildings and the resultant landscape for the use and delight of men."[57]

By presenting his philosophy of landscape design in terms of time-honored English naturalistic tradition—indeed, in adapting well-worn premises of mimetic art to suit his own rhetorical purpose—Eliot positioned his approach as the inevitable next phase in a trajectory already charted by Repton. Fused with Darwinian natural selection and a notion of cultural evolution as embodied in the rural landscapes of New England, William Wyndham's and Humphry Repton's notions of "fitness" or "conformity to purpose," in the context constructed by Eliot, gained a wholly new meaning.[58] This tacit reframing allowed Eliot to avail himself of the ascendant cultural authority of science in late-nineteenth-century America, while also firmly anchoring his ideas in a familiar and widely revered Anglo-American tradition. In suggesting that human culture developed according to natural laws of evolution, Eliot set the stage for a return to Repton's pragmatic approach to design, while also implying that the goal of attaining optimal fitness was really what naturalistic landscape design had been moving toward all along.

Conclusion

For readers like William A. Stiles, the appeal of Eliot's essay no doubt stemmed from the degree to which it effectively synthesized the rhetoric that had circulated through the pages of *Garden and Forest* during the previous nine years. Eliot not only subsumed the process of assimilating foreign styles to universal laws of nature, but he also sketched a coherent vision of how a future American style of landscape design might evolve. While *Garden and Forest*'s commitment to advancing the art and science of landscape gardening demanded that the journal maintain a cosmopolitan attitude with respect to the myriad varieties of this art, this imperative was in tension with the desire of many writers to nurture a truly distinctive national style of gardening. The American public's increasing fascination with foreign plants and garden art borrowed from other lands accentuated this tension. In response, contributors to *Garden and Forest* devised a design logic that evaded the contemporary and often bitter disputes about whether formal or natural gardens were "higher" or "lower" forms of art, or whether the appearance of "foreign" garden elements on American soil should be welcomed or turned away. They accomplished this by articulating a philosophy of garden-making that retained historical continuity with Old World design traditions, while also responding to late-nineteenth-century social conditions.

Garden and Forest contributors focused on how foreign influences might be woven into the larger project of nurturing a cosmopolitan yet truly distinctive national landscape. The history and character of American civilization itself seemed to preclude the outright rejection of foreign "immigrants," whether they were human, vegetable, or ideological. The imperative of treating all immigrants with respect and civility did not imply that all possessed the same capacity to contribute to American civilization, however. Some newcomers were presumed to be more highly evolved than others: those originating from places with climatic and environmental conditions resembling those found in North America were presumed to possess traits that would help them flourish in the New World. Accordingly, immigrants needed to be sorted on the basis of naturally inherited traits, and directed to their rightful place in society, and in the landscape. Garden and landscape design thus appeared as but one facet of the much greater project of forging disparate elements into a harmonious civilization—a civilization that would advance only by operating in harmony with the natural environment that gave it vitality and beauty.[59]

In late-nineteenth-century America, biological science offered a promising framework for defining the relations that would constitute this fortuitous linkage of nature and culture. The logic of garden making, as articulated in *Garden and Forest,* wove principles of science and art within a conceptual framework of environmental determinism, Darwinian natural selection, and an incipient ecological sensibility. While not divorced from aesthetic concerns, this mode of landscape design went well beyond simply creating ideal scenery. Instead, it strove to attain an optimal fit between human needs and local nature, a kind of ideal relationship that served human purposes yet also conserved and perfected natural beauty inherent in specific places. Scientific study, as a mode of inquiry and a source of knowledge about nature, was an essential tool for achieving this result. In its reassertion of *genius loci* as a fundamental principle of design, this philosophy was ostensibly timeless, yet in its appeal to contemporary science it was also undeniably "modern." In embracing this duality, *Garden and Forest* contributors also devised a response to foreign elements that was uniquely "American," and one that would prove useful in attempts to answer the growing popularity of "foreign trends" in gardening.

Notes

1. "Among the Wheelmen," *New York Times* (hereafter *NYT*), April 1, 1896, 6; "Bad Weather for Horses," *NYT,* March 30, 1896, 6; "Cape May Becoming Lively," *NYT,* March 29, 1896, 9; "City's Signs of Spring," *NYT,* April 1, 1896, 9; "Good Weather at Atlantic City," *NYT,* March 29, 1896, 21; "The Weather Forecast," *NYT,* March 28, 1896, 3; "Yesterday's Weather," *NYT,* March 29, 1896, 4.

2. William A. Stiles to Charles Eliot, March 28, 1896, and March 31, 1896, qtd. in Charles William Eliot, *Charles Eliot, Landscape Architect: A Lover of Nature and of His Kind, Who Trained Himself for a New Profession, Practised It Happily and through It Wrought Much Good,* introduction by Keith N. Morgan (Amherst, MA: University of Massachusetts, in association with Library of American Landscape History, 1999), 553.

3. Charles S. Sargent, "The Arnold Arboretum," in *Annual Reports of the President and Treasurer of Harvard College, 1887–88* (Cambridge, MA: Harvard University), 139. For further details about the founding and production of *Garden and Forest,* see Shen Hou, *The City Natural: Garden and Forest and the Rise of American Environmentalism* (Pittsburgh: University of Pittsburgh Press, 2013).

4. For a brief assessment of *Garden and Forest*'s place in Olmsted's biography, see Laura Wood Roper, *FLO: A Biography of Frederick Law Olmsted* (Baltimore: Johns Hopkins University Press, 1973), 474. Roper counts the discontinuance of *Garden and Forest* in 1897 as one of a number of "staggering reverses for the emerging profession of landscape architecture" during the 1890s.

5. See the obituary notice published in the October 13, 1897, issue of *Garden and Forest* (399–400) for a summary of Stiles's career, as well as a sense of the high esteem that backers of the journal had for him and his contributions to the publication. See also "Park Commissioner Stiles," *NYT,* October 7, 1897, 6; M. B. Coulston, "Stiles, William Augustus," in *Cyclopedia of American Horticulture . . . ,* ed. Liberty Hyde Bailey and Wilhelm Miller, 1724–1725 (New York: Macmillan, 1900); Phyllis Andersen, "'Master of a Felicitous English Style': William Augustus Stiles, Editor of *Garden and Forest,*" *Arnoldia* 60, no. 2 (2000): 39–42; Cynthia Zaitzevsky, "The Olmsted Firm and the Structures of the Boston Park System," *Journal of the Society of Architectural Historians* 32, no. 2 (1973): 167–74; Roper, *FLO,* 404.

6. Both Olmsted and Sargent supported the venture financially. Sargent also secured financial backing from many of the "Boston Brahmins" who had funded the arboretum.

7. In developing the journal's masthead, the founders of *Garden and Forest* apparently settled on *landscape art* as the best term to characterize the broad field of environmental design. During the 1890s, authors employed various terms when referring to the professional practice of landscape design, including *landscape architecture, landscape gardening, landscape art,* and *rural art.* The editors and other authors most frequently used *landscape gardening* in articles that discussed the topic. Throughout this essay, when discussing a particular primary text I adopt the term employed by the text's author. When speaking of the practice generally, I use the more generic term, *landscape design.* For a contemporary perspective on the terminology issue, see Mariana Griswold Van Rensselaer, "Landscape Gardening.—A Definition," *Garden and Forest* (hereafter *G&F*) 1, no. 1 (1888): 2. For a more recent discussion, see Joseph Disponzio, "History of the Profession," in *Landscape Architectural Graphic Standards,* ed. Leonard J. Hopper (Hoboken, NJ: John Wiley & Sons, 2007).

8. "Garden and Forest: An Illustrated Weekly Journal of Horticulture, Landscape Art and Forestry," *G&F* 1, no. 2 (1888): iii.

9. Since most editorial articles printed in *Garden and Forest* were unsigned, it is often difficult to attribute authorship to a particular individual. Sargent probably authored most of the articles pertaining to forestry and botany and many of the editorials about the theory and practice of landscape gardening. William A. Stiles also wrote about landscape gardening, however, and he almost certainly composed some of the editorials about public park controversies, particularly those concerning New York City's parks. Mariana Van Rensselaer, Mary Caroline Robbins, Charles Eliot, Sylvester Baxter, and other individuals also contributed editorial articles. Often, but not always, authorship by these individuals was acknowledged in a byline. Unless the identity of the author was specified in the journal, or is known from another source, I attribute editorials to the "editors" in a generic and collective sense.

10. Prominent *Garden and Forest* contributors included foresters Gifford Pinchot and Bernhard Fernow, botanists Charles E. Bessey and John Coulter, horticulturist Liberty Hyde Bailey, nature writer Mary Treat, art critic Mariana Van Rensselaer, as well as landscape architects Frederick Law Olmsted and Charles Eliot.

11. For approaches to viewing scientific and professional fields as discourse communities, see Brit-Louise Gunnarsson, "Sociohistorical Construction of Scientific Discourse," in *The Construction of Professional Discourse,* ed. Britt-Louise Gunnarsson, Per

Linell, and Bengt Nordberg (London: Longman, 1997), 99–126; Ellen Valle, "A Scientific Community and Its Texts: A Historical Discourse Study," in *Construction of Professional Discourse,* 76–98; Charles Bazerman and James G. Paradis, eds., *Textual Dynamics of the Professions: Historical and Contemporary Studies of Writing in Professional Communities* (Madison: University of Wisconsin Press, 1991). For the social processes involved in producing scientific and popular texts, see Greg Myers, *Writing Biology: Texts in the Social Construction of Scientific Knowledge* (Madison: University of Wisconsin Press, 1989); Christopher P. Wilson, "The Rhetoric of Consumption: Mass-Market Magazines and the Demise of the Gentle Reader, 1880–1920," in *The Culture of Consumption: Critical Essays in American History, 1880–1980,* ed. Richard Wightman Fox and T. J. Jackson Lears (New York: Pantheon, 1983), 39–64. For perspectives on how the production and genres of popular periodicals shaped habits and practices of readers, see David Paul Nord's essays on "communities of reception" in *Communities of Journalism: A History of American Newspapers and Their Readers* (Urbana: University of Illinois Press, 2001), 175–277.

12. See for example, "The Study of Botany by Horticulturists," *G&F* 1, no. 6 (1888): 62–63; P., "The Study of Botany," *G&F* 3, no. 109 (1890): 159; Mariana Griswold Van Rensselaer, "Botany for Young People," *G&F* 3, no. 105 (1890): 97–98.

13. The editors consistently upheld the validity of Darwinian evolutionary theory, a position that began with the first editorial to appear in *Garden and Forest:* "Asa Gray," *G&F* 1, no. 1 (1888): 1.

14. As one reader noted, the practices of both scientists and artists required "close" observation of nature and generally increased one's "powers of observation." George Cumming, "The Study of Botany," *G&F* 3, no. 123 (1890): 325. Professional scientists also echoed this view. See Edward L. Greene, "California Woods in Autumn," *G&F* 1, no. 36 (1888): 422–23; Van Rensselaer, "Botany for Young People."

15. Mariana Griswold Van Rensselaer, "Landscape Gardening.—A Definition," *G&F* 1, no. 1 (1888): 2; "Landscape Gardening.—II," *G&F* 1, no. 2 (1888): 14–15; "Landscape Gardening.—III," *G&F* 1, no. 3 (1888): 27; "Landscape Gardening.—IV," *G&F* 1, no. 4 (1888): 38–39. For an extended discussion of Van Rensselaer's four-part *Garden and Forest* essay on landscape design, see Judith K. Major, "Mariana Griswold Van Rensselaer's Landscape Gardening Manifesto in *Garden and Forest,*" *Landscape Journal* 26, no. 2 (2007): 183–200. For assessments of Van Rensselaer's place in American landscape design history, see Judith K. Major, "Mariana Griswold Van Rensselaer," in *Pioneers of American Landscape Design,* ed. Charles A. Birnbaum and Robin S. Karson (New York: McGraw-Hill, 2000), 403–4; Mariana Griswold Van Rensselaer, *Accents as Well as Broad Effects: Writings on Architecture, Landscape, and the Environment,* ed. David Gebhard (Berkeley: University of California Press, 1996); and Thaisa Way, *Unbounded Practice: Women and Landscape Architecture in the Early Twentieth Century* (Charlottesville: University of Virginia Press, 2009), 20–21, 25.

16. Van Rensselaer, "Landscape Gardening.—A Definition," 2.

17. Van Rensselaer, "Landscape Gardening.—IV," 39.

18. On the social construction of artists' identities, see Joanne Cubbs, "Rebels, Mystics, and Outcasts: The Romantic Artist Outsider," in *The Artist Outsider: Creativity and the Boundaries of Culture,* ed. Michael D. Hall and E. W. Metcalf Jr. (Washington, DC:

Smithsonian Institution Press, 1994), 77–93; Catherine M. Soussloff, *The Absolute Artist: The Historiography of a Concept* (Minneapolis: University of Minnesota Press, 1997).

19. Van Rensselaer's essay became a starting point for discussions about the definition of landscape gardening, and it immediately sparked a lively exchange about the various modalities of this art. See Liberty Hyde Bailey, "Landscape Gardening.—A Definition," *G&F* 1, no. 5 (1888): 58; "Notes [Landscape Horticulture]," ibid., 51.

20. Van Rensselaer, "Landscape Gardening.—A Definition," 2.

21. Mary Caroline Robbins, "Imagination in Gardening," *G&F* 7, no. 355 (1894): 492.

22. For example, see S. G. W. Benjamin, "Landscape-Gardening in Persia," *G&F* 2, no. 89 (1889): 530.

23. Robbins, "Imagination in Gardening," 492.

24. See "Park-Making as a National Art," *G&F* 10, no. 464 (1897): 11–12; "Park-Making," *G&F* 10, no. 512 (1897): 489–90. Professionally designed park systems were regarded as important cultural resources because they provided Americans with "great object-lessons" and "splendid flashes of inspiration" that portended "a time when our gardens will be in some adequate way an expression of the genius of the republic." Robbins, "Imagination in Gardening," 493.

25. Mariana Van Rensselaer's inaugural "definition" of landscape gardening also introduced this theme. In the final installment of her essay, Van Rensselaer admitted that Americans were "not as advanced in the art of gardening as we are in certain other arts." Van Rensselaer, "Landscape Gardening.—VI," 75.

26. "The Future of American Gardening," *G&F* 1, no. 2 (1888): 13.

27. Ibid.

28. In attempting to explain the development of American gardening culture, *Garden and Forest* writers adopted a narrative that mirrored themes of American historian Frederick Jackson Turner's "frontier thesis." First presented in 1893, Turner's thesis subsequently influenced many areas of American historiography. See Frederick Jackson Turner, *History, Frontier, and Section: Three Essays* (Albuquerque: University of New Mexico Press, 1993). For assessments of Turner's influence see Richard W. Slatta, "Taking Our Myths Seriously," *Journal of the West* 40, no. 3 (2001): 31–35; Allen G. Bogue, *Frederick Jackson Turner: Strange Roads Going Down* (Norman: University of Oklahoma Press, 1998); Kerwin Lee Klein, *Frontiers of Historical Imagination: Narrating the European Conquest of Native America, 1890–1990* (Berkeley: University of California Press, 1997); Wilbur R. Jacobs, *On Turner's Trail: 100 Years of Writing Western History* (Lawrence: University Press of Kansas, 1994); John B. Boles, "Turner, the Frontier, and the Study of Religion in America," *Journal of the Early Republic* 13, no. 2 (1993): 205–16; Robert H. Block, "Frederick Jackson Turner and American Geography," *Annals of the Association of American Geographers* 70, no. 1 (March 1980): 31–42; Richard Hofstadter, *Turner and the Sociology of the Frontier* (New York: Basic Books, 1968); Guy Stanton Ford, *Essays in American History, Dedicated to Frederick Jackson Turner* (New York: H. Holt and Company, 1910).

29. Profligate use of exotic plants in the landscape violated the essential principle that the gardener "must respect the frame" furnished by nature and work within "the general scheme which she prescribes." Van Rensselaer, "Landscape Gardening.—II," 14. Regard-

ing use of exotic plants in public parks, see also Mariana Griswold Van Rensselaer, "The Boston Public Garden," *G&F* 1, no. 29 (1888): 345–47; "Horticultural Fashions," *G&F* 1, no. 5 (28 March 1888): 49–50; "The Proper Use of Herbaceous Plants," *G&F* 1, no. 31 (1888): 361–62.

30. "The Use of Color in Our Parks," *G&F* 7, no. 334 (1894): 282.

31. "Native Plants for Ornamental Planting," *G&F* 10, no. 498 (1897): 349–50.

32. For example, the July 18, 1894, issue of *Garden and Forest* included an editorial article entitled "The Use of Color in Our Parks," which criticized the widespread planting of foreign species and showy cultivars. However, the same issue also included articles that described the botanical and horticultural qualities of exotic species and showy cultivars, such as "Deutzia Discolor, Var. Purpurascens," (284, 287), and J. N. Gerard, "Carnations and Pinks," (286–87). Moreover, as in all issues of *Garden and Forest,* the topical content of the journal was sandwiched between several pages of advertisements intended to entice readers to purchase ornamental ironwork, decorative "lawn vases," pansies, palms, bamboos, orchids, or their own hothouse outfitted with the most modern heating system.

33. "Artistic Aspect of Trees.—IV," *G&F* 1, no. 32 (1888): 373.

34. "Native Plants for Ornamental Planting," 349–50.

35. "The Planting of Shrubberies," *G&F* 10, no. 463 (1897): 1–2.

36. "English Gardens Unsuitable for America," *G&F* 9, no. 438 (1896): 282.

37. See Van Rensselaer, "Boston Public Garden"; "One Way to Make Parks Attractive," *G&F* 10, no. 483 (1897): 201–2; "Park-Making as a National Art," 11; "The Proper Use of Herbaceous Plants," *G&F* 1, no. 31 (1888): 361–62.

38. See "Park-Making," 489; "One Way to Make Parks Attractive," 201–2.

39. "The Planting of Home Grounds," *G&F* 4, no. 177 (1891): 326.

40. In *Garden and Forest* discussions about the relative virtues of exotic horticultural plants occurred alongside conversations about the phenomenon of uninvited, foreign "weeds" and insect "pests," which were observed to be invading landscapes across the continent. See for example, E. W. Hilgard, "Weeds of California—IV," *G&F* 4, no. 200 (1891): 604–5; "Legislation against Plant Pests," *G&F* 10, no. 491 (1897): 281–82; "Notes," *G&F* 3, no. 100 (1890): 48; "Recent Publications," *G&F* 1, no. 3 (1888): 35–36.

41. "Planting of Home Grounds," 326.

42. "Use of Color in Our Parks," 282.

43. Mariana Van Rensselaer noted that such plants were always "palpably out of place" in naturalistic plantings "[b]ecause they are known not to be natural products of our clime, and because they are formal, architectural, in expression." Van Rensselaer, "Boston Public Garden," 346. One of the earliest, fully developed debates about the role of exotic plants in American landscapes coalesced in a published exchange between Charles S. Sargent and Frederick Law Olmsted. See "Hardy Trees for a Trying Climate," *G&F* 1, no. 23 (1888): 265–65; Frederick Law Olmsted, "Foreign Plants and American Scenery," *G&F* 1, no. 35 (1888): 418–19.

44. "Formal Gardening," *G&F* 5, no. 219 (1892): 205. See also "Notes on Italian Gardens," *G&F* 6, no. 284 (1893): 322; Van Rensselaer, "Landscape Gardening.—A Definition," 2; and "Garden Design," *G&F* 10, no. 475 (1897): 121–22.

45. "Formal Gardening: Does It Conflict with the Natural Style?" *G&F* 6, no. 264 (1893): 119.

46. "Planting of Home Grounds," 325.

47. "Notes on Italian Gardens"; "Sculpture in Gardens," *G&F* 10, no. 474 (1897): 112.

48. "Formal Gardening," 120.

49. See, for example, "Garden Design," 121.

50. Charles Eliot, "Anglomania in Park Making," *G&F* 1, no. 6 (1888): 64.

51. Many *Garden and Forest* writings evoke the "survival-of-the-fittest" version of evolution popularized by Herbert Spencer. Although *Garden and Forest* contributors published little commentary on Spencer's ideas, the tremendous popularity of his *Principles of Biology* (London: Williams and Norgate, 1864) no doubt would have made his ideas familiar to many readers. An account of coursework in "The Evolution of Cultivated Plants" at Cornell University included sections from Spencer's *Principles,* as well as Darwin's *Origin of Species* (London: John Murray, 1859), Alfred Russel Wallace's *Darwinism* (London: Macmillan, 1889), Edward Drinker Cope's *Origin of the Fittest* (New York: Appleton, 1887), as well as writings by August Weismann and Asa Gray. Student, "Class Work in Horticulture at Cornell," *G&F* 9, no. 410 (1896): 7.

52. See Charles Eliot, "The Landscape Gardener," *G&F* 2, no. 51 (1889): 74–75; Charles Eliot, "The Waverly Oaks," *G&F* 3, no. 106 (1890): 117–18; "Boston's Proposed Metropolitan Park System," *G&F* 6, no. 259 (1893): 61–62; Sylvester Baxter, "Boston's New Metropolitan Parks," *G&F* 7, no. 306 (1894): 22–23; "Public Holdings in Massachusetts," *G&F* 7, no. 341 (1894): 351–52; "The Metropolitan Parks of Boston," *G&F* 8, no. 375 (1895): 171–72; "Park Work Near Boston," *G&F* 9, no. 427 (1896): 171–72; "A River Parkway," *G&F* 9, no. 448 (1896): 381–82. For a sense of how *Garden and Forest* editors promoted a rational approach for developing metropolitan park systems, see "Parks for Growing Cities," *G&F* 5, no. 207 (1892): 61; "Park Lands and Their Boundaries," *G&F* 9, no. 452 (1896): 421–22; "Park-making as a National Art," 11–12; Sylvester Baxter, "The Boston Metropolitan Park Movement," *G&F* 5, no. 207 (1892): 62–63; "The Boston Metropolitan Park Commission," *G&F* 5, no. 237 (1892): 421; "The Gift of a Tract of Land on the Charles River," *G&F* 6, no. 262 (1893): 98.

53. Charles Eliot to Chairman of the Boston Metropolitan Park Commission, October 6, 1892, in Charles William Eliot, *Charles Eliot,* 381.

54. Charles Eliot, "What Would Be Fair Must First Be Fit," *G&F* 9, no. 423 (1896): 132.

55. Ibid, 133. In this passage Eliot quoted William Angus Knight, *The Philosophy of the Beautiful* (London: John Murray, 1893), 2:36. Eliot omitted the subsequent line from Knight's text (36–37), which claimed fitness as a necessary but insufficient cause of beauty: "it does not follow that everything that Beauty consists in the actual fitness that has been evolved. It is true that nothing fitly evolved could be inharmonious, but that is not the same thing as saying that the beauty of what has been evolved is due to the fitness of its evolution." Elsewhere in *The Philosophy of the Beautiful,* Knight criticized the notion "that Beauty consists in utility" as another "inadequate or partial" theory. Eliot thus selectively appropriated Knight's words to support his own argument. While stopping short of arguing that fitness is in fact the cause of beauty, Eliot implied that it was at least a first principle.

56. Ibid.

57. Ibid.

58. Melanie Simo has similarly characterized Eliot's sources of inspiration for the essay. See Melanie Louise Simo, *100 Years of Landscape Architecture: Some Patterns of a Century* (Washington, DC: ASLA Press, 1999), 20.

59. Aside from commenting on the pleasant spring weather and the recreational activities of New Yorkers, the *New York Times,* in spring 1896, reported on an unprecedented "Spring flood of immigrants" to Ellis Island. The newspaper noted that while the island "presented a picturesque scene," many of the new arrivals were deemed "undesirable as acquisitions to this country's population"—remarks that echoed contemporary discussions about American landscapes and "vegetable immigrants" in *Garden and Forest.* "Ellis Island's Crowd: Immigrants Arriving in Numbers That Are Unprecedented," *NYT,* March 28, 1896, 9. For a provocative exploration of the parallels between the discourses of U.S. immigration policy and horticultural and agricultural policies in late-nineteenth- and early-twentieth-century America, see Philip J. Pauly, "The Beauty and Menace of Japanese Cherry Trees: Conflicting Visions of American Ecological Dependence," *Isis* 87 (1996): 51–73; and Philip J. Pauly, *Fruits and Plains: The Horticultural Transformation of America* (Cambridge, MA: Harvard University Press, 2007).

Growing Home

Thomas Affleck, Immigrant and Advisor in the American South

JAMES SCHISSEL

Mainstream America has long been associated with the country's Anglo-American sector. As a result, the influences of British immigrants have assumed a certain naturalized standing over time and have been taken for granted as inherently American. Therefore, it may seem unorthodox here, in a discussion of foreign trends on American soil, to concentrate on the life and work of Thomas Affleck (1812–1868), who migrated from Scotland in 1831, long after the first flux of settlers from the British Isles. Often referred to as "invisible immigrants," natives of England and Scotland who arrived on American soil were deemed by many to blend quickly and unobtrusively into the existing fabric of their new country.[1] Thomas Affleck, in his career as an author, nurseryman, horticultural advisor, and agricultural reformer, encountered gardening and agricultural traditions in his new country that to his eyes appeared unfamiliar, inefficient, and strange, and he devoted much of his professional energy to changing and improving existing American landscape practices. In particular, Affleck focused on a fairly narrow audience—southern planters—and through his work he attempted to guide his readership as it developed both landscapes of production and landscapes of pleasure. This essay maintains that landscape manipulation can be a strategy for creating and expressing identity and interprets the work of Thomas Affleck as an expression of his personal identity and as a form of advocacy for regional identity in the American South.[2]

Although Affleck's body of work as a nurseryman and writer has received very limited scholarly attention, his work is significant to American landscape history because it provides an essential voice for understanding the development of nineteenth-century landscapes in the South.[3] He disseminated horticultural knowledge in two ways: by supplying plants and through the written word. In 1848 Affleck opened Southern Nurseries, one of the earliest commercial plant nurseries in the Lower Mississippi River Valley. From his home base in Washington, Mississippi, Affleck played a vital role in the distribution of plants and horticultural advice throughout the American South. At a time when the majority of plant distribution and plant-related literature flowed through Europe and the northern United States, Affleck recognized a need for locally grown plants and information about plants aimed specifically at a southern audience. His publications cover a remarkable range of subjects, with individual examples treating landscape topics as diverse as bee breeding, hedging, and plantation recording and accounting methods for cotton and sugar.[4] Here, I concentrate on one ongoing publishing venture in Affleck's body of work: *Affleck's Southern Rural Almanac and Plantation and Garden Calendar* (published annually from the mid-1840s through the 1860s). Other contemporary publications focused on southern land practices, but most of these ventures were short-lived, lasting only several years. However, in Affleck's work we have a rare, sustained effort, spanning decades. Affleck's publications were popular, with estimated annual circulation figures for his almanac as high as one hundred thousand.[5]

From Scotsman to Southerner

Despite the popularity of his published work, relatively few copies have survived; fortunately, he left behind a sizable archive of diaries, personal letters, and business records, and from this treasure trove it is possible to reconstruct much of his life. Thomas Affleck was an avid letter writer and meticulous record keeper, and the letters he wrote—particularly during the years following his 1831 arrival in America—offer some insight into the young Scot's experience as an immigrant. Affleck's motives for moving to America were not uncommon in nineteenth-century Scotland, and his migration pattern once in America followed a fairly typical sequence of moves common among northern European immigrants.[6] It has been argued that Scots "displayed a compulsion to adapt, to change, to improve."[7] Whether we accept this broad description as a typical trait of the Scots, Affleck certainly demonstrated his desire to adapt and improve throughout his life.

Born in 1812 in Dumfries in the Scottish lowlands, Affleck was one of eleven children born to Thomas and Mary Hannay Affleck. His father was engaged as a merchant and importer of goods but provided unreliably for his family due to his habit of squandering money on inventions and speculations. Despite the fluctuations in income, the family enjoyed an impressive residence, moved among the highest social circles, and, by local standards, were considered a wealthy family. From an early age Affleck showed an interest in nature and cultivation, recording in his diary his delight in the flora and fauna he encountered on walks through the Scottish countryside, and he studied physical and natural science with great interest. Out of respect for his parents' wish that he become a doctor, Affleck entered the University of Edinburgh to study medicine; however, poor health and financial problems hastened his return to Dumfries, where he worked as a bank clerk under the direction of his uncle for several years.[8] During this period he spent his free time supplementing his formal education with a fierce appetite for reading about agriculture, horticulture, and natural history.[9] In addition to reading, he pursued his interest in farming by attending agricultural fairs, livestock auctions, and flower exhibits as often as possible.[10] As he developed his passions for nature and cultivation, Thomas Affleck became increasingly disenchanted with banking and increasingly determined to become a farmer. Observing that large tracts of land in Scotland became available primarily through inheritance, Affleck concluded that life in his native country would be incompatible with his desire to farm and, ultimately, decided to move to America to satisfy his agricultural aspirations.[11] In this sense Affleck was like many others emigrating from Scotland at the time. During the nineteenth century Scottish emigration intensified for several reasons, and agriculture-based rural life was a common thread among them. For example, stagnant or declining opportunities in rural areas coupled with increases in the population forced many residents to either move into urban areas or search for a rural mode of life outside Scotland. Similarly, the labor system for agricultural workers created a direct link between employment and housing. This system, based on annual or half-yearly contracts, provided laborers with housing as a significant part of their compensation; therefore, the loss of jobs for these agricultural laborers simultaneously meant the loss of homes.[12] Affleck left Scotland with his aspirations to farm and with his family's blessing. His father, in particular, encouraged the move. The elder Affleck was in the process of inventing a hydraulic tool for deepening, widening, and clearing rivers and for creating new navigational channels, and he requested that his son promote the instrument in his adopted country.[13]

Upon his arrival in America in 1831 at the age of nineteen, he worked briefly in New York as a clerk for a firm of wholesale merchants.[14] Shortly thereafter, Affleck joined relatives in Hickory, Pennsylvania, and spent the next three years there working as an accountant in dry goods stores in nearby Pittsburgh but continued his habits of nature walks and reading for self-improvement.[15] In 1834 Affleck's parents and siblings made plans to leave Scotland permanently for America, a decision prompted by the family's financial ruin in Scotland, resulting largely from the father's efforts to invent, patent, and promote the hydraulic tool. Viewing the West as a social equalizer, Affleck investigated frontier locations as a potential home for the family to spare them any embarrassment their reduced circumstances might cause.[16] In 1835 the Affleck clan settled in Clinton, Indiana, where father and son collaborated in a frontier mercantile business, which enjoyed some initial success. The younger Affleck's time in Indiana, however, was plagued with professional and personal crises. The mercantile business ultimately failed, and after only a year of marriage, Affleck suffered the deaths of his young wife, Margaret, and their infant son.[17]

Out of despair Affleck left Indiana abruptly with plans to return to Scotland, but severe illness forced him to stop in Cincinnati, where he recuperated under the care of a physician who encouraged him to pursue his interests in horticulture and agriculture for the sake of improved physical and mental health. Affleck remained in Cincinnati and developed a small produce farm, supplying markets in the city with the vegetables, melons, and flowers he grew. During this time of emotional recovery, Affleck reexamined his life, reconnected with his farming aspirations, and made many connections in Cincinnati.[18] Impressed by Affleck's knowledge, the publisher of *Western Farmer,* a journal based in Cincinnati, invited Affleck to serve as editor of the publication. Beginning in 1840, during his tenure as editor of the journal, Affleck was instrumental in expanding its scope to include horticultural pursuits, and as a result, the title changed to *Western Farmer and Gardener* to better reflect the aims of the periodical. Affleck used his position to promote the development of both local agricultural and horticultural societies, as he had witnessed the value of such organizations in Scotland as venues for dialogue and the exchange of ideas, equipment, livestock, seed, and plants.[19]

To support the journal's mission, Affleck worked as a traveling correspondent. He attended many fairs held by societies and reported his findings in the journal; the connections he made at the fairs shaped the professional and personal trajectories of his life.[20] In particular, while touring the South in 1841 he participated in the fair of the Agricultural, Horticultural, and Botanical Society of Jefferson College in Washington, Mississippi. During his time in Washington he met Anna Dunbar Smith, the young widow of a plantation owner and daughter of a prominent Scottish family who had settled in the nearby Natchez vicinity during the eighteenth century. His attraction to Anna, coupled with the agricultural promise he saw in

Fig. 1. Ingleside, Affleck residence, April 1936, front elevation. (Library of Congress, Prints and Photographs Division, HABS MISS, 1-WASH, 1-1)

the region, culminated in his swift resettlement in Washington, where he and Anna married and made their home, which Affleck christened with the Scottish name Ingleside (fig. 1). In 1842, shortly after their marriage, he made a shocking discovery about his new wife. Contrary to his assumption during courtship, the new Mrs. Affleck was not wealthy, despite her plantation ownership and family connections; in fact, she was heavily in debt. This discovery would influence his career in significant and long-lasting ways. Although Affleck attempted to manage multiple cotton plantations inherited by his wife and young stepson for several years, he would ultimately fail as a planter due to repeated unfavorable growing seasons. As a result, much of the land was lost to creditors, and Affleck was forced to abandon his career in agriculture and eke out alternative ways of supporting his family.

Writing and Planting the Southern Landscape

While managing the family's plantations, Affleck continued his writing career, publishing in a variety of formats such as New Orleans newspaper advice columns and agricultural journals, and most notably, he began producing southern rural almanacs in the mid-1840s, first editing *Norman's*

Southern Agricultural Almanac for New Orleans publisher B. M. Norman, which gradually evolved into *Affleck's Southern Rural Almanac and Plantation and Garden Calendar* (fig. 2). Aimed at the planter class and organized by month, these almanacs provided readers with planting and maintenance schedules for gardens and plantations, as well as detailed information about the cultivation of specific plants and Affleck's views on plant aesthetics and climate suitability. The basic format for each month included two sections, with one devoted to the planter's calendar and one devoted to the garden calendar. The planter's calendar contained advice directed at the business of the plantation staple crop, either cotton or sugar, including its planting and harvest cycles, crop rotation, fertilizers, and the management of enslaved laborers. For the garden calendar, Affleck devised subsections addressing the kitchen garden, fruit garden and orchard, rose garden, and shrub garden. Not surprisingly, these garden subsections aligned closely with the author's work as a nurseryman and the kinds of plants he offered for sale.

In 1848 Affleck opened Southern Nurseries, one of the earliest commercial plant nurseries in the Lower Mississippi River Valley. It was not until his arrival and marriage in Mississippi that his vision for a nursery business began to take shape. Mississippi was still a frontier landscape in many ways, and Affleck's desire to make it his permanent home spurred his interest in horticultural pursuits. It was during this period in December 1848 that Solon Robinson, a traveling correspondent for the *American Agriculturist,* found Affleck at Ingleside transitioning from failed, despondent planter to hopeful nurseryman. Robinson reported that on his "little place of 47 acres, at Washington, Mississippi, Affleck is now engaged in laying down into a nursery of fruits, shrubs, flowers, and plants—both out doors [*sic*], in hot houses, and forcing beds, with the intention of supplying that region, as well as the New Orleans market with such articles." From Robinson we also learn that Affleck had the assistance of an accomplished gardener from Scotland, and that he was eagerly awaiting the arrival of bulbs and plants ordered from a London nurseryman, as well as plants from other parts of the United States.[21]

Viewing the garden not only as a supply for sustenance but also as a source of culture, Affleck offered fruit trees, plants for the kitchen garden, and ornamental plants. Although new to the South, Affleck anticipated a kindred spirit in his readers, many of whom were also newly settled in the region. Because he targeted the planters and their families as his audience, migration and mobility were a fundamental part of their identity in their ongoing search for fertile land.[22] As a result, Affleck sought to strengthen

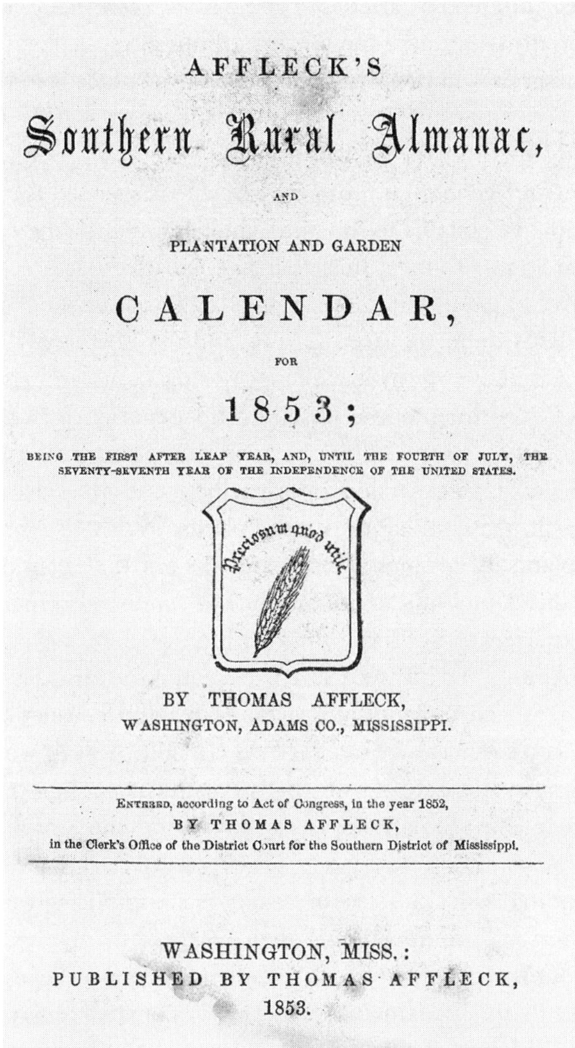

AFFLECK'S

Southern Rural Almanac,

AND

PLANTATION AND GARDEN

CALENDAR,

FOR

1853;

BEING THE FIRST AFTER LEAP YEAR, AND, UNTIL THE FOURTH OF JULY, THE SEVENTY-SEVENTH YEAR OF THE INDEPENDENCE OF THE UNITED STATES.

Preciosum quod utile.

BY THOMAS AFFLECK,
WASHINGTON, ADAMS CO., MISSISSIPPI.

ENTERED, according to Act of Congress, in the year 1852,
BY THOMAS AFFLECK,
in the Clerk's Office of the District Court for the Southern District of Mississippi.

WASHINGTON, MISS.:
PUBLISHED BY THOMAS AFFLECK,
1853.

Fig. 2. Title page, Affleck's *Southern Rural Almanac and Plantation and Garden Calendar* (1853).

the bonds between people and place by promoting the advice and materials to establish landscapes successful both in terms of production and beauty, a strengthened bond hopefully resulting in a sense of home and stability in the region.

His almanacs not only served as practical guides for readers but also became Affleck's primary marketing vehicle for Southern Nurseries, advertising his extensive variety of plants available for order. According to his 1854 catalog, Affleck offered 80 varieties of apple trees, 134 varieties of pear trees, and 174 different roses; these three plant groups alone reflect the extent of Southern Nurseries—impressive figures even by standards today. But what is perhaps more important than the range of cultivars is Affleck's emphasis on origin and suitability for the southern climate. As a proponent of native plants and second-generation nonnatives, Affleck stressed the importance of supplying plants suitable to the often challenging growing conditions of the American South. To meet this challenge, he advertised his nursery not only as a source of plants but, more importantly, as a service that tested and acclimated plants imported from Europe and the northern United States, a service that reduced the risks of lengthy shipments and spared buyers the gamble of experimentation. Based on his experiences when ordering plants from distant sources, Affleck became all too familiar with the potential pitfalls of slow transportation, poor packing, and other distance-related oversights resulting in unhealthy or dead plants.[23] With his emphasis on locally grown plants, he promoted his nursery as one that offered only plants tested for their adaptability to the South. His catalog also included native plants. He experienced southern flora with an outsider's eyes and a fresh perspective. Among the lush vegetation he noted the striking, ornamental qualities of many native plants and particularly admired the plentiful evergreens, both coniferous and broadleaf. As a result, Affleck would become an early American advocate of using native plants in a design context, viewing the native forests of Mississippi as a cache of potential profit, value, and beauty.[24]

Understanding Affleck's sense of beauty is a complicated task because, unlike designers with compositional advice, Affleck most often approached aesthetics from the perspective of a plantsman, concentrating on the appearance of individual specimens. Although he couched much of his plant-related advice in terms of climatic requirements and ideal methods of culture, Affleck also commented on the form, texture, and color of plants and, at times, recommended them for specific design applications. For example, in an 1854 Natchez newspaper, he offered hints on selecting and growing ornamental trees and shrubs, with the goal of advocating greater plant variety in the region. Addressing scales ranging from street plantings to small urban private gardens, Affleck expressed his disappointment that the local population restricted itself to a limited palette consisting of a handful of introduced plants and ignored the abundant supply of beautiful native plants, as well as other nonnative plants capable of flourishing in the climate. Affleck criticized Natchez city leaders for their "perpetual" use of the Pride of China or chinaberry tree (*Melia azedarach*) as a street tree, which he characterized as beautiful but "filthy" and "in very bad taste," and suggested as an alternative the native live oak (*Quercus virginiana*) for its ability to provide shade, its monumental scale, sculptural form, and longevity spanning multiple centuries.[25] The Pride of China's propensity to create litter and its susceptibility to breakage, typical of most fast-growing, short-lived trees, spurred Affleck's negative description, despite the tree's showy profusion of lavender blossoms; however, his disparaging remarks about this tree were atypical for the time and place. During this period, editors of a southern agricultural magazine so highly extolled the qualities of the Pride of China that they exclaimed, "we hold that man is a misanthrope indeed who loves not the China tree."[26] Far from misanthropic in his comments, Affleck's desire for comfortable, beautiful, long-lasting places for people prompted his dismissal of the popular tree in favor of native trees, such as live oaks, for streets and other public spaces.

Affleck's recommendations for ornamental trees and shrubs embraced both native and nonnative plants. Some nonnative plants Affleck promoted held personal significance, such as the mountain ash or rowan tree, about which he waxed uncharacteristically sentimental, describing it as "dear to every Scotchman's boyish recollections," and other nonnatives captured his attention for their outstanding physical qualities and their ability to be "at home" in the climate. But what is particularly noteworthy is the way Affleck underscores native plants. His tone brightens when he describes them, and his language is filled with a sense of belonging and affinity, teeming with phrases such as "our magnificent water oak," "our great southern cypress," and "our own native cedar."[27] And even though his letter is partly for marketing the plants available at his nearby nursery, so strong was Affleck's belief in the importance of cultivating native plants that he provided readers with instructions for transplanting them from the woods to the garden, thereby jeopardizing his potential profits from the sale of native plants. Because Affleck advocated both native and introduced plants, his predilection for native plants appears to spring not from any quest for ecological authenticity but, instead, from a desire to educate and strengthen the bonds between people and place through plants. Plants help us understand that beauty for Affleck was not tied solely to physical traits and that he did not grow and advocate ornamental plants for ornament alone. For Affleck, beauty was also based in practicality, plant performance, and, notably, longevity.

Notions of utility and value dominate much of Affleck's work, and, therefore, it is not surprising that he displayed the Affleck family motto prominently on the cover of his annual almanac: *Preciosum quod utile,* or "What is useful is valuable." His use of this device was intended, most likely, to impress his readers with his erudition and, therefore, to serve as a form of cultural capital. It also implies a familiarity with emblem books, which contained combinations of engravings and text that conveyed lessons in morality. Affleck may have known the *Emblemata* published by Sambucus in 1564, which includes an illustrated page for *Preciosum quod utile,* translated in the following way: "Many things are thought worthy by men of a high price, for they are rare, and the waves bring them from distant places. Empty superstition, worthy of general laughter! All the same, this rare horn is recommended by its utility. For, if men make so bold as to mix poison in the cups, this medicine averts all present danger. It is an ornament to the treasuries of kings, and it demands a price: this expense did not deserve faint praise!"[28]

The lesson conveyed by this emblem most likely appealed to Affleck for its emphasis on value, and he employed it as a framing device for his work in at least two significant ways. First, as a reference to the advice in his almanacs, Affleck interprets value in terms of the merits and benefits of his work to his readers. Second, he considers value in monetary terms, citing the southern authenticity of his plants and the acclimation process in the introduction to his catalog. For Affleck, the quality and dependability of his nursery stock translated into the prices he demanded, which were higher than those of his northern competitors.

Also, the emblem *Preciosum quod utile* alludes to exoticism in its reference to things from "distant places," a theme that aligns closely with Affleck's identity as a nurseryman and with many of the plants he imported. Ordering plants from established nurseries in the Northeast, such as Highland Nurseries in Syracuse, New York, and from nurseries in Europe, such as Vilmorin-Andrieux in France and T. Rivers and Son in England, Affleck obtained seedlings of plant varieties unavailable in the South. He grew them on the grounds of his nursery in Mississippi to test their climate suitability and used them for propagating additional generations of nursery stock. By doing so, he not only introduced new plants to the region, but he also certified them as authentic southern stock. In light of his focus on the adaptability and acclimation of plants, Affleck clearly viewed his business as a conduit between local people and distant places, and he bridged the gap with plants that gained value from his transformative care.

Critics of Acclimation

What exactly was this transformative process of acclimation so firmly entrenched in the foundation of Affleck's nursery work, and how was the concept received?

Affleck did not fully or clearly articulate his method, but from his writings it is clear that he used a vegetative method of propagation to replicate and maintain the qualities of the parent plant through a system of cuttings and grafts, fusing cuttings from northern-grown trees onto southern-grown root stocks (fig. 3). As the resulting trees put out new growth, he would repeat the process to create subsequent generations before authenticating them as acclimated plants fully adapted to the southern climate.

Reactions to his work and philosophy as a nurseryman ranged wildly. Newspapers in the 1850s in Little Rock, Arkansas, and Austin, Texas, praised Thomas Affleck as "intelligent and highly cultivated, and a perfect walking library on fruit and flowers" and they characterized his nursery near Natchez as "a paradise on earth." However, the ideas he promoted about plants, specifically the acclimation of fruit trees, were subject, at times, to criticism. Some southern correspondents in journals, such as the regional *Southern Cultivator* and Andrew Jackson Downing's nationally prominent *Horticulturist,* responded to Affleck with skepticism, dismissal, or hostility. In some instances, these writers simply claimed success with northern-grown fruit trees and gave advice for their treatment in the southern climate, such as one nameless contributor to the *Horticulturist,* identified by the editors only as "a very intelligent and observing lady" of Port Gibson, Mississippi, who reported her success with mulching fruit trees from northern nurseries.[29] She went on to advise that "Mr. Affleck, of the nurseries near Natchez, dwells very earnestly on the difficulty of acclimating such trees here; but mulching removes this, at least so my success hitherto goes to prove; and, experience apart, common sense would show us that if it is useful at the North, it must be much more so at the South, in our very long, scorching summers."[30] While "the lady" from Port Gibson merely dismissed Affleck's theory of acclimation as illogical, other contributors to the agricultural press actively sought to discredit Affleck by attacking him professionally and personally, painting the nurseryman as a crafty opportunist who aimed to take advantage of his customers and readers by appealing to their growing desire for all things southern.[31]

Two of Affleck's harshest critics, neighboring planters and brothers-in-law Martin Phillips and Spencer Montgomery, located three counties from

NOVEMBER.

PLANTER'S CALENDAR.

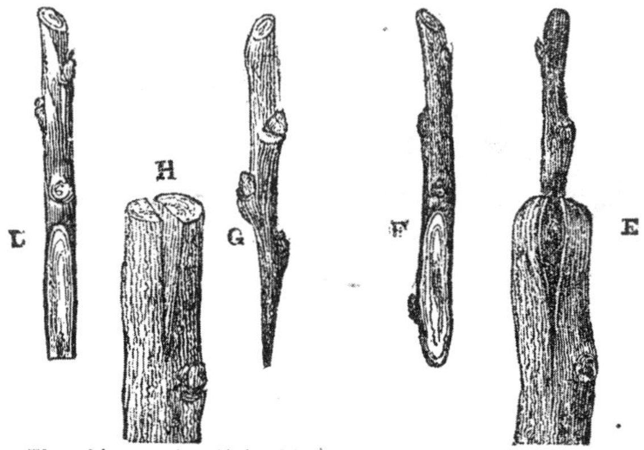

GRAFTING—The object to be attained by *Grafting*, as by *Budding*, is the multiplication of such varieties of fruit and and other trees as could not be readily and certainly reproduced from seed. It is performed in winter and early spring; and best, at such time as the sap begins to flow in the stock; the *scions* being kept back by being buried in dry, sandy soil, in a pit, on the north side of a wall or hill, and so covered as to be kept dry and cool until wanted. The scions or grafts should be well ripened shoots, with plump full buds, of the previous year's growth, taken from thrifty, bearing trees, when practicable. *Stocks* of any size and age may be used, if healthy and vigorous; and even old trees, if well supplied with young wood on which to graft. One or two year-old seedlings, however, are preferred, and commonly used. *Suckers* should never, under any circumstances, be made use of as stocks. The stock must be of the same *natural family* as the species to be grafted on it—as the Peach, Plum, Apricot, Almond &c., all of which may be grafted or budded the one on the other. It is folly to expect any good result from placing grafts of the Peach, for instance, on the China tree, or the Pear on the Sycamore, &c. All the different species of grape may be grafted on each other. A hardy and strong-growing native grape-vine, may almost always be successfully employed as a stock for the more delicate or capricious foreign grapes.

Cleft or *hedge* grafting is represented above; H is the stock; T and G the graft prepared for insertion, and should be from four to six buds in length. Care must be used in wedge and splice grafting that the inner bark of the scion is exactly applied to the inner bark of the stock. We prefer side or bark grafting, see above, F, E as the wood of many stocks is apt to die and rot at the heart, when cleft. This mode can only be practiced after the sap begins to flow so freely early in the spring, as that the bark will part readily from the wood. A perpendicular cut is made in the bark, E, which is gently raised, and the graft, F pushed down, so as to fit neatly. When large and old trees are to be filled with grafts of finer varieties, this is always the best plan. The old trees should be *cut in* the year before, so as to cause them to throw out a good supply of thrifty young wood on which to graft. In this way, old trees, which bear indifferent fruit, and especially pears and apples, may be at once furnished with an entire new head of some choice varieties, which will bear almost immediately.

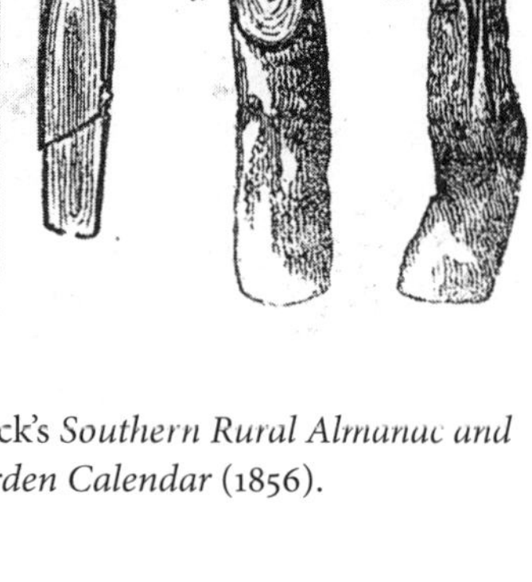

Fig. 3. Grafting methods, Affleck's *Southern Rural Almanac and Plantation and Garden Calendar* (1856).

Affleck, launched attacks against the nurseryman in 1853 in the *Southern Cultivator* and the *Horticulturist*.[32] They did not merely disagree with the concept of acclimating fruit trees but, instead, went so far as to accuse Affleck of deceit, claiming that he was attempting to circulate and teach erroneous information about southern pomology when he emphasized the necessity of southern-grown fruit trees and the inferiority of northern-grown trees. This information, they argued, was an unfounded justification for demanding elevated prices and merely a ruse for lining Affleck's pockets. To reinforce their positions, both Phillips and Montgomery provided personal accounts of their success with fruit trees of northern origin, claiming excellent growth and production of high-quality fruit, all possible in the southern climate—indeed, in the immediate neighborhood of Southern Nurseries—and at a fraction of Affleck's prices. Ultimately, these neighbors alleged that Affleck's process consisted of nothing more than ordering fruit trees from distant sources and keeping them at his southern nursery briefly—perhaps only a matter of days—before reselling them at inflated prices.

Angered not only by Affleck's wholesale rejection of northern fruit trees, Philips and Montgomery also founded their attacks on the ambiguity surrounding the nurseryman's acclimation process, especially in terms of his method and its duration. It is unclear why Affleck never fully divulged his method. Perhaps he was attempting to protect a trade secret, but by being evasive his method was misinterpreted, and as a result, he opened himself to accusations of chicanery and subterfuge. Most notably, Philips and Montgomery called attention to Affleck's claim that multiple generations were necessary to acclimate, or rehabituate, plants originating and grown in a colder climate before they could fully adapt and flourish in a new, warmer climate. His critics assumed, incorrectly, that Affleck propagated successive generations by seed instead of cuttings and grafts. Based on this misunderstanding, Philips and Montgomery proceeded to systematically undermine Affleck, pointing to the unpredictability of fruit seedlings, the time required from seed to fruit-bearing tree (much less the time required to repeat for multiple generations), and the fact that the catalog for Southern Nurseries only listed well-known cultivars and not new varieties that naturally result in fruit trees when propagated by seed (because fruit seedlings were rarely, if ever, true to the characteristics of the parent plant). By pointing to the sloth-like rate of propagation by seed, Philips and Montgomery sought to prove that Affleck had not resided in the South long enough to have already produced multiple generations of fruit trees.

To further undermine his reputation as an expert on southern horticulture and pomology, his critics shifted their discussion from the origins of plants to the origins of people. Philips and Montgomery strategically painted Affleck as an outsider to invalidate his work, and they derided "all this gasconade about 'acclimated fruit,'"[33] claiming that it might with the same propriety be argued that a foreigner could not live in the southern climate:

> I would far sooner grant something to the acclimating of men, when we would get clear of such as are not of us. Fruit trees, in my humble opinion, are, in one respect, like men; some are good in other places, and prove good here when at proper age; some never prove good here, whether any account in their native place or not. Some kinds of fruit may be good on one soil and not good on another, not because they were grown here or elsewhere.[34]

Affleck acknowledged the publication of what he described as "wondrously pungent, pointed, personal articles," and vigorously defended his stance on plant acclimation.[35] His response also showed that the references to his "foreignness" had hit a nerve:

> True, I am a Scotchman, born and educated, and do not feel that I have the slightest occasion to be ashamed of that fact. I came to these United States, of my own free will and consent, twenty-two years ago, immediately declared my intention of becoming a citizen, as provided by law; and have now cast my vote, generally with the Whigs, and always a conservative vote, for these sixteen or seventeen years. I became a citizen of the South, fifteen, and of Mississippi, twelve years ago, of my own choice—can native-born citizens say as much? I trow not. Most of them, I suspect, made very wry faces on their first introduction to Southern soil![36]

In this bitter exchange, notions of nativity, continuity, and adaptability figure prominently, and the language employed refers to the origins of people as much, if not more, than those of fruit trees. Throughout this battle of the pens several trajectories surface that may contribute to our general understanding of what has happened when something or someone foreign has converged with American soil. First, Affleck, Philips, and Montgomery each used his place of nativity to either validate his position or invalidate another's position, thereby claiming to be an insider or accusing another of being an outsider. For example, while attempting to forge an identity as a southern planter and nurseryman, Affleck remained proud of his Scottish heritage and did not make efforts to hide, forget, or erase his foreign origin. Instead, he claimed to be southern by choice, while Philips and Montgomery were southern by birth. As natives of South Carolina who had migrated to Mississippi around 1830, Philips and Montgomery stressed their southern heritage and their extensive experience with growing plants in a southern climate.[37]

Second, they each used time as a measure to quantify cultural affiliation and expertise by the passage of years lived continuously in one place or region. In this case Philips only broached the subject of time by distinguishing his twenty years of experience with fruit trees in Mississippi from the fifteen years prior in South Carolina; in total, he claimed thirty-five years of experience with southern fruit and, therefore, viewed his experiences in the two different climates as a continuous southern one. Affleck, on the other hand, counted his years and chose his numbers very carefully. There is a degree of elision in Affleck's response regarding his background. Taking the growing sectionalism of the 1850s into account, Affleck omitted any references to the places he lived during his first decade in America—New York, Pennsylvania, Indiana, Ohio—all located outside the margins of the South. His claim that he had been a citizen of the South for fifteen years at the time of publication is suspect because those years would have included his time in Cincinnati, Ohio, where he farmed and edited the *Western Farmer and Gardener.* It is unclear whether he was stretching the numbers to boost his credibility as a fruit grower, or whether he considered Cincinnati as a southern city, given its proximity to Kentucky.

The third link that came from this spirited debate was a person's willingness and ability to adapt to or assimilate into his or her new environs. Secure in his identity, Philips apparently found little need to adapt to the frontier landscape of Mississippi, viewing it as continuum of his early life in South Carolina. While writing under his pseudonym "Plebs," he vigorously defended and lauded the products of northern nurseries and his success with them. However, he quickly reminded his southern readers: "Now, sirs, I am no Northern man, nor the son of a Northern man, but I want even handed justice."[38]

Affleck, on the other hand, was eager to inform his audience of his loyalty to the region, stressing his choice to become a southerner. Also, his reference to political affiliation was most certainly to impress upon his readers that, despite his foreign birth and upbringing, he had fully assimilated into their society and shared their views and priorities.

The transformation of foreign seedling to southern plant at Thomas Affleck's nursery mirrors his life as an immigrant in striking ways. Undoubtedly, his nursery philosophy was based partially on a pragmatic foundation—his effort to earn money. His advocacy of native plants, for example, had a cost-saving benefit as he did not need to secure them from other growers and, therefore, increased his profit margin. And while it may be tempting in our time of increased environmental sensitivity to conjure images of him pillaging southern forests in order to profit from native plants, it is important to remember that he did not endorse native plants to the exclusion of all others. To the contrary, the vast majority of his nursery stock consisted of nonnative plants, and it is here, in his emphasis on acclimation of ornamentals and multigenerational plants, that the parallels with Affleck's life are most obvious. Much like the acclimation of plants, Affleck underwent a transformative process of acculturation from the time he left his native Scotland.

Selling South

In addition to the almanacs' roles as advisory organ and marketing tool for Southern Nurseries, these publications acted as promotional instruments for southern merchants and businesses. To subsidize publication costs of his annual almanac and garden calendar Affleck advertised many products and services by southern companies, therefore stressing regionalism by providing alternatives to imported goods.[39] In his address to potential advertisers Affleck boasted that his almanac was unparalleled as an advertising medium and "has been prepared with a view of being circulated in the families of the Planters in the South-West; and is to be found in almost every house."[40] While Affleck was no doubt puffing the popularity of the almanac in an effort to secure advertisers, his almanac attracted a wide range of advertisers primarily from nearby Natchez and New Orleans who sought to establish connections with plantation owners and their families. From these sponsorships we can learn much about the target audience—planters and their families—or at least the ways in which advertisers and Affleck perceived them and encouraged a certain image attainable through goods. Occupying anywhere from one-third to one-half of the annual almanac, hundreds of advertisements each year offered a wide range of services and goods from insurance companies, clothing businesses, seed suppliers, schools and colleges, and other merchants selling cotton gins, jewelry, fertilizers, silverware, guns, and medicinal remedies. The juxtaposition of such seemingly different goods as fine hats and shingle-making machines signals Affleck's efforts to appeal to both the working and leisure dimensions of plantation landscapes.

Through his publications and nursery business, Thomas Affleck sought to improve frontier landscape practices in an effort to advocate a degree of permanence. By promoting sustainable agricultural practices such as crop rotation and fertilizers, he used his work to eliminate the planter's inevitable quest for new fertile land in other regions; by offering dependable, predictable plants for sustenance and beauty, Affleck encouraged a deeper, long-lasting attachment to places that nourished the body and spirit; and by fostering a regional network of merchants and services, he enabled and simplified his audience's desire to create landscapes of production and pleasure. Although he moved many times himself, Affleck demonstrated a consistent loyalty and ability to adapt to the region he inhabited at any given time. The names he selected for his publications and business ventures reflect his emphasis on location and regionalism as he moved throughout America. Titles such as *Bee-Breeding in the West, Western Farmer and Gardener,* and *Southern Rural Almanac* and business names such as Southern Nurseries, located in Mississippi, and Central Nurseries, which he eventually established in Texas, all point to regional identity as a fundamental tenet of his professional work. Even the Scottish name Affleck chose for his Mississippi residence, Ingleside, which translates to "fireside or hearth," suggests the primacy and stability of the figurative center of family and home and, at the same time, conveys the potency of his memories of his native land.

Notes

1. Charlotte Erickson, *Invisible Immigrants: The Adaptation of English and Scottish Immigrants in Nineteenth-Century America* (Coral Gables, FL: University of Miami Press, 1972).

2. This premise of landscape manipulation is fundamental in studies of cultural heritage and, therefore, most commonly applied to generalized group interaction with the landscape. For a more specific example of individuals and small groups transforming the landscape for reasons of identity, see Sheila ffolliott, "Women in the Garden of Allegory: Catherine de Medicis and the Locus of Female Rule," in *Villas and Gardens in Early Modern Italy and France,* ed. Mirka Benes and Dianne Harris (Cambridge: Cambridge University Press, 2001), 207–24.

3. Despite its popularity, Affleck's work has not received significant scholarly treatment. Agricultural historians, accounting historians, and, only recently, landscape historians have noted Affleck's publications as a way for understanding antebellum society in the South. Only since 2000 have landscape historians begun to acknowledge Thomas Affleck's work. For bibliographic information see James Schissel, "Home Grown: Thomas Affleck's Advocacy of Regional Identity in the American South, 1848–1868" (PhD diss., University of Illinois at Urbana-Champaign, forthcoming).

4. Examples of Thomas Affleck's publications on these respective topics include the following titles: *Bee-Breeding in the West* (1841); "On the Hygiene of Cotton Plantations

and the Management of Slaves" (1850); *Cotton Plantation Record and Account Book* and *Sugar Plantation Record and Account Book* (1850–1860), through which he sought to systematize plantation management; and the posthumous publication *Hedging and Hedging Plants* (1869).

5. Affleck claims this quantity on the cover of his 1854 almanac. It is difficult to establish the accuracy of circulation figures because they were self-reported. Affleck received fees from advertisers based on his circulation numbers, so there is the possibility that the figures he reported were inflated to increase his income from the almanac advertisements.

6. For additional detail on nineteenth-century Scottish migration motives and patterns, see William E. Van Vugt, *British Buckeyes: The English, Scots, and Welsh in Ohio, 1700–1900* (Kent, OH: Kent State University Press, 2006).

7. Eric Richards, "Scotland and the Uses of the Atlantic Empire," in *Strangers with the Realm: Cultural Margins of the First British Empire,* ed. Bernard Bailyn and Philip D. Morgan (Chapel Hill: University of North Carolina Press, 1991), 84.

8. Thomas Affleck to Anna Smith, March 19, 1842, in Thomas Affleck Papers (Mss. 3, 4, 1110, 1263, 1264), Louisiana and Lower Mississippi Valley Collections, Hill Memorial Library, Louisiana State University, Baton Rouge.

9. Thomas Affleck diary, January 7, 1831, February 1, 1831, and January 8, 1832, in Thomas Affleck Papers.

10. Thomas Affleck diary, September 21, 1831, in Thomas Affleck Papers.

11. Thomas Affleck to John Graham, February 8, 1832, in Thomas Affleck Papers.

12. Thomas Martin Devine, "The Paradox of Scottish Emigration," in *Scottish Emigration and Scottish Society,* ed. T. M. Devine (Edinburgh: John Donald, 1992), 5–7. Also see Thomas Martin Devine, *Scotland's Empire and the Shaping of the Americas, 1600–1815* (Washington, DC: Smithsonian Books, 2003), especially chapter 5, "The Scottish Lowlands and North America to 1775," 94–118.

13. Correspondence indicates that Thomas Affleck had little faith in the project and did not actively promote the project in America despite requests from his father to do so.

14. Thomas Affleck diary, May 9–12, 1832, in Thomas Affleck Papers.

15. Thomas Affleck to Thomas Affleck Sr., July 2, 1832, in Thomas Affleck Papers.

16. Compare Affleck's reasons for moving west with William Cronon's discussion of the American frontier in "The Trouble with Wilderness," in *Uncommon Ground: Rethinking the Human Place in Nature,* ed. William Cronon (New York: W. W. Norton, 1996), 76–78. Thomas Affleck to Margarete Bruce, April 11, 1835, in Thomas Affleck Papers.

17. Thomas Affleck to Anna Smith, March 19, 1842, in Thomas Affleck Papers.

18. Andrew Hannay to Thomas Affleck, February 30, 1839, in Thomas Affleck Papers.

19. Eli J. Hooper, *Western Farmer and Gardener* 2 (1840–41): 1–2. Hooper, an agricultural editor in Cincinnati, hired Affleck to assist with editing the journal. In this piece Hooper relates to readers how Affleck came to join the publication and describes him as "evidently well-born," "conspicuous in his bearing and manners," and "well educated." For an overview of these societies in Scotland, see E. H. M. Cox, *A History of Gardening in Scotland* (London: Chatto and Windus, 1935), and particularly chapter 9, "Horticultural Societies and Flower Shows."

20. For an overview of the agricultural societies in America and their use of the Berk-

shire plan, which featured an annual fair as a distinguishing characteristic, see Albert Lowther Demaree, *The American Agricultural Press, 1819–1860* (New York: Columbia University Press, 1941), 9, 197–230.

21. Solon Robinson, *Solon Robinson, Pioneer and Agriculturist: Selected Writings,* vol. 2 (1846–51), ed. Herbert Anthony Kellar (Indianapolis: Indiana Historical Bureau, 1936), 139–41. This installation of Robinson's tour of the South and West was originally published in the *American Agriculturist,* March 1849, and reprinted in part in the *Ohio Cultivator,* April 1849.

22. For a fascinating discussion of the planter class, its mobility, and its views of the landscape, see James David Miller, *South by Southwest: Planter Emigration and Identity in the Slave South* (Charlottesville: University of Virginia Press, 2002). Chapter 6, "A Household with a View: The Social Landscape," is particularly helpful for understanding how planters and their families attempted to reconcile conflicting notions of economic success and social success.

23. For example, see Thomas Affleck to J. M. McCullough of Cincinnati, 1856, in which Affleck complains bitterly to McCullough, upon receiving a shipment of improperly packed, rotten plants that "it is the most incomprehensible thing to me that Northern and European nurserymen will not consider or inform themselves of the difference of climate!" Thomas Affleck Papers.

24. Thomas Affleck was an early advocate of native plants in America. The craze for all things native in American landscape design would not gain widespread notice until after the beginning of the twentieth century, most notably in the work of Danish-born Jens Jensen, who practiced in the American Midwest. Jensen scholars have argued whether his preference for native species was grounded in deeper racist beliefs. Despite this debate's grounding in the twentieth century, both arguments have merits relevant to Affleck's nineteenth-century career as a plantsman. Like National Socialist Germany, the structure of the antebellum South and its reliance on the institution of slavery clearly embraces the concept of racial superiority, and the letters of Thomas Affleck reflect his pro-slavery stance, as well as his ownership of enslaved laborers of African descent. Similarly, Affleck's advocacy of purebred livestock could be interpreted as a preference indicator. Considering his immigrant status, the other side of the debate (embracing native plants as a demonstration of loyalty to a new land) is equally applicable to Affleck. Future discussion in this regard is in order and will yield a significant context for understanding Thomas Affleck's body of work.

25. Affleck's letter to the editor was published in the *Natchez (Mississippi) Daily Courier,* October 23, 1854, and reprinted in George R. Stritikus, "A Nurseryman Evaluates Southern Gardens of the 1850s," *Magnolia* 12, no. 4 (Fall 1996): 1–4, 8–9.

26. Editors Daniel Lee, M. C. Redmond, and D. Redmond of the *Southern Cultivator* in 1857, qtd. in James R. Cothran, *Gardens and Historic Plants of the Antebellum South* (Columbia: University of South Carolina Press, 2003), 230.

27. *Natchez (Mississippi) Daily Courier,* October 23, 1854.

28. University of Glasgow Emblem Website/French Emblems at Glasgow Digitisation Project, http://www.emblems.arts.gla.ac.uk/french/emblem.php?id=FSAb118, accessed September 8, 2009.

29. Port Gibson is approximately thirty-five miles from Affleck's nursery.

30. *Horticulturist and Journal of Rural Art and Rural Taste* 8 (1853): 429.

31. The editors of *Southern Cultivator* in 1852 endorsed Thomas Affleck as a source of "well acclimated varieties of fruit and ornamental trees." This endorsement was credited by Martin Philips as the spark for his anti-Affleck letter, and the endorsement probably resulted in the other similar contributions to the agricultural press in 1853. For the endorsement, see *Southern Cultivator* 10 (December 1852): 368.

32. Martin Philips wrote under the pseudonym "Plebs" in his letter to the editors of the *Southern Cultivator.* See "'Acclimated' Fruit Trees," *Southern Cultivator* 11 (April 1853): 121. Affleck identified "Plebs" easily as Philips from the fruit-growing experience and biographical information outlined in the letter. Philips, a native of South Carolina, settled in Mississippi in 1830, where he became known for his farming abilities and agricultural writings. Like Affleck, he promoted fruit growing in the South and sold fruit trees, and he also was the senior editor of the short-lived weekly *Southwestern Farmer* (1841–46), published in Raymond, Mississippi. For biographical information on Martin Philips, see Alexander E. Cance, "Philips, M. W.," in *Cyclopedia of American Agriculture,* ed. Liberty Hyde Bailey (New York: Macmillan, 1909), 605. In 1853, Philips's brother-in-law and fellow farmer, Spencer Montgomery, submitted a scathing letter to the *Horticulturist* attacking Affleck's ideas about plant acclimation in the South. S. W. Montgomery, "Affleck's Almanac," *Horticulturist* 8 (1853): 328–30. For additional information on Montgomery and Philips, see Franklin L. Riley, "Diary of a Mississippi Planter, January 1, 1840 to April 1863," *Publications of the Mississippi Historical Society* 10 (1909): 305–481.

33. Montgomery, "Affleck's Almanac," 329.

34. "'Acclimated' Fruit Trees," 121.

35. "Letter from Mr. Affleck," *Southern Cultivator* 11 (December 1853): 365.

36. *Affleck's Southern Rural Almanac and Plantation and Garden Calendar for 1855,* 47. For a very similar response, see Affleck's rebuttal letter in *Southern Cultivator* 11 (December 1853): 365.

37. In this regard, however, Philips and Montgomery are referring to the South as a cultural construction and ignoring the differences in climate between the coastal Atlantic and the lower Mississippi River valley.

38. "'Acclimated' Fruit Trees," 121.

39. In some cases advertisements only gave the impression of local goods and services since local agents of northern companies also advertised in Affleck's almanac.

40. *Affleck's Southern Rural Almanac and Plantation and Garden Calendar for 1854,* title page.

A European "Northerner" in California

Richard Neutra as a Landscape Architect

JOHANNES STOFFLER

"Human nature is sometimes like an apple tree which has only to be grafted with the right stock to change completely the quality of its fruits."[1] Sigfried Giedion drew this comparison in 1951 to describe the Austrian American architect Richard Joseph Neutra (1892–1970). Giedion saw Neutra as an ennobling scion grafted onto the building activity that had occurred until then in California. He also saw him as an exceptional representative of a new and promising modernist domestic culture. With regard to Neutra's life story, Giedion's metaphor of the grafted apple tree seems appropriate in another, twofold sense: the breakthrough in Neutra's career as an architect only started when he "took root" in the new soil of California, where he had arrived in 1925, and secondly, the related profession of garden and landscape design seems grafted onto his architecture.

Neutra uniquely mastered both professions, and his evolution as a designer is evident from his numerous projects, first collected in *Richard Neutra: Buildings and Projects,* published in Zurich in 1951. The residences portrayed in the book were encompassed and permeated by carefully composed gardens. For many of these garden designs, the cultural or natural landscape in which they arose offered the leitmotif; Neutra strove, with or without the help of a landscape architect, to imitate and to enhance the landscape's inherent character by horticultural means. As scenic, staged "wilderness" created by the gardener's hand, the gardens surround his houses, flood in through the glass fronts, and permeate them through the patios and walkways. Neutra's interest in the outdoor space went far deeper than the distanced, framed view from inside the house as cultivated by the greater majority of CIAM (Congrès internationaux d'architecture moderne) architects. Unlike Le Corbusier, who perceived the garden as an artifact and sought to achieve an "un-designed" "Nature around the house," Neutra intended the garden as a cultural work to which he attributed an important mediatory role between the house and the surrounding landscape.[2] Garden and house interpenetrated each other to create a shared habitat that would have been practical, healthy, and beautiful.

Although Neutra's garden designs were very much indebted to the horticultural knowledge and exposure to plant physiognomy he gained in Switzerland, and to his assimilation of natural philosophy and study of the Japanese garden tradition prior to his move to the United States, his capacity to identify and interpret local site conditions allowed him to shape an original design language that, according to European critics, best represented the regional character and uniqueness of the California landscape.

In order to articulate the foreign trends that Neutra grafted onto American territory and culture, this essay examines the beginnings of Neutra's career as a garden designer in Europe by dwelling on the cultural context in which he worked, his collaboration with notable contemporary gardenists, and, in particular, his relationship to European modernist garden design.[3]

Neutra and Switzerland

Of all the countries of Europe, Switzerland seems closely interwoven with Neutra's life story. During the First World War, Neutra had served as an officer in the defeated Habsburg army. To recover after a malaria relapse he decided to travel to Switzerland, where, in early spring 1919, he found accommodation in a small convalescent home on Lake Zurich. The city of Zurich—as Neutra himself wrote—seemed to him, after the vicissitudes of war, "like an old coin, neatly cleaned and . . . distinctly solid and silvery," and he resolved to settle there for the time being.[4] This period of residence was to set the tone and direction of Neutra's life in many ways. Here, he met his wife-to-be, Dione, née Niedermann, who not only accompanied and supported Neutra throughout his life but also ensured that their shared Swiss network of friends and business contacts was constantly expanded.

After Neutra's emigration to the United States in 1923, Zurich became an important hub of his European network. It is in Zurich that Girsberger published the overview of his work, mentioned above, and it was there that lecture tours brought him—once in 1930 and many more times in the postwar years. It was not far from Zurich that Neutra built his three Swiss residences: Bucerius, Tillmanns-Schmidt, and Rentsch.

Moreover, Neutra's stay in Zurich in 1919 had a deep and lasting influence on his development as a designer of gardens. Absolutely penniless,

Neutra found no work as an architect and took a position as assistant with the renowned landscape gardeners Otto Froebels Erben. The company was regarded as the foremost Swiss landscape gardening firm, and its international reputation was particularly founded on its nursery business. It was one of the first in Switzerland to espouse and practice the reform gardening movement of the early twentieth century. The "Neue Gärten" (fig. 1), conceived by Otto Froebels Erben, disassociated itself from Switzerland's historicist landscape garden tradition to pursue the ideals of the Schweizerischer Werkbund (Artists and Designers Association). The "Neue Gärten" interpreted the garden as an architectural continuation of the house into the outdoor space. Zurich garden architect Gustav Ammann had been Otto Froebels Erben's artistic director since 1911. Ammann took a shine to his attentive assistant, just seven years his junior, and willingly shared his knowledge of plant breeding and propagation, the uses of plants, and garden design. He invited him to lunch with the family and sent him food packages after Neutra left Zurich for a Germany racked by economic crisis. With a loan of the then not inconsiderable sum of five hundred francs, Ammann made a significant contribution to Neutra's travel expenses to help him on his way to the United States in 1923. The cordial relationship and professional dialogue between the two is clearly demonstrated in Ammann's cor-

Fig. 1. Neue Gärten, catalogue of the Zurich landscape gardeners Otto Froebels Erben ca. 1915. (gta Archiv [NSL Archiv], ETH Zürich, estate of Gustav Ammann, 1-0202; © gta Archiv [NSL Archiv], ETH Zürich)

respondence through to Neutra's arrival in California in 1925.[5] And although his employment with Ammann lasted a mere eight months, from the spring to the fall of 1919, in retrospect Neutra regarded it as of crucial importance. In his 1962 autobiography he called Ammann "my master in the art of landscape design." In addition, in 1955, Neutra wrote in the foreword to Ammann's posthumously published book *Blühende Gärten:* "Gustav Ammann intensified my understanding that architecture was a production intimately interwoven with nature and the landscape in which it is inserted."[6] Even if this estimation may have been particularly sympathetic to honor the recently deceased Amman, it still shows Neutra's admiration of a designer who, in the course of his career, developed into one of Switzerland's leading landscape architects.

Gustav Ammann

Gustav Ammann's oeuvre comprises over 1,700 gardens and garden projects in Switzerland, especially in Zurich, and in neighboring European countries. His more than 230 publications on garden and landscape design made Ammann a driving force of his profession in Switzerland. He was a member of the Schweizerischer Werkbund and the Heimatschutz national heritage conservation association and also cultivated good relations with many foreign colleagues, especially the Germans Leberecht Migge, Peter Behrens, Karl Foerster, and Otto Valentin. Ammann was the principal garden designer for the Schweizerische Landesausstellung exhibition in 1939; he was cofounder and later president of the Swiss landscape gardeners association, the Bund Schweizerischer Gartengestalter, and shortly before his death, he was appointed secretary-general of the International Federation of Landscape Architects.

Essentially, Ammann's work can be regarded as including two creative phases. Many and well known, above all, are the commissions he executed after 1929, distinguished by—as Ammann himself stated—a "natural style of composition" (*natürliche Gestaltungsweise*).[7] The formal characteristics of these designs include unconstructed layouts and apparently "wild" scenic plantings. The natural composition style was a shaping force of the dominant modernist architectural commissions in Switzerland that included residences, housing estates, public schools, and open-air swimming pools; they also comprised many of Switzerland's "icons of modernism" from the 1930s, such as the Werkbundsiedlung Neubühl housing estate and the Allenmoos open-air swimming baths in Zurich.[8]

Fig. 2. Exuberant herbaceous planting: the Schweickhardt Garden, Zurich, 1919. (gta Archiv [NSL Archiv], ETH Zürich, Gustav Ammann estate, 1-0202; © gta Archiv [NSL Archiv], ETH Zürich)

Less well known, however, is Ammann's creative phase between 1911 and 1928. Neutra's time with Ammann lies within this "architectural garden" period, which saw the garden as the continuation of the rooms of a house under the open sky, often geometrically organized and symmetrically arranged. At first glance such designs differ distinctly from his "natural" works after 1929—in fact, while Neutra was learning from Ammann, this had already set the direction of his subsequent development. This is plain in the Schweickhardt Garden, laid out on Zürichberg in 1919, on which Neutra also worked. One interesting feature of the Schweickhardt Garden is that its architectural elements, such as the pergola, walls, and pathways were literally overrun by the vegetation (figs. 2 and 3). It is not surprising that in retrospect Ammann identified that postwar year, 1919, as the beginning of a period of transition: while in his early gardens the architectural form had taken precedence, it was now assigned a subordinate role, especially to the advantage of exuberant herbaceous plantings.[9] This was above all due to the influence of English Arts and Crafts gardens, whose mixed borders had also become possible in Switzerland thanks to the success of continental breeding. The planting schemes of gardener Gertrude Jekyll provided Ammann

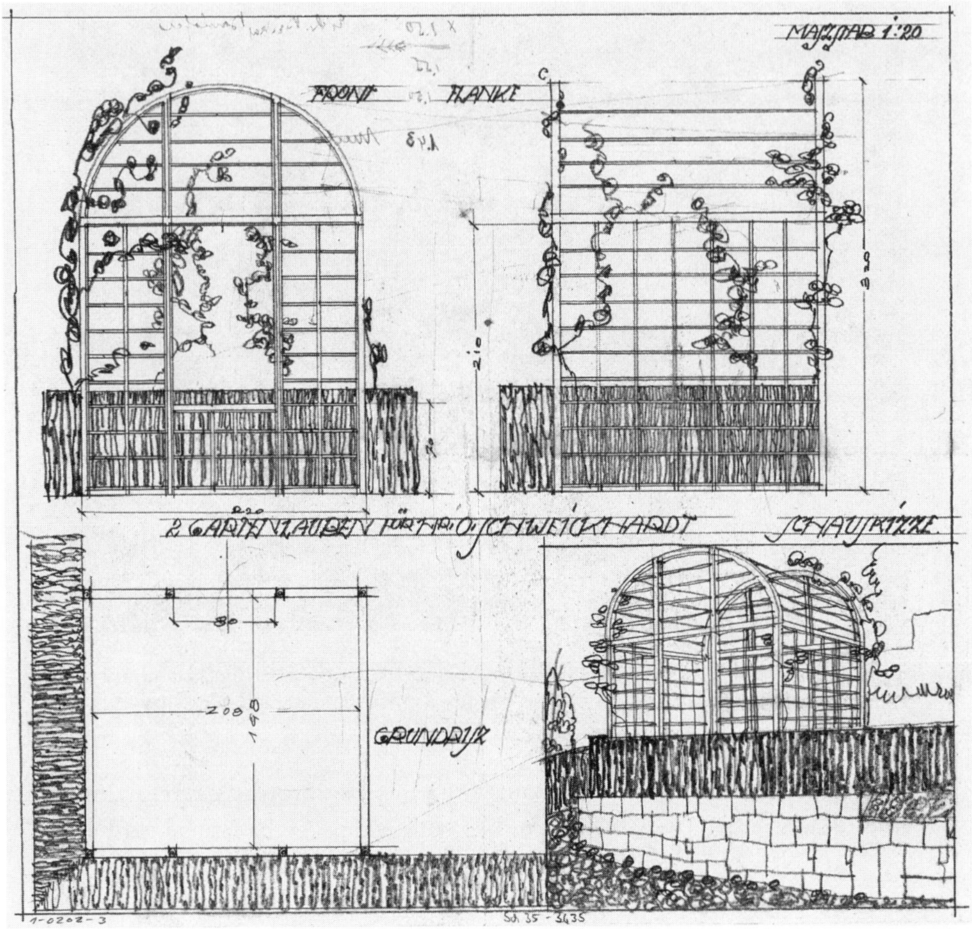

Fig. 3. The apprentice as draughtsman: sketch by Richard Neutra of a pergola in the Schweickhardt Garden, 1919. (gta Archiv [NSL Archiv], ETH Zürich, Gustav Ammann estate, 1-0202; © gta Archiv [NSL Archiv], ETH Zürich)

with a shining example and model for his own planting design. Amman knew Jekyll's work both firsthand and from such publications as *Wood and Garden* (1904), but the German herbaceous perennial breeder Karl Foerster also exerted a strong influence on Ammann through his publications.

A Language of Landscape

Along with his work as a draftsman, Neutra mainly carried out a gardener's everyday duties in the nurseries, as recorded in his diary: "Taking cuttings, pinching off buds, potting on, tying up seed heads, planting out, propagating, pricking out, sowing (. . .)! Sun, weariness—I'm deeply suntanned and work in my shirtsleeves."[10] Neutra comprehended the gardener's craft and the mastery of plants as design material, as the foundation of artistic design in the garden, writing: "In order to learn to paint, first you have to internalize the nomenclature of all the existing names of the colors. You have to experience the colors little by little. Application for the garden arts."[11] Ammann's work inspired Neutra: "Herr Ammann makes an ever-stronger impression when his planting schemes conjure up entire glorious gardens in my mind's eye." In his terse notes (fig. 4), Neutra describes plants, their growth habit, blooming period, and uses; he was interested in many herbaceous perennials and geophytes with a wilderness character such as wild tulips, veronica, and ferns. With regard to shrubs and trees, he mainly mentions those species that stand out for their picturesque growth habit and

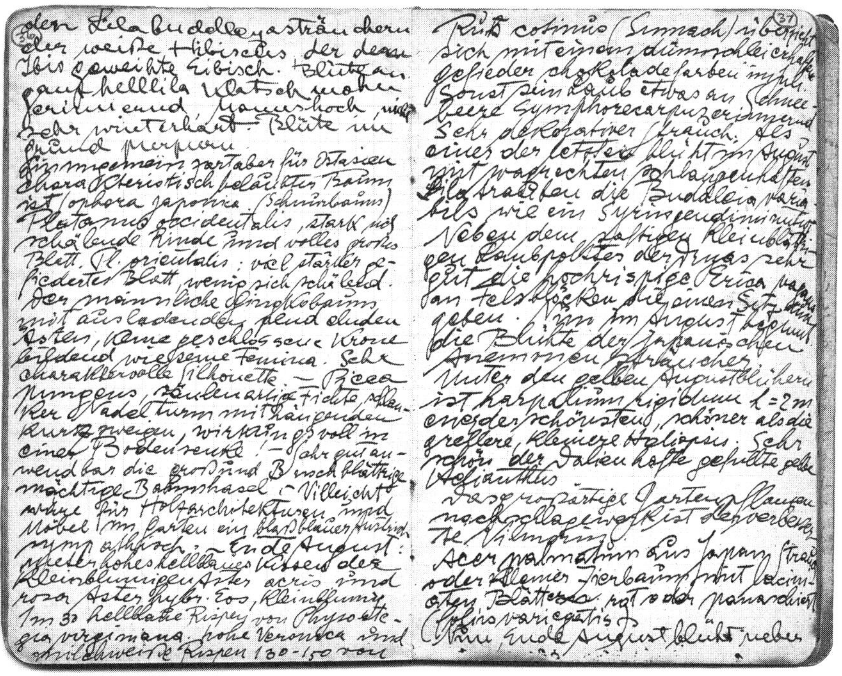

Fig. 4. Hungry for knowledge: notes on plants in Neutra's Zurich diary, summer 1919. University of California Los Angeles, Department of Special Collections, Richard and Dion Neutra Papers, Box 335, vol. 7, 36–37. (Permissions courtesy Dion Neutra, Architect © and Richard and Dion Neutra Papers, Department of Special Collections, Charles E. Young Research Library, UCLA)

hardiness, such as the newly introduced *Cotoneaster horizontalis* or the *Acer palmatum*.

In Ammann's library Neutra discovered Karl Foerster's 1913 book *Winterharte Blütenstauden und Sträucher der Neuzeit*, which for the first time provided a detailed overview of the herbaceous perennial species and varieties that would grow satisfactorily in the continental climate of Germany and northern Switzerland. Almost fifty years later, Neutra recalled in his autobiography how Ammann elucidated the book's approach in their conversations, and in this there lies an important key to understanding Neutra's notion of garden design. Foerster considered herbaceous perennials as "a way of marrying the flowering romanticism of the wilderness with the garden and . . . bringing something of the taste and aroma of the primeval solitude into our garden realm."[12] In this, Foerster was following the theories of German landscape gardener Willy Lange, who had also written the foreword to Foerster's publication. In his own book *Gartengestaltung der Neuzeit* (1907), Lange had called for a "Naturgarten"—a garden designed according to the principles of plant sociology and aesthetics. Lange was here taking up ideas that had been publicized by the German botanist Hermann Berge and the Irish garden writer William Robinson. Lange differentiated between the character of the location and the physiognomy of the individual plants, understanding the term *character* as a cultural leitmotif that was defined in a "Naturgarten" by the landscape. In the character of a landscape, both the biological and sociological suitability of the plant would be simultaneously revealed. "The landscape receives its 'character' through the plant societies; the plant communities draw the lines in the countenance of the landscape."[13] The term *physiognomy* was, however, intended by Lange as the specific adaptation of a plant to its location, which, for example, became apparent through its habit of growth. This definition was also, according to Lange, applicable to the garden arts: "I can," he concluded, "arrange the combinations and distribution of plants in the garden following the example of natural plant societies."[14] Lange valued exotic species as enrichment for the garden; the prerequisite for their use, however, was that their physiognomy fitted in with the character of a garden's location. The aim was not to copy natural locations but rather—as Lange wrote, "the enhancement of nature in the garden so that it becomes a work of art"[15] (fig. 5).

In the Froebel nurseries in Zurich and during his discussions with Ammann, Neutra also learned to distinguish "character" from "physiognomy," as he recalled in his autobiography: "The landscape designer can play up

Fig. 5. Enhanced woodland wilderness: planting scheme after Karl Foerster, 1913. From Karl Foerster, *Winterharte Blütenstauden und Sträucher der Neuzeit* (Leipzig, 1912), 186.

both cultural 'character' and natural 'physiognomy' to support his site creation and its allegiance to the surrounding of natural and cultural landscape. . . . I learned to arrange plants as to growth, size, color, and season of bloom. I recognized the associations which may link their character to peasant or castle gardens, or on the other hand, their physiognomy, seemingly indicating to everyone, not only to the botanist, say, a moisture-laden habitat, or a dry sandy spot, or a wind-swept hilltop, or a deeply eroded ravine, bravely reclaimed by 'native' vegetation. It all became a never-ending inspiration."[16] At the time of writing this, Neutra's stay with Amman was more than forty years in the past, but the memory was clear as day. Its essence, that is, Lange's ideas, was precisely rendered—because Neutra had been employing them in his work all his life.

After his emigration to the United States, Neutra continued to place these considerations about vegetation ecology at the forefront of his notion of contemporary gardens. This, he first elucidated in his contribution to the catalog of *Contemporary Landscape Architecture,* an exhibition staged in 1937 at the San Francisco Museum of Modern Art. Neutra posited that the "keynote" of modern architecture lay in the way it opened itself to the exterior space, for whose design, aspects of its use, and the biology of the site had to be given priority: "And the garden around it is laid out for the enjoyment of bodily exercise and mental relaxation in a setting that is an ensemble of plants which can keep natural company—which are not arbitrarily assembled like a masquerade party, in opposition to climate, exposures, soil conditions and biological decency."[17] The integration of the house and its garden with the natural surroundings and its flora were regarded by Neutra as vital: "Our relation to the natural setting is a biologically minded appreciation of the soil, in which all life is rooted and must remain rooted, to succeed."[18]

Neutra was convinced that he had discovered principles underlying the nature of the garden, which he also consequently sought to use for the benefit of his houses' dwellers. He conceived of house and garden as a kind of inspirited biotope in which the laws of nature and the spiritual dimension were equally strongly reflected. In his 1951 book *Mystery and Realities of the Site,* Neutra lamented the alienation of modern human beings from nature. The realities of a one-sided, profit-oriented civilization were hardly concerned with the significance and mysteries of a place. The garden and the house, he demanded, must however respond to and work with what he called the "biological memory" of the human race, its evolutionarily grounded need to be close to nature. Against the dread specter of the "realities," therefore, Neutra offered his idea of *biorealism,* a neologism by which he meant leading people back to an inspirited nature with the help of the latest scientific discoveries from the fields of biology, sociology, and technology, which should also be applied in architecture and garden design.[19] There—where Nature had been lost—is where she should be re-created for people.

Japanese Influences

With his idea of biorealism Neutra was building on monistic natural philosophy, a body of thought established by the German zoologist and natural philosopher Ernst Haeckel, whom Neutra had read and reflected upon during his Vienna years, that is, before World War I.[20] Monism was a populist scientific theory combining aspects of Darwin's theory of evolution with pantheism, which held that God was the equivalent of the natural universe.

It is hardly surprising that Neutra's comprehension of Far Eastern culture—and especially of Japanese gardens—was strongly influenced by this philosophical leitmotif. In his foreword to David H. Engel's *Japanese Gardens for Today* in 1959 he delineated the Japanese garden rather histrionically as the expression of "long-range values of equilibrium" and as "symbolic linking of time before the soul of man."[21]

Back in his Vienna years, Neutra had already concerned himself intensely with Japanese domestic culture.[22] His reading included—as he noted in his diary—F. Baltzer's 1903 essay *Das Japanische Haus: Eine bautechnische Studie,* which primarily addressed in detail the climatic and cultural conditions and structural characteristics of Japanese architecture. Neutra copied entire passages from Edwin S. Morse's *Japanese Homes and Their Surroundings,* published in 1886, which casts light upon his subsequent work; he was particularly struck by the way Japanese houses opened to the outside space by means of movable walls: "In the Japanese House . . . there are two or more sides, that have no permanent walls. . . . The screens may be opened by sliding them back, or they may be entirely removed thus throwing a number of rooms into one great apartment. In the same way the whole side of a house may be flung open to sunlight and air."[23] Morse's book also devoted a chapter to Japanese gardens, in which he noted, among other features, the gardens' "irregularly and grotesquely shaped stones and huge slabs of rock" or the "stone pathways, and curious trees and shrubs so characteristic of the Japanese gardens"[24] (fig. 6).

Neutra's early discovery of the "curious trees and shrubs" of East Asia is also apparent from his Zurich diaries. He studied the catalog of what was at that time the largest nursery in Europe, Veitch & Sons in London, which imported and propagated the beauties of Far Eastern flora in grand style. Also the catalog of Louis Boehmer & Co., based in Yokohama, then the principal exporter of Japanese plants to central Europe, drew Neutra's attention; his notes pulsate with passionate enthusiasm, writing of *Sophora japonica* as "an exceptionally delicate and for eastern Asia typically leaved tree" or declaring: "The tulip tree is a wonderful Chinese plant."[25]

When Neutra first traveled to Japan in 1930, his awareness of the country's gardens was already sharpened. Fêted as a celebrity by his Japanese hosts, Neutra was treated to an intense program of receptions and visits that also took him to Kyoto—"almost untouched in its antiquity," as he later reminisced. Japanese gardens remained a shaping experience: "Seeing, hearing, smelling a scent from the tiny garden court, enjoying one's inner senses of position and muscle strain in following a zigzag path and gently climb-

Fig. 6. The poetry of simplicity: view of a garden with stepping stones in Kyoto. From David H. Engel, *Japanese Gardens for Today* (Rutland, VT, 1959), 169. (© Tuttle Publishing)

ing a gooseneck bridge over the lotus pond—all seemed to make an art of subtly knowing man's many and fused responses."[26] Nevertheless, for all Neutra's admiration of Japanese culture, simply copying its gardens was out of the question. Rather, he was seeking ways of interweaving his own origins and the foreign into a new cultural material. Once in California, Neutra included single rocks, stepping stone paths, picturesque plantings, and occasionally even bonsai trees in his garden designs, firmly rooted in his European influences and at the same time responding to the climate and domestic culture of the region. "The author of this valuable book rightly warns against its being used superficially for the shallow imitation of fragments," admonished Neutra in his foreword to *Japanese Gardens for Today,* thus echoing the opinions of his earlier master and mentor Gustav Ammann.[27] In 1955 Amman warned, "Never, ever, may the garden architect be a simple copyist or snatcher of motifs." His proposal for the integration of the foreign into one's own creations describes Neutra's creative process as well: "Out of all these diverse influences, the main thing is now, with wise moderation, with restraint and tact, to select the happy mean from our climate and our habits of living . . . and to create freely, using today's technical possibilities, without being fixated on old forms."[28]

Quoting a Language of Landscape: The Kaufmann House Garden

While Neutra probably worked on every conceivable kind of commission from housing developments to public administration buildings in his career as an architect, the residential house was particularly well suited to illustrating his vision of a biorealistic life. Along with the Tremaine House it was above all the internationally fêted Kaufmann House, built in 1946, that clarified and exemplified Neutra's ideals, in some ways taken to extremes. Neutra's clients were the wealthy businessman Edgar J. Kaufmann and his wife, Liliane, who had commissioned Fallingwater near Pittsburgh from Frank Lloyd Wright some ten years earlier. The new house in the California desert near Palm Springs, at the foot of Mount San Jacinto, was to serve the couple as a winter vacation residence. The bungalow opened itself toward the garden through generously proportioned sliding glass doors and window fronts. Here, on the lee side of the building, was the swimming pool, set in sweeping lawns and loose groups of small shrubs and herbaceous perennial plantings.

Neutra himself was involved in laying out the garden, as he emphasized to the Kaufmanns: "from early sketches . . . visiting various nurseries, submitting plant lists, to digging up cacti and arranging boulders."[29] The character of the desert, horticulturally staged by Neutra as a leitmotif in diverse nuances, played an important role in the design. Most dominant was the character of the rocky desert on the side of the house looking toward the mountain, where one was exposed to the winds, and, after heavy rainfall, a watercourse between the rocks appeared. For this area, explained Neutra: "The natural desert planting between boulders we shall simply provide with a few glorified accents."[30] Along with the indigenous physiognomies (discussed with Lange) such as agave, prickly pear, and Washingtonia palms, the Australian tea tree *Leptospermum* with its luxuriant violet blooms bestowed colorful accents.[31] The plants for Neutra's plans were supplied by Walter's Nursery, a company founded by German immigrants in Los Angeles. From Walter's, Neutra acquired succulents but most especially a rich selection of herbaceous perennials, most of them from other parts of the world; by ordering cotoneaster, privet, and hibiscus, Neutra was using species that he had noted and described in his 1919 Zurich diary.

In the entrance area, too, Neutra enriched the aspects of the desert flora with attractive exotics; bougainvillea and yellow lantana bloomed here alongside yucca and pachycereus cacti. The structure of the plantings was created by species with pronouncedly sculptural qualities; while Neutra had favored large-leafed species such as philodendron or banana plants for other commissions, here he turned to bizarre desert shapes such as the ocatillo with its long upward-striving spiky shoots. The rocks were also an important design feature, bringing a characteristic of the desert into the garden to be deliberately stylized. The spatial tension created by the setting of single stones, and also the paving stones at the entrance, were reminiscent of Japanese models with which Neutra had been familiar since his trip to Japan in 1930 (fig. 7).

Neutra designed the area around the swimming pool as an obvious and striking contrast to the natural desert landscape. Here, he was clearly meet-

Fig. 7. Luxuriant desert vegetation: the entrance area of the Kaufmann House ca. 1950. From Richard and Dion Neutra, *Pflanzen Wasser Steine Licht* (Berlin, 1974), 37. (Permissions courtesy Dion Neutra, Architect)

ing a widespread desire of his clients, something he admitted as early as 1925 in a letter to Amman: "What entices us most—the dracaena, the grotesque Joshua tree, the multifarious cacti—is not so popular among the inhabitants; it is too familiar and above all too much of the desert. California culture means irrigation, erasing the desert and all its traces."[32] Liliane Kaufmann, too, had originally asked Neutra to refrain from the all-too-frequent use of cacti—and actually only a few rocks around the swimming pool remind residents and guests of the surrounding desert. The water for the pool was pumped from the property's own groundwater well and also generously sprinkled the plants at the heart of this private oasis. It circulated constantly on the hard surfaces of the outdoor space and thus prevented it from overheating by day and chilling at night. However, the immaculately green and practical lawn did more than promise a piece of American normality in the middle of the desert; it also contributed to the creation of a temperate microclimate, maintained with copious amounts of water. The nature of the garden included not only an aesthetic component—it was also functional.

A "Northerner" in California

Neutra's garden design for the Kaufmann House does not sit naturally in the panorama of U.S. landscape architecture during and after the Second World War. Some established garden history publications addressing modernist landscape architecture in the United States describe the late 1930s as a period of transition and departure from the formal Beaux-Arts garden as presented by Louise Shelton in her 1915 *Beautiful Gardens of America.*[33] Young designers mainly working in California, such as Garrett Eckbo (1910–2000), Lawrence Halprin (1916–2009), and also Thomas Church (1902–1978), were hailed as the rising generation of landscape architects seeking new forms of expression in the garden. Influenced by modernist architecture and arts, their designs experimented with abstract geometrical, but also organic, forms in the plan and largely avoided naturalistic interpretations of landscape elements. Neutra's garden designs, however, can hardly be included within these movements.

The cultural context of Neutra's design approach is apparent in the book *Modern Gardens* (1953) by British architect Peter Shepheard. Shepheard presented only a few examples of recent California garden designs, such as Thomas Church's Martin and Donnell Gardens; this was less a sign of his low consideration for the new, as presented by Church's garden, than it was of the fact that this new generation of California gardens was comprehended as still being in embryo. The other selections in the book, however, including the Kaufmann Garden, reflected the cultural origins of an author who openly professed his affinity for William Robinson's "Wild Garden." Like Neutra, Shepheard assigned the study of natural plant societies a central role in garden design: "The lessons to be learnt from a study of these natural patterns of growth . . . will suggest principles . . . for placing all plants in surroundings other than their natural ones."[34] Shepheard thus emphasized the significance of an artistic transformation process, from natural models through to the garden. The product was thereby a portrayal of the environment on the one hand, and an abstraction of its phenotypes on the other.

The majority of examples in Shepheard's book stood for this modernist design approach, which Brigitt Sigel and Erik de Jong recently described most appositely with the term *abstract naturalism*.[35] Apart from Neutra's Kaufmann House, this approach was most clearly apparent in the first, 1953 edition (in which no German examples were shown so soon after the war) and exemplified by work dating from the 1930s and 1940s in England, Denmark, Sweden, and Switzerland. Many of these examples also showed clear signs of their designers' involvement with the Japanese garden arts, incorporating such motifs as stepping stone paths, setting single stones, or Asiatic planting designs. Shepheard documented, for instance, Sven Markelius's private garden near Stockholm (fig. 8), a garden by Carl Theodor Sørensen at Øresund, the London South Bank Exhibition of 1951, and Gustav Ammann's Hauser Garden on Zürichberg from 1936[36] (fig. 9). In 1955 Ammann himself ascribed his work to an international circle of designers from central Europe and Scandinavia that he called, for the sake of simplicity, the "Nordländer" or "Northerners," among them Hermann Mattern (1902–1971), Sven Hermelin (1900–1984), and Mien Ruys (1904–1999).[37] In fact, over the preceding twenty-five years this circle had developed a comparable design vocabulary that had established itself within the traditionally close professional discourse in this part of Europe. In this respect, Neutra's garden design for the Kaufmann House may be read as an adaptation of the Northerners' design language to the American West. Like his European-based colleagues, Neutra grounded his designs in the leitmotif of the ambient natural landscape, apparently unsullied by modern civilization. These cultural components of the "character" of a landscape were interpreted through the materialization of the design; his selection and use of plants did not correspond

Fig. 8. Swedish garden landscape: the Markelius Garden in Kevinge (1933). (Photograph by Bo Törngren/Arkitektur- och designcentrum Stockholm)

solely to the location's natural plant society but also drew associatively on its aspects and enriched it with attractive garden plants. The innovative nature of Neutra's design achievement lay in the way it adapted the Northerners' design approach to California conditions, as it was not only the region's climatic zone and vegetation that set fundamentally different conditions for the design of a garden; its inhabitants' easygoing attitude to life and extravagant use of natural resources also offered new design parameters.

Fig. 9. A Northerners' garden: Ammann's Hauser Garden in Zurich (1936). (gta Archiv [NSL Archiv], ETH Zürich, estate of Gustav Ammann, 1-0202; © gta Archiv [NSL Archiv], ETH Zürich)

Back at the Roots

After the Second World War, Neutra's work attracted lively interest in Europe and Switzerland, being presented as forward-looking as early as September 1945 at the Kunstgewerbemuseum Zürich's *USA Baut* exhibition (fig. 10), which was supported by the U.S. Office of War Information with work by thirty-seven other architects including Frank Lloyd Wright, Walter Gropius, Marcel Breuer, and Philip Johnson. Alfred Roth expressed his hope that the exhibition would provide new impetus from the "greatest sister democracy" for Switzerland's architectural culture, which during the war had suffered "a serious deprivation of free professional and intellectual dialogue."[38] This view may have ignored the considerable achievements of Swiss architecture in the 1930s and 1940s as impressively described by the American writer on architecture G. E. Kidder-Smith in his book *Switzerland Builds;*[39] nevertheless it voiced the hunger for the new that had stirred in Switzerland with the advent of peace and the end of the country's isolation. Neutra's architecture, it seemed, caught the spirit of those times. "California Lifestyle" was the *Zürcher Tagesanzeiger*'s headline to its enthusiastic 1954 description of Neutra's architecture with "its large French doors, its often exotic-seeming transitions from outside to inside," praising them as being "grown into the landscape" and "living for our times."[40] Neutra enjoyed exceptional popularity in Switzerland, more so than his American colleagues; *Das Werk,* the leading Swiss journal of architecture and crafts, went so far as to describe him as "the most striking personality in American architecture."[41]

Neutra was primarily celebrated as an architect in Switzerland and his work disseminated through architectural publications; these were, however, appreciated by those circles of garden designers who cultivated a taste for seeking inspiration beyond their professional "garden gate." The expansiveness of Neutra's works and the way they used architectural geometries in the garden stood in direct opposition to the work of many Swiss garden designers, especially those of the older generations such as Walter Leder (1892–1985) and Johannes Schweizer (1901–1983), but also Gustav Ammann. The private gardens they had created during the war years were above all rightly seen as "overloaded with motifs" in their infatuation with detail and occasionally diffuse layouts.[42] Against this background, Neutra's spacious works offered the occasion for self-critical stocktaking to some Swiss garden designers—not least Neutra's earlier master and mentor. In 1955 Ammann devoted an entire chapter of his book to the "Californian Gardens," comprehending it together with Japanese and Italian gardens as a source of valuable inspiration for himself and his colleagues. Along with work by Lawrence Halprin, Emmet Layton, and Osmundson & Staley, Richard Neutra was comprehensively represented with the Tremaine (1948), Rourke (1949), and Brod (1951) gardens. The obvious differences between Neutra's garden designs and those of his younger California colleagues were not commented upon by Ammann; rather, he took the California examples as a general admonition to the Northerners' garden culture: "Gardens in California . . . particularly impress us Northerners by virtue of their clear-cut, practical lines and their breadth of conception, for at present we cannot do enough to deformalize our lay-outs or cultivate the picturesque."[43] In the years that followed, the younger generation of Swiss landscape architects did actually, along with Japanese and Scandinavian influences, look to the "American style . . . i.e. no hedges, open terrain, villas with swimming pool and everything very orderly," for creative inspiration.[44] The rather nebulous character of this definition by Swiss landscape architect Walter Bischoff (b. 1926) indicates, however, that this influence never developed into an autonomous style but was much more an amalgamation of local design praxis

Fig. 10. USA baut, poster for the exhibition at the Kunstgewerbemuseum Zürich in 1945. (Museum für Gestaltung, Zürich, poster collection; © 2014, ProLitteris, Zurich)

and the international cultural exchange that grew exponentially from the 1950s onward. "Nowadays," wrote Ammann in 1955, "when the distances between countries, between continents even, plays only a minor role, our outlook has been powerfully enriched. We are familiar with the ways and customs, forms and designs, plants and landscapes of the South and North. A vast amount of visual material is available to us, and we would like to see some fortunate picture from the gardens of far-off lands or times in our own garden."[45] Neutra's gardens are linked with and form part of this "visual material" in a most particular way. His oeuvre is rooted in the cultures of two continents. It does more than build a bridge between the European and North American modernist garden cultures—it also reminds us that a foreign trend on any soil does not generally indicate a one-way cultural transfer but is part of the living panorama of cultural exchange.

Notes

This essay is partly the result of my research while a Visiting Fellow at Harvard Graduate School of Design in 2010, which was made possible by a scholarship from the Swiss National Fund but even more so by the institutional and intellectual support of Christophe Girot and Dorothée Imbert. To them, and also to Marc Treib, Thomas Hines, and Erik de Jong for professional and academic advice and support, I would like to express my gratitude and appreciation.

1. Sigfried Giedion, "R.J. Neutra. Europäer und Amerikaner," in Willy Boesinger, *Richard Neutra: Buildings and Projects* (Zurich: Girsberger, 1951), 10.

2. Le Corbusier and Pierre Jeanneret, *Zwei Wohnhäuser* (Stuttgart: Wedeking & Co., 1927), 37.

3. While Neutra's architecture has been thoroughly researched and its relationship to the topography of his sites examined, the landscape gardening dimension of his work has not thus far been sufficiently appreciated. On Neutra's architecture see Thomas Hines, *Richard Neutra and the Search for Modern Architecture* (New York: Rizzoli, 2005), and Renata Wandel-Hoefer, "Zur Architektur Richard Neutras—eine Analyse seines theoretischen Werkes und der Umsetzung in seinen Bauten" (diss., Technische Hochschule Darmstadt, 1989). On the relationships between architecture and topography, see David Leatherbarrow, *Uncommon Ground: Architecture, Technology, and Topography* (Cambridge, MA: MIT Press, 2000). A first evaluation of Neutra as a landscape architect was provided by Hubertus Adam, "'The site, well treated, is a lasting source of happiness': Richard Neutra und die Landschaftsarchitektur," in *Richard Neutra in Europa: Bauten und Projekte, 1960–1970,* ed. Klaus Leuschel and Marta Herford, exhibition catalog by Marta Herford (Cologne: DuMont Buchverlag, 2010), 149–56. Neutra as a "horticultural exception" in modern architecture is discussed in Johannes Stoffler, "Neutra als Gärtner: Vom seltenen Bekenntnis eines Architekten zur Hortikultur," in Institut für Landschaftsarchitektur ETH Zürich, *Mies als Gärtner,* pamphlet no. 14 (Zurich, 2011), 56–62. Johannes Stoffler, "Pflanzenverwendung auf Transatlantisch: Richard Neutra als Gartengestalter," in *Topiaria Helvetica* (2012): 28–38, concentrates on the aspect of Neutra's use of plants related to specific passages from this considerably more extensive essay.

4. Richard Neutra, *Life and Shape* (New York: Appleton-Century-Crofts, 1962), 136–37.

5. NSL (gta) Archiv ETH Zürich, estate of Gustav Ammann.

6. Richard Neutra, introduction to Gustav Ammann, *Blühende Gärten* (Erlenbach-Zurich: Verlag für Architektur, 1955), 7.

7. Johannes Stoffler, *Gustav Ammann: Landschaften der Moderne in der Schweiz* (Zurich: gta-Verlag, 2008), 82.

8. Johannes Stoffler, "Modernism for the Public: Swimming Pool Landscapes in Swit-

zerland," in *Modernism and Landscape Architecture, 1890–1940,* ed. Therese O'Malley and Joachim Wolschke-Bulmahn (Washington DC: National Gallery of Art; New Haven, CT: Yale University Press, 2015).

9. Gustav Ammann, "Die Entwicklung der Gartengestaltung von 1900–1950," in *Der Gärtnermeister* 53, no. 41 (1950): 1–11.

10. Neutra Papers, University of California, Special Collections, Box 335, Diary vol. 7, June 1919. In the original German: "Stecklinge schneiden, Pincieren, Eintopfen, Samenstände stutzen, Verpflanzen, vermehren, Pickieren, säen, [. . .]! Sonne und Müdigkeit. Ich bin ganz und gar braungebrannt und arbeite im Hemd."

11. Neutra Papers, University of California, Special Collections, Box 335, Diary vol. 7, September 1919. In the original German: "Um die Malerei zu erlernen, hat man recht zuerst die Nomenklatur aller vorhandenen Farbennamen intus zu haben. Die Farben muss man erleben nach und nach. Anwendung auf die Gartenkunst."

12. Karl Foerster, *Winterharte Blütenstauden und Sträucher der Neuzeit* (Leipzig, 1913), 8. In the original German: "Möglichkeit, Blumenromantik der Wildnis dem Garten zu vermählen und etwas vom Schmuck und Aroma urweltlicher Einsamkeit . . . in unseren Gartenbereich hineinzuziehen."

13. Willy Lange, *Gartengestaltung der Neuzeit* (Leipzig: J. J. Weber, 1907), 147.

14. Ibid., 149.

15. Ibid., 151.

16. Neutra, *Life and Shape,* 137–38.

17. Richard Neutra, "Landscaping—A New Issue," in San Francisco Museum of Modern Art, *Contemporary Landscape Architecture and Its Sources,* exhibition catalog (San Francisco, 1937), 22.

18. Ibid.

19. Richard Neutra, "Der Gartenarchitekt—Seniorpartner des Architekten," in *Pflanzen Wasser Steine Licht,* ed. Hermann Exner and Dione Neutra (Berlin: Parey, 1974), 8.

20. Neutra, *Life and Shape,* 53.

21. Richard Neutra, foreword to David H. Engel, *Japanese Gardens for Today* (Rutland, VT: Charles E. Tuttle, 1959), xii.

22. Wandel-Hoefer, "Zur Architektur Richard Neutras," 67–84.

23. Neutra Papers, University of California, Special Collections, Box 335, Diary vol. 6, cited by Wandel-Hoefer, "Zur Architektur Richard Neutras," 72.

24. Edward S. Morse, *Japanese Homes and Their Surroundings* (New York: Harper, 1895), 275.

25. Neutra Papers, University of California, Special Collections, Box 335, Diary vol. 7, 36 and 44.

26. Neutra, *Life and Shape,* 227. The articles that Neutra published after his travels excluded the gardens (still in line with avant-garde principles) in favor of new architecture and engineering. See Richard Neutra, "Gegenwärtige Bauarbeit in Japan," *Die Form* 6, no. 1 (1931): 22–28; "Die Japanische Wohnung: Ableitung. Schwierigkeiten," *Die Form* 6, no. 3 (1931): 92–106; "Neue Architektur in Japan," *Die Form* 6, no. 9 (1931): 333.

27. Ammann revered Japanese culture but was familiar with it only through publications and exhibitions. For him, the Japanese garden showed a way to "what could be achieved through greater internalization, through ensoulment of the Material," as he pos-

ited in 1933. See Johannes Stoffler, "Es ist überall Erdbebenzeit: Gustav Ammann (1885–1955) und die Landschaft der Moderne in der Schweiz" (diss., ETH Zürich, 2006), 151.

28. The original English translation, "Under no circumstances must the landscape architect be concerned simply with imitation or with the reproduction of existing motifs," hardly does justice to the resoluteness of Ammann's original German, and the second half of the quotation is omitted. In the German it reads: "Aus all diesen verschiedenen Einflüssen nun kommt es darauf an, mit weiser Mäßigung, mit Zurückhaltung und Takt das unserem Klima und unseren Lebensgewohnheiten Gemäße auszuwählen . . . und mit den heutigen technischen Mitteln frei schaffen, ohne nach alten Formen zu schielen." Ammann, *Blühende Gärten,* 10 (German) and 24 (English).

29. Neutra Papers, University of California, Special Collections, Box 1179, letter from Neutra to Edgar Kaufmann, November 28, 1946.

30. Ibid., letter from Neutra to Liliane Kaufmann, April 20, 1946.

31. Ibid., Kaufmann House, plant list from Walter's Nursery, undated.

32. NSL (gta) Archiv ETH Zürich, Gustav Ammann estate, letter from Neutra to Ammann, undateable, around spring 1925. In the original German: "Was uns am meisten lockt, die Dracaenen, der groteske Josuahbaum, die vielerlei Kakteen, ist bei der Bevölkerung nicht so sehr beliebt, es ist ihnen zu gewöhnlich und vor allem zu wüstenhaft. Kalifornische Kultur heißt Bewässerung, Ausmärzen der Wüste mit allen ihren Spuren."

33. On modernist landscape architecture see, for example, Marc Treib, ed., *Modern Landscape Architecture: A Critical Review* (Cambridge, MA: MIT Press, 1993), and Marc Treib and Dorothée Imbert, eds., *Garrett Eckbo: Modern Landscapes for Living* (Berkeley: University of California Press, 1997).

34. Peter F. Shepheard, *Modern Gardens: Masterworks of International Garden Architecture* (New York: F. A. Praeger, 1954), 21.

35. Brigitt Sigel and Erik A. de Jong, *Der Seeuferweg in Zürich: Eine Spazierlandschaft der Moderne von 1963* (Zurich: Scheidegger & Spiess, 2010), 16.

36. Also worth mentioning in this connection are the following examples, all from Shepheard, *Modern Gardens:* Bernard Rudofsky (who emigrated from Austria-Hungary) in Brazil, 34–37; Karl Koch (influenced by his collaboration with Sven Markelius in Sweden) in Lincoln, Massachusetts, 54–55; Tayler and Green in England, 92–95; Sven Hermelin and Inger Wedborn in Sweden, 114–15; and Holger Blom and Erik Glemme in Sweden, 118–29.

37. Ammann, *Blühende Gärten,* 16, 26.

38. Alfred Roth (1946), "Bemerkungen zur neueren Amerikanischen Architektur," in *U.S.A. baut,* guide no. 167 to the exhibition at the Kunstgewerbemuseum Zürich from September 8 to October 7, 1945 (Basel, 1946), 14.

39. George Everald Kidder-Smith, *Switzerland Builds: Its Native and Modern Architecture* (New York: Albert Bonnier, 1950).

40. R. A. Braun, "Kalifornischer Lebensstil," in *Tages-Anzeiger für Stadt und Kanton Zürich,* January 22, 1954, n.p.

41. Alfred Roth, "Neue Arbeiten von Richard J. Neutra," in *Werk* 34, no. 10 (1947): 313.

42. Otto Valentien, "Eindrücke der heutigen Schweizer Gartengestaltung," *Garten und Landschaft* 63, no. 1 (1953): 15.

43. Ammann, *Blühende Gärten,* 26.

44. Mirjam Bucher Bauer, "Pioniere der Landschaftsarchitektur in der Schweiz: Interview with Walter Bischoff, Renens (Lausanne)," *Der Gartenbau* 17, no. 16 (2005): 17.

45. Ammann, *Blühende Gärten,* 22. Again, the English translation of Amman's text in the book does not accurately reflect the German original: "Wo die Distanzen zwischen den Ländern, ja zwischen den Erdteilen nur mehr eine geringe Rolle spielen ist unsere Anschauung gewaltig bereichert. Wir kennen Sitten und Gebräuche, Formen und Gestalten, Pflanzen und Landschaften des Südens und des Nordens. Ein ungeheures Bildermaterial steht uns zur Verfügung, und wir möchten manch beglückendes Bild aus Gärten ferner Länder oder Zeiten im eigenen Garten verwirklicht sehen" (8). The English quote above was translated by Mic Hale and the author.

PART 5

The Pull of the Orient

Political Landscapes

Japanese Gardens at San Francisco's World's Fairs of 1915 and 1939

KENDALL H. BROWN

While most studies in this anthology examine how Americans imported and appropriated foreign landscape styles in response to evolving ideas of Americanness, this essay looks at gardens in America from the standpoint of the exporter. It investigates how Japanese officials created Japanese gardens at world's fairs in America in order to clarify, and reify, Japanese identity. It places these desires within specific political contexts and traces American popular responses to these politicized foreign gardens. Although exposition gardens had a broad impact on American garden building and civic culture, it is important to understand the international dynamic at stake in the transmission of some garden styles. The creation of "Japanese gardens" on the international stage was critical in disseminating Japan's image abroad, where gardens served as cultural ambassadors, and in addressing domestic Japanese concerns over the nation's identity in an age of cultural anxiety and political turmoil for an imperial government in power only since 1868.

This essay investigates two Japanese gardens built at world's fairs in San Francisco: the Panama-Pacific International Exposition of 1915 and the Golden Gate Exposition of 1939–40[1] (fig. 1). As with the expositions in Chicago in 1893 and St. Louis in 1904, these fairs coincided with debate over Japan's aggressive foreign policies. As a result, Japan, perennially a major player in international expositions, made particularly large displays in 1915, a year of rabid anti-Japanese immigration sentiment in California, and in 1939, when Japan's war in China intensified diplomatic tension across the Pacific. Despite the rise of modernism as the de facto style for exposition architecture, at both fairs Japan presented a united front of historicizing architecture and landscape. Aware that, in the competitive cacophony of the exposition ground, nations benefited from a cohesive national style as a visual brand and an expression of ethnic community, Japanese officials

Fig. 1. "Full View, Japanese Pavilion, Treasure Island." San Francisco. Postcard, 1939. (Private collection)

continued the neotraditional styles that had garnered positive response at foreign fairs from the late nineteenth century.[2]

Several factors explain these fair gardens' success and thus the repetition of their forms. Most basically, in contrast to Japan's image as a modern, mechanized, and militaristic power, an identity witnessed in other displays at the fairs (and evident in newspaper headlines), the gardens presented the countervailing picture of Japan as ancient, agrarian, and artistic. Moreover, these hybrid gardens signaled Japan as the land of the samurai through their impressive scale, large stone ornaments, and overt references to warrior culture. Yet they also projected Japan as the realm of the geisha in their extravagant deployment of flowering trees, gentle water elements, and the presence of kimono-clad women. In addition, by fusing styles previously limited to a specific period, region, patron group, or function, these totalizing modern "Japanese gardens" provided a visual analog for the cohesion of the new national state. As modern reconstructions, both the exposition gardens and the Empire of Japan (*Dai nippon teikoku*) sought to cloak their originality and artifice in the guises of an exulted past and timeless nature. This recourse to nature traded on the West's cliché notion of a Japanese "love of nature" and added a spiritual dimension to the landscape by evoking Romantic ideas of physical and temporal escape into idyllic nature. These claims are neatly evoked in an advertisement for the Japanese exhibit at the 1939–40 New York World's Fair reproduced in a pamphlet. Showing two Japanese women in a Japanese garden, above a rendering of the garden-girdled pavilion, the text encapsulates the message. It begins, "Changeless, timeless Japan . . . its enduring charm takes its place naturally in 'The World of Tomorrow.'" And it closes, "When the Fair's modern world bewilders you, remember—and enjoy—the Japanese pavilion!"[3]

Before expanding upon these two particular expressions of, and reactions to, Japanese garden nationalism, it is useful to sketch the legacy of these exposition gardens in America. First, expo gardens created a vogue that produced hundreds of public Japanese gardens (fig. 2) and countless residential gardens. Second, the rhetoric of authenticity, essential to the political valence of exposition gardens, dominated the discourse on Japanese-style gardens through the twentieth century, and, arguably, retarded design evolution by the anxious reproduction of familiar (i.e., authentic) forms at the expense of key concepts or thoughtful adaptations. Third, the idea that expo gardens represented Japan's entire garden history led to the essentializing notion of "the Japanese garden" and, from the 1960s, the construction of "combination plate gardens" displaying side by side different historic styles.

Fig. 2. "G. T. Marsh & Co. Japanese Garden, Coronado Beach, California." Postcard c. 1915. (Private collection)

Fourth, the politicized identity of fair gardens as national symbols led to the postwar phenomenon of "friendship" or sister city gardens when, during the Cold War, American and Japanese cities collaborated to create Japanese-style gardens as statements of Japan's peaceful heritage and America's magnanimous internationalism. The study of fair gardens discloses this potent political legacy that has often disappeared beneath the familiar rhetoric of nature and spirit.

Japan at the World's Fairs

For visitors, fairs offered entertainment and education on a grand scale. For governments, expositions provided a competitive theater for performing economic viability and cultural identity. Powerful European nations participated in large numbers, signaling their progress by contrasting their material abundance with the backwardness of their colonies. Japan occupied a unique position in this brutal power dynamic, and its government exploited this singularity to craft a complex message in which gardens played a key role. Because of its status as an Asian country, Japan was initially considered among the backward nations, part of the static and passive Orient. Yet, by the 1890s, Japan was a colonizer in Asia and becoming an economic and military equal of Euro-America, abundantly able to represent itself and its colonial subjects. In the exhibition halls dedicated to science, industry, and education, Japan trumpeted its latest achievements. In its national pavilion, however, Japan promoted itself as a steadfast guardian of the past, building retrospective structures set in timeless gardens. Architecture and landscape together embodied a history both glorious and demonstrably still alive.

In the fairs' charged atmosphere, Japanese gardens were inherently political—and acknowledged as such. The creation of effective exposition gardens was learned gradually and is worth noting. Japanese gardens were built at American fairs beginning with the Philadelphia Centennial Exposition in 1876. There, and at Chicago's World's Columbian Exposition of 1893, the Japanese government focused on architecture. Gardens were small adjuncts to the Bazaar in Philadelphia and the Nippon Tea House in Chicago. It was the Japanese Village at the California Mid-Winter Exposition in San Francisco in 1894 that first integrated pavilions and gardens in a compelling representation of an idealized Japan. Built and run by Oriental antique dealer George Turner Marsh (1857–1932), after the Japanese government declined to participate in the fair, this pastoral environment had a dramatic impact on commercial "tea gardens." Its successor was the six-acre Imperial

Japanese Garden at St. Louis's Louisiana Purchase Exposition of 1904. The exposition took place as Japan was going to war with Russia, and the imperial government invested in lavish presentations in nearly every exhibition hall and in a "national pavilion" consisting of a series of buildings arranged on an elaborate hillside landscape. These structures included the Bazaar, the Formosan Tea Pavilion (displaying Japan's oldest colony), and a "replica" of Kyoto's Golden Pavilion staffed by "forty genuine geisha girls." The investment paid off when commentators such as Isaac Marcosson wrote, "While the Japanese soldiers and sails at the front use the latest inventions in warfare, their countrymen at the exposition are exploiting the arts of peace." He concluded, "In arrangement and detail the national pavilions show that, to the achievement of commerce and industry, the Japanese have brought the perfection of landscaped beauty, another expression of the genius of a people who, in the art of war and the pursuits of peace, are steadily making their way to a larger place in world power."[4]

San Francisco, 1915: The Imperial Japanese Garden and "Oriental Aggression"

While Japan's victories on the Korean Peninsula and at St. Louis earned it a place in the family of leading nations, escalating anti-Japanese immigration sentiment and pending legislation in California raised the stakes in Japanese garden diplomacy. The Panama-Pacific International Exposition was a prominent battleground in this political war. Held in San Francisco in 1915 to celebrate completion of the Panama Canal, which signaled the economic rise of the Pacific Coast and projected American power into the Pacific region, the fair had a clear political agenda. Because Washington politicians and San Francisco businessmen needed Japan's massive participation to cover costs and ensure popular success, the Japanese government used its involvement—pledging, then pulling its commitment between 1910 and 1914—to influence these allies to thwart the political initiatives of the anti-Japanese lobbies in Sacramento and Washington. Japan's opponents were led by state senator James Phelan (1861–1930), who, in legislative hearings, proclaimed, "Gentleman the exposition will be in California only one year, while the white race, I hope, will be here forever . . . Japan may not choose to exhibit at our fair, but we cannot sell our birthright for a tea garden."[5]

Groups such as the Japanese Exclusion League argued that Japanese could not be assimilated and should be ineligible for citizenship. After the 1907 "Gentleman's Agreement" halted immigration of Japanese males, California's Alien Land Law of 1913 prohibited alien Asians from owning land. Conservative newspapers endorsed anti-Japanese crusades to save Californians from the cultural degeneracy, racial mongrelization, and economic catastrophe of Japanese immigration. The usual refrain was that, while Japanese culture deserved respect, Japanese propaganda had blinded Americans to Japan's expansionist agenda. Phelan's equating of Japanese participation at the fair with a tea garden was echoed in a string of editorials in the *Sacramento Union* in January 1913. In "Labor Opposes Tea-Garden," the editors claimed, "We believe [labor] desires the Japanese burden off its shoulders just as much as it ever desired it, and that it will not be lured from its opposition by promise of the most beautiful tea-garden that the mind of the Oriental man has conceived." The next editorial asked, "Shall we consider the welfare of Californian citizens or shall we consider the tea-garden? The proposition is that we merely postpone action; tickle the Japs until we have secured what we desire from them, and then kick them out of the back door of their tea-garden. This is no secret . . . What is a thing like honor, as compared with a tea-garden at a world's fair. The Jap is a cunning boy . . . If he appears at the fair with his tea-garden it will be because he calculates that he can stave off action against himself longer."[6]

The editorial correctly predicted that Japan would choose constructive engagement. In June 1914, the Japanese government reasserted its acceptance after securing control over all concessions dealing with Japan, the price of Japanese goods in San Francisco, and a deposit waiver for Japanese workers. At the fairgrounds, Japan exerted its presence in impressive fashion. One local journalist wrote that Japan "seems to have a most intense desire to exhibit in every Palace" and that "Japan is the best represented of any of the foreign nations."[7]

The centerpiece was the three-acre Imperial Japanese Garden (fig. 3). The construction and display materials, sent in 551 crates, reportedly cost four million dollars. Expanding on the St. Louis model, the garden compound featured five large buildings and eight small pavilions set in a series of gardens. Entering at one corner through a formal gate, visitors were confronted by the Commissioner's Office, built in the Edo period (1615–1868) style reserved for the warrior caste. Pressed against it was the even more imposing Reception Hall, an oversized adaptation of Kyoto's famous Golden Pavilion. Designed by a team of carpenters and the university-trained architect Takeda Gōichi (1872–1938), the pastiche included exterior details in styles from the Kamakura (1185–1333), Muromachi (1392–1573), and Momoyama (1573–1615) periods. Like its inspiration, the building was cantilevered over a pond that connected with a sizable garden punctuated by other structures. To the north a path led to the Main Pavilion, created in a quasi-Heian period (794–1185) style. At the enclosure's north edge were the Formosa Teahouse and Japan Teahouse, landscaped by the Domoto Brothers with plants from the Yokohama Nursery Company. The remaining land was devoted to a pond-style stroll garden, designed by Izawa Hannosuke, who had worked on the gardens at the Japan-British Exhibition of 1910. The team of garden builders began work in October 1914. The large pond, bisected by two promontories connected by a bridge, extended around the Reception Hall. Several *azumaya* (viewing arbors) and a teahouse graced the low slope south of the pond, which was fed by a stream leading from a pump-driven waterfall. The garden featured seven stones of over three tons each as well as 257 small rocks—all transported from famous quarries in Japan, with granite from Bishu, Seto, and Ibaragi, blue and purple stone from Iyo, and black stone from Izu. Also brought from Japan were 1,360 trees in 36 Asian species. Most of the specimens were small, thus, just before the garden opened on February 24, 1915, Izawa added 109 trees purchased locally, then another 50 in July. Among the 4,400 small plants of 21 types, azalea, iris, bush clover, and sasa bamboo predominated.

English-language descriptions of the garden mixed superficial observation and the usual effusions. However, a Japanese-language guide to the fair suggests how the Japanese officials likely intended it: "The garden—in styles borrowed from each period in our country, and taking their essence and adding the taste of the modern period—is in a pure Japanese style."[8] Paralleling the architecture's eclectic historicism, the garden was intended to signal Japan's landscape heritage as understood by the first generation of modern garden historians. The pond garden recalls Edo period garden styles, and its extension under the Reception Hall may refer to Heian period Shinden-style gardens but more likely to their adaptation in the fifteenth century. One English-language guide to the fair explains that the prevailing style of the garden "is that of the Muromachi period," but also notes its "modern taste" is evident in extensive lawns.[9] The claim of purity signals an anxiety about the Japanese "tradition" that gave rise to the historicism of the entire garden. The eager acceptance of this message is witnessed in one author's conclusion that Japan "has shown the Western world a lesson in the beauty of simplicity."[10] This statement also deploys the ostensible purity of Japanese culture as a rebuke to the fair's jumble of neoclassical, neobaroque, and Spanish Revival buildings.

The Japanese garden was consistently extolled as among the fair's most

compelling displays. Discussion revolves around ideas of authenticity, refinement, workmanship, picturesqueness, and spiritual evocation—and links these qualities with Japanese culture in general. In Frank Todd's *The Story of the Exposition,* the first page of the chapter on the entire Japanese display at the fair, tellingly titled "In the Gardens of Japan," captures the flavor and substance of most accounts:

> These gardens had their own atmosphere. They were little plantations of the most delicate pattern, to which Japan itself had been in part transplanted. Shining pools and chattering streamlets gave spark and life, and even the gray stones of paths and bridges and stream beds, brought from Japan for the purpose and disposed as though in their island home, assumed pictorial form and relation. Still the garden growth was dainty, graceful, exquisitely refined by an art practised through centuries and brought in this fashion to America, to demonstrate that the most pleasing art forms are those that interpret nature to use through a clear but tinted glass. . . . Every rock and shrub was placed with such almost meticulous care that it formed a significant part of the beauty and harmony of the picture.[11]

Todd and others paint the garden as a landscape picture come to life, every part vital, harmonious, and profound. This view of Japan was surely associated with the Japanese landscape tradition represented by popular woodblock prints. Indeed, the cover illustration of the Japanese exposition association's pamphlet, *Japan and Her Exhibits,* features a print by Ando Hiroshige (1797–1858) showing Mt. Fuji rising peacefully over a scene of fishing boats adrift near a seaside hamlet.

Perhaps the most remarkable aspect of the Imperial Japanese Garden at the Panama Pacific International Garden was its almost wholly positive reception given the political tensions attending its creation. Nineteen million people visited the fair, and it seems that, once inside, citizens and journalists were willing and able to suspend disbelief, overwhelmed by the sheer scale and artifice. Yet, once visitors emerged from their encounter with appealing gardens and other manifestations of Japanese culture, their preexisting political attitudes seem not to have changed in kind. After the 1915 fair, anti-

Fig. 3, opposite. Plan of the Japanese Garden in the Grounds of the Panama Pacific International Exposition, San Francisco. From the booklet "Japan and Her Exhibits" (Tokyo: Exposition Society of Japan, 1915). (Donald G. Larson Collection on International Expositions and Fairs, Special Collections Research Center, Henry Madden Library, California State University, Fresno)

Japanese sentiment grew markedly in California, resulting in the Alien Land Act of 1920 and the Immigration Act of 1925 and culminating in Executive Order 9066 of 1942, which "evacuated" Japanese Americans from the West Coast and moved most into Relocation Camps.

San Francisco, 1939–1940: "Dynamic" Japan on the Lake of Nations

Given Americans' favorable attitude toward Japanese culture but increasingly negative disposition toward Imperial Japan, it is not surprising that at international expositions over the next quarter century, the Japanese government created buildings in premodern styles, surrounded them with appealing gardens, and staffed them with smiling women. This recipe was repeated at Paris in 1925, Philadelphia in 1926, Liege in 1930, and Chicago in 1933—even though it clashed with those fairs' modernist architecture and progressive orientation.[12]

The Japanese government invested deeply in the two competing American fairs of 1939: the New York World's Fair and the San Francisco Golden Gate Exposition. Desperate for Japanese participation given limited European presence, American politicians muted their public criticism of Japan before and during the fairs. However, tension over Japan's invasion of China simmered. In his speech opening the Golden Gate Exposition, Franklin Roosevelt cited the man-made Treasure Island site as "an outstanding example of territorial extension without aggression."[13] The Japanese, facing an international relations crisis after invading China in 1937 but enjoying a booming war economy, participated in both fairs on a large scale, initially hoping to secure American participation in the planned Tokyo exposition of 1940. After that exposition was canceled, some of the money was invested at the American fairs.

Brimming with national pride, the Japanese government promised its citizens in the spring of 1938 to reveal a new "three-dimensional essence" at these fairs. Whereas during the previous forty-seven expositions, Japan had followed the spirit of the fairs in emphasizing products and culture, at these two future-oriented expositions, Japan would show its "substance" (*jishutsu*), not just its "form" (*katachi*). And rather than presenting a "static" view, these expositions would display "dynamic, modern Japan."[14] Such was the rhetoric. In reality, fair planners hewed to the familiar formula of historically oriented buildings set in elegant pond-and-stream style gardens. And in spirit, the garden-ringed pavilions were intended as antidotes to Western modernity and to Japan's negative publicity.

Fig. 4. "Night View of Japan Pavilion." From the booklet "The Japan Pavilion Welcomes World Visitors." (San Francisco, 1939). (Private collection)

The only dramatic break with the architecture of previous fairs was a shift from wood to concrete and stucco, so that Japanese design idioms were given a seeming solidity and mass along with the "clean" surface of modern architecture. For the two American fairs, Japanese officials chose the conservative architects Kishida Hideto (1899–1966) and Uchida Yōzō (1885–?) to design a Shinto shrine–style structure in New York and Oguma Yoshikuni, who had just completed the National Diet building, to create a modern version of a castle fused with a palatial samurai residence in San Francisco (fig. 4). Tamura Tsuyoshi (1890–1979) of Tokyo Imperial University designed the gardens around both pavilions. In relation to the large concrete buildings, the gardens were intended to convey a "flavor of subtle elegance."[15]

Sakurai Nagao (1896–1973), a garden builder for the Imperial Household Agency, was charged with constructing both gardens. Believing that stones were key, Sakurai scoured the Oku-Tama and Oku-Chichibu regions west of Tokyo, gathering about 150 tons of rock, with some of the 200 stones weighing up to 5 tons. He also acquired small trees and shrubs from Japan but used large trees gathered in America. Aware of garden politics, Sakurai told reporters, "I want to show characteristic Japanese techniques so that this garden will contribute to friendship between Japan and America. As the

Americans are now much interested in Japanese gardens, I am considering offering to draft a Japanese design for American gardens, if desired, free of charge."[16]

In contrast to the intimate Heian-style garden in New York, the larger garden in San Francisco was more carefully integrated with the pavilion, which occupied 18,000 of the 50,000 square foot area. The original scheme called for a large Japanese compound, formed on two sides by the massive main pavilion, with a three-story pagoda-like turret at the conjunction of the two perpendicular halls. As built, the L-shaped main hall was slightly truncated, and the square hall was brought closer, so the entire complex was shaped like the letter *C* written in block script. The architectural identity of the hybrid building was uncertain, with reporters calling it a "typical feudal castle," a "samurai's house," and even a Buddhist temple. The pavilion's saving grace was its location on a large pond opening on to the Lake of Nations. The pavilion was best seen from across the pond, the structure rising out of a landscape that softened its sharp contours. Visitors could access the pavilion directly from the west or from the south via a beautiful curved wooden bridge that crossed the inlet of the lagoon and led to the Hall of Festivities, appended to the main pavilion. Given the arrangement of national pavilions around the central lake, which symbolized the Pacific Ocean, Japan presented a congenial face to its neighbors at the fair.

The garden was accomplished in design and execution. If photos (fig. 5) can be trusted, it was the only exposition garden to convey the sensibility of premodern Japanese pond gardens in its dynamic composition, balance of large stones with mature trees, and restrained use of plants. Sakurai was a master of arranging stones, and his 150 tons of high-quality Japanese stone conveyed a natural shoreline. His placement of a large, low *yukimi* lantern on an outcrop near one edge of the bridge and a dramatic *Kasuga* lantern on the opposite shore discloses the kind of sensitive arrangement that marked the entire garden. A corner of the inlet featured a series of small islands: one including another *yukimi* lantern, while a slightly larger island was in the tortoise-and-crane style with a single pine. So compelling was the design that a decade later Garrett Eckbo used a photo of it in his book *Landscape for Living*.[17]

Anxious about public perception, the Japanese government issued publicity to clarify the desired effect. Even as the pavilion was under construction, a press release described the garden and then concluded, "the visitor is entranced and held by the beauty and spell of the Oriental setting. Pretty Nipponese maidens, dressed in the traditional kimono, await to extend a

Fig. 5. "Japanese Garden, Hall of Festivities in Background, Treasure Island." Golden Gate Exposition, San Francisco. Postcard, 1939. (Private collection)

smiling welcome and to serve all who enter in the manner of hospitality for which the Japanese people are noted."[18] Such self-promotion was required as, for the first time, the American press was unmoved.

For visitors entering via the bridge, the garden was an effective transition from the hectic world of the modern fair, with its "colonial modern" architecture, to the feminine, tranquil, and largely traditional presentation of modern Japan inside the building. Japan's official pamphlet treats the garden as an important adjunct to the pavilion. It explains that the garden is in the "*kairyu* style" perfected during the Edo period. More critically, the garden and the pavilion's exhibits worked in tandem to express the continuity of Japanese culture, its artistry, and its feminine sensibility—all characteristics calculated to counter Japan's burgeoning militarism. At the Hall of Festivals, a detached building reached by crossing the garden on a bridge, visitors could see films on folk dance, displays of folk crafts and festivals, and an ikebana arrangement showing "the typical Oriental simplicity and emphasis on small detail [that is] of great interest to women."[19]

The emphasis on feminine premodern Japan found in the displays was stressed in the promotional materials where photos often featured women in the garden. A booklet, entitled "Japan" and distributed by the Board of Tourist Industry, featured a photo of a kimono-clad woman holding a doll on the cover, cherry blossoms on the first page, and the garden on the back cover. In that photo (fig. 6), two kimono-clad women pose in the garden. Japanese culture was displayed in the pavilion and frequently was performed in the garden, which hosted a flower festival (*hanamatsuri*) and a beauty contest.[20] At night the garden was lit with hundreds of paper lanterns, and a master cormorant fisher from the Imperial Household demonstrated nocturnal fishing from his special boat. Japan Day, June 23, 1940, featured a large parade with Western and Japanese floats, various Japanese foods and entertainments, and speeches promoting peace and friendship. On the next day, the Nazis carved up France and recognized the Vichy government; a week later Japan's Imperial Army advanced into French Indo-China. At the fair, the Japanese jammed American radio broadcasts from Treasure Island aimed at "Occupied China" when these began to criticize Japan.[21]

Both the New York and San Francisco gardens were destroyed at the fairs' close. A plan to create a large, new Japanese garden on the site of the Czech pavilion and donate it to the City of New York was never realized. In San Francisco, all of Treasure Island was turned into a military base. Although

Fig. 6. Back cover of the booklet "Japan." Board of Tourist Industry, Japanese Government Railways (San Francisco, 1940). (Donald G. Larson Collection on International Expositions and Fairs, Special Collections Research Center, Henry Madden Library, California State University, Fresno)

Japanese designers planned elaborate structures and gardens for the occupied cities of the Greater East Asia Co-Prosperity Sphere, these were never created. Apparently the only Japanese garden built abroad by the Japanese government between 1940 and 1945 was constructed in 1941 at the Berlin Flower Show. Called a "replica of an ancient Japanese garden," it included a pond, a red-lacquer bridge, and a lantern.[22] In America, the war years saw the destruction of some extant Japanese gardens, the renaming of others, and the creation of new Japanese gardens only at the Internment Camps where Japanese Americans sought solace, beauty, and, perhaps, a measure of defiance.

Conclusion: The Lasting Impact of Exposition Gardens

Given the concurrent histories of the popular success of Japanese gardens at American world's fairs and, from around 1910, the deteriorating political relations that resulted in the Pacific War, one might conclude that Japanese fair gardens ultimately failed in their goal of influencing American politics. Although the Americans were charmed by Japanese culture and gardens, this fascination was easily distinguished and thus separated from attitudes toward the Japanese nation when it became an economic or political competitor. Arguably, because of the success of the early gardens, the Japanese government perpetuated the feminine-pastoral-historic presentation of Japan and encouraged a fantasy image that was then easily detached from political realities precisely because it was so manifestly a daydream.

Yet, the fair gardens may well have impacted policy in more nuanced ways by delaying or softening actions, as Phelan and others predicted. Perhaps one can find evidence of such mitigation in the degree of Theodore Roosevelt's support for Japan in the Russo-Japanese War in the wake of the Louisiana Purchase Exposition, in the delay of anti-Japanese legislation in California following Japan's participation at the Panama-Pacific Exposition, and in Franklin Roosevelt's reluctance to embargo Japan until the summer of 1941, after the New York and San Francisco fairs of 1939 and 1940. Because Japan both participated at these fairs en masse and presented a compelling image, the nation created an aura of goodwill that was more slowly eroded. In a longer view, perhaps the best measure of the success of exposition gardens is the rapid reappearance of public Japanese gardens in America after World War II. No doubt these gardens were partly manifestations of America's "Cold War Orientalism" that sought to construct a new and "true" view of Japan as a bulwark against Communism. Yet the swift revival of cultural exchange was built on a foundation laid before the war. More specifically, the prewar exposition gardens gave rise to the postwar phenomenon of Japanese gardens at fair-like amusement parks including Sea World in San Diego from 1962, the Japanese Village and Deer Park in Buena Park, California, from 1967 to 1972, and the lavish Japanese village at Disney's EPCOT Center, completed in 1982.

The deeper legacy of Japan's presentations at American expositions is found in the intangible realm of American attitudes. Unlike the permanence intended for most buildings and gardens, fairs bloomed extravagantly for a season or two. In large part it was their temporality, in tandem with their mighty scale, that gave expositions purchase in the collective imagination. As Neil Harris enumerates, expositions formed "assumptions about the social functions of public spaces," spawned institutions as different as amusement parks and museums, underscored ideas about the hierarchical nature of aesthetic, social, and racial structure, and propagated the commodification of culture; "above all, they performed as sites for self-discovery." In this last regard, they served to "reaffirm belief" in the past and the future as well as in a shared sense of American identity.[23]

The success of Japanese gardens at the fairs demonstrated that Asia was now part of the American public space. Unlike the fantastic chinoiserie of earlier eras, this Asian culture had sufficient weight and dimension to be taken on its own terms, or an approximation of them. Japanese gardens raised a fundamental question about the cultural dimension of nature since the Japanese seemed to have a definition of nature that, although paralleling Western concepts in some ways, also diverged as surely as Buddhism and Shinto differ from Christianity. Even as expositions provided a sense of political and aesthetic structures that could be controlled within the larger order represented by the world's fairs, they planted the seeds that had the potential to undermine those structures. Hence, part of the pleasure of deracinated Japanese gardens was the tension inherent in gardens that were located within Western spaces but simultaneously existed outside, and beyond, them. This tension may explain in part the intense animosity toward "Oriental tea gardens" by xenophobes like Phelan, who ran for the U.S. Senate in 1920 on the pledge to "Keep California White."

Neil Harris holds that fairs served to encourage "self-discovery" and to "reaffirm belief" because travel to them was a mass movement to an idealized destination that functioned as a "social restorative."[24] The key means of restoring faith in American society was through a shared experience of the past and the future. This optimistic attitude stemmed from a sense of progress relative to the past and an affirmative orientation toward the future, as promised by the technology on display. However, when figuring Japanese gardens into the equation, the addition of the living Japanese past to the American landscape substantially enriched prospects for the American future. The role of Japan in American society was in part that of an exotic frontier to be experienced and partially tamed. More critically, these gardens soothed the anxiety of an industrializing society estranged from the kinds of spiritual authority ascribed to nature and artistic refinement. The ideals attributed to Japanese gardens showed that American belief in the redemptive power of art and nature was shared by the Japanese, who, happily, had perfected their expression and translated it into an exportable form. Although the Japanese government "sold" a politicized ideal of Japan through exposition gardens, Japanese and American entrepreneurs continued to market Japanese gardens between the fairs. These commercial "Japanese tea gardens" pointed to the possibility of a future American landscape that not only looked different but also held the possibilities of reaffirming modern American cultural identity while challenging it in relatively safe ways.

Notes

1. Two studies of specific American fair gardens are Kendall H. Brown, "Rashōmon: The Multiple Histories of the Japanese Tea Garden in Golden Gate Park," *Studies in the History of Gardens and Designed Landscapes* 18, no. 2 (1998): 93–119, and Seiko Goto, "The First Japanese Garden in the Western World: The Garden in the Louisiana Purchase Exposition," *Studies in the History of Gardens & Designed Landscapes* 27, no. 3 (2007): 244–53. For a broad discussion of exposition gardens, see Kendall H. Brown, "Fair Japan: Japanese Gardens at World's Fairs, 1876–1940," *Sitelines* 4, no. 1 (2008): 10–16, and Cathy Jean Maloney, *World's Fair Gardens: Shaping American Landscapes* (Charlottesville: University of Virginia Press, 2012).

2. The sameness of Japanese exposition displays is discussed in Angus Lockyer, "Expo Fascism? Ideology, Representation, Economy," in *The Culture of Japanese Fascism*, ed. Alan Tansman (Durham, NC: Duke University Press, 2009), 276–95.

3. The advertisement's authorship is unknown, but it was likely made by the Board of Tourist Industries. The garden at the New York pavilion was atypical in its small size, its link to only one historical era and style (the tenth-century aristocratic garden style), and its allusion to the natural scenery around the Grand Shrine at Ise, the seat of imperial power.

4. Isaac Marcosson, "Japan's Extraordinary Exhibit," *World's Work* 4, no. 8 (August 1904): 51–53.

5. James Phelan, qtd. in Roger Daniels, *The Politics of Prejudice: The Anti-Japanese Movement in California and the Struggle for Japanese Exclusion* (Berkeley: University of California Press, 1962), 60.

6. “That Jap Tea Garden,” *Sacramento Union,* January 16, 1913.

7. Elizabeth Deitrick, *Best Bits of Panama Pacific International Expo at San Francisco* (San Francisco: Galen, 1915), 9. For example, at the Palace of Horticulture, Japan, represented by the Yokohama Nursery Co., was the only foreign exhibitor.

8. *Panama taiheiyo bankoku hankurankai sandō jimu hōkoku* (Tokyo: Nōshō musho, 1917), 154. This report by the Ministry of Agriculture describes the site in detail, listing the designers and construction companies of each feature.

9. *The Blue Book: A Comprehensive Official Souvenir View Book Illustrating the Panama Pacific International Exposition of San Francisco* (San Francisco: Robert Reid, 1915), n.p.

10. Ben Macomber, *The Jewel City* (San Francisco: John H. Williams, 1915), 165.

11. Frank Morton Todd, *The Story of the Exposition: Being the Official History of the International Celebration Held at San Francisco in 1915 to Commemorate the Discovery of the Pacific Ocean and the Construction of the Panama Canal* (New York: G. P. Putnam's Sons, 1915), 3:210.

12. The sole exception, the Japanese Pavilion and attendant landscape at the Paris International Exposition of 1936, is discussed in Jonathon Reynolds, *Maekawa Kunio and the Emergence of Japanese Modernist Architecture* (Berkeley: University of California Press, 2001), 104–7.

13. “Text of F. R. Speech Opening Exposition,” *San Francisco Chronicle,* February 19, 1939, 13.

14. “Beikokumin no kimo o nuku rittai nihon no iki,” *Tokyo Asahi shinbun,* April 19, 1938, 4.

15. Ibid.

16. *Japan Times,* December 10, 1938, 8.

17. Garret Eckbo, *Landscape for Living* (New York: Duell, Sloan, and Pearce, 1950), 128–29.

18. “Japan Presents Her $500,000 Pavilion to the World,” *San Francisco Chronicle,* February 17, 1939, 3.

19. *San Francisco Chronicle,* February 21, 1939, 13.

20. “Yobimono nihonkan no joō senkyo,” *Tokyo Asahi shinbun,* March 23, 1939, 1.

21. “Japanese Jam Radio,” *New York Times,* October 3, 1939, 13.

22. “Berlin Flower Show Opens,” *Japan Times,* May 31, 1941, 7.

23. Neil Harris, “Expository Expositions: Preparing for the Theme Parks,” in *Designing Disney's Theme Parks,* ed. Karal Ann Marling (New York: Flammarion, 1997), 19–22.

24. Ibid., 27.

The Garden Network

George Rogers Hall's Horticultural Activism

SARA A. BUTLER

In 1889 Charles Sprague Sargent, first director of the Arnold Arboretum and founder of *Garden and Forest,* visited Bristol, Rhode Island, to report on George Rogers Hall's collection of rare Japanese plants. Sargent could hardly believe what he found there. He glowed that the "*Zelkowa Keaki*" [a Japanese relative of the elm] was "the only specimen of this plant I remember to have seen growing in the United States, and I have never seen one a quarter of the size in Europe." In the "garden near the house," he found the "finest specimen of *Quercus dentata* [Daimyo oak, native to Japan] which I have seen." He praised Hall's *Taxus cuspidata* [Japanese yew] as "by far the finest specimen I have ever seen." He judged Hall's half-dozen Tiger-tail spruces [native to Japan] to be the "best specimens of *Picea polita* I have seen" and raved about a "perfect specimen of *Thuiopsis dolabrata*" [conifer from Japan]. Summarizing the significance of the collection, he proclaimed, "Hall's Japanese plants . . . have grown into what, I believe, are the finest specimens of certain species which can be found in the eastern states. Some of them I have not seen equaled in Europe."[1] Sargent trained his focus on plants, all but ignoring the garden in favor of the trees; he offered only passing comments about the organization of Hall's plantations and made no mention at all of landscape style or aesthetics.

Contemporaries and horticultural historians have rightly celebrated Hall for his transformative botanical introductions (fig. 1). Sargent described him as the "first American who sent Japanese plants to the United States, in any considerable numbers, at least."[2] Historians regularly echo this assessment.[3] In doing so, however, they have overlooked the fact that Hall was not just a pioneering importer; he was also a gardener, at the center of a horticultural network of exchange. While the terms *network* and *web* today call to mind digital communication of information, they provide a useful means for visualizing the dynamics of exchange of tangible goods in the nineteenth century.[4] Hall's associates included Sargent as well as historian and horticul-

Fig. 1. George Rogers Hall, no date, unidentified photographer. (Collection of Margaret Howe Ewing)

turist Francis Parkman, railroad entrepreneur and amateur botanist Horatio Hollis Hunnewell, seed merchant and journalist Charles Mason Hovey, and nurseryman Samuel Bowne Parsons. Collectively, they honed a physical and social infrastructure that not only facilitated the dissemination of Hall's imports but also shaped the aesthetics of gardening with Japanese plants. Personally involved in gathering, shipping, distributing, propagating, popularizing, and educating, Hall sought to make a place for Japanese botanicals in American gardens. A study of his activities offers an illuminating window into the workings of nineteenth-century horticultural activism.

Hall's networking and gardening were bound together. The hub of his horticultural web was his Bristol estate. Although only partially intact today, a portion of that property, which became known as North Farm, contains, in the leafy southeast quadrant, elements of the sole surviving landscape cultivated by the pioneering plantsman (fig. 2). While Hall saw Japanese gardens firsthand during the late Tokugawa period, the landscape he planted in Rhode Island neither imitated nor introduced to the United States Japanese garden design principles. Hall was not indifferent to landscape aesthetics. His inspirations, however, were the sweeping Japanese countryside rather than the compact Japanese garden and the imagery of botanical bounty brought together through cross-cultural exchange. The collection he laid out in Rhode Island was shaped by what he had seen and also by the relationships he built.

Those who have examined Hall's career and importations have not taken into account his gardens and network. The significance of the latter, as we shall see, is revealed in previously unexamined correspondence and drawings. Examining Hall's interest in plants and his gardening in East Asia,

Fig. 2. Aerial view of North Farm, Bristol, Rhode Island, c. 1970, unidentified photographer. Text added by Sara A. Butler and Kathryn Klesseck. (Collection of the North Farm Homeowners Association)

along with his interactions with like-minded individuals in the United States, sheds new light on the process of, and changing objectives in, introducing foreign trends on American soil in the late nineteenth century. Peeling back layers of subsequent reworkings, Hall's Rhode Island garden emerges as a demonstration landscape. Its cultural and aesthetic value was recognized in the early twentieth century by Charles A. Platt, whose redesign of a portion of the property constitutes a pioneering example of landscape preservation.

A Network for Exporting: Hall in Asia

George Rogers Hall, born in Bristol in 1820, graduated from Trinity College in Hartford, Connecticut, in 1842 and from Harvard Medical School in 1846. Soon after completing his studies he made a momentous career choice, deciding to go to China to establish a medical practice in the treaty port at Shanghai. In 1850 he returned home briefly to marry Helen Beal of Kingston, Massachusetts. The couple then traveled together to Shanghai, where they had three sons.[5]

Hall took an interest in native plants and cultivated grounds in the Chinese port city. As letters make clear, his garden contained both Eastern and Western plants. The Halls imported "Summer Savory," highly prized by his wife because "it will taste so home-like." He also planted chrysanthemums, which his wife proclaimed were "the favorite flower with the Chinese."[6] Hall also traveled to collect local botanicals, with an eye to introducing some to the United States.[7] He sent the *Amaryllis hallii* to Charles M. and Phineas B. Hovey, the famed Boston seed and nurserymen, for propagation and distribution.[8] In China, Hall not only established a garden for personal use and pleasure; he also began to cultivate a set of associates, a rudimentary network, for exchanging plants between East and West.

In 1854, just four years after her arrival, his wife and the children left Shanghai because of political unrest. It was not long after her departure that Hall decided to turn from medicine to trade. He began as a dealer, exporting a variety of Japanese and Chinese decorative arts, including porcelain, lacquerwork, jade, bronzes, and ivory. He also speculated in gold and silver. With the opening of Japan following Matthew Perry's historic visits in 1853–54, Hall moved to that country in 1859, where he worked for Walsh & Co.—later Walsh, Hall & Co.—an American trading house. He acquired a prominent site on the Bund in Yokohama.[9] There he built a "fine house," similar to those of other foreign merchants.[10] From Japan, he summarized his personal ambitions to his wife: "My tastes and habits are such that poverty is almost unbearable . . . If neither of us had lived differently from the majority of persons in New England it would be comparatively easy to live on a small income and . . . we should pass . . . away with the common herd, and our children would be left with an inheritance of our good name (I hope) but nothing more. I look forward for something better."[11] Through trade he hoped to advance himself and his family.

Procuring botanicals was one of his pursuits, and in Japan Hall crafted a broader horticultural network. Robert Fortune, the famed Scottish plant hunter, became an acquaintance, and it is likely that he shared some of his collection with Hall.[12] To exchange seeds with Japanese cultivators, the American traveled widely within the allowed treaty boundaries around Yokohama, often with Francis Hall, a journalist, also an American but not a relative, who later took George Rogers Hall's position at Walsh & Co.[13] On one trip, the two Halls visited a Japanese gardener who "showed us with some pride some tomatoes and turnips growing in his garden, the seeds of which H. [presumably George Rogers Hall] had given him last April." That same day they found in a "lotus pond . . . some pure white blossoms" that they requested a local to mark for harvest the following spring. "He wanted no pay"; instead, "it was agreed that it should be an interchange of presents."[14] Fortune later recalled that in Japan he bought plants from "[i]tinerant florists and nurserymen."[15] George Rogers Hall made similar purchases. One contemporary reported, "It being known that he [Hall] was a buyer, plants were brought him from the interior," adding admiringly, "until his collection was as rich as any botanical collectors [*sic*] could make it."[16]

To cultivate and display his acquisitions, George Rogers Hall established a garden, illustrated in Utagawa Hiroshige II's 1861 woodblock print, *Picture of a Mercantile Building in Yokohama*[17] (fig. 3). Within the grounds, fenced beds with serpentine edges overflow with flowers, beneath evergreen and deciduous trees. The nearest border displays flowers of a single type: individual buoyant blossoms, all of the same color, tied down by taut, slender stems, floating above cresting waves of foliage. They appear to be chrysanthemums, native to Asia, first imported to the West in the seventeenth century. If so, the American pitted his gardening prowess against that of native enthusiasts. Francis Hall noted that the chrysanthemum was the "favorite flower of priest and peasant" and that "multiplied varieties" were "trophies of Japanese horticultural skill."[18] Near the fence along the water, a small gate and a gnarled bonsai pine anchor meandering ribbons of green and white that flow past islands of red and yellow masses. Despite the schematic qual-

Fig. 3. Picture of a Mercantile Building in Yokohama, 1861, by Utagawa Hiroshige II. (Fred & Isabel Pollard Collection, 1962.016.001 a-c, photo © Art Gallery of Greater Victoria; photo credit Robert Matheson)

ity of the medium, the print illustrates George Rogers Hall's preference for sorting botanicals by type, a predilection that he would exhibit again later on his Bristol grounds. Not illustrated is the kitchen garden bearing crops from home. Hall noted that he grew "beets, lettuce, tomatoes and cauliflowers, and few heads of celery."[19] His gardening placed Japanese and American plants together and on view.

Hall's garden also functioned as an exchange point between East and West. Here, he processed plants for shipment, anticipating that one year "[m]any new flowers and shrubs will ornament my grounds . . . I hope to save seed and specimens to send or take home."[20] Fortune praised Hall's "very interesting collection of the plants of Japan" and warmly recalled his "valuable information and assistance."[21] That information and assistance included exportation. Hall's garden was the nexus of a network for gathering botanicals and a clearinghouse for ornamentals leaving the country collected by the two plant hunters.

Prior to his departure from Yokohama on January 3, 1862, Hall shipped several large collections of Japanese plants and seeds to the United States.[22] One, containing kousa dogwood, umbrella pine, variegated ginkgo, sawara false cypress, rhododendrons, and a new crabapple, arrived in the Boston area in 1861 prior to Hall's departure from Japan.[23] F. Gordon Dexter was to deliver them to Francis L. Lee of Chestnut Hill. By the time they arrived, however, Lee had enlisted in the Union Army. Anticipating his absence, he entrusted the leafy treasures to his friend Francis Parkman, the historian who was also one of Boston's most celebrated horticulturists.[24] Parkman incorporated Hall's plants in his garden on the shores of Jamaica Pond. There Sargent was likely to have seen Hall's novel introductions, prior to the founding of the Arnold Arboretum in 1872, perhaps fueling his interest in Japanese plants.[25]

Parkman propagated and showed plants he obtained from Hall. His entries into exhibitions at the Massachusetts Horticultural Society built interest in Japanese imports and in Hall. One of the first was the "rare and very beautiful Lily, recently brought from Japan," possibly a "*new species,*" shown by Parkman and nurseryman William H. Spooner in July 1862. Although the organization's published account did not mention Hall by name, by outlining the hands that the botanicals passed through—from Dexter to Lee to Spooner and Parkman—the author made the identity of the sender entirely clear.[26] Hall was identified as the source in the *Magazine of Horticulture,* the first horticultural journal published in the United States, compiled and edited by Charles Hovey.[27] More importantly, publications like these built a market for Hall's botanicals.

Hall returned to the United States with more than just botanical treasure. Although he had seen a number of gardens with Francis Hall, he made no mention of them in his correspondence. Instead, he reserved comment for the Japanese landscape. For example, in an early letter to his wife, George Rogers Hall described the countryside as "without exception . . . the most charming I [have] ever seen or expect to see."[28] By comparison, Francis Hall described in detail in his journal a garden the two saw near Kamakura and mused as he wrote about the singular opportunity his geographic situation presented him. Description gave way to dreams of transplantation as he recalled, "one little mia in front of which, out of a spot of ground not four rods square, was a complete epitome of Japanese landscape garden. Every thing was there in dwarfed proportions, trees, lines of hedges, ponds, rockwork, old walls of mossy stone, flowering plants, and bits of green turf. Could I have set this down in the Central Park it would have been its greatest wonder and completest triumph of the gardener's skill."[29] Like his fellow sightseer, Francis Hall ultimately returned to the United States. Although he never realized his Japanese garden in Central Park, George Rogers Hall did plant a landscape informed by his travels and experiences in Japan. Yet the garden he crafted in Rhode Island, inspired by the memory of the Japanese landscape rather than specific gardens, bore no resemblance to the ones his traveling companion had documented and envisioned earlier.

A Network for Disseminating: Hall in the United States

Back in New England, Hall retooled his network for gathering plants as one for distributing them. In March 1862, soon after his return, he delivered a shipment of Japanese horticultural materials in person to Parsons & Sons Company, of Flushing, New York.[30] There the nurserymen could hardly believe their good fortune, gushing in the *Horticulturist:* "Dr. Hall of Japan, whom we had for some time well known by reputation," walked into the offices, introducing himself as someone who had "resided at Yokohama, and being greatly interested in trees and plants, had . . . collected in his garden [there] all of any interest which Japan contained." He also had gathered "a large quantity of seeds of trees and plants, many of them unknown either in Europe or this county." The author then proudly announced that the doctor "proposed to place them all in our hands for propagation and culture." With these, the commercial nursery made available the first introductions of kobus magnolia, star magnolia, hinoki cypress, zelkova, new varieties of Japanese maples, and more.[31]

Hall's interactions with the Parsons nursery illuminate the economics behind his activities. In delivering botanicals to a prominent nursery in an established center of horticulture, Hall made a savvy affiliation and mutually profitable alliance. While the firm had been in business since 1838, with the materials from Hall, they scored an immediate first, becoming a leading distributor of Japanese plants. Hall's choice of Parsons & Sons might seem at first curious. After all, he had strong ties to the Boston horticultural community and had years earlier sent his amaryllis to the nursery co-owned by Charles Hovey, a leading figure in American horticulture. However, it turns out that Hall did not select Parsons; instead, they had recruited him.[32] While others have suggested that Hall's exchange with Parsons & Sons was purely altruistic, in fact, he did not simply donate his plants and seeds to the nursery.[33] They were placed there on the condition that they be used for propagation for three years and then sold. Hall, after all, was a trader, and he quite reasonably received a portion of the sales.[34] If he accelerated the rate of dissemination of Japanese plants, he did so by affiliating with a well-known commercial nursery and tying into their already established network.

Hall's spider web of connections tied him to horticultural circles in Boston, Newport, New York, and beyond. Horticulture appealed to early-nineteenth-century Boston elites as a cultural symbol of status and sophistication.[35] Hall was a member of the next generation, but his attitudes were similar. Further, he was more than a collector, importer, and gardener. He was also a popularizer, who forged intellectual and social ties that facilitated the distribution of Japanese plants in the United States. Tracing the threads of his network demonstrates the pervasiveness of his contributions.

Exchanges of botanicals were common among Boston horticultural enthusiasts. Plants mapped social interactions. Hall, Sargent, Parkman, Hunnewell, and others were all part of the same network, directly or indirectly. Prior to his return to the United States, Hall had sent a specimen to "Prof. [presumably, Louis] Agassiz" of Harvard University and plants to Agassiz or Dexter "to forward to his friends."[36] Sargent gave seeds and cuttings of rare plants to Arnold Arboretum patrons as well as to nurseries.[37] While it is unknown if Hall presented any botanicals to the director, the Bristolian did seek to augment his own collection with new "Japanese novelties" from the Bostonian.[38] Hunnewell, a pillar of the Boston horticultural community, was part of Hall's network. Some plants for his impressive estate in Wellesley, Massachusetts, came from Sargent. Although it is not known if any of the Japanese plants on his grounds came from Hall, the two men certainly knew each other.[39] On September 10, 1873, Hunnewell recorded that he had hosted a dinner meeting of the Horticultural Club and that the group also included "Dr. Hall."[40] Japanese plants did go to family members: Hall's daughter and a grandson planted zelkovas at their home in Milton, Massachusetts.[41]

In Boston, where Hall lived prior to moving to Bristol, he affiliated with the Massachusetts Horticultural Society and remained a member from 1863 until his death. The oldest horticultural association in the nation was a vehicle for distributing plants and information about them in the United States. Even before he joined, Hall had contributed to the educational program, supplying the botanical materials for propagating the new lily that Parkman and Spooner displayed in July 1862. While still in Japan, Hall had anticipated exhibiting plants he collected.[42] Later, he did so at the Society and in 1868 won a "First Class Certificate of Merit" for one of his entries.[43] There, he also shared with others a book from his library that illustrated Japanese variegated plants, to spur interest in the imports he championed.[44] Hall remained an admired figure well after his death. In a 1916 address to the organization, famed Asian plant hunter Ernest Henry "Chinese" Wilson reminded his audience that "garden-lovers of this country should treasure the name of this gentleman for the plants he introduced."[45]

Hall's contributions were widely acknowledged during his lifetime. Hovey repeatedly called attention to his efforts, crediting the Rhode Islander for his horticultural introductions and requesting in print that Hall write about his experiences in Japan, which, unfortunately, the plantsman did not do.[46] Sargent, too, published articles acknowledging Hall's contributions, and in 1893 noted that the specimen for the zelkova illustrated in *Garden and Forest* came from Hall.[47]

Hall's estate became both a pilgrimage site and informal educational facility, as horticultural enthusiasts, in addition to Sargent, visited and studied the garden. Four years after Sargent's 1889 article, E. W. Davis of Providence, Rhode Island, traveled to see the grounds and penned an update. He admired the zelkovas, suggesting that they would "make an excellent street tree," as they, indeed, have. He noted that the *Pinus thunbergii* was "producing seed," and that Hall's "plantation is full of seedling Pines of this species." He lamented that the rare Daimyo oak had "never recovered after having been removed to a new position, and is dead." Like Sargent earlier, he touted the potential of the Japanese yew.[48] It was Sargent's account that had piqued Davis's interest and prompted his visit and published assessment.

Hall's garden not only attracted amateurs and professionals but also shaped the Arnold Arboretum. While it is tantalizing to speculate that seeing Hall's plants earlier in Parkman's garden had encouraged Sargent's interest in Asian plants, it is certain that Hall's plantings in Bristol served as a resource for the celebrated institution the arborist founded. Not only did Sargent visit the estate, but he anticipated at least one return during Hall's lifetime, acknowledging in 1898, "It will give me a great deal of pleasure to see your collection again."[49] Whether or not the Boston director made that trip, he did travel with colleagues to the estate in the years after Hall's death. Photographs, taken during his visits in 1916 and 1919, documented the growth of the plantings[50] (fig. 4). In compiling this record, the professional arborists not only collected visual specimens for the Arnold Arboretum reference library but also paid homage to the inspirational collection that predated the planting, beginning in 1886, of their own grounds.[51]

Hall's imports spread into American horticulture and sank roots into U.S. soils not only through personal gifts of exchange but also by way of nurseries promoting sales through publications. Commercial advertising and journal articles sold seeds, bulbs, and plants. Interconnected horticul-

Fig. 4. J. S. Ames, "*Taxus cuspidata* . . . Prof. Sargent standing," Estate of the late George Rogers Hall, Bristol, Rhode Island, November 1916. (Image #2366, Image Collection, Arnold Arboretum Horticultural Library of Harvard University, Jamaica Plain, Massachusetts; © President and Fellows of Harvard College. Arnold Arboretum Archives)

tural institutions and societies, nurserymen-entrepreneurs, and the gardening press popularized foreign plants, as the case of Hall's amaryllis illustrates so well. As noted above, Hall had sent samples of the botanical from his garden in Shanghai for commercial sale back home. In 1890, a writer for *Garden and Forest* documented the acquisition lineage, "brought originally from China by Dr. George R. Hall, of Bristol, Rhode Island." Both the accompanying illustration and the wistfully evocative description from Hall—"often planted by the Chinese in their cemeteries"—tempted readers to buy an exotic with an intriguing backstory. The writer also considerately explained how shoppers could purchase, noting that the plant was "distributed by the Messrs. Hovey, the Boston seedmen."[52] Part educational, part sales document, such journal articles helped stimulate the desire to acquire.

In a similar way, Parsons & Sons' 1862 report in the *Horticulturist* on Hall's visit to the nursery coupled information with promotion. Inventorying the bounty that Hall had turned over to them, the writer crowed competitively: "a collection so rich and so varied has never been obtained from any country, even by the best English collectors." Equally smitten, the editor rhapsodized: "So much horticultural treasure is almost enough to turn one's head," predicting that the "splendid collection now placed in the hands of the Messrs. Parsons will . . . mark a new era in our history."[53] The "infotisement," intended to enlighten and to sell plants, also spread the fame of both Hall and his distributor.

Plants that Hall first imported soon anchored the collections of others. In Newport, on the grounds of the Theodore K. Gibbs house, Bethshan, a Daimyo oak was planted, most likely in the 1880s or 1890s.[54] The species was among the trees Hall had delivered to Parsons & Sons, although his own specimen succumbed prior to Davis's visit.[55] While the Bethshan plant may or may not have come from Parsons & Sons or Hall, it did constitute an early planting of a tree that Hall was the first to introduce. Similarly, zelkovas, originally imported by Hall, are frequently identified with him. They, too, were among the plants he delivered to Parsons & Sons, and several survive on the Bristol grounds from his time. His grandson recalled seeing seedlings of the tree on the estate and, as previously noted, transplanting some in Milton with his mother.[56] Arborists of the late nineteenth century marveled over them. Sargent suggested that they could be grown for timber, and Davis, as indicated above, urged their use as street trees.[57] A photograph in the Arnold Arboretum archives shows a well-established zelkova, planted next to the street in front of a modest house in Warren, Rhode Island, not far from Hall's garden (fig. 5). The image, taken on the same day in 1925 as others at the former Hall estate, hints suggestively at a connection between this tree and Hall.[58] More importantly, the photograph, shot by Wilson, the famed Asian plant hunter, documents how Hall's plants, originally cherished as rarities, were, by the early twentieth century, distributed widely across the American landscape.

Cultivating Japanese Botanicals: The Hub of Hall's Network

Hall's network radiated from the Bristol property purchased by his father, Benjamin Hall, in 1832.[59] The working farm, two miles north of the down-

Fig. 5. E. H. Wilson, "*Zelkowa serrata . . .*" Warren, Rhode Island, November 18, 1925. (Image #13946-[M268], Image Collection, Arnold Arboretum Horticultural Library of Harvard University, Jamaica Plain, Massachusetts; © President and Fellows of Harvard College. Arnold Arboretum Archives)

town, was bordered by the Narragansett Bay on the west and on the east by the road that now links Providence to Newport. The farmhouse (c. 1799), today on a separate property, was set back a short distance from the road. George Rogers Hall inherited the house and farm in 1873.[60] Earlier, around 1870, some eight years after his return, he began the transformation of parts of the site, planting Japanese yew as well as zelkova, Yeddo spruce, Tigertail spruce, and others.[61] His grounds also displayed native species, such as the Cucumber magnolia. By the time of Sargent's 1889 visit, Hall had established an impressive collection.

A few literary references and pictorial records hint at the layout of the Bristol grounds. A letter from Hall's son, Chandler Prince Hall, provides one clue. Born in Shanghai in 1851, he followed in his father's footsteps, moving to Japan in 1874.[62] He remained there, working for Walsh, Hall & Co., until his death from small pox in 1897.[63] In 1880, he wrote to his two sisters about his pleasant memories of "the old place" in Bristol, asking, "Please write me about the place how it looks especially the groves of Japanese Trees."[64] The son's letter indicates that his father had planted Japanese trees in groups, separate from the rest of his collection. In the account of his visit, Sargent gave a sketchy description of a single, and presumably different, component of Hall's garden, noting, "The plantations are confined, in the main, to the

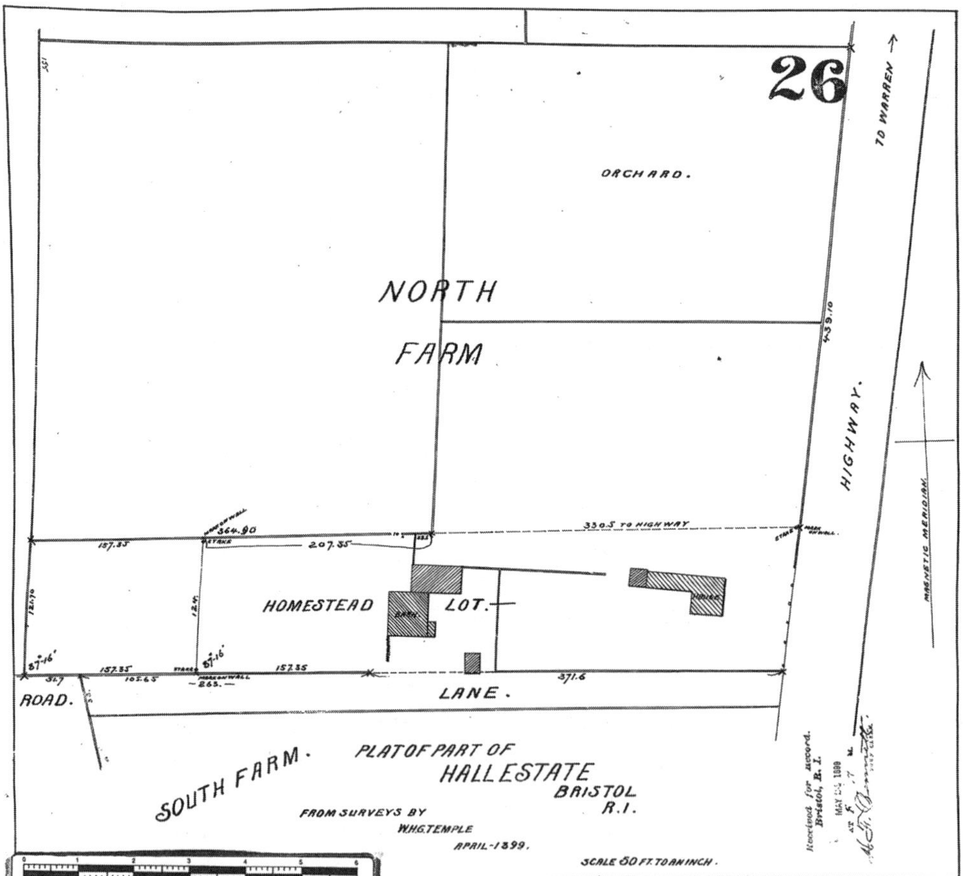

Fig. 6. W. H. G. Temple, "Plat of Part of Hall Estate, Bristol, R.I.," April 1899. (Clerk's Office, Town Hall, Bristol, Rhode Island)

Fig. 7. J. Murray Howe II, "The Lane, Bristol, July 3d 1893." (Sketchbook in the collection of Margaret Howe Ewing)

northern and eastern sides of an open field, on the top of the ridge."[65] This ridge runs north–south on the eastern side of the property. Hall's grandson, James M. Howe Jr., in an article accompanying a catalog of some of Hall's imports, described some of the components of the Bristol garden. While he did not pinpoint locations geographically, the elements he identified included a "great evergreen border," containing "some fifty or more varieties of trees," a "deciduous section," and a "garden back of the house," containing the "original Japanese Yew."[66] Hall's notable collection is invisible on an April 1899 survey that shows the location of the farmhouse, walls, barns and outbuildings, and an orchard (fig. 6). An 1893 sketch by Hall's son-in-law, J. Murray Howe II, offers one of the earliest illustrations of the plantings (fig. 7). Looking east along the lane, unbounded by the walls shown on the later survey, in the distance three trees frame the terminus to the lane and another row parallels the pathway on the right. Within each of the two groupings, the artist rendered bark and foliage similarly, suggesting that Hall planted trees of like kinds together. Taken together, the evidence of these written and visual sources indicates that a garden containing a mix of trees, shrubs, and flowering plants stood behind the house, that the "great evergreen border" was either between the house and orchard or south of the house, and that Hall sorted some plantings into groups by type.

Hall's activities on the grounds of his Bristol estate included improving and ameliorating plants. Windbreaks and judicious site selection aided acclimatization for tender plants. Sargent noted that Hall employed Japanese false cypresses as "wind-breaks."[67] Howe reported later that a "hardy Orange (*Poncirus trifoliata*) which occasionally bears fruit" remained on the site.[68] Such experimentation was not unique to Hall, of course, but instead was part of a broad undertaking in the period. In an unsigned 1890 article in *Garden and Forest,* the author pointed out an important contemporary challenge: to improve tree stock by hybridization and discrimination, observing, "For the ordinary collector of tree-seeds in the nursery or the forest a seed is a seed." The article proposed an alternative approach—"tree-culture," careful seed selection based on close study—as the means to improvement. The writer concluded by pointing to the leadership role professionals should play: "by making such experiments . . . arboreta, botanic gardens and our agricultural experiment stations can do practical and useful work."[69] Yet, Sargent's visit to Hall's estate the previous year and his praise for the Bristol gardener's successes reveal he recognized the crucial contributions also made by diligent nonprofessionals. At the conclusion of his report on the Bristol estate, Sargent applauded the valuable efforts of amateur arborists, singling out Hall and Hunnewell for mention.[70] Together, the two articles confirmed that the late-nineteenth-century quest to enhance tree culture in the United States was to be a collaborative effort of professionals and amateurs. Hall was a volunteer scientific gardener in the Sargent network. His estate was an amateur research facility as well as an ornamental garden.

George Rogers Hall did not imitate Japanese garden aesthetics as Francis Hall had dreamed of doing in 1861, and, in fact, Japanese-style gardens in the United States postdated his work in Bristol. Josiah Conder's landmark 1893 *Landscape Gardening in Japan* introduced Japanese garden design principles to the West.[71] That same year, Beatrix Farrand saw the Japanese pavilion at the World's Columbian Exposition in Chicago and described its setting as a "poor representation of a Japanese garden."[72] The earliest Japanese-style gardens on private estates in the United States generally date to the turn of the century.[73] By comparison, Hall, working earlier in Bristol and recalling the captivating Japanese landscape, employed imported plants and bigness of scale rather than miniaturization as an aesthetic.

Although Hall's garden was not unique in incorporating Japanese plants in the late nineteenth century, it was, nonetheless, groundbreaking. Clay

Lancaster identified the first Japanese garden in the United States as the grounds of the Japanese Bazaar at the 1876 Centennial International Exhibition in Philadelphia. Like a portion of Hall's garden, it showcased Japanese specimens planted in orderly rows, rather than Japanese garden design principles.[74] While Hall left no records dating his work in Bristol, Sargent claimed the planting of Hall's Japanese botanicals on the estate began "about 1870," approximately six years before the fair.[75] Some of these plants presumably formed the "groves of Japanese Trees" the son recalled.[76]

No other landscape rivals Hall's "groves" for primacy as the earliest American garden in which Japanese plantings dominate. Parkman had incorporated Hall's exotics into the garden he had begun earlier on the shores of Jamaica Pond. There, he sorted some groupings, such as maples, by genus rather than by place of origin. Such a planting pattern suggests that, unlike Hall, who laid out a collection of Japanese trees as a unit, Parkman distributed the Eastern imports throughout his garden.[77] As noted above, the Japanese plants at the Parsons nursery, following their use for propagation, were to be sold, rather than to remain in Flushing.[78] The disposition of the botanicals Hall sent to others, such as Agassiz, is unknown. Hall's groves of imports, then, constituted the earliest known garden of Japanese plants in the United States planted by an American. His estate was not only one of the earliest grounds to include Japanese plants but also the first collection in the country that contained plants gathered, propagated, and selected in Japan by the gardener. Today, the Bristol estate holds fragments of the only garden planted by Hall with material from the first wave of direct importations from Japan.

Read literally, Chandler Hall's statement indicates a specific section of his father's estate contained almost exclusively Japanese plants. If so, standing apart from the groves of Japanese trees was another area, organized quite differently. This part of his landscape exhibited plants from Japan co-mingled with those from other locales. Photographs taken in 1916 and 1919 of trees on the former Hall estate reveal specimens pulled together from locations across the globe to create an imposing and expansive wall of green. Their maturity suggests they had been planted by Hall or at his direction. In one vignette, two firs, one from Greece and the other from the Middle East, joined a spruce from Japan (fig. 8). This section, not sorted by genus, species, or country of origin, exhibits the clearest expression of Hall's tribute to the networked world in which he operated. Branches intertwined, metaphorically linking far-flung parts of the globe together. The visual rhetoric articulated an ideal of interconnectivity, celebrating Hall's

Fig. 8. E. H. Wilson, "*Abies cephalonica* Lh. . . . on right; *Picea polita* Carr. . . . on left; *Abies cilicica* Carr. in rear," Estate of the late George Rogers Hall, Bristol, Rhode Island, September 27, 1919. (Image #1398-[M510], Image Collection, Arnold Arboretum Horticultural Library of Harvard University, Jamaica Plain, Massachusetts; © President and Fellows of Harvard College. Arnold Arboretum Archives)

own globe-spanning career as well as contact between East and West. Here, the doctor-turned-gardener dramatized the height of the trees by fronting them with a broad, sweeping agricultural field (fig. 9). No intervening plantings mitigated the immense scale or the vertical rush of the towering trees. If not directly a recapitulation of the Japanese countryside he had admired, the landscape created an aestheticized vision of a new, improved American forest self-consciously reimagined by bringing together native and imported trees. In this landscape Hall promoted Japanese plants, not as exotic curiosities, but as suitable co-inhabitants of an American garden.

Trees, in particular, held great power for Hall and his family. In 1860 he wrote his wife from Japan, "I can imagine you and the boys at Kingston occasionally roving through those fine woods which delighted me so much."[79] Later, he urged her to cultivate his interest in their sons: "I have written Father to have the boys make him a visit in the spring and transplant some trees in a lot . . . with their own hands. There will be some sentiment in this operation and I know that it will be gratifying to their Grandfather to see them show so much interest."[80] The concern did take hold, as Chandler Hall's fond recollection of the groves of Japanese trees indicates. For the son, the imported, rather than native, trees—the only specific element on the estate he identified in his letter—were a potent icon of home.

Hall viewed his cultivation of Japanese botanicals as a tool for both social and societal advancement. Gathering seeds and plants promised not only

Fig. 9. Great evergreen border, Estate of George Rogers Hall, Bristol, no date, unidentified photographer. (Collection of Margaret Howe Ewing)

future personal enjoyment—the pleasure of "seeing some of the beautiful trees and shrubs growing in our grounds"—but also a means to enhance his status—"I shall get some credit for sending it [a specimen] there if it arrives safely."[81] He sought not only to improve the flora of his own country, but also, in so doing, to advance himself and his family. Horticultural and personal cultivation were intertwined.

Although no document from Hall spells out the impulses that inspired his gardening in Bristol, and no map from his hand indicates the organization of his garden, his actions speak louder than words or sketches. In contrast to contemporary "arboricultural nationalists," who shunned foreign plants, Hall was a "cosmopolitan," endorsing exotics as appropriate for American gardens and forests.[82] While he left no manifesto, his position was built into the fabric of his garden. His choice to import horticultural materials but not Japanese garden aesthetics was a call to naturalize foreign botanicals rather than to isolate and segregate stylistic novelties. Like his home, which proudly displayed curios from Asia in a Federal style house and his New England stone walls, ornamented with Asian guardian lions, Hall's plantings endorsed integration of foreign plants. His garden was a physical record of his travels, his entrepreneurialism, his vibrant intellectual and commercial network, and his social and philosophical attitudes. It also documented his exchanges. As noted previously, in 1898, one year before his death, Hall sought to add to his collection.[83] Exchanges, networking, and interconnectivity, both physically and symbolically, were the foundations of Hall's garden.

Yet, despite Hall's substantial contributions, some of the satisfaction he had anticipated from Japan was short-lived. His wife died in 1864 soon after the birth of their twin daughters. Unfortunate investments, particularly in Florida, where he spent a number of winters, dogged him. In 1874 he traveled a final time to Japan. He died at the home of one of his daughters in Milton on December 24, 1899.[84]

The Organization and Transformation of the Hall Garden

Well into the twentieth century, Hall's descendants owned the southern half of the property, using it as a vacation home. Elizabeth G. Clark and her husband, Providence financier Howard L. Clark, acquired the northern parcel, which contained a portion of Hall's gardens, around the turn of the century. They hired Charles Platt to design a new fashionable country house and garden. Called North Farm, their estate exhibited many of the formal characteristics found in the architect's Italian-inspired work: extensive, framed lawn with sculpture, house sited for views of the bay, pergola, and a formal, geometric garden. Yet the Platt landscape at North Farm did not draw exclusively from the Italian tradition, because it incorporated portions of Hall's earlier garden.[85]

Period documentation of the Clark garden provides further insight into the organization of the landscape Hall had created. Platt's 1902 site plan, drawn by C. C. Grant, shows the Clark-owned portion of Hall's garden, as it was only two and one-half years after the plantsman's death (fig. 10). As a note on the drawing points out, light lines with hatching denoted existing plantings; groupings shown in outline were new (fig. 11). If Platt removed any earlier plants, as journalist and editor Herbert Croly suggested, their locations were not indicated on the drawing.[86] Eighteen years after Sargent's visit and five years after the Platt drawing, another journalist toured North Farm to report on recent changes to the former Hall estate. Cross-referencing the plan with the nearly contemporary 1907 newspaper description offers the best insight into the organization of Hall's garden as it survived in the Clark period.[87] Platt's plan illustrated a garden containing four major components from Hall's time. Although the site plan lacks a north arrow, Grant oriented the drawing to place north at the top of the sheet. North of the "Farm House," rows of deciduous and evergreen trees, sorted by genus, framed rectangular corridors. Some were zelkovas, one of which remains today. Three hemlocks, standing today in the line of the row indicated on the plan, are Japanese. These trees are most likely the remnants of the groves of Japanese trees that Chandler Hall recalled. In Hall's day, this section had been a botanical showcase for propagation and display. West of the "Farm House," Platt's drawing showed an informally planted walled pocket garden, containing a variety of trees encircling a large Japanese yew. The centerpiece was a variety of the now-ubiquitous evergreen that was planted first in Bristol by Hall.[88] To the west, south of a new formal garden, rows of unidentified plants framed rectangular corridors for the display of specimens. In the center of the plan, a row of larches and a curving border of unidentified plants partially encircled a large open field. No part of the Platt plan resembled the imposing "plantations," bordering the north and east sides of an "open field, on the top of the ridge," described earlier by Sargent or the "great evergreen border," noted by Howe. Instead, it is most likely that the two descriptions reference the same plantings in Hall's garden

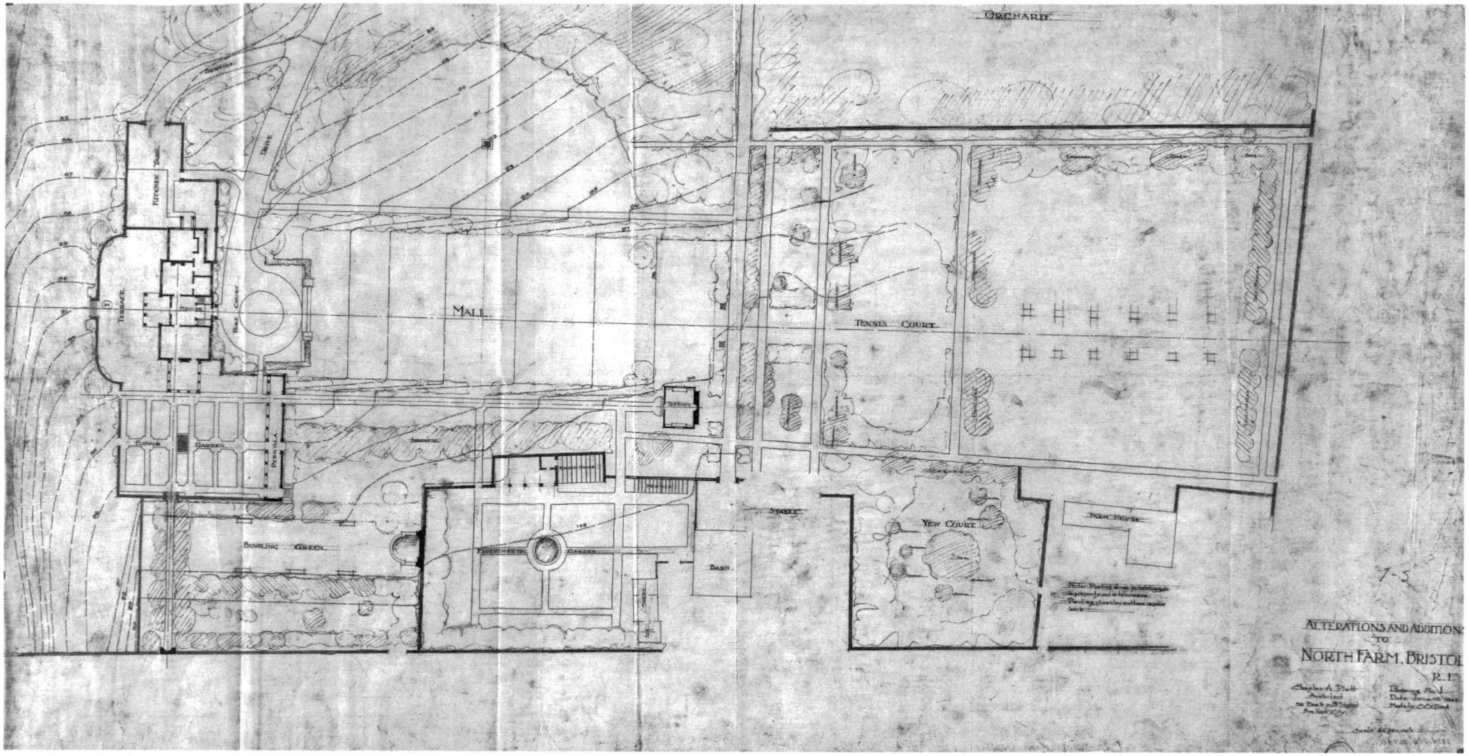

ORCHARD
TERRACE
KITCHEN YARD
HOUSE
BOX COURT
DRIVE
MALL
TENNIS COURT
FLOWER GARDEN
PERGOLA
BOWLING GREEN
STABLE
BARN
YEW COURT
FARM HOUSE
7-5
ALTERATIONS AND ADDITIONS TO NORTH FARM, BRISTOL R.I.
Charles A. Platt Architect

and that the grouping, still intact in the aerial photograph (c. 1970), stood on the southern parcel retained by Hall's heirs (fig. 2, on the adjacent property, south of the south boundary of North Farm, and fig. 9).

The decision to retain portions of the Hall landscape is especially noteworthy. The Clarks and Platt chose to preserve the remains of the Hall garden as relics, "to attract the attention of horticulturists and connoisseurs of garden lore" and "to form a harmonious whole."[89] No correspondence survives to indicate who urged the retention of the Hall plantings. Yet, Platt's aversion to incorporating existing landscaping in his designs and the absence of Japanese influences in his other work coupled with Howard Clark's longstanding amateur interests in natural science and collecting suggest the impulse came from the client.[90] Either way, whether initiated by the designer or the patrons, the outcome was the same. Attentive to the stature of the Hall landscape, the architect and the owners together created a new composition that incorporated and complemented the old. In retaining the historic plants, the Clarks assumed stewardship of the notable collection, and Platt's deference to the historic garden constituted an early act of landscape preservation by a designer. Platt's "proto-preservationism" predated the "full flowering of the landscape preservation movement in the 1920s and 1930s," exemplified in the work of Arthur Shurcliff at Colonial Williamsburg.[91] However, unlike Shurcliff's work, the historic American landscape that the North Farm designer and clients saved was anchored by a venerable collection of Japanese trees.

Platt tenderly stitched the new garden into and around Hall's mature collection in the southeast quadrant of the site (fig. 2). The new house and terrace, situated on the brow of the slope leading down to the bay, were positioned perpendicular to Hall's rows, "so that the house might appear to have been there when the trees were planted."[92] Platt's Italian Renaissance–inspired pergola and his formal garden—configured differently today—stood apart from the valued earlier plantings. The landscape architect artfully employed the earlier imports as a leafy green backdrop to enhance the pale columns of the middle ground (fig. 12). He slotted a bowling green into Hall's green corridors and cut a mall through the open field between Hall's larches and the new hemicycle. A tennis court, shown on the Platt

Fig. 10, opposite. Charles A. Platt, Architect, "Additions and Alterations to North Farm, Bristol, R.I.," drawing by C. C. Grant, June 10, 1902. ("Charles A. Platt architectural records and papers, 1879–1981 [bulk, 1882–1933]," Avery Architectural and Fine Arts Library, Columbia University)

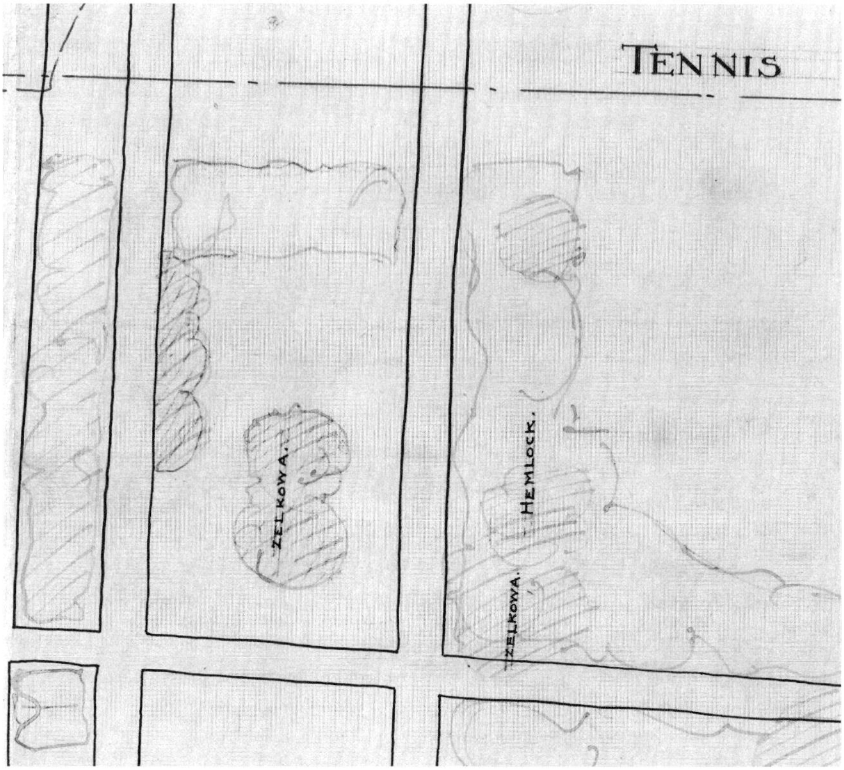

Fig. 11. Detail of Charles A. Platt, Architect, "Additions and Alterations to North Farm, Bristol, R.I.," drawing by C. C. Grant, June 10, 1902. ("Charles A. Platt architectural records and papers, 1879–1981 [bulk, 1882–1933]," Avery Architectural and Fine Arts Library, Columbia University)

plan between rows of Japanese trees, apparently was not built. The 1907 visitor described this area "[b]eyond the study" as "a wilderness of trees and shrubs, a veritable arboretum, containing some of the rarest trees and shrubs to be found in this country."[93] By this time, Hall's mature Japanese trees had become the armature for a very different garden that, nonetheless, paid homage to the Hall legacy.

Today, portions of Hall's and Platt's landscape remain intact on the eighty-four-acre grounds of a condominium complex, also known as North Farm. The redevelopment of the site for the new use began in 1973 and continued through a series of phases until the 1990s. By the time this second transformation began, Platt's house for the Clarks had been demolished. One of the terraces survives, as do the pergola, a reconfigured portion of the formal garden, foundations of the greenhouses, and the mall. Sited to preserve large swaths of the former meadows, three hundred condominiums cluster in boxy masses, framing open meadows that nod to the earlier agricultural use. Others are threaded in among the trees of Hall's early arboretum. Only a few remnants of the great evergreen border remain on the property to the south, now a residential subdivision. Thus, the most substantial surviving portions of the Hall garden ornament the grounds of North Farm.

Conclusion

George Rogers Hall transformed the content of American gardens and shaped American landscape taste with his groundbreaking introduction of Japanese botanicals. Today, a wide array of his imports, ranging from zelkovas to Japanese yews to new varieties of Japanese maples, are basic building blocks of the American landscape, and *Amaryllis hallii, Malus halliana* [Hall's crabapple], and *Lonicera japonica var. Halliana* [Hall's honeysuckle] bear his name. His own garden proudly displayed Japanese plants, giving physical expression to a vision of a new American garden that celebrated cross-cultural exchange. Honing the imagery for a cosmopolitan garden

Fig. 12. Charles A. Platt, Pergola and remaining portion of the formal garden, North Farm, Bristol, Rhode Island. (Photograph by Sara A. Butler)

rather than isolating and segregating a design curiosity, he created a landscape that not only was inspired by his travels but that also paid tribute to the networked world he helped to build.

Hall merits interest for the horticultural web he honed to facilitate importation and dissemination. Through his network, a stream of botanicals flowed from the hands of Western plant hunters and local gardeners in Japan, nurtured by personal exchanges and educational initiatives and aided by horticultural institutions, the gardening press, and his own estate in Bristol, to plant enthusiasts, commercial nurseries, and gardens across the United States. At each stage Hall had a hand. His grounds were the nucleus of the system, and there he inscribed a tangible record of the attitudes he endorsed and the relationships he forged. His collection was known to, served as a resource for, and was documented by the makers of the oldest public arboretum in the United States. It shaped the Arnold Arboretum collection in ways that are both recoverable and speculative. Beyond his own day, the incorporation of his historic plantings within a later garden at North Farm constituted a precocious act of landscape preservation. Platt's plan documented not one garden but two, for it also displayed the earliest known and most complete plan of a portion of Hall's plantings. The North Farm landscape contains a fragment of the only surviving garden of the pioneering plantsman, horticultural activist, and tastemaker, who built networks for botanical exchange between East and West.

Notes

I am especially grateful to Margaret Howe Ewing, who generously shared materials from her collection, Lisa E. Pearson of the Arnold Arboretum Horticultural Library, and Raffaella Fabiani Giannetto.

1. C. S. S. [Charles Sprague Sargent], "The Forest: Some Japanese Trees in New England," *Garden and Forest: A Journal of Horticulture, Landscape Art, and Forestry* 2, no. 89 (November 6, 1889): 537–38. "Zelkova" is an alternate spelling.

2. Ibid., 537.

3. Peter Barnes, "Japan's Botanical Sunrise: Plant Exploration around the Meiji Restoration," *Curtis's Botanical Magazine* 18, no. 2 (May 2001): 121; Alice M. Coats, *The Plant Hunters, Being a History of the Horticultural Pioneers, Their Quests and Their Discoveries, from the Renaissance to the Twentieth Century* (New York: McGraw-Hill, 1969), 79; Elizabeth May McClintock and Richard G. Turner, *The Trees of Golden Gate Park and San Francisco* (Berkeley, CA: Heyday Books/Clapperstick Institute, 2001), 182; Frederick McGourty Jr., "Hall—Of Hall's Honeysuckle," *Plants & Gardens* 23 (1967): 85; Stephen A. Spongberg, *A Reunion of Trees: The Discovery of Exotic Plants and Their Introduction into North American and European Landscapes* (Cambridge, MA: Harvard University Press,

1990), 145–55; Stephen A. Spongberg, "The First Japanese Plants for New England," *Arnoldia* 50, no. 3 (1990): 2–11; Judith Sumner, *American Household Botany: A History of Useful Plants, 1620–1900* (Portland, OR: Timber Press, 2004), 336.

4. Historians of the nineteenth century employ the imagery of "networks" to examine the dynamic of exchange in the period. See Melody Barnett Deusner, "A Network of Associations: Aesthetic Painting and Its Patrons, 1870–1914" (PhD diss., University of Delaware, 2010); Philip J. Pauly, *Fruits and Plains: The Horticultural Transformation of America* (Cambridge, MA: Harvard University Press, 2007).

5. On Hall see "Dr. Hall, Collector," *Horticulture* 1, no. 3 (September 1, 1923): 42; George E. Gifford Jr., "George Rogers Hall: 'Pills and Plants,'" *Harvard Medical Alumni Bulletin* 47, no. 2 (1972): 22–24; James M. Howe Jr., "George Rogers Hall, Lover of Plants," *Journal of the Arnold Arboretum* 4 (April 1923): 91–98; F. G. Notehelfer, "A Sketch of the Life of Francis Hall," in *Japan through American Eyes: The Journal of Francis Hall, Kanagawa and Yokohama, 1859–1866,* ed. F. G. Notehelfer (Princeton, NJ: Princeton University Press, 1992), 33–37; Spongberg, *A Reunion of Trees,* 145–55; Spongberg, "First Japanese Plants," 2–11. For a lively account see Richardson Wright, "Pills and Plants: The Tale of Dr. George R. Hall, Who Eventually Chose between Them," in *Gardener's Tribute* (New York: J. B. Lippincott, 1949), 119–42.

6. Helen Beal Hall to Mother [Mrs. Thomas P. Beal], March 9, 1851, Folder: Beal family (March–June 1851), Box 2 of 4, and Helen Beal Hall to Thos. P. Beal for Elizabeth Beal, undated, Folder: Beal family (1850s), Box 2 of 4, Beal Family Papers, Massachusetts Historical Society, Boston, Massachusetts.

7. Wright, "Pills and Plants," 129.

8. S. W., "New or Little Known Plants: Lycoris squamigera," *Garden and Forest* 3, no. 111 (April 9, 1890): 176. Also noted in Gifford, "George Rogers Hall," 22, 24.

9. Notehelfer, *Japan through American Eyes,* 33–35. The location of Hall's house is identified in Joseph Heco, *Narrative of a Japanese* (San Francisco: American-Japanese Publishing Assn., n.d.), 1:216–17, qtd. in Notehelfer, *Japan through American Eyes,* 102–3n6.

10. John M. Brooke's assessment is in George M. Brooke Jr., ed., *John M. Brooke's Pacific Cruise and Japanese Adventure, 1858–1860* (Honolulu: University of Hawaii Press, 1986), 183.

11. [George Rogers Hall], Yokohama, to [Mrs. George Rogers Hall], December 21, 1860, private collection of and transcribed by Margaret Howe Ewing.

12. Spongberg, *A Reunion of Trees,* 155.

13. For information on Francis Hall, see Notehelfer, *Japan through American Eyes,* 3–62; F. G. Notehelfer, "Visions of Early Yokohama: Francis Hall in Treaty Port Japan," *Asian Art* 3 (Summer 1990): 8–35; F. G. Notehelfer, "Before the Restoration: Francis Hall's Description of Bakumatsu Japan," *Zinbun: Memoirs of the Research Institute for Humanistic Studies, Kyoto University* 21 (1986): 1–30.

14. Francis Hall, Thursday, August 8, 1861, qtd. in Notehelfer, *Japan through American Eyes,* 364.

15. Robert Fortune, *Yedo and Peking: A Narrative of a Journey to the Capitals of Japan and China* (London: John Murray, 1863), 184–85.

16. Parsons & Co., Flushing, March 20, 1862, "Japanese Trees," *Horticulturist and Journal of Rural Art and Rural Taste* 17 (1862), 186.

17. For the attribution of the ownership of the compound, see Ann Yonemura, *Yokohama: Prints from Nineteenth-Century Japan* (Washington, DC: Arthur M. Sackler Gallery and Smithsonian Institution Press, 1990), 88–89; and Notehelfer, "Visions of Early Yokohama," 21–23.

18. Francis Hall, Wednesday, November 6, 1861, qtd. in Notehelfer, *Japan through American Eyes,* 379–80.

19. [George Rogers Hall] to [Mrs. George Rogers Hall], December 21, 1860, Ewing collection.

20. George [Rogers Hall] to [Helen Beal Hall], undated, partial letter, Ewing collection.

21. Fortune, *Yedo and Peking,* 60–61.

22. Hall's departure date is noted in Francis Hall, Friday, January 3, 1862, qtd. in Notehelfer, *Japan through American Eyes,* 390.

23. Spongberg, "First Japanese Plants," 2, 4–5; Howe, "George Rogers Hall," 96–97.

24. Gifford, "George Rogers Hall," 24; Spongberg, *A Reunion of Trees,* 145.

25. S. B. Sutton, *Charles Sprague Sargent and the Arnold Arboretum* (Cambridge, MA: Harvard University Press, 1970), 199. Sargent probably encountered Hall's plants at the Massachusetts Horticultural Society, where Parkman exhibited regularly.

26. "New and Rare Japan Lily," *Transactions of the Massachusetts Horticultural Society for the Year 1862* (Boston: Henry W. Dutton & Son, 1863), 6–7; Walter Muir Whitehill, "Francis Parkman as Horticulturist," *Arnoldia* 33, no. 3 (May 1973): 174.

27. "Floricultural Notices: Lilium Auratum," *Magazine of Horticulture, Botany, and All Useful Discoveries and Improvements in Rural Affairs* 29 (August 1863): 312–13. Also noted in "Dr. Hall, Collector," 42. For information on Hovey, see B. June Hutchinson, "A Taste for Horticulture," *Arnoldia* 40, no. 2 (January 1980): 31–48; Pauly, *Fruits and Plains,* 58–61, 69–73.

28. George [Rogers Hall], Yokohama, to Mrs. G. R. Hall, Kingston, Massachusetts, November 10, 1859, Ewing collection.

29. Francis Hall, Sunday, March 17, 1861, qtd. in Notehelfer *Japan through American Eyes,* 315. A *mia,* usually spelled *"miya,"* is a Shinto shrine. Francis Hall apparently also frequently used the term to refer to a Buddhist temple. Ibid., 119n19.

30. For information on Parsons & Sons Company, see L. H. Bailey, *The Standard Cyclopedia of Horticulture,* 2nd ed. (New York: Macmillan, 1917), Charles A. Birnbaum, *Samuel Parsons Jr., and the Art of Landscape Architecture* (Bronx, New York: Wave Hill, 1994); and Charles A. Birnbaum, "Samuel Parsons Jr.," in *Pioneers of American Landscape Design,* ed. Charles A. Birnbaum and Robin Karson (New York, McGraw-Hill, 2000), 287–91.

31. Parsons & Co., "Japanese Trees," 186–87. Plants that Hall delivered to Parsons & Sons Company are also identified in Howe, "George Rogers Hall," 97–98, and Spongberg, "First Japanese Plants," 7–8.

32. S. B. Parsons, Flushing, New York, to Townsend Harris, May 30, 1861, James Parsons & Sons Co. Papers, Box 15 (letter book 2), Special Collections Department and University Archives, Frank Melville Jr. Memorial Library, Stony Brook University, Stony Brook, New York.

33. "Dr. Hall, Collector," 42.

34. Parsons & Co., Flushing, Queens, to Geo. R. Hall, September 1862, James Parsons & Sons Co. Papers.

35. Tamara Plakins Thornton, *Cultivating Gentlemen: The Meaning of Country Life among the Boston Elite, 1785–1860* (New Haven, CT: Yale University Press, 1989), 180–81. For an overview of the various functions and contributions of nurserymen in antebellum America, see Therese O'Malley, "From Practice to Theory: The Emerging Profession of Landscape Gardening in Early Nineteenth-Century America," in *Botanical Progress, Horticultural Innovation and Cultural Change,* ed. Michel Conan and W. John Kress (Washington, DC: Dumbarton Oaks Research Library and Collection, 2007), 223–37.

36. George [Rogers Hall], to [Mrs. G. R. Hall], undated, partial letter; and George [Rogers Hall], Yokohama, to Nellie [Helen Beal Hall], February 14, 1861, Ewing collection.

37. Sutton, *Charles Sprague Sargent,* 186–87.

38. C. S. Sargent to George R. Hall, April 21, 1898, Folder: Beal Family (1880–1898), Box 4 of 4, Beal Family Papers.

39. Japanese plants in Hunnewell's garden are noted in "Garden Gossip," *Magazine of Horticulture, Botany, and All Useful Discoveries and Improvements in Rural Affairs* 29 (July 1863): 264–66, and "Garden Gossip," *Magazine of Horticulture, Botany, and All Useful Discoveries and Improvements in Rural Affairs* 30 (July 1864): 269–71.

40. Horatio Hollis Hunnewell, *Life, Letters, and Diary of Horatio Hollis Hunnewell: Born July 27, 1810, Died May 20, 1902; with a Short History of the Hunnewell and Welles Families, and an Account of the Wellesley and Natick Estates* (Boston: Privately printed, 1906), 2:71.

41. Howe, "George Rogers Hall," 93.

42. George [Rogers Hall] to Nellie [Helen Beal Hall], February 14, 1861.

43. "Prizes Awarded for Plants, Flowers and Bouquets," *Transactions of the Massachusetts Horticultural Society for the Year 1868* (Boston: Henry W. Dutton & Son, 1869), 67.

44. "Japanese Trees and Shrubs," *Magazine of Horticulture, Botany, and All Useful Discoveries and Improvements in Rural Affairs* 30 (August 1864): 281.

45. Ernest H. Wilson, "Flowers and Gardens of Japan," Address to the Massachusetts Horticultural Society, January 8, 1916, in *Transactions of the Massachusetts Horticultural Society for the Year 1916, Part 1* (Boston: Printed for the Society, 1916), 17.

46. "Ornamental Foliaged Trees," *Magazine of Horticulture, Botany, and All Useful Discoveries and Improvements in Rural Affairs* 31 (November 1865): 322; "Arboriculture," *Magazine of Horticulture* 32 (January 1866): 11; Editor [C. M. Hovey], "The Striped Japanese Maize," *Magazine of Horticulture* 33 (March 1867): 92; and "Floricultural Notices: Lilium Auratum," 312–13. The anticipated report on Japan from Hall is noted in "Floriculture," *Magazine of Horticulture* 31 (January 1865): 9.

47. C. S. S., "The Forest: Some Japanese Trees," 537–39; E. W. Davis, Providence, Rhode Island, "Correspondence: Japanese Trees in Rhode Island," *Garden and Forest* 6, no. 298 (November 8, 1893): 468–69; J., "Notes from the Arnold Arboretum," *Garden and Forest* 2, no. 66 (May 29, 1889): 260; and C. S. S., "Notes on the Forest Flora of Japan—XVIII," *Garden and Forest* 6, no. 284 (August 2, 1893): 323–25.

48. Davis, "Correspondence: Japanese Trees," 468–69.

49. Sargent to George R. Hall, April 21, 1898, Beal Family Papers.

50. "Hall Estate Photographs, Warren [*sic*], Rhode Island," Image Collection, Arnold Arboretum Library, Jamaica Plain, Massachusetts.

51. The Arnold Arboretum's photograph collection is noted in Sutton, *Charles Sprague Sargent,* 332. The date is from ibid., 71.

52. S. W., "New or Little Known Plants," 176–77.

53. Parsons & Co., "Japanese Trees," and accompanying editor's note, 187.

54. The estimate of the planting date is from Fred Hall, gardener at Bethshan for many years beginning in 1906. Fred Hall, interview by Richard Champlin (April 1976), in Richard Champlin, "Newport Estates and Their Flora," *Newport History* 53, part 2, no. 178 (Spring 1980): 51–52.

55. Howe, "George Rogers Hall," 98.

56. Ibid., 93.

57. C. S. S., "Notes on the Forest Flora," 324; Davis, "Correspondence: Japanese Trees," 468.

58. "Hall Estate Photographs," Image #13946-(M268).

59. Deed of sale from Nathaniel Bullock to Benjamin Hall, February 6, 1832 (recorded February 7, 1832), Bristol, Rhode Island, Land Evidence Book 12, 354, Clerk's Office, Town Hall, Bristol, Rhode Island.

60. "Death of Hon. Benjamin Hall," *Bristol (RI) Phoenix*, January 11, 1873, 2. Will of Benjamin Hall (d. 8 January 1873), November 3, 1870, and probate record, March 3, 1873, Will Book 5, 499–501, Clerk's Office, Town Hall, Bristol, Rhode Island, and obituary of George Rogers Hall, *Milton (MA) News*, December 30, 1899, 5.

61. Howe, "George Rogers Hall," 98.

62. Although Howe dates Hall's return to Japan to 1875, Notehelfer, quoting a report in the *Japanese Weekly Mail* of George Rogers Hall's arrival in Yokohama from San Francisco, notes that father and son traveled together to Japan in 1874. Howe, "George Rogers Hall," 92; Notehelfer, *Japan through American Eyes,* 36n122.

63. Howe, "George Rogers Hall," 92.

64. CH [Chandler Prince Hall], Yokohama, to Sisters [Helen and Elizabeth], January 26, 1880, Folder: Beal Family (1880–1898), Box 4 of 4, Beal Family Papers.

65. C. S. S., "The Forest," 537.

66. Howe, "George Rogers Hall," 93.

67. C. S. S., "The Forest," 538.

68. Howe, "George Rogers Hall," 94. Also noted in "Japanese Trees Used to Beautify a Famous Bristol Estate," *Providence (RI) Sunday Journal*, April 21, 1907, sec. 4, 5.

69. "The Improvement of Trees," *Garden and Forest* 3, no. 140 (October 29, 1890): 521–22.

70. C. S. S., "The Forest," 539.

71. Noted in Azby Brown, foreword to *Landscape Gardening in Japan, with the Author's 1912 Supplement to Landscape Gardening in Japan,* by Josiah Conder (New York: Kodansha International, 2002), 7–8.

72. Beatrix Farrand, Journal, 1893, qtd. in Patrick Chassé, *The Abby Aldrich Rockefeller Garden: A Visitor's Guide* ([Maine?]: David Rockefeller, 1996), 18.

73. Clay Lancaster, *The Japanese Influence in America* (New York: Abbeville Press, 1983), 192–215.

74. Ibid., 50, 190.

75. C. S. S., "The Forest," 537.

76. CH [Chandler Hall] to Sisters, January 26, 1880.

77. Benjamin Watson, "Notes in Regard to Trees, Shrubs, and Herbaceous Plants, on the Estate of the Late Mr. Francis Parkman, of Jamaica Plain, Mass., November 1984," TMs, 3, Vertical file: Francis Parkman, Massachusetts Horticultural Society, Wellesley, Massachusetts.

78. Parsons & Co. to Geo. R. Hall, September 9, 1862.

79. George [Rogers Hall], Kanagawa, to Mrs. G. R. Hall, Kingston, MA, June 10, 1860, Ewing collection.

80. George [Rogers Hall] to Mrs. G. R. Hall, c/o Mssrs. Beal & Hooper, Haymarket Square, Boston, December 29, 1860, Ewing collection.

81. Ibid.; George [Rogers Hall] to [Mrs. G. R. Hall], undated, partial letter, Ewing collection.

82. The distinction is from Pauly, *Fruits and Plains*, 82–88.

83. Hall's request is acknowledged in Sargent to George R. Hall, April 21, 1898, Beal Family Papers.

84. Howe, "George Rogers Hall," 92–95; and obituary of George Rogers Hall.

85. For a brief discussion of North Farm, see Rhode Island Historical Preservation & Heritage Commission, *Historic Landscapes of Rhode Island* (Providence, RI: The Commission, 2001), 82–83.

86. Herbert Croly, "The Architectural Work of Charles A. Platt," *Architectural Record* 15, no. 3 (March 1904): 219.

87. "Japanese Trees Used to Beautify."

88. The Yew Court does not survive. Although a plaque on the grounds today identifies another yew on the property as the first planted in the United States, Hall's original planting of the variety died in 1927. Elizabeth Hall Howe, manuscript margin notes on a copy of Howe, "George Rogers Hall," 98, Ewing collection.

89. "Japanese Trees Used to Beautify."

90. Platt's preferences are noted in Keith Morgan, email message to author, April 7, 2011. Howard Clark's membership in the American Entomological Society and his "fascination" with the field is noted in "Howard Lee Clark Dead in 70th Year," *Providence (RI) Journal*, November 4, 1926, sec. 2, 2.

91. The term *proto-preservationism* is from Charles A. Birnbaum and Mary V. Hughes. They did not use it to describe Platt's work. Charles A. Birnbaum and Mary V. Hughes, "Introduction: Landscape Preservation in Context, 1890–1950," in *Design with Culture: Claiming America's Landscape Heritage*, ed. Charles A. Birnbaum and Mary V. Hughes (Charlottesville: University of Virginia Press, 2005), 4–5. For an overview of Shurcliff's career, see Elizabeth Hope Cushing, "Arthur Asahel Shurcliff (Shurtleff)," in Birnbaum and Karson, *Pioneers of American Landscape Design*, 351–56.

92. Croly, "Architectural Work of Charles A. Platt," 219.

93. "Japanese Trees Used to Beautify."

Contributors

KENDALL H. BROWN, Professor, School of Art, California State University, Long Beach, has most recently published *Quiet Beauty: The Japanese Gardens of North America* (2013).

SARA A. BUTLER, Professor of Art and Architectural History at Roger Williams University in Bristol, Rhode Island, teaches courses on the history of American art and architecture and on the history of landscape architecture. She earned a Ph.D. in architectural history from the University of Virginia, where she also coauthored *University of Virginia: The Campus Guide.*

EMILY T. COOPERMAN, PhD, an architectural and landscape historian and independent scholar, is principal of ARCH Preservation Consulting. Her publications include *William Birch: Picturing the American Scene,* with Lea Carson Sherk (2010), and an edited reprint of William Birch's 1808 *Country Seats of the United States of North America* (2008).

REBECCA WARREN DAVIDSON, PhD, Cornell 1994, is an independent scholar particularly interested in the role of printed images and texts in the reception and transmission of garden design knowledge. Among her publications are a biographical and critical introduction to the reprint edition of *The Spirit of the Garden,* a 1923 work by pioneering landscape architect Martha Brookes Hutcheson (2001); the Princeton University Library exhibition catalogs *Heroic Pastorals: Images of the American Landscape* (2002) and *Unseen Hands: Women Printers, Binders, and Book Designers* (2005); and "Opposites Attract: The Garden Art of Charles Platt, Maxfield Parrish, and Edith Wharton," in the proceedings of the conference "Edith Wharton and the American Garden" (2010).

RAFFAELLA FABIANI GIANNETTO, PhD, teaches courses in landscape architecture history and theory and in design at the University of Pennsylvania. She is the author of *Medici Gardens: From Making to Design* (2008), for which she received the Elisabeth Blair MacDougall Book Award, and *Paolo Bürgi Landscape Architect, Discovering the (Swiss) Horizon: Mountain, Lake, and Forest* (2009).

JOHN DIXON HUNT is Emeritus Professor of the history and theory of landscape at the University of Pennsylvania, where he continues to offer seminars. He is a visiting professor at Harvard's GSD.

ELIZABETH HYDE, PhD, is an Associate Professor in the Department of History at Kean University. She is the author of *Cultivated Power: Flowers, Culture, and Politics in the Reign of Louis XIV* (2005) and editor of and contributor to *A Cultural History of Gardens in the Renaissance* (2013). She is currently researching French and American botanical exchange through the mission of André Michaux and writing a cultural history of "how-to" books in the early modern period.

ERIC MACDONALD is Associate Professor in the University of Georgia, College of Environment and Design, where he teaches landscape architecture and historic preservation. His *Garden and Forest* research was supported by an award from the Graham Foundation for Advanced Studies in the Fine Arts and a 2008–2009 fellowship in Garden and Landscape Studies at Dumbarton Oaks Research Library and Collection.

JAMES SCHISSEL is a PhD candidate in the Department of Landscape Architecture at the University of Illinois at Urbana–Champaign. His research on nineteenth-century American vernacular landscapes has been recognized and supported through numerous awards including a fellowship in the Garden and Landscape Studies Program at the Dumbarton Oaks Research Library and Collection, the Douglas Dockery Thomas Fellowship in Garden History and Design, and a Dianne Woest Fellowship in the Arts and Humanities at the Historic New Orleans Collection.

JILL SINCLAIR is a British landscape historian and independent scholar who has lived and worked in the United States, France, and India. Her book, *Fresh Pond: The History of a Cambridge Landscape,* was published by the MIT Press in 2009, and she is a regular contributor to journals, including *Historic Gardens Review, Journal of the Garden History Society,* and *Design Philosophy Papers.*

JOHANNES STOFFLER, Dr. sc. nat. ETH Zürich, is a practicing landscape architect and researcher in the field of garden history and garden conservation. He is executive committee member of the Swiss Society for Historical Gardens, the Swiss Foundation for Landscape Architecture, and ICOMOS Switzerland/Garden Conservation. His publications include *Gustav Ammann: Landschaften der Moderne in der Schweiz* (2008); *Lebendiges Garte-*

nerbe (2009); and "Modernism for the People: Swimming Pool Landscapes in Switzerland," in *Modernism and Landscape Architecture, 1890–1940*, edited by Therese O'Malley and Joachim Wolschke-Bulmahn (2015).

CAREN YGLESIAS, PhD, AIA, is a practicing architect and teaches landscape architecture at the Academy of Art University in San Francisco and the University of California, Berkeley. Recent publications include *The Innovative Use of Materials in Architecture and Landscape Architecture: History, Theory and Performance* (2014), a book chapter on materiality, visuality, and design education methods called "Seeing Air" in *Visuality/Materiality: Images, Objects and Practices* (2012), and *The Complete House and Grounds: Learning from Andrew Jackson Downing's Domestic Architecture* (2011).

Index

Italicized page numbers refer to illustrations.